BRYANT AND STRATTON'S

COMMERCIAL ARITHMETIC.

IN TWO PARTS.

DESIGNED

FOR THE COUNTING ROOM, COMMERCIAL AND AGRICULTURAL COLLEGES, NORMAL AND HIGH SCHOOLS, ACADEMIES, AND UNIVERSITIES.

BY

E. E. WHITE, A.M.,
SUPT. PUB. SCHOOLS, PORTSMOUTH, OHIO.

J. B. MERIAM, A.M.,
CASHIER CITY BANK, CLEVELAND, OHIO.

AND

H. B. BRYANT, AND H. D. STRATTON,
FOUNDERS AND PROPRIETORS OF THE "NATIONAL CHAIN OF MERCANTILE COLLEGES," LOCATED AT NEW YORK, PHILADELPHIA, ALBANY, BUFFALO, CLEVELAND, DETROIT, CHICAGO, AND ST. LOUIS.

NEW YORK:
OAKLEY AND MASON.
1866.

ELECTROTYPED BY
SMITH & McDOUGAL,
82 & 84 Beekman St.

J. M. JOHNSON,
Printer and Binder,
BUFFALO, N. Y.

PREFACE.

EVERY book—and especially every text-book—should have a twofold reason for its existence: first, a want which it is designed to meet, and, secondly, an adaptedness to supply that want. A work which meets these conditions needs no apology for its appearance.

The preparation of the present treatise was undertaken at the earnest solicitation of Messrs. BRYANT and STRATTON. Their intimate acquaintance with the wants of business students, resulting from an extensive experience in Commercial Instruction, revealed to them an urgent demand for such a work, and suggested its general plan.

The Authors have also been engaged, many years, as teachers of Arithmetic and Commercial Calculations in the first schools and commercial colleges of the country, or in some of the most practical departments of business. The result of this experience is the conviction that a work presenting fully the applications of arithmetic to actual business, and discussing thoroughly the general principles of mercantile transactions, has long been a *desideratum.* True, there are some excellent works on arithmetic, in which considerable space is devoted to business forms and transactions. In no one of these, however, with which we are acquainted, are these subjects treated with sufficient fullness or thoroughness for commercial students. By searching through half a score of the best arithmetics now published, most of the information designed may possibly be obtained. The present treatise embodies this information in one volume, and presents, in part, our idea of what is needed.

PART FIRST is designed to afford a review of elementary arithmetic. In its preparation it has been assumed that the student possesses some knowledge of numbers. *Fractions*, common and decimal, and *Ratio* and *Proportion* are treated with considerable thoroughness on account of their great importance.

PART SECOND is devoted mainly to *Commercial Calculations.* Aside from clear and exact definitions, concise rules, and lucid explanations, we have endeavored to present a system of *general principles* relating to the different subjects which will enable the student more fully to understand the *nature* and true *theory* of business transactions. To secure accuracy, portions of the manuscript have been submitted to the supervision of business men familiar with the subjects treated of.

As the value of such a work as this greatly depends upon the character of its problems, we have aimed to present, as far as possible, those occurring in actual business, without *specially preparing them* for the place they occupy.

Experience and observation have taught us, in relation to money, banks, interest, and exchange, that business students need something more than rules, forms, and tables. They want the theory too. The various and contradictory opinions upon these subjects set forth by business men of even considerable experience, prove a lack of knowledge of first principles which should incite the student to a very thorough examination for himself. Money has intrinsic properties, and is controlled by natural laws, some of the most important of which we have endeavored to present.

The nature of Interest, and the principles of Exchange and Balance of Trade are also fully explained, and, if found correct, will necessarily expose some radical but popular errors. The problems submitted will be found to contain satisfactory facts and statistics supporting our views.

The difference between simple, annual, and compound interest, and the operation of the different rules for finding the amount due on notes when "partial payments" have been made, are illustrated by diagrams. The treatment of annual interest is the joint work of the authors, and is believed to be worthy of special attention.

In the Equation of Payments and the Equation of Accounts we have aimed to make the student a *rule to himself*. The rules and processes recommended are the results of a clear analysis, leading the student with "open eyes" into the usual perplexities of these subjects.

The first 116 pages of the work, also the articles on Equation of Payments, Equation of Accounts, Cash Balance, Annuities, Partnership, Alligation, Duodecimals, Involution and Evolution, were prepared by Mr. E. E. WHITE; the articles on Interest, Partial Payments, Currency and Money, Banks and Banking, Exchange, Prommissory Notes, Stocks and Bonds, Progression and Mensuration, by Mr. J. B. MERIAM. Partnership Settlements and a portion of the Supplement were written by Messrs. BRYANT and STRATTON, to whom we also acknowledge our indebtedness for valuable materials and suggestions.

The work has been extended beyond its first design, to adapt it to advanced classes in our High Schools and Academies, and is now believed to be sufficiently elementary and extensive for that purpose.

E. E. WHITE.
J. B. MERIAM.

December, 1860.

In committing this work to the hands of the gentlemen who are known as its authors, we have been actuated by the sole purpose of producing a book which should possess all the requisites of a first-class business Arithmetic in a greater degree than any previous work. We are aware that many books are already extant which may well dispute the ground as elaborately scientific essays upon the properties of numbers, but we are as fully conscious that few, if any, can be found which will so completely answer the demands of the student of Accounts or the practical business man, as the present treatise.

The principal authors of this work are men of large experience and ripe judgment, both in the general acceptation and in their respective departments of life. Mr. White has been for many years connected with public education in such capacities as would essentially prepare him to appreciate the wants of the learner, while his associate, Mr. Meriam, has had equal advantages in the more practical details of business, as well as ample experience in teaching. We think it would be difficult, if not impossible, to combine better qualifications for this particular work.

To be brief, the book suits us; and while we shall heartily adopt it in our extensive chain of business schools, we shall have no delicacy in pressing its claims upon educators and business men throughout the country, feeling, as we do, that in promoting its general circulation, we are doing much for the cause which is dearer to us than all others, that of Practical Education.

H. B. Bryant.
H. D. Stratton.

TABLE OF CONTENTS.

PART FIRST.

PART SECOND.

CONTENTS.

PART FIRST.

NUMERATION AND NOTATION.

ART. 1. Numbers are composed of orders, the value of whose unit increases from right to left in a ten-fold ratio, that is, ten units of any order make one unit of the order next higher. The names of the first twelve orders are as follows:

12th Order, or Hundreds of Billions.	11th Order, or Tens of Billions.	10th Order, or Billions.	9th Order, or Hundreds of Millions.	8th Order, or Tens of Millions.	7th Order, or Millions.	6th Order, or Hundreds of Thousands.	5th Order, or Tens of Thousands.	4th Order, or Thousands.	3d Order, or Hundreds.	2d Order, or Tens.	1st Order, or Units.
0	0	0	0	0	0	0	0	0	0	0	0

For convenience in reading or writing numbers, we divide the orders into periods of three figures each. The three orders which compose any period are called *Units, Tens, Hundreds* of that period. The following table presents the names of the periods and the manner of reading them:

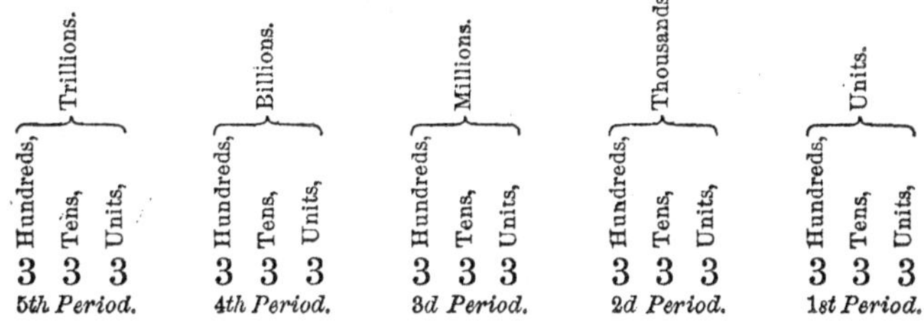

Trillions.			Billions.			Millions.			Thousands.			Units.		
Hundreds,	Tens,	Units,	Hundreds,	Tens,	Units,	Hundreds,	Tens,	Units,	Hundreds,	Tens,	Units,	Hundreds,	Tens,	Units,
3	3	3	3	3	3	3	3	3	3	3	3	3	3	3
5th Period.			*4th Period.*			*3d Period.*			*2d Period.*			*1st Period.*		

The names of the periods above Trillions are Quadrillions, Quintillions, Sextillions, Septillions, Octillions, Nonillions, Decillions, etc.

ART. **2.** To read a number composed of more than three figures, we have the following

RULE.

Begin at the right hand and divide the number into periods of three figures each. Then, commencing at the left hand, read the figures of each period as if it stood alone, adding the name of the period.

Remark.—1. The name of the first or unit period is generally omitted.

2. Beginners should first be taught to read and write numbers composed of not more than *three* figures. Perfect accuracy in this is very important.

Examples.

1. 203.
2. 230.
3. 40404.
4. 3060800.
5. 402300060.
6. 3700070707.
7. 30303030303.
8. 4000400040004.
9. 32400423000203.
10. 801001089006007.

Note.—In separating a number into periods, use a *comma.*

ART. **3.** To write a number by figures, we have the following

RULE.

Beginning at the left hand, write the figures of each period as if it were to stand alone, taking care to fill up the vacant orders or periods with ciphers.

Note.—We may begin at the right hand instead of the left. The latter is preferable, however.

Examples.

1. Express in figures forty millions, four hundred and six thousand, and five.

Explanation.—First write 40, and place after it a comma to separate it from the next lower period, thus : 40, ; next write 406 in thousand's period, and place a comma, thus : 40,406, ; then write 5 in unit's period, and fill up the two vacant orders with ciphers, thus : 40,406,005.

2. Express in figures sixty-five billions, twenty thousand, and eighty.

Explanation.—Write 65, and place after it a comma, thus : 65, ; then, as the next period (millions) is not given, fill it with ciphers, and place after it a comma ; thus : 65,000, ; then write 20, with a comma after it, in thousand's period, filling the vacant order with a cipher, thus : 65,000,020, ; lastly write eighty in unit's period, filling the vacant order with a cipher, thus : 65,000,020,080.

3. Express in figures thirty thousand and thirty.

4. Four hundred millions, five thousand and sixty.

5. Forty billions, forty thousand and forty.

6. Ten trillions, two hundred millions, one hundred and one.

7. Thirty-five millions and twenty-five thousand.

8. Two billions, three hundred and forty-five millions.

9. Nine trillions, ninety-nine millions, nine hundred and ninety-nine.

10. Forty trillions and ten.

ANALYSIS OF NUMBERS.

ART. 4. In addition and multiplication of numbers it is necessary to reduce units of a lower order to units of a higher ; in subtraction and division to reduce units of a higher order to units of a lower. It is, also, often necessary to change the form of a number, that is, take from it as many hundreds, or tens, etc., as possible, and read the rest in units ; or to reduce a part of the units of a higher order to some lower, and express the true value of the whole. A few examples will make these changes plain to the pupil.

1. How many units in 4 tens?
2. How many units in 4 hundreds?
3. How many tens in 6 hundreds?
4. How many tens in 6 thousands?
5. How many hundreds in 3 millions?
6. How many hundreds in 2 ten-thousands?
7. How many tens in 25 thousands? *Ans.* 2500.
8. How many tens in 40 units?
9. How many tens in 400 units? *Ans.* 40.
10. How many hundreds in 2000 units?
11. How many hundreds in 200 tens?
12. How many millions in 2400000 tens? *Ans.* 24.
13. How many thousands in 400 tens?
14. What is the greatest number of hundreds that can be taken from 34674? *Ans.* 346.
15. Divide 30460 into hundreds and units.
Ans. 304 hundreds and 60 units.
16. Divide 23046203 into ten-thousands and units.
Ans. 2304 ten-thousands and 6203 units.
17. Change the form of 23046.

Explanation.—By reducing the orders, a great number of forms may be given to the number. The following are some of the results: 1 ten-thousand, 130 hundreds, and 46 units; 129 hundreds, 14 tens, and 6 units; 22 thousands, 9 hundreds, 13 tens, and 16 units; and 2 ten-thousands, 304 tens, and 6 units. By writing the changed form above the natural, we may have:

1 12 9 14 6   2 2 10 3 16   1 12 10 3 16   20-29-13-16
23046; or 23046; or 23046; or 2 3 0 4 6.

Note.—The student should study the above changes closely. See that they are clearly understood.

ADDITION.

ART. 5. The two most important qualities of an accountant are accuracy and rapidity. Every accountant must know that his results possess *absolute accuracy.* In business, he is sometimes obliged to spend hours, and even days, in detecting an error of a few cents in a trial balance sheet. Rapidity in the performance of his work is of almost equal importance. The most rapid computers are, generally, the most accurate.

It is not good policy to wait for the practice of actual business to impart this skill. The persevering student can easily acquire a high degree of proficiency, and thus bring to his business one of the surest elements of success.

Addition is not only the basis of all numerical operations, but is actually the most frequently used in all departments of business. It is, also, in adding that the young accountant possesses the least skill and is most liable to make mistakes. For these reasons, the student should regard no labor too great which is necessary to master it. To aid him in acquiring facility and certainty in adding columns of figures, the following methods and suggestions are recommended.

Let it be required, for example, to add the following numbers:

637
584
796
839
376
458
749
276
968

Ans. 5683

Process.—Beginning at the bottom of the right hand column, and *naming only results,* add thus: 14, 23, 31, 37, 46, 52, 56, 63; then adding the 6 tens to the second column, add it in the same manner—12, 19, 23, 28, 35, etc. The student should never permit himself *to spell* his way up a column of

2

figures in this manner, viz.: 8 and 6 are 14, 14 and 9 are 23, 23 and 8 are 31, 31 and 6 are 37, etc. It is just as easy to name only the *results*, and much more rapid.

Proof.—To test the accuracy of the result, add the columns downward.

Examples.

1. Add 57, 63, 246, 788, 565, 399, 464, and 555.
2. Add 36, 69, 304, 5698, 4536, 40864.
3. Add 28, 47, 55, 66, 77, 88, 99, and 23.
4. What is the sum of 309+384+679+436+358+804+506+988+777?
5. What is the sum of 14+16+34+86+37+65+56+78+35+49+12+15+8+9+76?

LEDGER COLUMNS.

ART. **6.** In adding long columns of figures, as in a Ledger, the following method is sometimes used:

Add the columns in order, and place the footings under each other upon a separate piece of paper (testing the accuracy of the same by proof); point off the right hand figure (except in the last column) and add the left hand figure or figures to the next column, thus:

	Process.
$57.45	
28.75	4.7
36.87	4.7
4.56	6.1
98.88	29
6.25	
49.38	
9.63	
$291.77	

The figures, expressing the sum of the left hand column, together with the figures cut off on the right, *read upwards*, will be the sum total. The advantage of this method is two-fold: 1. The partial results being preserved, it is easier to detect errors.—Any column may be re-added without the trouble of adding the preceding. 2. The total sum when written is correct, and the page is not defaced by erasures and corrections.

The student should write out long ledger columns on slips of paper, and daily practice in adding them, being as careful to obtain a correct result as he would be in actual business.

The following ledger columns are given merely as examples. The student can easily increase the number of them to any extent.

1.	2.	3.	4.
3.25	32.56	75.50	19.50
8.37	8.15	284.38	23.86
2.50	6.33	3287.15	12.45
12.35	17.09	111.01	14.52
9.00	.90	43.96	25.48
.88	.75	263.55	42.54
.93	3.25	1900.09	8.60
4.65	21.87	1356.63	9.37
5.48	22.20	15.20	8.80
10.12	7.15	7.15	.65
1.20	4.32	13.48	.73
9.15	78.90	3456.38	.38
7.75	18.88	348.54	11.25
18.64	3.33	2.75	.86
9.15	1.38	52.30	2.95
13.48	.63	900.90	5.92
4.96	.49	4658.30	9.52
8.30	50.63	222.56	.88
4.55	24.88	914.53	.99
3.08	15.33	64.50	6.01
1.13	10.00	49.87	7.83
2.63	16.56	302.58	1.50
7.87	7.77	1256.29	2.00
4.33	5.00	10.10	3.85
0.00	4.33	100.98	5.38
.85	12.34	78.60	1.53
.90	17.15	44.50	12.60
5.00	20.00	253.63	19.30
8.00	8.50	77.88	22.33
12.00	8.76	1860.12	10.19
15.00	5.48	973.53	9.81
6.50	17.10	19.10	8.76
5.80	22.05	28.25	12.57
7.26	7.29	39.10	18.19
	8.99	135.00	7.63

THE ADDING OF SEVERAL COLUMNS.

ART. 7. Considerable practice will enable the accountant to add two or more columns at one operation. There is often an advantage in adding in this manner. Beyond two columns, or at most three, the method may be more skillful than practical. The following will illustrate the method of adding two columns:

	86
	75
	68
	34
	59
Ans.	322

Process.—59 plus 30=89, plus 4=93, plus 60=153, plus 8=161, plus 70=231, plus 5=236, plus 80=316, plus 6=322.

It will be seen that the process consists simply in adding the tens first and then the units. By naming only the *results*, we have 89, 93; 153, 161; 231, 236; 316, 322.

The units may be added first and then the tens, thus: 63, 93; 101, 161; 166, 236; 242, 322.

Three or more columns may be added in a similar manner, thus:

	223
	425
	384
	256
Ans.	1288

Operation.—256+4=260, 260+80=340, 340+300=640, 640+5=645, 645+20=665, 665+400=1065, 1065+3=1068, 1068+20=1088, 1088+200=1288.

By naming only results, we have: 260, 340, 640; 645, 665, 1065; 1068, 1088, 1288.

Examples.

1. Add 25, 68, 67, 83, 37, 46, 99, 87, and 34.
2. Add 38, 46, 92, 37, 83, 46, 52, 53, and 46.
3. Add 286, 356, 396, 423, 345, 660, and 780.
4. Add 384, 236, 112, 345, 784, 569, and 963.

SUBTRACTION.

Art. 8. Ex. 1. From 3084 take 2793.

```
29184 Minuend changed in form.
 3084 Minuend.
 2793 Subtrahend.
  291 Remainder.
```

Remarks.—1. That the changed minuend above is equivalent to the given minuend is evident from the fact that 30 hundreds+8 tens=29 hundreds+18 tens.

2. Upon the principle that the difference between two numbers is the same as the difference between these numbers *equally increased*, instead of changing the form of the minuend, we can add 10 to the minuend figure when it is less than the lower subtrahend figure, and add 1 to the *next* higher order of the subtrahend. It is plain that 1 added to a higher order is the same as 10 added to the next lower. We do not *borrow* this 10 however, nor do we *pay* any thing by adding the 1. These terms ought not to be used.

Examples.

2. From 406309 take 347278.
3. From 100102 take 90903.
4. From 5000050 take 86432.
5. From one billion take one million and one.
6. From 32670804 take 3867498.
7. From 30006070 take 4906007.
8. From 40 hundreds take 25 tens. *Ans.* 3750.
9. From 205 tens take 264 units.
10. From 230 tens take 12 hundreds. *Ans.* 1100.
11. From 2 millions take 2 thousands.
12. From 16 tens take 75 units.
13. From 101 thousand take 56 hundreds.
14. From 1 ten take 8 units.

MULTIPLICATION.

ART. **9.** Ex. 1. Multiply 3464 by 306.

```
Multiplicand,     3464
Multiplier,        306
               -------
                 20784
                10392
               -------
Product,       1059984
```

Proof by excess of 9's.—Add the figures of the multiplicand, casting out the 9's and setting the excess at the right. Proceed in the same manner with the multiplier, setting the excess under that of the multiplicand. Multiply these excesses together and cast the 9's out of the result. Then cast out the 9's in the original product, and, if the work is correct, the last two excesses will agree. Although this is not always an absolute test of the correctness of a result, it is sufficiently so for common purposes.

Ex. 2. Multiply 23045 by 70800.

```
                                *Proof.*
             23045              5 Excess.
               70800            6   "
           ----------           --
             184360             30 } 3 "
           161315                  }
           ----------              }
Product,   1631586000              } 3 "
```

Examples.

3. Multiply 405678 by 34006.
4. Multiply 38674506 by 30080.
5. Multiply 46923000 by 46702.
6. Multiply 83400607 by 33000.
7. Multiply 843464 by 30706.
8. Multiply 708000 by 4700.
9. How many feet would a horse travel in 109 days at the rate of 35 miles per day? (A mile contains 5280 feet.)
10. How much can 508 men earn in 65 days, if each man receives 3 dollars per day?

DIVISION.

Art. **10.** Ex. 1. Divide 2920464 by 60843.

```
60843)2920464(48 Quotient.
      243372
      ------
       486744
       486744
       ------
```

Suggestion.—Make 6 your trial divisor and 29 your first trial dividend. The second trial dividend is 48.

Ex. 2. Divide 2406874 by 30400.

```
304|00)24068|74(79 Quotient.
       2128
       ----
        2788
        2736
        -----
          5274 Remainder.
```

Examples.

3. Divide 304608 by 304.
4. Divide 6743207 by 6200.
5. Divide 340068 by 27.
6. Divide 84306200 by 308000.
7. Divide 8408 by 24.
8. Divide 345602 by 18.
9. Divide 4060703 by 33.
10. Divide 412304 by 30300.

CONTRACTIONS IN MULTIPLICATION AND DIVISION.

Art. **11.** There are abbreviated methods of multiplying and dividing numbers, which the expert accountant can often use with great advantage. With a little practice a person may readily multiply by two, three, or even more figures, at a single operation. The process of division may be abbreviated in a similar though less practical manner. Many of these methods, together with their explanations, are too complex for insertion here. The living teacher can best present such processes. Unless the student is made *familiar* with them, they are of no practical importance.

ART. 12. When the multiplier is 14, 15, 16, etc.

Ex. 1. Multiply 3425 by 15.

Operation.

$$\begin{array}{l} 3425 \times 15 \\ \underline{17125} \\ 51375 \text{ Product.} \end{array}$$

Remark.—It is not necessary to put down any part of the operation. The result may be written at once by the following

RULE.

Multiply by the unit's figure, adding, after the unit's place, the figures of the multiplicand.

Examples.

2. Multiply 34809 by 13.
3. Multiply 4876 by 18.
4. Multiply 369403 by 17.
5. Multiply 369403 by 13.
6. Multiply 369403 by 16.
7. Multiply 369403 by 15.
8. Multiply 369403 by 14.

ART. 13. When the multiplier is 31, 41, 51, etc.

Ex. 1. Multiply 3425 by 51.

Operation.

$$\begin{array}{r} 3425 \times 41 \\ \underline{13700} \\ 140425 \text{ Product.} \end{array}$$

RULE.

Multiply by the ten's figure and add the product to the proper orders of the multiplicand.

Examples.

2. Multiply 3486 by 71.
3. Multiply 864 by 51.

4. Multiply 86047 by 41.

5. Multiply 38967 by 91.

ART. 14. When the multiplier consists of two figures, the product may be written at once.

Ex. 1. Multiply 675 by 56.

$$675 \times 56 = 37800.$$

Explanation.—The process is based upon the fact that units multiplied by units give units, tens by units tens, tens by tens hundreds, hundreds by units hundreds, hundreds by tens thousands, etc.

We first multiply 5 units by 6 units=30 units=3 tens and 0 units. Write 0 units. Multiply 7 tens by 6 units=42 tens, and add 3 tens, (received from the units,)=45 tens, and to this add 5 tens by 5 units=25 tens, which gives 70 tens=7 hundreds and 0 tens. Write 0 tens.

Multiply 6 hundreds by 6 units=36 hundreds, and add the 7 hundred, received from the tens, which gives 43 hundreds. Then multiply the 5 tens by 7 tens=35 hundreds, and add 43 hundreds=78 hundreds=7 thousands and 8 hundreds. Write 8 hundreds. Multiply 6 hundreds by 5 tens=30 thousands, and add the 7 thousands received from hundreds=37 thousands. Write 37 thousand. The product is 37800.

Examples.

2. Multiply 38765 by 34. By 45.
3. Multiply 68753 by 48. By 84.
4. Multiply 23086 by 96. By 69.
5. Multiply 6784 by 37. By 73.
6. Multiply 8745 by 43. By 34.
7. Multiply 6321 by 98. By 89.

ART. 15. When the multiplier is a convenient part of 10, 100, 1000, etc.

RULE.

Multiply by 10, 100, 1000, *etc.* (by annexing ciphers) *of which the multiplier is a part, and take the same part of the product.*

Ex. 1. Multiply 357 by $33\frac{1}{3}$.

Operation.

$$\begin{array}{r} 3)\underline{35700} \\ 11900 \end{array} \text{ Product.}$$

Explanation.—Since $33\frac{1}{3}$ is one third of 100, $33\frac{1}{3}$ times 357 must equal $\frac{1}{3}$ of 100 times 357.

Note.—The following are some of the convenient parts often occurring: of 10—$2\frac{1}{2}$, $3\frac{1}{3}$; of 100—$12\frac{1}{2}$, $16\frac{2}{3}$, 25, $33\frac{1}{3}$, 50; of 1000—125, $166\frac{2}{3}$, 250, $333\frac{1}{3}$, 500, $666\frac{2}{3}$.

Examples.

2. Multiply 528 by $3\frac{1}{3}$. By $2\frac{1}{2}$.
3. Multiply 124860 by $12\frac{1}{2}$. By $16\frac{2}{3}$.
4. Multiply 80648 by 25. By $33\frac{1}{3}$.
5. Multiply 10368 by 125. By $166\frac{2}{3}$.
6. Multiply 62208 by $333\frac{1}{3}$. By $666\frac{2}{3}$.

Art. **16.** To divide by a convenient part of 10, 100, 1000, etc.

RULE.

Multiply by the quotient, found by dividing 10, 100, 1000, *etc.*, (as the case may be) *by the given divisor, and divide the result by* 10, 100, 1000, *etc.*

Ex. 1. Divide 850 by $16\frac{2}{3}$.

Operation.

$$\begin{array}{r} 850 \\ \underline{6} \\ 51.00 \end{array} \quad \textit{Ans. } 51.$$

Explanation.—Since 100 is 6 times $16\frac{2}{3}$, 100 is contained as many times in 6 times a given number as $16\frac{2}{3}$ is in the number itself.

Examples.

2. Divide 465 by $2\frac{1}{2}$. By $3\frac{1}{3}$.
3. Divide 54604 by $12\frac{1}{2}$. By $16\frac{2}{3}$.
4. Divide 8364 by 25. By $33\frac{1}{3}$.
5. Divide 64575 by 125. By 500.
6. Divide 647500 by $166\frac{2}{3}$. By $333\frac{1}{3}$.
7. Divide 2564 by $6\frac{1}{4}$. By 250.

FEDERAL MONEY.

ART. **17.** TABLE.

10 mills (m)	make	1 cent,	marked	ct.
10 cents	"	1 dime,	"	d.
10 dimes	"	1 dollar,	"	$
10 dollars	"	1 Eagle,	"	E.

E.	$	d.	ct.	m.
1=	10=	100=	1000=	10000
	1=	10=	100=	1000
		1=	10=	100
			1=	10

Remark.—Dimes and eagles are not mentioned in ordinary business transactions. In writing dollars and cents together, a point, called the *separatrix* (.), is placed between the dollars and cents ; and, since cents occupy two places, the first figure at the right of cents is mills. It is not customary to separate cents and mills.

Examples.

1. How many mills in 28 cents ? In 37½ cents ?
2. How many cents in 15 dimes ? In 16½ dimes ?
3. Reduce $12.50 to mills.
4. Change $90 to mills.
5. How many cents in 2 eagles, 5 dollars, and 8 dimes ?
6. Reduce 4360 cents to dollars.
7. Add the following: $9.60, $12.70, $45.37½, $.06, $1.50, $4.98, $68.33, $8.39, $60, and $.80.
8. Sold a carriage for $120.75, a horse for $90.60, a harness for $15.60, and a saddle for $13.12½ ; what was the amount received ? *Ans.* $240.075.
9. From $108 take 12½ cents. *Ans.* $107.875.
10. Bought a barrel of flour for $6.37½, and sold it for $5.87½ ; what did I lose ? *Ans.* $.50.
11. Bought a house and lot for $1500. Paid $40 for a front fence, $110.90 for painting house, $9.75 for fruit trees,

and \$15 for other improvements. I then sold the property for \$1800. What did I gain?

12. What will be the cost of 45 barrels of flour at \$5.80 per barrel?

13. What will 80 bushels of coal cost at 15 cents per bushel?

14. What will be the cost of 60 bushels of wheat at \$1.12$\frac{1}{2}$ per bushel; 146 bushels of corn at 66$\frac{2}{3}$ cents a bushel; and 45 bushels of oats at 25 cents a bushel?

15. How many bushels of coal at 12$\frac{1}{2}$ cents a bushel can be bought for \$125?

Suggestion.—The dividend and divisor must be reduced to the same denomination. Change both to mills. 125.000÷.125=1000. *Ans.* 1000 bushels.

16. How many pounds of butter at 16 cents per pound must be given for 15 barrels of flour at \$8 per barrel?

17. How many barrels of flour at \$5.62$\frac{1}{2}$ per barrel can be bought for \$225? *Ans.* 40 barrels.

18. How many half-dimes would it take to pay for 16 cows at \$16.37$\frac{1}{2}$ per head?

19. A drover bought 105 head of cattle at \$57 per head. He paid for their pasturage one month \$250, and then sold them at \$60 per head. What did he gain by the transaction? *Ans.* \$65.

BILLS.

ART. 18. *A Bill of Goods,* or simply a *Bill,* is a written statement of goods sold and their prices.

It contains the time and place of the transaction and the names of the parties.

A bill is drawn *against* the purchaser, and in *favor* of the merchant or seller.

A bill is receipted by writing the words *Received payment* at the bottom and affixing the seller's name. A bill may be receipted by a clerk, agent, or any authorized person, as in bills 2 and 3.

When sales are made at different times, the dates of the several transactions may be written at the left.

A bill presenting a debit and credit *account* between the parties and the balance due, may be written as in bill 7.

If the party against whom the bill is drawn is not able to pay it when presented, he may acknowledge the same by giving a *due-bill.* This will prevent all subsequent dispute as to the correctness of the claim. A bill may be receipted by means of a *due-bill,* as in bills 4 and 5.

1. CLEVELAND, July 1, 1859.

MR. JOHN COOK,

Bought of *Samuel Bliss.*

15 lbs. Rio Coffee,	@ 16c.	$2.40
50 lbs. W. I. Sugar,	@ $8\frac{1}{2}$c.	4.25
36 lbs. Pearl Starch,	@ $12\frac{1}{2}$c.	4.50
8 gals. Molasses,	@ 40c.	3.20
90 lbs. Butter Crackers,	@ 9c.	8.10
45 lbs. Picnic Crackers,	@ 11c.	4.95
		$27.40

Received payment, SAML. BLISS.

2. BUFFALO, Jan. 1, 1860.

PETER HIND,

Bought of *James Fink & Co.*

1859.			
July 15.	9 yds. Silk,	@ $0.95	
" "	8 yds. Ribbon,	@ .45	
" "	12 yds. Muslin,	@ .15	
Sept. 9.	3 yds. Cassimere,	@ 1.75	
" "	$2\frac{1}{2}$ yds. Broadcloth,	@ 4.50	
" "	6 yds. Doeskin,	@ $1.12\frac{1}{2}$	
" "	1 Cravat,	@ 1.25	
Oct. 15.	4 prs. Boots,	@ 5.20	
" "	2 doz. Hose,	@ 2.40	
" "	$\frac{1}{2}$ doz. Sleeve Buttons,	@ .48	
" "	$3\frac{1}{2}$ yds. Linen,	@ .60	
Nov. 30.	$1\frac{1}{2}$ doz. Collars,	@ 2.25	
" "	2 doz. Handkerchiefs,	@ 1.40	
" "	3 Vests,	@ 2.40	
			$79.765

Received payment, JAMES FINK & Co.
per SMITH.

3. NEW YORK, Jan. 1, 1859.

MR. JOHN SMITH,

To *Hurd & Brothers*, Dr.

1858.				
Aug. 20.	To 12 yds. Broadcloth,	.	@ $3.50	.
" "	" 16 yds. Cassimere,	.	@ 1.12	.
" "	" 17 yds. Drilling, .	.	@ .11	.
Sept. 25.	" 12 doz. Spools Cn. Thread,		@ .60	.
" "	" 7 yds. Gingham, .	.	@ .25	.
" "	" 34 yds. Fine Muslin,	.	@ .18	.
" "	" 5 yds. Red Flannel,	.	@ .62½	.
" "	" 2½ yds. Silk Velvet	.	@ 4.00	.
Oct. 9.	" 12 gross Shirt Buttons,		@ .75	.
" "	" 15 doz. Wool Hose,	.	@ 3.00	.
" "	" 3 prs. Kid Gloves,	.	@ 1.25	.
" "	" 2 doz. Linen Napkins,	.	@ 2.40	.
" "	" 2 doz. Shirt Bosoms,	.	@ 4.80	.
Nov. 1.	" 11 yds. Drilling, .	.	@ .10	.
" "	" 5 yds. Jean, . .	.	@ .75	.
" "	" 2 Silk Hdks., . .	.	@ 1.00	.
" "	" 12½ yds. Vel. Ribbon,	.	@ .20	.
				$171.485

Received payment,

JOHN STILL,
for HURD & BROTHERS.

4. CHICAGO, July 1, 1859.

JOSEPH CAMP,

To *Geo. W. Colburn*, Dr.

1859.				
Apr. 3.	To 3 doz. Scythes,	. .	@ $9.00	.
" 8.	" 1½ doz. Hoes, .	. .	@ 5.00	.
May 1.	" 6 doz. Rakes, .	. .	@ 1.75	.
				$45.00

Received payment by due-bill,

July 15, 1859. GEO. W. COLBURN.

5. CINCINNATI, June 20, 1859.

AMOS KENT, ESQ.,

To *W. B. Cook & Co.*, Dr.

To 1 doz. Webster's Unabridged Dictionary,	@	$50.00	
" 12 doz. Robinson's Arithmetic, . .	@	9.00	
" 5 doz. Sanders' Fifth Readers, . .	@	7.20	
" 9 doz. Wells's Grammar, . . .	@	3.00	
" $2\frac{1}{2}$ doz. Small Testaments, . . .	@	1.20	
			$224

July 1. Settled by due-bill,

W. B. COOK & CO.

6. PORTSMOUTH, July 1, 1859.

MR. J. H. POE,

Bought of *Wm. Miller*.

1859.					
May	3.	75 lbs. Sugar, ...	@ $6\frac{1}{4}$c	.	
"	"	9 lbs. Tea, ...	@ 65c	.	
"	"	21 gals. Golden Syrup, . .	@ 70c	.	
June	1.	10 lbs. Spice, ...	@ 20c	.	
"	"	12 lbs. Pepper, ...	@ 25c	.	
"	"	12 lbs. Ginger, ...	@ 18c	.	
"	"	15 lbs. Coffee, ...	@ $12\frac{1}{2}$c	.	
"	10.	20 lbs. Dried Apples, . .	@ 10c	.	
"	"	18 lbs. Dried Peaches, . .	@ $12\frac{1}{2}$c	.	
"	"	2 bu. Onions, ...	@ 80c	.	
"	15.	13 lbs. Mackerel, . . .	@ 8c	.	
"	18.	9 lbs. Smoked Herrings, .	@ 20c	.	
"	20.	25 lbs. Rice, ...	@ 5c	.	
"	"	12 lbs. Dried Beef, . .	@ $12\frac{1}{2}$c	.	
"	"	5 Sacks Table Salt, . .	@ 20c	.	
"	"	5 bu. Corn Meal, . . .	@ 80c	.	
"	27.	17 lbs. Soda Crackers, . .	@ 9c	.	
					$52.24

Received payment,

WM. MILLER.

7. St. Louis, Jan. 1, 1859.

Reed & Spry,

To *Hall, Smith & Co.*, Dr.

1859.						
July	7.	To 15 yds. Cambric, .	@	9c	.	
"	"	" 50 yds. Print, . .	@	$12\frac{1}{2}$c	.	
"	"	" 6 yds. Cassimere, .	@	$1.60	.	
"	20.	" 33 yds. Sheeting, .	@	11c	.	
"	"	" $6\frac{1}{2}$ yds. Broadcloth, .	@	$$4.37\frac{1}{2}$	.	
"	"	" 3 yd. Velvet, . .	@	3.00	.	
Aug.	30.	" 20 yds. French Print,	@	17c	.	
"	"	" 15 yds. Lyonese, .	@	70c	.	
						$65.42

Cr.

Sept.	1.	By 40 bu. Coal, . .	@	11c	.	
"	9.	" 6 Cords of Wood, .	@	$ 3.00	.	
Oct.	20.	" Cash, . . .	@	16.00	.	
Nov	25.	" 8 Days' Labor, . .	@	1.50	.	
						$50.40
		Balance due, ...				$15.02

Received payment,

Hall, Smith & Co.,
per Hibbs.

GREATEST COMMON DIVISOR.

Art. **19.** *Integers*, or whole numbers, are divided into two classes, *prime* and *composite*.

A prime number can be exactly divided only by itself and unity; as 2, 3, 5, 7, 11, etc.

A composite number can be exactly divided by other numbers besides itself and unity; as 4, 9, 21, etc.

The factor of a number is one of two or more numbers which multiplied together will produce the given number. The factors of 12 are 2, 3, 4, 6, 1, and 12, since each of these numbers multiplied by another will produce 12.

The prime factors of a number are all the prime numbers which multiplied together will produce the given number. The prime factors of 12 are 1, 2, 2 and 3.

Two or more numbers are said to be *prime with respect to each other* when they have no common factor ; as 8, 21, and 35.

The divisor of a number is any number that will exactly divide it. Thus 4 is a divisor of 12, 16, and 24.

Note.—Every factor is a divisor and *vice versa.*

A common divisor of two or more numbers is *any* number that will exactly divide each of them. Thus 4 is a common divisor of 16, 32, and 64.

The greatest common divisor of two or more numbers is the *greatest* number that will exactly divide each of them. Thus 16 is the greatest common divisor of 16, 32, and 64.

ART. **20.** To find the greatest common divisor of two or more numbers.

Ex. 1. What is the greatest common divisor of 63 and 105 ?

FIRST METHOD.

$63=3\times3\times7$
$105=3\times5\times7$
$3\times7=21$. *Ans.*

Explanation.—3 and 7 are the only factors common to 63 and 105, hence they are the only common divisors, and their product must be the greatest common divisor.

SECOND METHOD.

```
63)105(1
   63
   42)63(1
      42
      21)42(2
         42
      21 Ans.
```

Explanation.—That the last divisor is the greatest common divisor is evident from the following analysis :

$42=21\times2$; hence 21 will divide 42.
$63=42+21=21\times2+21\times1=21\times3$; hence 21 will divde 63.

$105=63+42=21\times3+21\times2=21\times5$; hence will also divide 105.'

RULE.

Resolve the numbers into their prime factors. The product of the factors common to all the numbers will be the greatest common divisor. Or,

Divide the greater number by the less ; the less number by the first remainder; the first remainder by the second remain-

der; the second remainder by the third, and so on until nothing remains. The last divisor will be the greatest common divisor.

Note.—The greatest common divisor is chiefly used in reducing fractions to their lowest terms. See Art. 24.

Find the greatest common divisor of the following numbers:

2. 56 and 98.
3. 69 and 161.
4. 168 and 392.
5. 85 and 136.
6. 126 and 294.
7. 148 and 296.
8. 16, 32, and 86.

Suggestion.—First find the greatest common divisor of two of the numbers; then use the greatest common divisor of these two numbers as a new number, and find the greatest common divisor of it and the third number.

9. 92, 138, and 161.
10. 2048 and 2560.

LEAST COMMON MULTIPLE.

Art. **21.** *A multiple* of a number is any number it will exactly divide; thus 24 is a multiple of 6.

A common multiple of two or more numbers is *any* number each of them will exactly divide. Thus 96 is a common multiple of 8, 12, 16, and 24.

The least common multiple of two or more numbers is the *least* number each of them will exactly divide. Thus 48 is the least common multiple of 8, 12, 16, and 24.

It is evident that the multiple of a number must contain all its prime factors, otherwise it can not contain the number itself. It follows from this, that a common multiple of two or more numbers must contain *all* the prime factors of each of the numbers, and that the *least* common multiple of two or more numbers must contain all the prime factors *only the greatest number* of times they are found in any of the numbers.

ART. **22.** To find the least common multiple of two or more numbers.

Ex. 1. What is the least common multiple of 21, 63, 108 ?

FIRST METHOD.

$21=3\times7$
$63=3\times3\times7$
$108=3\times3\times3\times2\times2$
$3\times3\times3\times4\times7=756$ *Ans.*

Explanation.—The multiple of 108 must contain the factor 3 three times and the factor 2 twice; the multiple of 63 must contain the factor 3 at least twice and 7 once; the multiple of 21 must contain the factor 3 at least once and 7 once. It is evident that a number that contains the factor 3 three times, the factor 7 once, and the factor 2 twice, is the least common multiple of 21, 63, and 108.

RULE.

Resolve each of the given numbers into its prime factors. The product of the different factors, each factor being taken the greatest number of times it occurs in any of the numbers, will be the least common multiple.

Note.—This method is not often used.

SECOND METHOD.

3)21—63—108
7)7—21— 36
3)1— 3— 36
1— 1— 12
$3\times3\times12\times7=756$ *Ans.*

Explanation.—It is evident that by this method the same result is obtained as by the former method, viz: the *greatest* number of times each prime factor enters in *any* of the numbers. 756 contains the factor 3 three times, 2 twice, and 7 once ($12=2\times2\times3$).

RULE.

Arrange the numbers on a horizontal line, divide by any prime number that will exactly divide two or more of the numbers, and write the quotients and undivided numbers in a line beneath. Divide this line of numbers in the same manner as the first, and so on until no prime number will exactly divide two numbers. The product of all the divisors and undivided numbers will be the least common multiple required.

Find the least common multiple of the following numbers:

2. 8, 12, 16, 24, and 36.
3. 9, 15, 21, and 75.
4. 3, 8, 9, 15, and 32.
5. 17, 34, 68, and 5.
6. 8, 12, 16, 35, and 84.
7. 3, 4, 5, 6, 8, 10, and 12.
8. 5, 4, 6, 9, and 7.
9. 7, 8, 49, 98, and 168.
10. $\frac{2}{3}$, $\frac{3}{4}$, $\frac{5}{6}$, and $\frac{2}{5}$.

Suggestion.—Reduce fractions to a common denominator, and then find the least common multiple of their numerators.

11. $2\frac{1}{2}$, 5, $3\frac{1}{3}$, and $4\frac{1}{2}$.

COMMON FRACTIONS.

ART. **23.** If a unit or a body, as an apple, an orange, etc., be divided into four *equal* parts, one of these parts is one-fourth of the whole; two, two-fourths; three, three-fourths; four, four-fourths—which are respectively written $\frac{1}{4}$, $\frac{2}{4}$, $\frac{3}{4}$, $\frac{4}{4}$. These expressions are called fractions; the number above the line being called the *numerator*, and the number below the line the *denominator*. Hence, "*a fraction is an expression for one or more of the equal parts of a unit.*"

It is evident that the denominator shows into how many equal parts the unit has been divided; the numerator, how many of these equal parts are taken. The numerator and denominator are called *terms* of the fraction.

A fraction may also be regarded as an expressed division, the numerator being the dividend and the denominator the divisor. $3 \div 4$ may also be written $\frac{3}{4}$; the value of the fraction being the *quotient.* 4 is contained in 3 three-fourths of a time.

A common or vulgar fraction is one in which both terms are written ; as $\frac{3}{4}$, $\frac{8}{7}$, $\frac{9}{10}$, etc.

Common fractions are divided into three classes, *simple, compound,* and *complex.*

A simple or single fraction has but one numerator and one denominator, each being a whole number ; as $\frac{5}{6}$ and $\frac{7}{5}$.

A compound fraction consists of two or more simple fractions connected by the word of ; as $\frac{2}{3}$ of $\frac{3}{4}$, and $\frac{2}{5}$ of $\frac{6}{7}$ of $2\frac{1}{2}$.

A complex fraction has a fraction for one or both of its terms ; as $\frac{\frac{2}{3}}{\frac{3}{4}}$, $\frac{\frac{2}{3}}{7}$, and $\frac{\frac{7}{2}}{3}$.

Simple fractions are divided into *proper* and *improper.*

A proper fraction is one whose numerator is less than its denominator ; as $\frac{3}{4}$, $\frac{7}{8}$, etc.

An improper fraction is one whose numerator is equal to or greater than its denominator ; as $\frac{4}{4}$ and $\frac{9}{5}$.

A mixed number is composed of a whole number and a fraction ; as $12\frac{1}{2}$, $16\frac{2}{3}$, etc. The fraction is added to the whole number, $12\frac{1}{2}$ being the same as $12+\frac{1}{2}$.

It is evident from the very nature of a fraction that *both of its terms may be multiplied or divided by the same number without changing its value.*

The value of a fraction may be *increased,* 1. By adding to its numerator. 2. By multiplying its numerator. 3. By subtracting from its denominator. 4. By dividing its denominator.

The value of a fraction may be decreased, 1. By adding to its denominator. 2. By multiplying its denominator. 3. By subtracting from its numerator. 4. By dividing its numerator.

ART. **24.** To reduce a fraction to its lowest terms.

Ex. 1. Reduce $\frac{24}{56}$ to its lowest terms.

$4)\frac{24}{56}=2)\frac{6}{14}-3\frac{3}{7}$ *Ans.* Or, $8)\frac{24}{56}=\frac{3}{7}$ *Ans.*

Explanation.—Since both terms of a fraction may be divided by the same number without changing its value, divide both numerator and denominator by 4. The result is $\frac{6}{24}$.

Again, divide both terms of this fraction by 2; the result is $\frac{3}{7}$, which can not be reduced lower, since no number greater than 1 will divide both of its terms. Or divide by 8, the *greatest* number that will divide both terms of the fraction; the result is $\frac{3}{7}$.

RULE.

Divide both terms of the fraction by any number that will divide each of them without a remainder, and proceed until they are prime to each other. Or,

Divide both terms of the fraction by their greatest common divisor.

Examples.

2. Reduce $\frac{63}{84}$ to its lowest terms.
3. Reduce $\frac{16}{128}$ to its lowest terms.
4. Reduce $\frac{45}{105}$ to its lowest terms.
5. Reduce $\frac{72}{168}$ to its lowest terms.
6. Reduce $\frac{150}{720}$ to its lowest terms.
7. Reduce $\frac{96}{144}$ to its lowest terms. *Ans.* $\frac{2}{3}$.
8. Reduce $\frac{360}{1032}$ to its lowest terms. *Ans.* $\frac{15}{43}$.
9. Reduce $\frac{4158}{9702}$ to its lowest terms. *Ans.* $\frac{3}{7}$.
10. Reduce $\frac{504}{1386}$ to its lowest terms. *Ans.* $\frac{4}{11}$.

ART. **25.** To reduce a fraction to higher terms.

Ex. 1. Reduce $\frac{3}{4}$ to twelfths.

$\frac{1}{4}=\frac{3}{12}$, $\frac{3}{4}=\frac{3\times 3}{12}=\frac{9}{12}$ *Ans.* Or, $\frac{3}{4}\times 3=\frac{9}{12}$ *Ans.*

Explanation.—Since 1 fourth equals 3 twelfths, 3 fourths must equal 3 times 3 twelfths, which is 9 twelfths. *Ans.* $\frac{9}{12}$. Or, since both terms of a fraction may be multiplied by the same number without changing its value, multiply both numerator and denominator by 3.

Examples.

2. Reduce $\frac{3}{7}$ to sixty-thirds. *Ans.* $\frac{27}{63}$.
3. Reduce $\frac{5}{12}$ to sixtieths. *Ans.* $\frac{25}{60}$.
4. Reduce $\frac{5}{19}$ to fifty-sevenths.
5. Reduce $\frac{8}{21}$ to eighty-fourths.
6. Reduce $\frac{7}{5}$ to fifteenths.

7. Reduce $\frac{56}{9}$ to twenty-sevenths.

8. Reduce $\frac{5}{6}$, $\frac{7}{8}$, and $\frac{2}{3}$ to twenty-fourths.

Ans. $\frac{20}{24}$, $\frac{21}{24}$, and $\frac{16}{24}$.

9. Reduce $\frac{5}{7}$, $\frac{3}{5}$, and $\frac{3}{14}$ to seventieths.

10. Reduce $\frac{7}{12}$, $\frac{5}{8}$, $\frac{3}{4}$, and $\frac{9}{16}$ to forty-eighths.

ART. **26.** To reduce an improper fraction to a whole or mixed number.

Ex. 1. Reduce $\frac{49}{5}$ to a mixed number.

$$49 \div 5 = 9\tfrac{4}{5} \text{ Ans.}$$

Explanation.—Since 5 fifths make 1, there will be as many ones in 49 fifths as 5 is contained times in 49, which is $9\frac{4}{5}$.

RULE.

Divide the numerator by the denominator.

Examples.

2. Reduce $\frac{19}{5}$ to a mixed number.
3. Reduce $\frac{25}{4}$ to a mixed number.
4. Reduce $\frac{57}{19}$ to a whole number.
5. Reduce $\frac{125}{12}$ to a mixed number.
6. Reduce $\frac{121}{17}$ to a mixed number.
7. Reduce $\frac{315}{95}$ to a mixed number. *Ans.* $3\frac{6}{19}$.
8. Reduce $\frac{75}{3}$ to a whole number. *Ans.* 25.
9. Reduce $\frac{87}{17}$ to a mixed number. *Ans.* $5\frac{2}{17}$.
10. Reduce $\frac{161}{9}$ to a mixed number. *Ans.* $17\frac{8}{9}$.

ART. **27.** To reduce a whole or mixed number to an improper fraction.

Ex. 1. Reduce $5\frac{3}{4}$ to an improper fraction.

$$\frac{5 \times 4}{4} + \frac{3}{4} = \frac{23}{4} \text{ Ans.}$$

Explanation.—Since there are 4 fourths in 1, in 5 there are 5 times 4 fourths=20 fourths, and 20 fourths+3 fourths= 23 fourths. *Ans.* $\frac{23}{4}$.

RULE.

Multiply the whole number by the denominator of the fraction, to the product add the numerator, and under the result place the denominator.

Examples.

2. Reduce $44\frac{2}{3}$ to an improper fraction.
3. Reduce $3\frac{60}{105}$ to an improper fraction. *Ans.* $\frac{375}{105}$.
4. Reduce $56\frac{3}{4}$ to an improper fraction.
5. Reduce $1236\frac{9}{20}$ to an improper fraction. *Ans.* $\frac{24729}{20}$.
6. Reduce $5\frac{5}{720}$ to an improper fraction.
7. Reduce $23\frac{9}{16}$ to an improper fraction. *Ans.* $\frac{377}{16}$.
8. Reduce $133\frac{13}{15}$ to an improper fraction.
9. Reduce $563\frac{4}{5}$ to an improper fraction. *Ans.* $\frac{2819}{5}$.
10. Reduce $8006\frac{13}{17}$ to an improper fraction. *Ans.* $\frac{136115}{17}$.
11. Reduce 24 to fourths. *Ans.* $\frac{96}{4}$.
12. Reduce 35 to twentieths. *Ans.* $\frac{700}{20}$.
13. Reduce 312 to twelfths.
14. Reduce 19 to twenty-fifths.
15. Reduce 1008 to ninths.

ART. **28.** To reduce compound fractions to simple ones.

Ex. 1. Reduce $\frac{4}{5}$ of $\frac{5}{6}$ to a simple fraction.

$$\frac{4}{5} \text{ of } \frac{5}{6} = \frac{4 \times 5}{5 \times 5} = \frac{20}{30} \textit{ Ans.}$$

Explanation.—$\frac{1}{5}$ of $\frac{1}{6}$ is $\frac{1}{30}$, and $\frac{1}{5}$ of $\frac{5}{6}$ is 5 times $\frac{1}{30}$ or $\frac{5}{30}$, and if $\frac{1}{5}$ of $\frac{5}{6}$ is $\frac{5}{30}$, $\frac{4}{5}$ of $\frac{5}{6}$ is 4 times $\frac{5}{30}$, or $\frac{20}{30}=\frac{2}{3}$ *Ans.* This is in effect multiplying the numerators together and also the denominators.

RULE.

Multiply the numerators together for the numerator of the simple fraction, and the denominators together for its denominator.

Note.—If there are whole or mixed numbers, first reduce them to improper fractions.

Examples.

2. Reduce $\frac{3}{4}$ of $\frac{5}{8}$ of $\frac{8}{9}$ to a simple fraction. *Ans.* $\frac{5}{12}$.
3. Reduce $3\frac{1}{3}$ of $2\frac{1}{2}$ of $\frac{3}{10}$ to a simple fraction. *Ans.* $2\frac{1}{2}$.
4. Reduce $2\frac{1}{2}$ of $1\frac{9}{15}$ of $\frac{2}{3}$ to a simple fraction.
5. Reduce $\frac{4}{5}$ of $\frac{7}{8}$ of $2\frac{1}{2}$ to a simple fraction.
6. Reduce $\frac{2}{3}$ of $1\frac{1}{2}$ of $\frac{3}{7}$ of $2\frac{1}{3}$ to a simple fraction. *Ans.* $\frac{1}{1}$.
7. Reduce $\frac{2}{5}$ of 6 to a simple fraction.
8. Reduce $\frac{2}{3}$ of $2\frac{1}{2}$ of 3 to a simple fraction.

CANCELLATION.

Art. 29. The above operations may be abbreviated by indicating the multiplications to be performed, and then cancelling the factors common to both terms, as shown in the following examples.

Ex. 1. Reduce $\frac{3}{4}$ of $\frac{8}{9}$ of $\frac{6}{7}$ of $2\frac{1}{3}$ to a simple fraction.

$$\frac{\cancel{3}\times\overset{2}{\cancel{8}}\times\overset{2}{\cancel{6}}\times\cancel{7}}{\cancel{4}\times\underset{\cancel{3}}{\cancel{9}}\times\cancel{7}\times 3}=\frac{4}{3}=1\tfrac{1}{3}\ \textit{Ans.}$$

2. Reduce $\frac{2}{3}$ of $\frac{3}{4}$ of $\frac{4}{5}$ of $\frac{5}{6}$ of $\frac{6}{7}$ of $1\frac{1}{6}$ to a simple fraction.

$$\frac{\cancel{2}\times\cancel{3}\times\cancel{4}\times\cancel{5}\times\cancel{6}\times\cancel{7}}{\cancel{3}\times\cancel{4}\times\cancel{5}\times\cancel{6}\times\cancel{7}\times\underset{3}{\cancel{6}}}=\tfrac{1}{3}\ \textit{Ans.}$$

Note.—1 remains as a factor in the numerator.

3. Reduce $\frac{1}{3}$ of $4\frac{1}{5}$ of $\frac{9}{14}$ of $\frac{7}{8}$ to a simple fraction.

4. Reduce $\frac{8}{9}$ of $2\frac{13}{16}$ of $\frac{7}{25}$ of $\frac{2}{3}$ to a simple fraction.

Ans. $\frac{7}{15}$.

5. Reduce $\frac{2}{3}$ of $\frac{4}{5}$ of $\frac{5}{6}$ of $\frac{6}{10}$ of $12\frac{6}{7}$ to a simple fraction.

Ans. $3\frac{3}{7}$.

6. Reduce $\frac{2}{7}$ of $3\frac{1}{2}$ of $\frac{6}{11}$ of $\frac{11}{12}$ of $\frac{7}{15}$ of $7\frac{1}{2}$ to a simple fraction.

Remark.—The principle of cancellation may often be used with great advantage. Whenever, to obtain a certain result, several multiplications and divisions are to be performed, indicate the operations and cancel the factors common to the multipliers and divisors.

7. Divide the product of 24, $16\frac{2}{3}$, 8, $33\frac{1}{3}$ by 12, $16\frac{2}{3}$, and $66\frac{2}{3}$.

$$\frac{\overset{\cancel{2}}{\cancel{24}}\times\cancel{16\tfrac{2}{3}}\times 8\times\cancel{33\tfrac{1}{3}}}{\cancel{12}\times\cancel{16\tfrac{2}{3}}\times\underset{\cancel{2}}{\cancel{66\tfrac{2}{3}}}}=8\ \textit{Ans.}$$

8. Multiply 48, 32, 5280 and 27 together, and divide the result by 16, 264, 54 and 6. *Ans.* 160.

9. How many cords of wood in a pile 144 feet long, 12 feet high and 3 feet wide?

$$\frac{\overset{\overset{9}{\cancel{18}}}{\cancel{144}}\times\overset{3}{\cancel{12}}\times 3}{\cancel{8}\times\cancel{4}\times\underset{2}{\cancel{4}}}=\frac{81}{2}=40\tfrac{1}{2}\ \textit{Ans.}$$

10. Multiply 9, 8, 18, 45, 36, 90, 81 together and divide the result by 72, 180, 27, 24, 4 and 18. *Ans.* $25\frac{5}{16}$.

ART. **30.** To reduce fractions to a common denominator.

Ex. 1. Reduce $\frac{3}{4}$, $\frac{5}{8}$, $\frac{5}{6}$, $\frac{2}{3}$ and $\frac{7}{12}$ to equivalent fractions having a common denominator.

Solution. First Method.—It is evident upon a little inspection that each of the fractions can be changed to *twenty-fourths.* According to Art. 24, $\frac{3}{4}=\frac{18}{24}$, $\frac{5}{8}=\frac{15}{24}$, $\frac{5}{6}=\frac{20}{24}$, $\frac{2}{3}=\frac{16}{24}$, and $\frac{7}{12}=\frac{14}{24}$. Hence $\frac{3}{4}$, $\frac{5}{8}$, $\frac{5}{6}$, $\frac{2}{3}$ and $\frac{7}{12}$ are respectively equal to $\frac{18}{24}$, $\frac{15}{24}$, $\frac{20}{24}$, $\frac{16}{24}$ and $\frac{14}{24}$, fractions having a common denominator.

Second Method.—The least common multiple of 4, 8, 6, 3 and 12 (denominators) found by Art. 22, is 24, which, being divided by 4, 8, 6, 3 and 12 respectively, give the multipliers by which both terms of their respective fractions are to be multiplied. $\frac{3\times6}{4\times6}=\frac{18}{24}$, $\frac{5\times3}{8\times3}=\frac{15}{24}$, $\frac{5\times4}{6\times4}=\frac{20}{24}$, $\frac{2\times8}{3\times8}=\frac{16}{24}$, and $\frac{7\times2}{12\times2}=\frac{14}{24}$.

RULE FOR SECOND METHOD.—*Find the least common multiple of the denominators. Then divide the least common multiple by the denominator of each fraction and multiply both of its terms by the quotient.*

Note.—The first method is the one generally used. In ordinary examples, the common denominator can be seen at a glance.

Examples.

Reduce the following fractions to equivalent fractions having a common denominator.

2. $\frac{3}{4}$, $\frac{5}{8}$, $\frac{6}{7}$, $\frac{5}{14}$, $\frac{9}{28}$.
3. $\frac{5}{6}$ and $\frac{7}{16}$.
4. $\frac{1}{4}$, $\frac{3}{5}$, $\frac{1}{3}$, $\frac{5}{8}$.
5. $\frac{2}{3}$, $\frac{3}{7}$, $\frac{5}{6}$, $\frac{1}{2}$.
6. $\frac{1}{2}$ of $\frac{2}{3}$, $2\frac{1}{2}$, $\frac{5}{6}$. *Ans.* $\frac{2}{6}$, $\frac{15}{6}$, $\frac{5}{6}$.
7. $\frac{2}{5}$ of $\frac{5}{6}$, $\frac{3}{8}$, $2\frac{1}{3}$.
8. $\frac{1}{3}$, $\frac{1}{4}$, $\frac{1}{5}$, $\frac{1}{6}$, $\frac{1}{8}$, $\frac{1}{12}$.
9. $\frac{2}{3}$, $\frac{4}{5}$, $\frac{5}{6}$, $\frac{7}{8}$.
10. $\frac{3}{4}$, $\frac{7}{8}$, $\frac{6}{7}$, $\frac{5}{9}$.

ADDITION OF COMMON FRACTIONS.

ART. **31.** Ex. 1. What is the sum of $\frac{2}{3}$, $\frac{3}{4}$, $\frac{5}{6}$ and $\frac{7}{8}$?

$\frac{2}{3}+\frac{3}{4}+\frac{5}{6}+\frac{7}{8}=$

$\frac{16}{24}+\frac{18}{24}+\frac{20}{24}+\frac{21}{24}=\frac{75}{24}=3\frac{1}{8}$ *Ans.*

Ex. 2. Add $\frac{2}{3}$ of $\frac{3}{5}$, $\frac{5}{6}$ of $\frac{6}{7}$ and $2\frac{1}{3}$.

$\frac{2}{3}$ of $\frac{3}{5}=\frac{2}{5}$, $\frac{5}{6}$ of $\frac{6}{7}=\frac{5}{7}$, $2\frac{1}{2}=\frac{5}{2}$

$\frac{2}{5}+\frac{5}{7}+\frac{5}{2}=$

$\frac{28}{70}+\frac{50}{70}+\frac{175}{70}=\frac{253}{70}=3\frac{43}{70}$ *Ans.*

RULE.

Reduce the fractions to a common denominator; then add their numerators, and under their sum place the common denominator.

Notes.—1. First reduce mixed numbers to improper fractions, and compound fractions to simple ones.

2. The integers may be set aside and subsequently added to the sum of the fractions.

Examples.

3. Add $\frac{3}{4}$, $\frac{2}{5}$, $\frac{2}{3}$ and $\frac{1}{2}$. *Ans.* $2\frac{19}{60}$.
4. Add $\frac{2}{3}$ of $\frac{3}{8}$ and $\frac{9}{10}$. *Ans.* $1\frac{3}{20}$.
5. Add $\frac{2}{3}$, $\frac{5}{8}$ and $\frac{4}{7}$. *Ans.* $1\frac{145}{168}$.
6. Add $5\frac{1}{2}$, $3\frac{3}{8}$, $5\frac{2}{3}$. *Ans.* $14\frac{13}{24}$.
7. Add $\frac{2}{5}$ of $2\frac{1}{2}$ and $\frac{3}{7}$ of $2\frac{1}{3}$. *Ans.* 2.
8. Add $1026\frac{11}{20}$, $1875\frac{3}{4}$ and $5634\frac{4}{9}$. *Ans.* $8536\frac{134}{180}$.

Suggestion.—First add the fractions.

9. Add $37\frac{1}{2}$, $18\frac{3}{4}$, $33\frac{1}{3}$ and $81\frac{1}{4}$. *Ans.* $170\frac{5}{6}$.
10. Add $\frac{2}{3}$, $\frac{9}{34}$ of $4\frac{1}{4}$, $563\frac{5}{9}$, and $\frac{3}{4}$ of $3\frac{5}{9}$.
11. Add $\frac{1}{2}$, $\frac{1}{3}$, $\frac{1}{4}$, $\frac{1}{5}$ and $\frac{1}{6}$.
12. Add $\frac{3}{5}$, $\frac{5}{8}$, $\frac{3}{10}$, and $\frac{6}{7}$ of $1\frac{1}{6}$.
13. Add $\frac{1}{2}$, $\frac{1}{3}$, $\frac{1}{4}$, $\frac{1}{5}$, and $\frac{1}{6}$.
14. Add $\frac{2}{3}$ of $\frac{3}{5}$ and $12\frac{1}{2}$.
15. Add $105\frac{2}{3}$ and $98\frac{1}{12}$.

SUBTRACTION OF COMMON FRACTIONS.

ART. **32.** Ex. 1. From $\frac{6}{7}$ take $\frac{2}{3}$.

$$\tfrac{6}{7}-\tfrac{2}{3}=\tfrac{18}{21}-\tfrac{14}{21}=\tfrac{4}{21}\ \textit{Ans.}$$

Ex. 2. From $2\frac{1}{2}$ take $\frac{3}{4}$ of 2.

$$2\tfrac{1}{2}=\tfrac{5}{2},\ \tfrac{3}{4}\text{ of }\tfrac{2}{1}=\tfrac{6}{4}$$

$$\tfrac{5}{2}-\tfrac{3}{2}=\tfrac{2}{2}=1\ \textit{Ans.}$$

RULE.

Reduce the fractions to a common denominator; then subtract their numerators, and under the result place the common denominator.

Note.—Mixed numbers may be subtracted without reducing them to improper fractions.

3. Subtract $\frac{2}{3}$ from $\frac{3}{4}$. *Ans.* $\frac{1}{12}$.
4. Subtract $\frac{2}{11}$ from $\frac{2}{7}$.
5. From $\frac{1}{3}$ of $\frac{3}{4}$ take $\frac{2}{5}$ of $\frac{2}{11}$. *Ans.* $\frac{39}{220}$.
6. From $\frac{3}{4}$ of $\frac{4}{9}$ take $\frac{1}{3}$.
7. From $\frac{1}{3}$ of $\frac{3}{4}$ take $\frac{3}{10}$ of $\frac{1}{8}$. *Ans.* $\frac{17}{80}$.
8. From $820\frac{2}{3}$ subtract $56\frac{3}{4}$.

$$\begin{array}{r} 820\tfrac{2}{3},\ \tfrac{8}{12} \\ 56\tfrac{3}{4},\ \tfrac{9}{12} \\ \hline 763\tfrac{11}{12}\ \textit{Ans.} \end{array}$$

9. From $250\frac{1}{5}$ subtract $225\frac{4}{7}$.
10. From $993\frac{3}{4}$ take $546\frac{7}{8}$. *Ans.* $446\frac{7}{8}$.
11. From $\frac{3}{4}+\frac{7}{8}+\frac{4}{9}$ take $\frac{3}{4}$ of $\frac{8}{9}+\frac{9}{10}$ of $\frac{5}{6}$. *Ans.* $\frac{47}{72}$.
12. From $\frac{2}{3}$ of 12 take $\frac{3}{4}$ of 9.
13. From 1000 take $156\frac{2}{3}$.
14. From 9 take $\frac{1}{2}$ of $\frac{3}{4}$.
15. From $56\frac{7}{12}+89\frac{3}{4}$ take $5\frac{4}{5}+81\frac{7}{10}$. *Ans.* $59\frac{23}{240}$.
16. From $\frac{1}{2}$ of 13 take $\frac{4}{5}$ of 8. *Ans.* $\frac{1}{10}$.
17. From $3\frac{1}{2}$ of 5 take $2\frac{1}{3}$ of 7. *Ans.* $1\frac{1}{6}$.
18. From $\frac{5}{7}$ of 42 take $\frac{2}{7}$ of 48. *Ans.* $16\frac{2}{7}$.
19. From $\frac{2}{3}$ of $19\frac{1}{2}$ take $\frac{2}{5}$ of $7\frac{2}{3}$. *Ans.* $9\frac{14}{15}$.
20. From $875\frac{2}{3}$ take $599\frac{7}{8}$.

MULTIPLICATION OF COMMON FRACTIONS.

ART. **33.** To multiply a fraction by a whole number.

Ex. 1. Multiply $\frac{5}{12}$ by 4.

$\frac{5\times4}{12}=\frac{20}{12}=\frac{5}{3}=1\frac{2}{3}$ *Ans.* Or, $\frac{5}{12\div4}=\frac{5}{3}=1\frac{2}{3}$ *Ans.*

Explanation.—4 times $\frac{5}{12}$ is $\frac{20}{12}=\frac{5}{3}$, or $1\frac{2}{3}$. It is evident that the same result is obtained by dividing the denominator by 4.

RULE.

Multiply the numerator of the fraction by the whole number, or divide the denominator.

2. Multiply $\frac{7}{64}$ by 16. *Ans.* $1\frac{3}{4}$.
3. Multiply $\frac{16}{21}$ by 3. *Ans.* $2\frac{2}{7}$.
4. Multiply $\frac{56}{81}$ by 9. *Ans.* $6\frac{2}{9}$.
5. Multiply $\frac{23}{1000}$ by 25.

ART. **34.** To multiply a whole number by a fraction.

Ex. 1. Multiply 15 by $\frac{3}{4}$.

$15\times\frac{3}{4}=\frac{45}{4}=11\frac{1}{4}$ *Ans.* Or, $15\div4=3\frac{3}{4}$, $3\frac{3}{4}\times3=11\frac{1}{4}$ *Ans.*

Explanation.—Since $\frac{3}{4}=\frac{1}{4}$ of 3, $\frac{3}{4}$ times 15 is $\frac{1}{4}$ of 3 times 15, or 45, and $\frac{1}{4}$ of $45=11\frac{1}{4}$ *Ans.* Or, since 1 times 15 is 15, $\frac{1}{4}$ times 15 is $\frac{1}{4}$ of $15=3\frac{3}{4}$, and $\frac{3}{4}$ times 15 is 3 times $3\frac{3}{4}=11\frac{1}{4}$ *Ans.*

Ex. 2. Multiply 5280 by $\frac{5}{8}$.

```
8)5280              5280
   660                 5
     5      Or, 8)26400
  3300 Ans.         3300 Ans.
```

RULE.

Multiply the whole number by the numerator of the fraction and divide the product by the denominator. Or,

Divide the whole number by the denominator of the fraction and multiply the quotient by the numerator.

3. Multiply 56 by $\frac{5}{8}$. *Ans.* 35.

4. Multiply 5280 by $\frac{3}{50}$. *Ans.* $316\frac{4}{5}$.

5. Multiply 329 by $5\frac{1}{2}$. *Ans.* $1809\frac{1}{2}$.

Suggestion.—Multiply by $\frac{1}{2}$, and then by 5, adding results.

6. Multiply 435 by $16\frac{2}{3}$. *Ans.* 7250.

Note.—By changing the whole number to a fraction ($12=\frac{12}{1}$), the above ten examples may be solved as in the following article.

ART. **35.** To multiply one fraction by another.

Ex. 1. Multiply $\frac{3}{4}$ by $\frac{7}{8}$.

$$\frac{3}{4}\times\frac{7}{8}=\frac{3\times 7}{4\times 8}=\frac{21}{32}\ \textit{Ans.}$$

Explanation.—Since $\frac{3}{4}$ is $\frac{1}{4}$ of 3, $\frac{3}{4}$ times $\frac{7}{8}$ must equal $\frac{1}{4}$ of 3 times $\frac{7}{8}$. 3 times $\frac{7}{8}$ is $\frac{21}{8}$, and $\frac{1}{4}$ of $\frac{21}{8}$ is $\frac{21}{32}$.

Ex. 2. Multiply $\frac{3}{7}$ by $\frac{2}{3}$ of $\frac{14}{15}$.

$$\frac{\cancel{3}}{\cancel{7}}\times\frac{2}{\cancel{3}}\text{ of }\frac{\overset{2}{\cancel{14}}}{15}=\frac{4}{15}\ \textit{Ans.}$$

RULE.

Multiply the numerators together, and also the denominators. Or,

Indicate the multiplication to be performed, and cancel the factors common to the numerators and denominators.

Note.—It is not necessary first to reduce compound fractions to simple ones.

Examples.

2. Multiply $\frac{3}{5}$ by $\frac{5}{6}$.
3. Multiply $\frac{7}{12}$ by $\frac{8}{21}$. *Ans.* $\frac{2}{9}$.
4. Multiply $\frac{5}{8}$ by $\frac{7}{9}$.
5. Multiply 56 by $\frac{7}{8}$. *Ans.* 49.
6. Multiply $\frac{9}{16}$ by 24. *Ans.* $13\frac{1}{2}$.
7. Multiply $8\frac{1}{2}$ by $7\frac{2}{3}$. *Ans.* $65\frac{1}{6}$.
8. Multiply 111 by $9\frac{2}{3}$.
9. Multiply $\frac{3}{4}$ of $\frac{16}{27}$ by $\frac{8}{10}$ of $\frac{25}{32}$. *Ans.* $\frac{5}{18}$.
10. Multiply $\frac{5}{9}$ of $\frac{9}{10}$ by $\frac{9}{11}-\frac{3}{4}$. *Ans.* $\frac{3}{88}$.
11. Multiply $\frac{3}{4}$ of 8 by 9 times $\frac{2}{3}$.

12. Multiply $8\frac{3}{4}-6\frac{7}{8}$ by $9\frac{2}{3}+\frac{4}{5}$. *Ans.* $19\frac{5}{8}$.
13. Multiply 256 by $12\frac{5}{16}$. *Ans.* 3152.
14. Multiply $12\frac{1}{2}$ by $16\frac{2}{3}$. *Ans.* 208.

DIVISION OF COMMON FRACTIONS

ART. **36.** To divide a fraction by a whole number.

Ex. 1. Divide $\frac{9}{10}$ by 3.

$$\frac{9 \div 3}{10}=\frac{3}{10} \textit{ Ans.} \quad \text{Or, } \frac{9}{10 \times 3}=\frac{9}{30}=\frac{3}{10} \textit{ Ans.}$$

Explanation.—To divide a number by 3 is to take $\frac{1}{3}$ of it; $\frac{1}{3}$ of $\frac{9}{10}=\frac{3}{10}$, or $\frac{1}{3}$ of $\frac{9}{10}=\frac{9}{30}=\frac{3}{10}$.

RULE.

Divide the numerator of the fraction by the whole number, or multiply its denominator.

Examples.

2. Divide $\frac{27}{32}$ by 9.
3. Divide $\frac{14}{25}$ by 7.
4. Divide $6\frac{1}{2}$ by 9. *Ans.* $\frac{13}{18}$.
5. Divide $6084\frac{2}{3}$ by 5.

$$5)\underline{6084\frac{2}{3}}$$
$$1216,\ 4\frac{2}{3} \text{ undivided}$$

$4\frac{2}{3}=\frac{14}{3}\div 5=\frac{14}{15}$. Hence $6084\frac{2}{3}\div 5=1216\frac{14}{15}$ *Ans.*

6. Divide $308\frac{2}{3}$ by 12. *Ans.* $25\frac{13}{18}$.
7. Divide $32006\frac{1}{5}$ by 9. *Ans.* $3556\frac{11}{45}$.
8. Divide $1000\frac{5}{12}$ by 5. *Ans.* $200\frac{1}{12}$.

ART. **37.** To divide a whole number by a fraction.

Ex. 1. Divide 12 by $\frac{3}{4}$.

```
   12            Or, 3)12
    4                  4
 3)48                  4
   16 Ans.            16 Ans.
```

Explanation.—Since 1 is contained in 12 twelve times, $\frac{1}{4}$ is contained in 12 four times 12 times, or 48 times, and $\frac{3}{4}$, one third of 48 times, or 16 times. Or, 3 is contained in 12 four times, and $\frac{3}{4}$, or $\frac{1}{4}$ of 3, four times 4 times, or 16 times.

RULE.

Multiply the whole number by the denominator of the fraction, and divide the product by the numerator. Or,

Divide the whole number by the numerator, and multiply the result by the denominator.

Examples.

2. Divide 16 by $\frac{3}{9}$.
3. Divide 256 by $\frac{16}{21}$. *Ans.* 336.
4. Divide 225 by $12\frac{1}{2}$.
5. Divide 30864 by $\frac{1}{4}$. By $\frac{2}{3}$. *Ans.* to last, 46296.
6. Divide 50 by $6\frac{1}{4}$. By $3\frac{1}{3}$.
7. Divide 284 by $\frac{2}{3}$ of $\frac{3}{8}$. *Ans.* 1136.

Note.—By reducing the whole number to an improper fraction the above 15 examples may be solved as in the following article.

ART. **38.** To divide one fraction by another.

Ex. 1. Divide $\frac{9}{20}$ by $\frac{3}{4}$.

$$\frac{9}{20} \div \frac{3}{4} = \frac{9}{20} \times \frac{4}{3} = \frac{3}{5} \textit{ Ans.}$$

Explanation.—Since $\frac{3}{4}$ is equal to $\frac{1}{4}$ of 3, the quotient of $\frac{9}{20}$, divided by 3, or $\frac{9}{60}$, will be four times too small, and hence the quotient of $\frac{9}{20}$, divided by $\frac{1}{4}$ of 3, or $\frac{3}{4}$, is equal to 4 times $\frac{9}{60}$, or $\frac{36}{60} = \frac{3}{5}$. Observe that this is, in effect, the same as multiplying the dividend by the divisor inverted.

RULE.

Invert the divisor and proceed as in multiplication of fractions.

Examples.

2. Divide $\frac{3}{5}$ by $\frac{1}{2}$.
3. Divide $\frac{2}{3}$ by $\frac{4}{9}$. *Ans.* $1\frac{1}{2}$.
4. Divide $7\frac{1}{2}$ by $8\frac{1}{3}$.
5. Divide $4\frac{1}{2}$ by $6\frac{1}{4}$. *Ans.* $\frac{18}{25}$.
6. Divide $18\frac{3}{4}$ by $15\frac{1}{5}$.

7. Divide $\frac{2}{3}$ of $\frac{3}{4}$ by $\frac{1}{2}$ of $5\frac{1}{2}$. *Ans.* $\frac{2}{11}$.
8. Divide $\frac{1}{4}$ of $4\frac{1}{2}$ by $\frac{1}{3}$ of $5\frac{1}{2}$.
9. Divide $\frac{3}{5}$ of 8 by $\frac{2}{3}$ of 7. *Ans.* $1\frac{1}{35}$.
10. Divide $12\frac{1}{2}$ of $\frac{1}{2}$ by $8\frac{1}{3}$ of $\frac{1}{3}$.
11. Divide $\frac{9}{20}+4\frac{4}{5}$ by $4\frac{7}{8}-3\frac{11}{12}$. *Ans.* $5\frac{11}{23}$.
12. Divide $\frac{9}{16}$ of $\frac{16}{27}-\frac{1}{3}$ of $\frac{7}{14}$ by $5\frac{1}{2}-4\frac{7}{8}$.
13. Divide $125\frac{3}{4}-62\frac{4}{5}$ by $37\frac{1}{2}$. *Ans.* $1\frac{509}{750}$.
14. Divide $4\frac{1}{2}+6\frac{2}{3}$ by $\frac{5}{11}$.
15. Divide $9\frac{1}{10}+4\frac{1}{2}\times\frac{5}{8}$ by $6\frac{3}{8}$. *Ans.* $1\frac{443}{510}$.

ART. **39.** To reduce a complex fraction to a simple one.

Ex. Reduce $\frac{\frac{4}{5}}{\frac{8}{9}}$ to a simple fraction.

$$\frac{\frac{4}{5}}{\frac{8}{9}}=\frac{4}{5}\div\frac{8}{9}=\frac{4}{5}\times\frac{9}{8}=\frac{9}{10}\ \textit{Ans.}$$

Explanation.—It is evident that a complex fraction is only an indicated division of one fraction by another, in which the numerator is the dividend, and the denominator the divisor. In the example $\frac{4}{5}$ is the dividend, and $\frac{8}{9}$ the divisor. We may proceed as in division, or it is plain that the same result may be obtained by multiplying the extremes, 4 and 9, for a numerator, and the means, 5 and 8, for a denominator.

RULE.

Divide the numerator of the complex fraction by the denominator as in division of fractions.

Examples.

2. Reduce $\frac{\frac{5}{6}}{\frac{7}{12}}$ to a simple fraction.
3. Reduce $\frac{\frac{2}{3}}{\frac{3}{4}}$ to a simple fraction. *Ans.* $\frac{8}{9}$.
4. Reduce $\frac{3\frac{1}{3}}{33\frac{1}{3}}$ to a simple fraction.
5. Reduce $\frac{6\frac{2}{3}}{11\frac{1}{9}}$ to a simple fraction. *Ans.* $\frac{3}{5}$.

6. Reduce $\frac{\frac{5}{3}}{4}$ to a simple fraction.

7. Reduce $\frac{\frac{3}{4}}{5}$ to a simple fraction. *Ans.* $\frac{3}{20}$.

8. Reduce $\frac{\frac{2}{3} \text{ of } \frac{3}{4}}{\frac{1}{2} \text{ of } \frac{2}{5}}$ to a simple fraction. *Ans.* $2\frac{1}{2}$.

MISCELLANEOUS PROBLEMS.

ART. **40.** 1. What is the sum of $\frac{2}{3}$, $\frac{3}{4}$, $\frac{5}{6}$, and $\frac{7}{12}$?

2. What is the difference between $\frac{7}{8}$ and $\frac{2}{3}$?

3. Multiply $\frac{2}{3}$ by $3\frac{1}{2}$.

4. Divide $\frac{2}{3}$ by $3\frac{1}{2}$.

5. What is the sum, difference, product, and quotient of $3\frac{1}{2}$ and $2\frac{1}{3}$?

6. What will be the cost of $15\frac{1}{2}$ pounds of butter at $16\frac{2}{3}$ cents a pound? *Ans.* \$2.58$\frac{1}{3}$.

7. At \$4$\frac{1}{2}$ per yard, how many yards may be bought for \$11$\frac{4}{7}$? *Ans.* $2\frac{4}{7}$.

8. At $28\frac{4}{7}$ cents per bushel, how many bushels of oats may be bought for $16\frac{2}{3}$ cents? *Ans.* $\frac{7}{12}$ bushels.

9. How many pounds in four bags, the first containing $360\frac{7}{8}$, the second $580\frac{4}{5}$, the third $296\frac{3}{4}$, and the fourth $375\frac{9}{10}$? *Ans.* $1614\frac{13}{40}$ lbs.

10. In 5 hogsheads of sugar containing, respectively, $945\frac{1}{2}$ $1054\frac{9}{10}$, $963\frac{4}{7}$, $901\frac{23}{28}$, and $899\frac{5}{8}$, how many pounds?

11. A man has 4 lots; the first containing $320\frac{11}{12}$ acres, the second $225\frac{5}{8}$, the third $160\frac{2}{3}$, and the fourth $278\frac{3}{9}$; how many acres in all? *Ans.* $986\frac{7}{72}$ A.

12. A man owes the following sums: to A \$32.56$\frac{1}{4}$, to B \$44.95$\frac{9}{10}$, to C \$32.72$\frac{7}{8}$, to D \$53.31$\frac{3}{20}$, to E 192.05$\frac{7}{15}$. How much does he owe in all?

13. A farm is divided into 5 fields, containing, respectively, as follows: $20\frac{2}{3}$, $56\frac{9}{11}$, $36\frac{4}{5}$, $9\frac{4}{5}$, and $102\frac{13}{22}$ acres. How many in all? *Ans.* $226\frac{223}{330}$ A.

14. A man purchased $\frac{7}{8}$ of a yard of velvet at the rate of \$3.62$\frac{1}{2}$ per yard; what did it cost him? *Ans.* \$3.17$\frac{3}{16}$.

15. A man owned $\frac{2}{3}$ of a boat, and sold $\frac{1}{2}$ of $\frac{3}{8}$ of his share for $2400. At that rate, what was the whole worth of it?

Ans. $19200.

16. James has $\frac{3}{4}$ of an orange. He gives Horace $\frac{1}{2}$ of this amount, and then divides the remainder equally between three boys. What part does each of the three boys receive?

Ans. $\frac{1}{8}$.

17. If $\frac{5}{8}$ of a barrel of flour costs $5, how much will 2 bags of flour cost, one containing $\frac{2}{3}$ of a barrel, and the other $\frac{5}{6}$ of a barrel?

Ans. $12.

18. Bought $\frac{2}{3}$ of $\frac{5}{8}$ of $5\frac{1}{2}$ yards of broadcloth at the rate of $3.50 per yard. Required the cost of it. *Ans.* 8.02\frac{1}{12}$.

19. What will be the cost of $7\frac{1}{2}$ yards of muslin at $12\frac{1}{2}$ cents per yard, and $12\frac{1}{2}$ yards of gingham at $18\frac{3}{4}$ cents per yard?

Ans. 3.28\frac{1}{8}$.

20. I purchased 7 loads of coal, each containing $15\frac{3}{4}$ bushels, at $12\frac{1}{2}$ cents per bushel. Required the cost. *Ans.* 13.78\frac{1}{8}$.

21. A owns $\frac{5}{8}$ of a vessel, and sells $\frac{3}{4}$ of his share to B for $45000. What part of the vessel has he left, and what is it worth at that rate? *Ans.* $\frac{5}{32}$ left, worth $15,000.

22. A owns $\frac{5}{8}$ of a ship. He sells $\frac{2}{3}$ of his share to B for a certain sum, and $\frac{1}{3}$ of what he then owns to C for $5,000. What was the value of the whole ship at C's rate of purchase?

Ans. $72000.

23. A owns $\frac{5}{12}$ of an acre of land, and B $\frac{3}{8}$ of an acre. How much does A own more than B? How many times more? How much do they both own?

Ans. to the last, $\frac{19}{24}$.

24. I have $1000 and wish to lay out 346\frac{5}{9}$ of it in sugar at $8\frac{1}{3}$ cents per pound, and the remainder in coffee at $11\frac{3}{4}$ cents per pound. How many pounds of coffee do I buy?

Ans. $5561\frac{97}{423}$ lbs.

25. A merchant directed his agent to lay out $\frac{5}{8}$ of $2354 in wheat at $87\frac{1}{2}$ cents per bushel; $\frac{3}{10}$ of it in rye at $56\frac{1}{4}$ cents per bushel; and the remainder in oats at $31\frac{1}{4}$ cents per bushel. How many bushels of each did he purchase?

Ans. to last, $564\frac{24}{25}$ bus. of oats.

26. What will $8\frac{1}{3}$ pounds of sugar cost at $18\frac{3}{4}$ cents per pound?

27. A has $6\frac{2}{3}$ acres in one lot and $7\frac{3}{4}$ in another; B has $5\frac{4}{5}$ times as much as A. How many has he? *Ans.* $83\frac{37}{60}$ A.

28. What will $\frac{2}{5}$ of $\frac{5}{6}$ yards of cloth cost at $\frac{3}{7}$ of $\frac{5}{9}$ dollars per yard?

29. A merchant owns $\frac{7}{8}$ of a mercantile establishment worth $64,000. He sells $\frac{3}{5}$ of his share to B, and $\frac{1}{2}$ the remainder to C. How much does he receive from B and C respectively, and what part has he remaining? *Ans.* From B, $33600.
From C, $11200.
Has left, $\frac{7}{40}$.

30. A merchant has $33\frac{7}{10}$ yards of cloth, from which he wishes to cut an equal number of coats, pants, and vests. What number of each can he cut if they contain $3\frac{3}{4}$, $2\frac{7}{8}$, and $1\frac{4}{5}$ yards respectively? *Ans.* 4.

31. A merchant owns $\frac{9}{16}$ of a stock of goods; $\frac{3}{4}$ of the whole stock were destroyed by fire, and $\frac{7}{10}$ of the remainder damaged by water. What part of the whole stock remained uninjured? How much did the merchant lose, provided the uninjured goods are sold at cost for $5400, and the damaged at half cost?
Ans. $\frac{3}{40}$ uninjured.
Merchant Loses, 33,918.75.

DECIMAL FRACTIONS.

ART. **41.** *A decimal fraction* is a fraction whose denominator is some power of ten, thus $\frac{5}{10}$, $\frac{3}{100}$, $\frac{12}{100}$ are decimal fractions.

In writing a decimal fraction the denominator is omitted, the numerator being written in such a manner as to indicate the denominator. This is done by continuing the decimal scale used in writing whole numbers below or to the right of the order of units.

The first order at the right of units is *tenths*, the second *hundredths*, the third *thousandths*, etc.

A point (.), called the *decimal point* or *separatrix*, is placed between the order of *units* and the order of *tenths*. The orders at the left of the decimal point express a *whole number;* the orders at the right a *decimal fraction*, or simply a *decimal.*

The names of the orders at the right and left of the decimal point, and the relation of decimals to whole numbers, are shown in the following

TABLE.

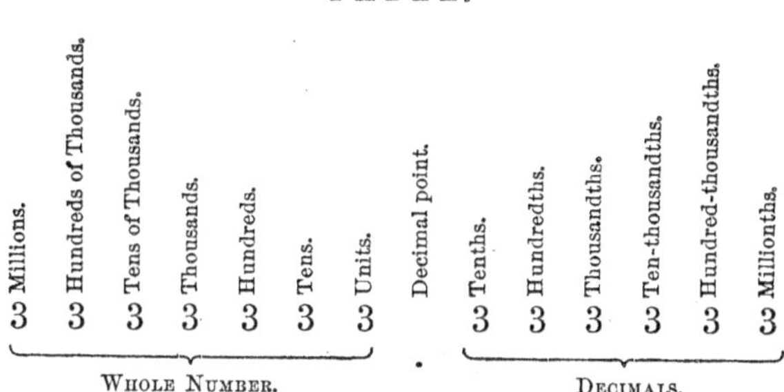

The orders at the right of the decimal point are called *decimal places.* Thus in .0223 there are four decimal places.

The denominator of a decimal fraction is 1 with as many ciphers annexed as there are decimal places in the numerator. Thus the denominator of .00035 is 100000.

Since the value of decimal orders decreases in a tenfold ratio from left to right, every cipher placed between decimal figures and the decimal point, thus removing them one place to the right, diminishes their value *tenfold.* Thus .025 is one-tenth of .25.

Ciphers placed at the right of decimal figures do not change their value. Thus .250=.25 and .8700=.87.

A whole number and a decimal written together constitute a mixed number, or a mixed decimal, as 25.037.

Note.—When the denominator of a decimal fraction is written, it is usually considered a common fraction; the term decimal being only applied when the denominator is *understood.* The above definition of a decimal fraction is, however, strictly correct.

NUMERATION OF DECIMALS.

ART. **42.** In reading a decimal expressed in figures, two things are necessary: 1st. To ascertain what the figures express as a *whole number.* 2d. To ascertain the *order of the right hand figure.* In a whole number, the right hand figure is always *units.* In a decimal, it is found by commencing at the decimal point and naming each order toward the right.

Ex. 1. Express in words .002015607.

Explanation.—Commence at the *right hand* and separate the figures into periods as in whole numbers, thus: 2.015.607. Next commence at the decimal point and name the orders to the last decimal figure, which is *billionths.* Then read the decimal as a whole number, adding the name of the last decimal figure, thus: two millions, fifteen thousand, six hundred and seven *billionths.* Hence the following general

RULE.

Read the figures as in whole numbers and add the name of the last decimal order.

Examples.

Express in words the following decimals:

2. .01012305
3. .000027
4. .500006
5. 207.0084

Suggestion.—Read the whole number as *units,* and then the decimal.

6. 7080.00607008
7. .002005505
8. .006
9. 600.06
10. 1000.001
11. 25000000.000250
12. 206.000000206

NOTATION OF DECIMALS.

Art. **43.** Ex. 1. Express in figures ten thousand five hundred and five millionths.

Explanation.—Write the numerator of the decimal as a whole number, thus: 10505. Then place the decimal point so that the right hand figure may be *millionths*, filling up the vacant order with a cipher, thus: .010505.

RULE.

Write the decimal as a whole number, and place the decimal point so that the right hand figure shall be of the same name as the decimal.

Examples.

Express in figures:

1. Twenty-five *thousandths.*
2. Twenty-five *millionths.*
3. Twenty-five *hundredths.*
4. Two hundred and five *ten-thousandths.*
5. Two hundred and five *ten-millionths.*
6. Twenty thousand and five *millionths.*
7. Two thousand and four *ten-thousandths.*
8. Six hundred and fifty units and thirty-seven thousandths.
9. One unit and one millionth.
10. Five thousand units and five thousandths.
11. Two thousand five hundred and six *hundredths.*.

Note.—The above is an improper decimal. The point falls between the figures, thus: 25.06.

12. Nine millions, fifteen thousand, and twenty-five *millionths.*
13. Eight thousand and forty *ten millionths.*
14. One million and one *millionths.*

REDUCTION OF DECIMALS.

ART. **44.** A whole number may be changed to a mixed decimal, or a decimal to an equivalent decimal of a lower order *by annexing ciphers.* Thus: .025=.025000, and 325.=325.000. This is, in effect, multiplying both terms of a fraction by the same number.

A mixed decimal may be reduced to an improper decimal fraction by removing the decimal point and writing the denominator, thus: $205.025=\frac{205025}{1000}$. The following examples will make the student familiar with these changes:

1. Reduce .205 to millionths. *Ans.* .205000.
2. Reduce .0225 to ten-millionths.
3. Reduce .14 to hundred-thousandths.
4. Reduce .0205 to billionths.
5. Reduce .02301 to billionths.
6. Reduce .5 to millionths.
7. Reduce 25. to thousandths. *Ans.* 25.000.
8. Reduce 404. to hundredths.
9. Reduce 4. to millionths.
10. Reduce 40. to ten-thousandths.
11. Reduce 62.5 to thousandths. *Ans.* 62.500.
12. Reduce 6.02 to millionths.
13. Reduce 4.506 to billionths.
14. How many *tenths* in 40 *units?* *Ans.* 400.
15. How many millionths in 5 thousandths? *Ans.* 500.
16. How many thousandths in 62.304? *Ans.* 62304.
17. How many millionths in 36.0304? *Ans.* 36030400.
18. How many hundredths in 400? *Ans.* 40000.
19. How many tenths in 6 tens?
20. How many millionths in one million?

ART. **45.** To reduce a decimal to an equivalent common fraction.

Ex. Reduce .25 to an equivalent common fraction.

$.25=\frac{25}{100}=\frac{1}{4}$. *Ans.*

RULE.

Supply the denominator, and reduce the fraction to its lowest terms.

Examples.

Reduce the following decimals to equivalent common fractions:

1. .20506.		7. 62.25.	*Ans.* $62\frac{1}{4}$.
2. .250.	*Ans.* $\frac{1}{4}$.	8. 6.225.	
3. .75.		9. 80.025.	*Ans.* $80\frac{1}{40}$.
4. .125.	*Ans.* $\frac{1}{8}$.	10. 8.0375.	
5. .0075.		11. 15.02.	*Ans.* $15\frac{1}{50}$.
6. .0125.	*Ans.* $\frac{1}{80}$.	12. 120.0125.	

ART. **46.** To reduce common fractions to an equivalent decimal.

Ex. Reduce $\frac{3}{4}$ to a decimal.

$$4\overline{)3.00}$$
$$.75 \text{ } Ans.$$

Explanation.—$\frac{3}{4}=\frac{1}{4}$ of 3; but 3=3.00, hence $\frac{3}{4}=\frac{1}{4}$of 3.00 =.75.

RULE.

Annex ciphers to the numerator and divide by the denominator. Point off as many decimal places as there are annexed ciphers.

Examples.

2. Reduce $\frac{5}{8}$ to a decimal.
3. Reduce $\frac{7}{25}$ to a decimal.
4. Reduce $\frac{3}{125}$ to a decimal. *Ans.* .024.
5. Reduce $\frac{9}{400}$ to a decimal.
6. Reduce $\frac{3}{2500}$ to a decimal.
7. Reduce $12\frac{3}{4}$ to a mixed decimal. *Ans.* 12.75.
8. Reduce $25\frac{3}{40}$ to a mixed decimal.
9. Reduce $300\frac{3}{400}$ to a mixed decimal.
10. Reduce $\frac{256}{8}$ to a mixed decimal.
11. Reduce $6.37\frac{3}{4}$ to a mixed decimal. *Ans.* 6.3775.
12. Reduce $.07\frac{1}{8}$ to a pure decimal. *Ans.* .07125.

ADDITION OF DECIMALS

ART. **47.** Ex. 1. Add 6.025, 65.37, 100.0035, and .875.

```
   6.025
  65.37
 100.0035
    .875
 ________
 172.2735 Ans.
```

Explanation.—Since decimals are written upon the same scale as whole numbers, they are added in the same manner.

RULE.

Write the numbers so that the figures of the same order shall stand in the same column.

Add as in whole numbers, and point off in the result as many decimal places as are equal the greatest number found in any of the numbers added.

Note.—The decimal points of the several decimals added and of the answer stand in the same column.

Examples.

Ex. 2. Add $.37\frac{3}{4}$, $.0256\frac{1}{2}$, .00015, $.5\frac{1}{3}$, $.27\frac{1}{3}$, and .026.

$.37\frac{3}{4} = .3775$
$.0256\frac{1}{2} = .02565$
$.00015 = .00015$
$.5\frac{1}{3} = .53333\frac{1}{3}$
$.27\frac{1}{3} = .27333\frac{1}{3}$
$.026 = .026$

$1.23596\frac{2}{3}$ *Ans.*

3. What is the sum of 256 thousandths, 3005 millionths, 207 ten-thousandths, 45 hundred-thousandths, 7 hundredths, and 20037 millionths?

4. Add .00675, 4.5689, 3.00007, 2.05, $3.6800\frac{3}{5}$, .9375, 8.75, 6.4375.

5. What is the sum of 307 millionths, $56\frac{1}{4}$ ten-thousandths, $68\frac{3}{4}$ hundredths, 5 hundred-thousandths, $256\frac{1}{4}$ tenths, $18\frac{3}{4}$ ten-millionths, and 25 hundredths? *Ans.* 26.568483875.

6. Add 375 ten-thousandths, 375 thousandths, 375 hundredths, 375 tenths, and 375 units. *Ans.* 416.6625.

7. A man bought 4 barrels of molasses, each containing

respectively $30.37\frac{1}{2}$, $31\frac{1}{2}$, 33.6756, and $28.6\frac{5}{8}$ gallons. How many gallons in all?

8. A man bought 5 lots, containing, respectively, $26.62\frac{1}{2}$, 220.2007, $56.9\frac{7}{8}$, $5.8\frac{3}{16}$, and $150.68\frac{3}{4}$ acres. How many acres in all? *Ans.* 460.31945.

9. Add 360.00025, 3.75, 567.893, 60,000.637, 200.050006, .0003625, 20.05.

10. Find the sum of $2\frac{7}{8}$, .625, $6\frac{9}{40}$, $3.6\frac{7}{250}$, 26.3125, 5.6, $.8\frac{13}{80}$.

SUBTRACTION OF DECIMALS.

ART. **48.** Ex. 1. From 60.025 take 3.0825.

```
60.0250
 3.0825
56.9425 Ans.
```

Explanation.—Same as in addition.

RULE.

Write the numbers as in addition of decimals, subtract as in whole numbers, and point off as in addition of decimals.

Examples.

2. From $.37\frac{1}{2}$ take $.0187\frac{3}{4}$.

$.37\frac{1}{2} = .375000$

$.0187\frac{3}{4} = .018775$

$.356225$ *Ans.*

3. From 4.05 take 2.00075.

4. From 8.1 take $5.37\frac{5}{8}$.

5. From 362 ten-thousandths take 1056 millionths. *Ans.* .035144.

6. From 875 thousandths take 62 ten-millionths.

7. From $100.001\frac{4}{5}$ take 93.00075. *Ans.* 7.00105.

8. A man bought $8.75\frac{31}{160}$ yards of linen at one time and 29.0056 at another. He afterwards sold $25\frac{13}{16}$ yards. How many has he left?

9. From 7 tenths take 7 ten-millionths.

10. From 10001 ten-thousandths take 10001 ten-millionths.

MULTIPLICATION OF DECIMALS.

ART. **49.** Ex. 1. Multiply 2.5 by .25.

2.5
.25
.625 *Ans.*

Explanation.—$2.5=\frac{25}{10}$, $.25=\frac{25}{100}$, and hence $2.5\times.25=\frac{25}{10}\times\frac{25}{100}=\frac{625}{1000}=.625$.

RULE.

Multiply as in whole numbers, and point off as many figures in the product as there are decimal places in the multiplicand and multiplier.

Note.—If there are not enough figures in the product, prefix ciphers. Thus: $1.6\times.016=.0256$; $.01\times.003=.00003$.

Examples.

2. Multiply 37.5 by 4.5.
3. Multiply $16.37½ by 3 hundredths.
4. What is 12 hundredths of $100.15?
5. What is 7 tenths of .201 thousandths?
6. Multiply .0015 by .125.

DIVISION OF DECIMALS.

ART. **50.** All the examples in Division of Decimals fall under one of three cases, viz.:

1. When the decimal places in the dividend *equal* those of the divisor.

2. When the decimal places of the dividend *exceed* those of the divisor.

3. When the decimal places of the dividend are less than those of the divisor.

These three cases are illustrated in the following examples:

Ex. 1. Divide 6.25 by .25.

.25)6.25
25. *Ans.*

Explanation.—Since the quotient arising from dividing one number by another of the same denomination is a whole number, 625 hundredths divided by 25 hundredths must give 25 units.

Ex. 2. Divide .864 by 3.6.

```
3.6).864.(.24 Ans.
     72
     ---
     144
     144
     ---
```

Explanation.—36 tenths (3.6) is contained in 8 tenths (the same denomination) 0 times; hence there are no units in the quotient. 36 tenths is contained in 86 hundredths 2 tenths of a time and 14 hundredths remaining. 36 tenths is contained in 144 thousandths 4 hundredths of a time. Hence .864÷3.6=.24.

Ex. 3. Divide 13.2 by .033.

```
.033)13.200
     ------
       400.
```

Explanation.—13.2 = 13.200 = 13200 thousandths, which divided by 33 thousandths must give 400, a whole number.

RULE.

FIRST CASE.—*Divide as in whole numbers; the quotient will be in units.*

SECOND CASE.—*Divide as in whole numbers, and point out as many places in the quotient as the decimal places of the dividend exceed those of the divisor.*

THIRD CASE.—*Make the decimal places of the dividend equal to those of the divisor by annexing ciphers, and then proceed as in whole numbers. The quotient will be in units.*

Note.—In either case, if there is a remainder, the division may be continued by annexing ciphers; *but each cipher thus annexed will give one decimal figure in the quotient.*

Proof.—It is well for the student to test the correctness of his answer by multiplying the divisor by the quotient. If the quotient is correct, the product will be the dividend.

Examples.

4. Divide 6.25 by 2.5. *Ans.* 2.5.
5. Divide 6.25 by .025. *Ans.* 250.
6. Divide .625 by 25.
7. Divide 25.6 by .016.
8. Divide 256 by .16.
9. Divide .256 by 160. *Ans.* .0016.
10. Divide .001 by 100.
11. Divide .0025 by 50.

12. Divide 4.2 by $31\frac{1}{4}$.

13. Divide \$16 by \$0.25.

14. Divide 3 by 1.25. *Ans.* .024.

Note.—In this example, we annex two ciphers to make the division possible ; this gives two decimal places in the dividend. We add another cipher to obtain the quotient figure 4 ; thus making in all *three* decimal places.

15. Divide 5 by 400.

16. Divide 9 by 1500.

17. Divide 6.4 by 80.

18. Divide .1 by $.12\frac{1}{2}$. *Ans.* .08.

19. Divide $6\frac{2}{5}$ by .08.

20. Divide $16\frac{2}{3}$ by $.033\frac{1}{3}$.

CONTRACTIONS.

ART. **51.** To divide a decimal by 10, 100, 1000, etc., *remove the decimal point as many places to the left as there are ciphers in the divisor.*

Note.—If there are not figures enough in the number, prefix ciphers.

Examples.

1. Divide 6.25 by 100. *Ans.* .0625.
2. Divide .25 by 10.
3. Divide .45 by 1000.
4. Divide .01 by 100.

ART. **52.** To multiply a decimal by 10, 100, 1000, etc., *remove the decimal point as many places to the right as there are ciphers in the multiplier.* Thus: $62.5 \times 100 = 6250$; $4.3 \times 10 = 43$.

$$\text{Multiply} \left\{ \begin{array}{r} \$43.50 \\ 150. \\ 1.68 \\ 456.30 \\ 1000. \\ 38. \\ 5.60 \end{array} \right\} \text{by } 100.$$

REDUCTION OF DENOMINATE NUMBERS.

ART. **53.** *A denominate number* is composed of concrete units of different weights, measures, etc.

Denominate numbers are of two kinds, simple and compound.

A simple denominate number is composed of units of a single denomination, as 10 pounds; 12 hours.

A compound denominate number, or simply a compound number, is composed of units of several denominations of the same weight, measure, etc., as 5 days 16 hours 20 minutes.

Reduction is the process of changing the form of a denominate number without altering its value.

Remark.—In treating of Denominate Numbers, we omit both tables and rules. The student is supposed to be familiar with the tables in common use.

ART. **54.** To reduce a denominate number of a higher denomination to a simple denominate number of a lower.

Examples.

1. Reduce 5 lb. 6 oz. 10 pwt. 18 gr. of silver to grains.

```
lb. oz. dwt. gr.
 5   6   10  18          Ans. 31938 gr.
12
66  oz.
 20
1330 pwt.
  24
31938 gr.
```

2. How many seconds in 10 hours?

```
  10  h.                 Ans. 36000 s.
  60
 600  m.
  60
36000 s.
```

3. Reduce $\frac{7}{9}$ lb. of butter to drams. *Ans.* $199\frac{1}{9}$ dr.

$$\overset{\text{lb.}}{\tfrac{7}{9}}\times 16=\overset{\text{oz.}}{\tfrac{112}{9}}, \times 16=\overset{\text{dr.}}{\tfrac{1792}{9}}=199\tfrac{1}{9}\text{ dr.}$$

4. Reduce $\frac{7}{320}$ yd. to inches. *Ans.* $\frac{63}{80}$ in.

$$\overset{\text{yd.}}{\tfrac{7}{320}}\times 3=\overset{\text{ft.}}{\tfrac{21}{320}}, \times 12=\overset{\text{in.}}{\tfrac{63}{80}}. \textit{ Ans. } \text{Or, } \tfrac{7\times 3\times 12}{320}=\tfrac{63}{80}\text{ in.}$$

5. Reduce .48 yd. to nails. *Ans.* 7.68 na.

$$\begin{array}{r l} .48 & \text{yd.} \\ 4 & \\ \hline 1.92 & \text{qr.} \\ 4 & \\ \hline 7.68 & \text{na.} \end{array}$$

6. Reduce $12\frac{1}{2}$ bu. to pints. *Ans.* 800 pt.
7. In $\frac{7}{8}$ of an acre how many perches? *Ans.* 140 p.
8. Reduce 12 h. 20 m. to seconds. *Ans.* 44400 s.
9. Reduce $\frac{3}{4}$ hhd. of wine to pints. *Ans.* 378 pt.
10. Reduce .375 T. to pounds (Avoirdupois). *Ans.* 750 lb.
11. In .7 of a bushel how many pints? *Ans.* 44.8 pt.
12. In 8.75 yd. how many nails? *Ans.* 140 na.
13. Reduce $2\frac{2}{3}$ days to minutes. *Ans.* 3840 m.
14. Reduce $5\frac{3}{4}$ cords to solid feet. *Ans.* 736 s. ft.
15. In .45 of a rod how many inches? *Ans.* 89.1 in.
16. Reduce 12 cubic feet to cubic inches. *Ans.* 20736 c. in.
17. Reduce 13.5 hhd. of beer to quarts. *Ans.* 2916 qt.
18. Reduce 5 lb. 6 oz. 12 pwt. of gold to pwt. *Ans.* 1332 pwt.
19. Reduce 5.24 lb. of calomel to ounces. *Ans.* 83.84 oz.
20. Reduce 7 lb. (Troy weight) to grains. *Ans.* 40320 gr.
21. Reduce .65 of a yard to quarters. *Ans.* 2.6 qr.
22. In .24 of a ream of paper how many sheets? *Ans.* 115.2 sheets.
23. In $\frac{2}{5}$ of a barrel of flour how many pounds? *Ans.* $78\frac{2}{5}$ lb.
24. Reduce 7 lb. $8\frac{2}{3}$ oz. of butter to drams. *Ans.* $1930\frac{2}{3}$ dr

25. In $\frac{3}{500}$ lb. of brass how many ounces? *Ans.* $\frac{12}{125}$ oz.

ART. **55.** To reduce a simple denominate number of a lower denomination to a denominate number of a higher.

Examples.

1. Reduce 15969 gr. to pounds.

Ans. 2 lb. 9 oz. 5 pwt. 9 gr.

```
24)15969 gr.
 20)665  pwt.  9 gr.
  12)33  oz.   5 pwt.
      2  lb.   9 oz.
```

2. Reduce $\frac{7}{9}$ of an inch to the fraction of a yard.

in. ft. yd.

$\frac{7}{9} \times \frac{1}{12} = \frac{7}{108}, \times \frac{1}{3} = \frac{7}{324}$. *Ans.* $\frac{7}{324}$ yd.

Explanation.—$\frac{7}{9}$ of an inch is $\frac{7}{9}$ of $\frac{1}{12}$ of a ft., which is $\frac{7}{108}$ ft., and $\frac{7}{108}$ of a foot is $\frac{7}{109}$ of $\frac{1}{3}$ of a yard $= \frac{7}{324}$ yd.

3. Reduce .48 of a nail to the decimal of a yard.

Ans. .03 yd.

```
4).48 n.
 4).12 qr.
    .03 yd.
```

4. Reduce 25.6 dr. to the decimal of a pound.

Ans. .1 lb.

```
16)25.6 dr.
 16)1.6 oz.
     .1 lb.
```

5. Reduce 414 gal. wine to hhd. *Ans.* 6 hhd. 36 gal.

6. Reduce 2461 pwt. to pounds.

Ans. 10 lb. 3 oz. 1 pwt.

7. Reduce 1357 pts. to bushels. *Ans.* 21 bu. 6 qts. 1 pt.

8. Reduce 98 furlongs to miles. *Ans.* 12 m. 2 fur.

9. Reduce 307200 perches to square miles. *Ans.* 3 sq. m.

10. Reduce 4032 gills to hhd. of wine. *Ans.* 2 hhd.

11. Reduce $\frac{3}{10}$ gal. to the fraction of a hhd. *Ans.* $\frac{1}{336}$.

12. Reduce $\frac{7}{15}$ hours to the fraction of a day. *Ans.* $\frac{7}{360}$.

13. Reduce $6\frac{2}{5}$ pt. to the fraction of a bu. *Ans.* $\frac{1}{10}$.

14. Reduce 645 in. to yd. *Ans.* 17 yds. 2 ft. 9 in.

15. Reduce 2176 cu. ft. to cords. *Ans.* 17 cords.

16. Reduce $1152\frac{4}{5}$ qt. to hhd. *Ans.* 4 hhd. 36.2 qt.

17. Reduce 623 nails to yards. *Ans.* 38 yd. 3 qr. 3 na.

18. Reduce 23.04 drams to lbs. *Ans.* .09 lb.

19. Reduce 184.8 hours to weeks. *Ans.* 1.1 weeks.

20. How many acres in a street 5 rods wide and $2\frac{1}{2}$ miles long? *Ans.* 25 acres.

ART. **56.** To find what part one denominate number is of another?

Note.—The first ten examples contain abstract numbers, and are designed to introduce denominate numbers.

Examples.

1. 8 is what part of 12? *Ans.* $\frac{2}{3}$.

Explanation.—1 is $\frac{1}{12}$ of 12, and 8 is 8 times $\frac{1}{12}$ of 12, which is $\frac{8}{12}$ of $12=\frac{2}{3}$ of 12.

2. 9 is what decimal part of 15? *Ans.* .6.

Explanation.—9 is $\frac{9}{15}$ of 15, and $\frac{9}{15}$ changed to a decimal is .6.

3. $\frac{2}{3}$ is what part of $\frac{3}{4}$? *Ans.* $\frac{8}{9}$.

$\frac{\frac{2}{3}}{\frac{3}{4}}=\frac{8}{9}$. Or, $\frac{2}{3}=\frac{8}{12}$ and $\frac{3}{4}=\frac{9}{12}$; $\frac{9}{12}\div\frac{8}{12}=\frac{8}{9}$. Since $\frac{1}{12}$ is $\frac{1}{9}$ of $\frac{9}{12}$, $\frac{8}{12}$ is 8 times $\frac{1}{9}$ of $\frac{9}{12}=\frac{8}{9}$ of $\frac{9}{12}$.

4. What part of $6\frac{1}{2}$ is $2\frac{2}{3}$? *Ans.* $\frac{16}{39}$.

$\frac{2\frac{2}{3}}{6\frac{1}{2}}=\frac{\frac{8}{3}}{\frac{13}{2}}=\frac{16}{39}$. Or, $2\frac{2}{3}=\frac{8}{3}=\frac{16}{6}$ and $6\frac{1}{2}=\frac{13}{2}=\frac{39}{6}$; $\frac{16}{6}\div\frac{39}{6}=\frac{16}{39}$.

5. 15 is what part of 12? *Ans* $\frac{5}{4}$.

6. 27 is what part of 48? *Ans.* $\frac{9}{16}$.

7. What decimal part of 72 is 54? *Ans.* .75.

8. What decimal part of $\frac{5}{6}$ is $\frac{2}{3}$? *Ans.* .8.

9. What decimal part of 10 is $4\frac{1}{2}$? *Ans.* .45.

10. What part of .45 is .09? *Ans.* $\frac{1}{5}$.

11. 2 ft. 6 in. is what part of a yard? *Ans.* $\frac{5}{6}$.

2 ft. 6 in.=30 in., and 1 yd.=36 in.; 30 in.÷36 in.$=\frac{5}{6}$.

Suggestion.—Reduce denominate numbers to the same denomination.

12. What part of a week is 5 d. 10 h.? *Ans.* $\frac{65}{84}$.

13. What part of 2 acres is 3 R. 25 p.? *Ans.* $\frac{21}{64}$.

14. What decimal part of 5 hours is 40 minutes? *Ans.* $.13\frac{1}{3}$.

15. What decimal part of 5 gals. is 3 qts. 1 pt.? *Ans.* .175.

16. What part of $5 is 87½ cents? *Ans.* $\frac{7}{40}$.

17. What decimal part of a gallon is 3 pints? *Ans.* .375.

18. What part of .45 lb. Troy is .45 oz.? *Ans.* $\frac{1}{12}$.

19. $\frac{3}{4}$ oz. is what part of $\frac{2}{3}$ lb. Avoirdupois? *Ans.* $\frac{9}{128}$.

20. 4 quires of paper is what decimal part of a ream? *Ans.* .2.

21. What part of a mile is 6 fur. 16 rds.? *Ans.* $\frac{4}{5}$.

22. What decimal part of a pound is 10 oz. 4 pwts.? *Ans.* .85.

23. What decimal part of a bushel is 3 pks. 4 qts.? *Ans.* .875.

24. What part of a week is 3 d. 17 h. 36 m.? *Ans.* $\frac{3}{15}$.

ART. **57.** To reduce a fraction of a higher denomination to integers of a lower.

Examples.

1. Reduce $\frac{3}{5}$ of a day to integers. *Ans.* 14 h. 24 m.

$$\overset{\text{d.}}{\tfrac{3\times24}{5}}=\overset{\text{h.}}{\tfrac{72}{5}}=\overset{\text{h.}}{14\tfrac{2}{5}},\ \overset{\text{h.}}{\tfrac{2\times60}{5}}=\overset{\text{m.}}{24}.$$

2. Reduce .85 of a day to integers. *Ans.* 20 h. 24 m.

$$\begin{array}{r} .85\text{ d.} \\ 24 \\ \hline 20.40\text{ h.} \\ 60 \\ \hline 24.00\text{ m.} \end{array}$$

3. Reduce .375 hhd. to integers. *Ans.* 23 gals. 2 qts. 1 pt.

4. Reduce .9 lbs. Troy to integers. *Ans.* 10 oz. 16 pwts.

5. Reduce $\frac{5}{6}$ rod to integers. *Ans.* 4 yds. 1 ft. 9 in.

6. Reduce .5625 cwt. to integers. *Ans.* 2 qrs. 6 lbs. 4 oz.

7. Reduce $30\frac{7}{16}$ hhds. to integers. *Ans.* 30 hhds. 27 gals. 2 qts. 2 gills.

8. Reduce $\frac{5}{9}$ mile to integers. *Ans.* 4 fur. 17 rds, 4 yds. 10 in.

9. Reduce 250.35 lbs. Troy to integers. *Ans.* 250 lbs. 4 oz. 4 pwts.

10. Reduce .8 mile to integers. *Ans.* 6 fur. 16 rods.

11. Reduce £$\frac{2}{3}$ to integers. *Ans.* 13s. 4d.

12. Reduce .45 peck to integers. *Ans.* 3 qts. 1.2 pts.

13. What is the value of $\frac{2}{5}$ week ? *Ans.* 2 d. 19 h. 12 m.

14. What is the value of .75 bu. ? *Ans.* 3 pecks.

15. What is the value of $\frac{9}{16}$ day ? *Ans.* 13 h. 30 m.

ADDITION OF DENOMINATE NUMBERS.

ART. **58.** Ex. 1. Add together 5 lbs. 6 oz. 13 pwts. 22 grs. ; 12 lbs. 9 oz. 18 pwts. ; 7 oz. 19 pwts. 21 grs. ; 24 lbs. 11 oz. 18 grs.

lbs.	oz.	pwts.	grs.	
5	6	13	22	
12	9	18	00	
	7	19	21	
24	11	00	18	
43	11	12	13	*Ans.*

Explanation.—Having written numbers of the same denomination in the same column, add, reducing as far as possible the lower denominations to a higher. In this example, the sum of the grains is 61 grs.= 2 pwts. 13 grs. Write 13 grs., and add the 2 pwts. to the column of pwts., and proceed as before.

2. A man purchased 4 loads of corn : the first contained 25 bu. 3 pks. 7 qts. 1 pt. ; the second, 30 bu. 2 qts. ; the third, 37 bu. 1 pk ; the fourth, 29 bu. 1 pk. 7 qts. 1 pt. How much did he buy ? *Ans.* 122 bu. 3 pks. 1 qt.

3. Find the sum of 5 gals. 3 qts. 1 pt. ; 10 gals. 1 pt. 1 gill ; 25 gals. 1 pt. ; 19 gals. 1 qt. 1 gill ; and 30 gals. 1 pt. 3 gills. *Ans.* 90 gals. 2 qts. 1 pt. 1 gill.

4. A man has 4 farms. The first contains 110 A. 3 R. 25 P. ; the second, 95 A. 1 R. 20 P. ; the third, 205 A. 0 R. 15 P. ; and the fourth, 90 A. 3 R. 35 P. How many acres in all ? *Ans.* 502 A. 1 R. 15 P.

5. I purchase of a merchant 19 yds. 3 qrs. of cloth; of a second, 25 yds. 3 qrs. 2 na.; of a third, 17 yds. 3 na. How many yards did I buy? *Ans.* 62 yds. 3 qrs. 1 na.

SUBTRACTION OF DENOMINATE NUMBERS.

ART. 59. Ex. 1. From 12 lbs. 6 oz. take 7 lbs. 9 oz. 13 pwts. 22 grs.

11	17	19	24	Minuend changed in form.
lbs.	oz.	pwt.	grs.	
12	6	00	00	Minuend.
7	9	13	22	Subtrahend.
4	8	6	2	Remainder.

Ex. 2. From 3 m. 7 fur. 30 rds. take 5 fur. 38 rds. 10 ft. 9 in.

8	6	69	$15\frac{1}{2}$	12	Minuend changed in form.
m.	fur.	rds.	ft.	in.	
3	7	30	00	0	
	5	38	10	9	
3	1	31	$5\frac{1}{2}$	3	
			$\frac{1}{2}=$	6	
3	1	31	5	9	*Ans.*

3. From 1 m. take 4 fur. 3 rds; 4 yds. 2 ft. 6 in.

4. From 2 T. 4 cwt. take 17 cwt. 2 qrs. 8 lbs.

5. How long from June 12, 1855, to April 3, 1859?

	mo.	da.	
1859	4	3	
1855	6	12	
3	9	21	*Ans.*

6. How long from the signing of the Declaration of Independence, July 4, 1776, to the battle of New Orleans, January 8, 1815? *Ans.* 38 yrs. 6 mo. 4 da.

7. From the battle of Lexington, April 18, 1775, to the battle of Montebello, May 5, 1859? *Ans.* 84 yrs. 17 da.

8. How long from the battle of Saratoga, Sept. 7, 1777, to Perry's victory, Sept. 19, 1813? *Ans.* 36 yrs. 12 da.

MULTIPLICATION OF DENOMINATE NUMBERS.

ART. **60.** Ex. 1. Multiply 5 fur. 35 rds. 16 ft. 9 in. by 5.

m.	fur.	rds.	ft.	in.	
	5	35	16	9	
				5	
3	5	20	$\frac{1}{2}$	9	
				$\frac{1}{2}=6$	
3	5	20	1	3	*Ans.*

2. What is the distance round a square field, each side of which is 35 rds. 5 yds. 2 ft. 9 in. in length?

Ans. 3 fur. 24 rds. 1 yd. 2 ft.

3. What is the weight of 5 watch chains, each containing 1 oz. 7 pwts. 13 grs. of gold? *Ans.* 6 oz. 17 pwts. 17 grs.

4. Bought 7 loads of corn, each containing 29 bu. 3 pks. 7 qts. 1 pt.; how much corn did I buy?

Ans. 209 bu. 3 pks. 4 qts. 1 pt.

5. Bought 11 pieces of broadcloth, each containing 34 yds. 1 qr. 3 na.; how many yards did I buy?

Ans. 378 yds. 3 qrs. 1 na.

6. How much wine in 7 casks, each containing 75 gals. 3 qts. 1 pt.? *Ans.* 531 gals. 0 qts. 1 pt.

DIVISION OF DENOMINATE NUMBERS.

ART. **61.** Ex. 1. Divide 1 m. 3 fur. 28 rds. 5 yds. 2 ft. 8 in. by 5.

	m.	fur.	rds.	yds.	ft.	in.
5)	1	3	28	5	2	8
		2	13	4	1	$5\frac{1}{5}$.

2. A man divided 1578 acres of land equally between 7 children; what was the share of each?

Ans. 225 A. 1 R. $28\frac{4}{7}$ P.

3. A piece of cloth containing 36 yds. 3 qrs. will make 5 suits of clothes; how much cloth in each suit?

Ans. 7 yds. 1 qr. $1\frac{3}{4}$ na.

4. Seven men purchased 8 cwt. 3 qrs. 20 lbs. of sugar. What was the share of each? *Ans.* 1 cwt. 1 qr. 2 lbs. $13\frac{5}{7}$ oz.

5. Four men agreed to share equally 3 sacks of coffee, each containing 2 cwt. 1 qr. 15 lbs. What was the share of each?

Ans. 1 cwt. 3 qrs. 5 lbs.

MISCELLANEOUS PROBLEMS.

ART. **62.** Ex. 1. What will .65 of a ream of paper cost at 20 cents a quire? *Ans.* \$2.60.

2. What will $\frac{5}{8}$ of a ream of paper cost at $\frac{3}{4}$ of a cent per sheet? *Ans.* \$2.25.

3. What will $\frac{3}{8}$ of a barrel of beef cost at $6\frac{1}{4}$ cents a pound?

Ans. \$4.69.

4. What must be the height of a wood-bed that is 12 feet long and $3\frac{1}{2}$ feet wide to hold just one cord? *Ans.* $3\frac{1}{21}$ ft.

5. What will it cost to excavate a cellar $18\frac{1}{2}$ feet long, $15\frac{1}{2}$ feet wide, and 9 feet deep, at 20 cents per cubic yard?

Ans. \$19.12.

6. How many cords of wood in a pile 40 feet long, $7\frac{1}{2}$ feet high, and 4 feet wide? *Ans.* $9\frac{3}{8}$ cords.

7. What will .75 of a hhd. of wine cost at 75 cents a pint?

Ans. \$283.50.

8. Bought 12 barrels of flour at \$6.50 per barrel, and sold the same at retail at 4 cents a pound. How much did I gain?

Ans. \$16.08.

9. The cabin of the steamer Bostona is 165 feet long and 18 feet wide. What will it cost to carpet the same with Brussels carpeting $\frac{3}{8}$ of a yard wide at 80 cents a yard?

Ans. \$704.

10. At 25 cents a sq. yd., what will it cost to plaster the ceiling of a room $18\frac{1}{2}$ feet long and 16 feet wide?

Ans. \$8.22.

11. At 20 cents a sq. yd., what will it cost to plaster both sides of a partition wall 52 feet long and $13\frac{1}{2}$ feet high, and another wall 149 feet long and 11 feet high? *Ans.* \$52.02.

12. A gentleman's garden 200 feet long and 180 feet wide is enclosed by a tight board fence $5\frac{1}{2}$ feet high? What will it cost to paint the fence at 10 cts. per sq. yd.? *Ans.* \$46.44.

13. How many bricks, each being 8 in. long and 4 in. wide, will it take to surround the above garden with a walk 6 feet in width? What will be the cost of the bricks at \$4 per 1000?
Ans. 21168 bricks; \$84.67 cost.

14. A miller ground 5000 bushels of wheat, taking from each bushel 4 quarts of wheat as toll. How many bushels of wheat does he grind for his customers, and what does he receive for the work, wheat being worth $87\frac{1}{2}$ cents a bushel?
Ans. 4375 bushels, \$546.87$\frac{1}{2}$.

15. What will be the cost of 25 boards, each being 15 ft. long and 10 in. wide, at \$30 per thousand? *Ans.* \$9.37$\frac{1}{2}$.

16. What cost 9 cwt. 1 qr. 18 lbs. 12 oz. at \$6.40 per cwt.?
Ans. \$60.40.

17. What will 10 lbs. 8 oz. 8 pwts. of gold cost at \$300 per pound? *Ans.* \$3210.

18. What will $3\frac{3}{4}$ hhds. of molasses cost at 10 cents per quart? *Ans.* \$94.50.

19. What will be the cost of papering the walls of a room 40 feet long, 30 feet wide, and 9 feet high, at 30 cents a bolt, each bolt being 9 yards long and 18 inches wide?
Ans. \$9.33$\frac{1}{3}$.

20. A farmer sold 30 bu. 2 pks. 1 qt. $1\frac{5}{9}$ pts. of clover seed at \$3.60 per bushel. How much did he receive?
Ans. \$191.10.

21. How many bushels of coal will a boat 100 feet long, 42 feet wide, and 4 feet deep contain, a bushel of coal being $1\frac{5}{9}$ of a cubic foot? *Ans.* 10800.

22. If there are 6 yds. 3 qrs. 2 na. in one suit of clothes, how many yards will clothe an army of 128,000 men?
Ans. 880,000.

PRACTICE.

ART. 63. Many of the examples met with in common business, may be easily solved by exercising a little tact, especially where the prices used contain an aliquot part of a dollar, or where the cost of compound quantities is required.

A few examples will illustrate this method.

The aliquot parts of a dollar in common use are shown in the following

TABLE.

50 cts. $=\frac{1}{2}$ of \$1.00	25 cts. $=\frac{1}{2}$ of 50 cts.
25 " $=\frac{1}{4}$ of \$1.00	$12\frac{1}{2}$ " $=\frac{1}{2}$ of 25 "
$12\frac{1}{2}$ " $=\frac{1}{8}$ of \$1.00	$6\frac{1}{4}$ " $=\frac{1}{2}$ of $12\frac{1}{2}$ "
$6\frac{1}{4}$ " $=\frac{1}{16}$ of \$1.00	$16\frac{2}{3}$ " $=\frac{1}{2}$ of $33\frac{1}{3}$ "
$33\frac{1}{3}$ " $=\frac{1}{3}$ of \$1.00	$8\frac{1}{3}$ " $=\frac{1}{2}$ of $16\frac{2}{3}$ "
$16\frac{2}{3}$ " $=\frac{1}{6}$ of \$1.00	$16\frac{2}{3}$ " $=\frac{1}{3}$ of 50 "
$8\frac{1}{3}$ " $=\frac{1}{12}$ of \$1.00	$6\frac{1}{4}$ " $=\frac{1}{8}$ of 50 "

Ex. 1. Required the cost of 24 yds. of muslin at $12\frac{1}{2}$ cts. a yd.

Solution.—At \$1.00 a yd. it is worth \$24.00.

At $12\frac{1}{2}$ cts. a yd. it is worth only $\frac{1}{8}$ of \$24.00, which is \$3.00. *Ans.*

Ex. 2. Find the cost of 56 yds. at $37\frac{1}{2}$ cts. a yd.

Solution.—At \$1.00 a yd. the cost=\$56.00.

At 25 cts. a yd. the cost=$\frac{1}{4}$ of \$56.00=\$14.00.

At $12\frac{1}{2}$ cts. a yd. the cost=$\frac{1}{2}$ of \$14.00=\$7.00.

The sum of the last two results=\$21.00. *Ans.*

Ex. 3. Required the cost of 56 bbls. of flour at $\$6.87\frac{1}{2}$ a bbl.

50 cts. =	$\frac{1}{2}$	\$56.00	=the cost at \$1.00 a bbl.
		$6.87\frac{1}{2}$	
		\$336.00	=the cost at \$6.00 a bbl.
25 " =	$\frac{1}{2}$	28.00	= " " " .50 "
$12\frac{1}{2}$ " =	$\frac{1}{2}$	14.00	= " " " .25 "
		7.00	= " " " $.12\frac{1}{2}$ "
		\$385.00	= " " " $\$6.87\frac{1}{2}$ "

Note.—See table of aliquot parts.

Ex. 4. Required the cost of 75 gals. of wine at $\$3.93\frac{3}{4}$ a gal.

50 cts. =	$\frac{1}{2}$	\$75.00 = the cost at \$1.00 a gal.
		$3.93\frac{3}{4}$
		\$225.00 = the cost at \$3.00 a gal.
		37.50 = " " " .50 "
25 " =	$\frac{1}{2}$	18.75 = " " " .25 "
$12\frac{1}{2}$ " =	$\frac{1}{2}$	9.375 = " " " $.12\frac{1}{2}$ "
$6\frac{1}{4}$ " =	$\frac{1}{2}$	4.6875 = " " " $.06\frac{1}{4}$ "
		\$295.3125 = " " " $\$3.93\frac{3}{4}$ "

Ex. 5. Find the cost of 25 bu. at $\$1.16\frac{2}{3}$ a bu.

$16\frac{2}{3}$ cts. =	$\frac{1}{6}$	\$25.00 = the cost at \$1.00 a bu.
		$4.16\frac{2}{3}$ = " " " $.16\frac{2}{3}$ "
		\$29.166 = " " " $\$1.16\frac{2}{3}$ "

Ex. 6. Required the cost of 75 yds. at $43\frac{3}{4}$ cts. a yard.

25 cts. =	$\frac{1}{4}$	\$75.00 = the cost at \$1.00 a yd.
$12\frac{1}{2}$ " =	$\frac{1}{2}$	18.75 = " " " .25 a yd.
$6\frac{1}{4}$ " =	$\frac{1}{2}$	9.375 = " " " $.12\frac{1}{2}$ "
		4.6874 = " " " $.06\frac{1}{4}$ "
		\$32.8125 = " " " $.43\frac{3}{4}$ "

Ex. 7. Required the cost of 45 bu. at $56\frac{1}{4}$ cts. a bu.

50 cts. =	$\frac{1}{2}$	\$45.00 = the cost at \$1.00 a bu.
$6\frac{1}{4}$ " =	$\frac{1}{8}$	22.50 = " " " .50 "
		2.8125 = " " " $.06\frac{1}{4}$ "
		\$25.3125 = " " " $.56\frac{1}{4}$ "

Ex. 8. Find the cost of 9762 bu. at 25 cts. a bu.

25 cts. =	$\frac{1}{4}$	\$9762. = the cost at \$1.00 a bu.
		\$2440.50 = " " " .25 "

Ex. 9. Required the cost of 7 yds. 3 qrs. at 75 cts. a yd.

2 qrs. =	$\frac{1}{2}$	\$0.75 = the cost of 1 yd.
		7
		\$5.25 = " " " 7 yds.
1 "	$\frac{1}{2}$	.375 = " " " 2 qrs.
		.1875 = " " " 1 qr.
		\$5.8125 = " " " 7 yds. 3 qrs.

Ex. 10. Required the cost of 256 bu. of corn at $18\frac{3}{4}$ cts. a bu.

$12\frac{1}{2}$ cts. =	$\frac{1}{8}$	\$256.00 = the cost at \$1.00 a bu.
	$\frac{1}{2}$	32.00 = " " " $.12\frac{1}{2}$ "
$6\frac{1}{4}$ "		16.00 = " " " $.06\frac{1}{4}$ "
		\$48.00 = " " " $.18\frac{3}{4}$ "

Ex. 11. Find the cost of 15 lbs. 15 oz. of butter at 25 cts. a lb.

8 oz.=	$\frac{1}{2}$	$0.25	=the cost of 1 lb.
		15	
		3.75	= " " " 15 lbs.
4 " =	$\frac{1}{2}$	125	= " " " 8 oz.
2 " =	$\frac{1}{2}$	625	= " " " 4 "
1 " =	$\frac{1}{2}$	3125	= " " " 2 "
		15625	= " " " 1 "
		$3.984375	= " " " 15 lbs. 15 oz.

Ex. 12. Required tne cost of 9 lbs. 7 oz. of cheese at $12\frac{1}{2}$ cts. a lb.

4 oz.=	$\frac{1}{4}$	$0.125	=the cost of 1 lb.
		9	
		1.125	= " " " 9 lbs.
2 " =	$\frac{1}{2}$	3125	= " " " 4 oz.
1 " =	$\frac{1}{2}$	15625	= " " " 2 "
		78125	= " " " 1 "
		$1.1796875	= " " " 9 lbs. 7 oz.

Ex. 13. Required the cost of 5 cwt. 3 qrs. 10 lbs. of sugar at $9.50 a cwt.

2 qrs.=	$\frac{1}{2}$	$9.50	=the cost of 1 cwt.
		5	
		$47.50	= " " " 5 cwt.
1 "	$\frac{1}{2}$	4.75	= " " " 2 qrs.
5 lbs.=	$\frac{1}{5}$	2.375	= " " " 1 "
5 " =	$\frac{1}{5}$	475	= " " " 5 lbs.
		475	= " " " 5 "
		$55.575	= " " " 5 cwt. 3 qrs. 10 lbs.

Ex. 14. Find the cost of 15 gals. 3 qts. 1 pt. of molasses at $68\frac{3}{4}$ cts. a gal.

2 qts.=	$\frac{1}{2}$	$0.6875	=the cost of 1 gal.
		15	
		1.03125	= " " " 15 gals.
1 "	$\frac{1}{2}$	34375	= " " " 2 qts.
1 pt. =	$\frac{1}{2}$	171875	= " " " 1 "
		859875	= " " " 1 pt.
		$10.9141125	

Ex. 15. Required the cost of 875 bu. at $\$1.06\frac{1}{4}$ a bu.

$6\frac{1}{4}$ cts.=	$\frac{1}{16}$	$875.00	=the cost at $1.00 a bu.
		54.69	= " " " $.06\frac{1}{4}$ "
		$929.69	= " " " $\$1.06\frac{1}{4}$ "

Ex. 16. If a man walk 24 m. 7 fur. 25 rds. in one day; how far can he walk in 5 d. 11 h. 50 m.?

Ans. 137 m. 0 fur. 23$\frac{55}{144}$ rds.

Remark.—This example may be solved in the same manner as the preceding; the only difference is, the multiplicand (24 m. 7 fur. 25 rds.) is a compound number.

Ex. 17. What will be the cost of 3 qrs. 2 na. at $4.50 a yd.?

Ans. $3.94.

Ex. 18. Required the cost of 13 cwt. 3 qrs. 20 lbs. of cheese at $9.12½ a cwt. *Ans.* $127.29.

Ex. 19. Find the cost of a ham, weighing 15 lbs. 13 oz. at 13 cts. a lb. *Ans.* $2.06.

Ex. 20. What will be the cost of 17 A. 1 R. 15 P. of land at $25.25 per acre? *Ans.* $437.93.

Ex. 21. Find the cost of 19 yds. at $4.37½ a yd.

Ex. 22. What are 156 bu. 3 pks. 7 qts. 1 pt. of wheat worth at 93¾ cts. a bu.? *Ans.* $147.17.

Ex. 23. Find the cost of 87½ yds. at 87½ cts. a yd.

Ans. $76.56.

Ex. 24. If a man walk 27 m. 5 fur. 15 rds. in one day; how far can he walk in 15 d. 10 h. 45 m.?

Ans. 439 m. 1 fur. 26 rds.

Ex. 25. If a man earn 6 lb. 15 oz. 15 dr. of cheese in one day; how much can he earn in 7 d. 7 h.?

Ans. 51 lbs. 5 oz. 6¼ dr.

Ex. 26. A man can plow 2 A. 1 R. 25 P. in a day? how much can he plow in 5¾ days? *Ans.* 12 A. 3 R. 13¾ P.

Ex. 27. Find the cost of 6 T. 5 cwt. 3 qrs. 20 lbs. of hay at $16.62½ a T. *Ans.* $104.57.

Ex. 28. Required the cost of 10 loads of coal, each containing 15½ bu. at 12½ cts. a bu. *Ans.* $19.37½.

Ex. 29. What will be the cost of making 29 m. 7 fur. 35 rds. of road at $975.75 a mile? *Ans.* $29257.25.

Ex. 30. Required the cost of 10 cords 75 ft. of wood at $2.87½ a cord. *Ans.* $30.43.

Ex. 31. Required the cost of 55 bbls. of flour at $6.68¾ a bbl. *Ans.* $367.81¼.

RATIO.

ART. 64. *Ratio* is the relation of one number to another of the same kind, and is expressed by their quotient. Thus the ratio of 8 to 12 is expressed by 12÷8, or $\frac{12}{8}$; and the ratio of 5 to 3 by 3÷5, or $\frac{3}{5}$.

A ratio is commonly expressed by separating the two numbers by a colon. Thus the ratio of 8 to 12 is written 8 : 12; the ratio of 5 to 3 is written 5 : 3.

The two numbers are called *terms* of the ratio—the first, or *divisor*, being called the *antecedent*, and the second, or *dividend*, the *consequent*.

When the antecedent is *less* than the consequent, the value of the ratio is greater than 1, and the ratio is called *increasing*; when the antecedent is *greater* than the consequent, the value of the ratio is less than 1, and the ratio is called *decreasing*.

Ratios are of three kinds; *simple*, *complex*, and *compound*.

A simple ratio is the ratio of two whole numbers, as 5 : 6, and 12 : 5.

A complex ratio is the ratio of two fractional numbers, as $\frac{3}{4} : \frac{5}{6}$, $2\frac{1}{2} : 5\frac{1}{2}$, and 2.5 : .5.

A compound ratio is the product of two or more simple ratios, as (5 : 4) × (3 : 2) × (3 : 4).

Compound ratios may be written in the form of fractions, as $\frac{4}{5} \times \frac{2}{3} \times \frac{4}{3}$. In stating problems, the ratios are written under each other without the sign of multiplication, as

5 : 4
3 : 2
3 : 4

A compound ratio may be reduced to a simple one by multiplying all the antecedents together for a new antecedent and all the consequents for a new consequent.

Note.—The numbers that form a ratio must be either both abstract, or both concrete. When concrete, they must be of the same denomination, or such as may be reduced to the same denomination, otherwise a *division* is impossible. 5 men have no ratio to 10 hogs, nor 3 pens to 6 hens.

What is the value of each of the following ratios:

1. 7 : 14. *Ans.* 2.
2. 6 : 3. *Ans.* $\frac{1}{2}$.
3. 15 : 45.
4. 3 : 9.
5. 6 : 2.
6. 45 : 15.
7. $\frac{3}{4} : \frac{2}{3}$.
8. $2\frac{1}{2} : \frac{5}{6}$.
9. $\frac{2}{5} : \frac{7}{10}$.
10. 1.5 : .45.
11. .25 : .6.
12. 2.5 : 10.
13. 10 : 2.5.
14. $5 : $15.
15. $0.75 : $3.
16. 2 ft. 6 in. : 10 ft.
17. 2 lb. 8 oz. : 10 oz.
18. 10 oz. : 2 lb. 8 oz.
19. $(\frac{3}{4} : \frac{5}{6}) \times (\frac{5}{6} : \frac{2}{3}) \times (\frac{2}{3} : 2\frac{2}{3})$.
20. $\left\{\begin{array}{l} 5 : 6 \\ 6 : 7 \\ 2\frac{1}{3} : \frac{3}{4} \\ 8 : 5 \end{array}\right.$ *Ans.* $\frac{9}{32}$.

PROPORTION.

ART. **65.** *A Proportion* is an equality of ratios.

Four numbers are in proportion when the ratio of the first to the second equals the ratio of the third to the fourth; thus 4, 6, 8 and 12 are in proportion.

The equality of two ratios may be expressed by the sign of equality, thus 4 : 8=6 : 12; or by four dots, thus 4 : 8 : : 6 : 12. The last method is the more common, and is read 4 is to 8 as 6 is to 12.

The first ratio of a proportion is called the *first couplet;* the second, the *second couplet.*

The first and third terms of a proportion, being the antecedents of the two ratios, are called *antecedents;* the second and fourth, being consequents of the two ratios, are called *consequents.*

The first and fourth terms of a proportion are called *extremes;* the second and third terms, *means.*

Both ratios of a proportion must be of the same kind, that is, both *increasing*, or both *decreasing*, otherwise they cannot be equal. Hence, in every proportion, if the first term is *less* than the second, the third term is *less* than the fourth, and if the first term is *greater* than the second, the third term is *greater* than the fourth.

As ratios may be expressed in the form of fractions (see Art. 64), the proportion 4 : 8 : : 6 : 12 may be written $\frac{8}{4}=\frac{12}{6}$. By multiplying each of these equal fractions by 6 (the denominator of the second), we have $\frac{8\times 6}{4}=12$, and by multiplying each of these equal quantities by 4 (the denominator of the first fraction), we have $8\times 6=12\times 4$. But 8 and 6 are the *means* of the above proportion, and 12 and 4 its extremes. Hence,

In every proportion, the product of the means equals the product of the extremes.

Therefore,

1. *If the product of the two means of a proportion be divided by either extreme, the quotient will be the other extreme.*

2. *If the product of the two extremes of a proportion be divided by either mean, the quotient will be the other mean.*

It follows from the above, that if any three terms of a proportion are given, the remaining term may be found. Find the missing term in each of the following proportions :

1. 15 : 20 : : 90 : —.
2. — : 16 : : 90 : 20.
3. 45 : 90 : : — : 28.
4. 27 : — : : 108 : 12.
5. $\frac{2}{3}$: $\frac{3}{4}$: : $\frac{5}{6}$: —.
6. $2\frac{1}{2}$: — : : $\frac{2}{5}$: 4.
7. $\frac{2}{3}$: $\frac{3}{4}$: : — : $\frac{5}{6}$.
8. 2.5 : 62.5 : : 15 : —.
9. 3.6 : 7.2 : : — : 9.4.
10. $2\frac{1}{2}$: $7\frac{1}{2}$: : $\frac{1}{4}$: —.
11. $\frac{1}{3}$: $\frac{1}{12}$: : — : $\frac{1}{5}$.
12. $\frac{1}{2}$: $\frac{1}{3}$: : $\frac{1}{4}$: —.

SIMPLE PROPORTION.

ART. **66.** *A Simple Proportion* is an equality of two simple ratios.

The method of finding the fourth term of a simple proportion, the other three being given, or of solving problems by means of a simple proportion, is sometimes called the *Rule of Three.*

In stating a problem in simple proportion, the first and second terms must be of the same denomination ; also the third and the answer sought.

Ex. 1. If 5 men can do a piece of work in 18 days, how many men can do it in 10 days ?

STATEMENT.

10 days : 18 days : : 5 men : *Ans.*
5
10)90
9 men, 4th term, or *Ans.*

Explanation.—The answer (or fourth term) is to be in men, therefore 5 men is the third term. If 5 men can do a piece of work in 18 days, it will require more men to do the same work in 10 days (less time). Hence the second ratio is *increasing,* and the first must be increasing, or 18 days must be made the second term. Hence, 10 days : 18 : : 5 men : *Ans.* or 9 men.

RULE.

Place the number of the same denomination as the answer sought for the third term. If the answer is to be GREATER *than the third term, place the greater of the other two numbers for the second term, and the less for the first; if the answer is to be less than the third term, place the* LESS *of the two numbers for the second term, and the greater for the first.*

Then divide the product of the second and third terms by the first; the quotient will be the fourth term, or answer.

Examples.

2. If 5 peaches cost as much as 7 apples, how many apples can you buy for 35 peaches ? *Ans.* 49 apples.

3. What will 450 feet of lumber cost at $17 per thousand? *Ans.* $7.65.

4. If 150 cows cost $1800, how many cows can be bought for $132?

5. If 5 men can mow 8 acres of grass in one day, how many men can mow 32 acres in the same time? *Ans.* 20 men.

6. If a horse travels 15 miles in 1 h. 40 m., how far, at this rate, can it travel in 12 hours?

7. If a 5 cent loaf of bread weigh 4 ounces when flour is $4 per barrel, what should be the weight of a loaf when flour is $7.50 per barrel?

8. If 5 yards of cloth cost $17, how many yards can be bought for $102? *Ans.* 30 yds.

9. A man received $45 for 30 days' work, how much should he receive for 25 days' work? *Ans.* $37.50.

10. If 12 oz. of pepper cost 20 cents, what will 7 lbs. of pepper cost? *Ans.* 1.86\frac{2}{3}$.

11. A merchant failing can pay but 70 cents on each dollar of his indebtedness. He owns A $1690, B $2000, and C $1100; what will each receive? *Ans.* C $770.

12. A merchant failing owes A $900, B $1200, C $1400, and D $1500. His property is valued at $2800; what will each creditor receive? *Ans.* D $840.

COMPOUND PROPORTION.

ART. **67.** *A Compound Proportion* is an equality of two compound ratios, or of a compound ratio and a simple one.

In solving problems in Compound Proportion, sometimes called the Double Rule of Three, the second ratio is always *simple.* The first ratio may be reduced to a simple ratio by multiplying the antecedents together for a new antecedent, and the consequents together for a new consequent. Hence, every compound proportion may be reduced to a simple one.

6

The third term of a compound proportion must be of the same denomination as the answer sought, and each of the simple ratios that compose the compound ratio must be of like denominations.

Ex. 1. If 5 men can mow 20 acres of grass in 3 days by working 8 hours each day, how many men will it take to mow 80 acres of grass in 4 days, working 6 hours each day?

Ans. 20 men.

STATEMENT.

$$\left.\begin{array}{r} 20 \text{ A.} : 80 \text{ A.} \\ 4 \text{ days} : 3 \text{ days} \\ 6 \text{ hours} : 8 \text{ hours} \end{array}\right\} :: 5 \text{ men} : \textit{Ans.} \quad \text{Or, } \frac{80 \times 3 \times 8 \times 5}{20 \times 4 \times 6} = 20$$

Explanation.—The answer required being in men, place 5 men for the third term. If it take 5 men to mow 20 acres, it will require *more* men to mow 80 acres in the same time; hence, 80 acres must be made the second term of the first simple ratio of the compound ratio. If it take 5 men when they work 3 days, it will require *less* men when they work 4 days; hence, 3 days is the second term of the second simple ratio. If it take 5 men when they work 8 hours per day, it will require *more* men when they work but 6 hours per day; hence, 8 hours is the second term of the third simple ratio. Reducing the compound ratio to a simple one, we have $20 \times 4 \times 6 : 80 \times 3 \times 8 :: 5 : \textit{Ans.}$, from which we find the fourth term to be 20.

By Cancellation.—Instead of stating a problem in compound proportion in the above form, it is more convenient to arrange the third and second terms in one column, the first terms in another column, and cancel the factors common to the two. The correctness of the process is evident from the fact, that the product of the third and second terms constitutes a *dividend*, and the product of the first terms a *divisor*. The quotient is the fourth term.

$$\begin{array}{r|l} & 5 \\ \cancel{20} & \cancel{80}\ 4 \\ \cancel{4} & \cancel{3} \\ 2\ \cancel{6} & \cancel{8}\ 4 \end{array}$$

$5 \times 4 = 20$ *Ans.*

$$\text{Or, } \frac{5 \times \overset{4}{\cancel{80}} \times \cancel{3} \times \overset{4}{\cancel{8}}}{\cancel{20} \times \cancel{4} \times \underset{2}{\cancel{6}}} = 20 \ \textit{Ans.}$$

RULE.

Place the number of the same denomination as the answer sought for the third term. Arrange the first and second terms of each of the simple ratios of the compound ratio as in SIMPLE PROPORTION.

Then, multiply the second and third terms together, and divide their product by the product of the first terms. The quotient will be the answer. Or,

Arrange the third and second terms in one column, the first terms in another at the left hand, and cancel all the factors common to the two. Then, divide the product of all the uncancelled factors of the right hand column by the product of all the uncancelled factors in the left hand column. The quotient will be the answer.

Note.—In determining which number of each ratio is to be the second term, reason from the number in the *condition.*

Examples.

2. If $900 produce $50 in 9 months, what sum will produce $450 in 5 months? *Ans.* $14580.

3. If it cost $25 to lay a sidewalk 10 feet wide and 90 feet long, what will it cost to make a walk 6 feet wide and $\frac{1}{5}$ of a mile long?

4. If 16 men can excavate a cellar 90 feet long, 40 feet wide, and 10 feet deep in 15 days of 8 hours each, in how many days of 9 hours each can 3 men excavate a cellar 60 feet long, 36 feet wide, and 8 feet deep? *Ans.* $34\frac{2}{15}$ days.

5. If 30 men, by working 8 hours a day, can in 9 days dig a ditch 40 rods long, 12 feet wide, and 4 feet deep, how many men, by working 12 hours a day for 12 days, can dig a ditch 300 rods long, 9 feet wide, and 6 feet deep?

PART SECOND.

PERCENTAGE.

ART. **68.** *Per cent.* is a contraction of the Latin phrase *per centum*, which signifies *by the hundred.*

Percentage includes all those operations in which 100 is the basis of computation.

The *rate per cent.* is the number of *hundredths.* Hence, any *per cent.* of a number is so many *hundredths* of it. Thus,

5 *per cent.* of a number is 5 *hundredths* of it.
30 *per cent.* of a number is 30 *hundredths* of it.
$3\frac{1}{2}$ *per cent.* of a number is $3\frac{1}{2}$ *hundredths* of it.
$\frac{1}{2}$ *per cent.* of a number is $\frac{1}{2}$ *hundredths* of it.
125 *per cent.* of a number is 125 *hundredths* of it.
And so on.

Note.—Instead of the words "per cent.," it is now customary to use the character % : thus, 12 per cent. is written 12 % ; $2\frac{1}{2}$ per cent., $2\frac{1}{2}$%.

ART. **69.** The rate per cent. may be expressed decimally by writing it as so many hundredths. Thus,

1 per cent. is written .01
7 per cent. is written .07
$5\frac{1}{2}$ per cent. is written $.05\frac{1}{2}$; or .055
15 per cent. is written .15
100 per cent. is written 1.00
$\frac{1}{2}$ per cent. is written $.00\frac{1}{2}$; or .005
$\frac{1}{4}$ per cent. is written $.00\frac{1}{4}$; or .0025
$2\frac{1}{3}$ per cent. is written $.02\frac{1}{3}$
$\frac{1}{20}$ per cent. is written $.00\frac{1}{20}$; or .0005

Exercises.

1. Express decimally 10 per cent.
2. Express decimally $12\frac{1}{2}$ per cent.
3 Express decimally $1\frac{3}{4}$ per cent. *Ans.* $.01\frac{3}{4}$.
4. Express decimally $\frac{5}{8}$ per cent.
5. Express decimally $\frac{1}{10}$ per cent. *Ans.* .001
6. Express decimally 2 per cent.
7. Express decimally 120 per cent.
8. Express decimally 250 per cent.
9. Express decimally $1\frac{1}{2}$ per cent.
10. Express decimally $\frac{1}{2}$ of 3 per cent. *Ans.* .015.
11. Express decimally $\frac{1}{3}$ per cent.
12. Express decimally 500 per cent. *Ans.* 5.00.

CASE I.

ART. **70.** To find a given per cent. of any number or quantity.

Ex. 1. Sold a house and lot, which cost me $1450.75, at a gain of 15%. What was the gain?

```
 1450.75
     .15
$217.6125
```

Explanation.—Since 15% is .15, the gain was 15 *hundredths* of $1450.75.

Some persons prefer, and it is sometimes more convenient, to find the percentage as follows:

```
 $14.5075
       15
$217.6125
```

Explanation.—1 per cent. of any number is .01 of it (which is found by removing the decimal point *two* places to the left), and 15 per cent. is 15 times as much as 1 per cent.

RULE.

Multiply the given number by the rate per cent. EXPRESSED DECIMALLY. Or,

Remove the decimal point TWO *places to the left, and multiply by the rate per cent.* AS A WHOLE NUMBER.

Examples.

2. What is 8 per cent. of 500 miles?
3. What is 6 per cent. of $$72.37\frac{1}{2}$? *Ans.* $4.3425.

4. Find 32 per cent. of 1200 men.

5. Find 25 per cent. of 12 hours 30 minutes.

Ans. 3 h. 7 m. 30 s.

6. What is 1000 per cent. of $1000? *Ans.* $10000.

7. What is $\frac{3}{8}$ per cent. of $320?

Note.—The second rule is most convenient in solving such examples as the above. Thus, $\frac{3}{8}$ of $3.20=$1.20.

8. What is $\frac{1}{2}$ per cent. of $15.80?

9. What is $1\frac{1}{3}$ per cent. of 1050 sheep? *Ans.* 14 sheep.

10. Find $\frac{1}{20}$ per cent. of 134500 bushels. *Ans.* $67\frac{1}{4}$ bu.

11. $33\frac{1}{3}$ per cent of any number is what part of it?

Ans. $\frac{1}{3}$.

12. What is $33\frac{1}{3}$ per cent. of 252 cattle? *Ans.* 84 cattle.

Note.—When the rate per cent. is a convenient part of 100, take the same part of the given number. Thus, $33\frac{1}{3}$ per cent. of 252 is $\frac{1}{3}$ of 252=84.

13. What is $16\frac{2}{3}$ per cent. of 1200 hogs? *Ans.* 200 hogs.

14. Find $66\frac{2}{3}$ per cent. of 660 men. *Ans.* 440 men.

15. Find 75 per cent. ($\frac{3}{4}$) of 4852. *Ans.* 3639.

16. Find 15 per cent. of 25 per cent. of $13.60.

Ans. $0.51.

17. Find $87\frac{1}{2}$ per cent. ($\frac{7}{8}$) of 1632 feet. *Ans.* 1428 feet.

18. A merchant failing was able to pay his creditors but 40 per cent. He owes A $3500, B $1200, C $1134, D $650. What will each receive?

Ans. A $1400, B $480, C $453.60, D $260.

19. A person at his death leaves an estate worth $1500; 12 per cent. of which he received from his wife; 20 per cent. from speculation; 30 per cent. from rise of property; 25 per cent. from the estate of an uncle; and the remainder from his father. How much did he receive from each source?

Ans. to last, $195.

20. A has an income of $1100 per year; he pays 10 per cent. of it for board; $\frac{1}{2}$ per cent. for washing; 2 per cent. for incidentals; 15 per cent. for clothing; 9 per cent. for other expenses. What does each item cost, and how much has he left? *Ans.* He has left $698.50.

CASE II.

ART. 71. To find what per cent. one number is of another.

Ex. 1. 6 is what per cent. of 25?

$$\frac{6}{25} = \frac{6.00}{25} = .24. \quad \textit{Ans. } 24 \text{ per cent.}$$

Explanation.—6 is $\frac{6}{25}$ of 25, which changed to a decimal (Art.) equals 24 hundredths; or 24 *per cent.*

Ex. 2. 12 cents is what per cent. of $3?

$$\frac{12}{300} = \frac{12.|00}{3|00} = .04. \quad \textit{Ans. } 4 \text{ per cent.}$$

Explanation.—Since only quantities of the same denomination can be compared, reduce $3 to cents, and proceed as above.

RULE.

Reduce the numbers to the same denomination. Annex two ciphers to the number which is to be the rate per cent., and divide the result by the other number.

Examples.

3. What per cent. of $40 is $12? *Ans.* 30%.
4. What per cent. of 120 yards is 20 per cent. of 90 yards?
5. $2\frac{1}{2}$ dimes is what per cent. of $5? *Ans.* 5%.
6. 40 men is what per cent. of 150 men?
7. 150 men is what per cent. of 40 men?
8. The cent (new coinage) contains 22 parts copper and 3 parts nickle; what per cent. of it is copper and what per cent. nickle? *Ans.* Copper 88%. Nickle 12%.
9. 15 per cent. is what per cent. of 60 per cent.? *Ans.* 25%.
10. A person whose annual income is $450 pays $125 for board, $140 for clothing, $25 for books, and $30 for sundries; what per cent. of his income is each item, and what per cent. remains? *Ans.* to last, $28\frac{8}{9}$%.
11. A merchant failing owes $3500; his property is valued at $2100. What per cent. of his indebtedness can he pay? *Ans.* 60%.

CASE III.

ART. **72.** To find a number when a certain per cent. of it is given.

Ex. 1. A merchant sells 40 per cent. of his stock for \$3500; what is the value of his whole stock at this rate:

$\frac{\$3500}{40}\times 100=\$8750$. *Ans.*

Explanation.—Since \$3500 is 40 per cent. of his stock, 1 per cent. is $\frac{1}{40}$ of \$3500, or \$87 50, and 100 per cent., or the whole stock, 100 times \$87.50, or \$8750.

Ex. 2. A person pays \$13.50 a month for board, which is 30 per cent. of his salary, what is his salary?

$$\frac{\$13.50}{30}\times 100=\frac{\$1350}{30}=\$450. \ Ans.$$

RULE.

Divide the given number by the given rate per cent. and multiply the quotient by 100. Or,

Annex two ciphers to the given number, and divide the result by the rate per cent.

Note.—When the given number contains cents (see Ex. 2, above), remove decimal point two places to the left, instead of annexing two ciphers.

Examples.

3. 45 is 10 per cent. of what number?

4. \$3.60 is 15 per cent. of what number?

5. \$5.62½ is 12½ per cent. of what number? *Ans.* \$45.

6. Sold cloth for \$3.50 per yard, which was 70 per cent. of its cost; what was the cost of the cloth per yard? *Ans.* \$5.

7. A boy spent 60 per cent. of his money for toys, and 25 per cent. for candies, and had 15 cents remaining; how many cents had he at first? *Ans.* \$1.00.

8. The assets of a merchant are \$45000, which is 60 per cent. of his indebtedness; what is his indebtedness?

Ans. \$75000.

9. The deaths in a certain city, during the year, are 980, which is 3½ per cent. of the population; what is the number of inhabitants? *Ans.* 28000.

CASE IV.

ART. **73.** A number being given which is a given per cent. *more* or *less* than another number, to find the required number.

Ex. 1. Sold broadcloth at $5 per yard and made 25 per cent.; what did the cloth cost per yard?

100
25
125)500
4
$4 \times 100 = 400$ cents.
Ans. $4.

Explanation.—Since I gain 25 per cent., I receive 125 cents for every 100 cents the cloth cost; hence the cloth cost as many times 100 cents as I receive times 125 cents, which is 4, and 4 times 100 cents is $4.

Or thus:

1.00
.25
1.25)5.00
$4. *Ans.*

Since I gain 25 per cent., the sum received is 125 per cent. of the cost; hence, $5 is $\frac{125}{100}$ of the cost, which is found by dividing by 1.25.

When the given per cent. is a convenient part of 100, it may be solved by using the common fraction; thus, $\frac{25}{100} = \frac{1}{4}$, $\frac{4}{4} + \frac{1}{4} = \frac{5}{4}$; hence, $5 is $\frac{5}{4}$ of the cost.

Ex. 2. A drover lost 12 per cent. of a flock of sheep by disease, and then had 2200; how many sheep in the flock at first?

100
12
88)2200
25
$25 \times 100 = 2500$ *Ans.*

Or,

$$\frac{2200 \times 100}{88} = 2500 \text{ Ans.}$$

Explanation.—Since he lost 12 per cent. of his sheep, for every 100 sheep at first there remained but 88; hence, the flock at first contained as many times 100 sheep as there remained times 88, or 25 times 100 sheep=2500 sheep.

Or thus:

Since he lost 12 per cent. of his flock, there remained 88 per cent.; hence, 2200 sheep must be $\frac{88}{100}$ of his original flock, which is 2500 sheep.

RULE.

Divide the given number by 100, *increased or diminished by the rate per cent., and multiply the quotient by* 100. Or,

Divide the given number by 1, *increased or diminished by the rate per cent. expressed* decimally.

Examples.

3. 168 is 20 per cent. more than what number? *Ans.* 140.

4. $63.75 is 15 per cent. less than what? *Ans.* $75.

5. The population of a certain city is 25000, which is 25 per cent. more than it was in 1850; what was the population in 1850? *Ans.* 20000.

6. A grocer sells flour as follows:

Extra Family,	$5.50	per bbl.
Superfine,	$4.75	" "
Fine,	$4.25	" "

and makes a profit of $12\frac{1}{2}$ per cent.; what was the cost of each brand? *Ans.* to last, $$3.77\frac{7}{9}$.

7. A cargo of corn being injured, the owner was obliged to sell the same for $28000, which was at a loss of 30 per cent.; what was the cost of the cargo? *Ans.* $40000.

8. The sales of a dry goods firm amount to $90000 per year; $\frac{2}{5}$ of the sales were made at a profit of 25 per cent.; $\frac{3}{10}$ at a profit of 35 per cent.; and the remainder at a profit of 20 per cent.; what was the cost of goods? *Ans.* $71300.

APPLICATIONS OF PERCENTAGE.

ART. **74.** The four preceding cases underlie the whole subfect of Percentage in all its numerous and important applications. The importance of fully understanding them can not be urged too strongly upon one who wishes to become a competent accountant. It is not enough to be able to solve the examples in accordance with the directions of the rules. Rule accountants are always liable to make serious errors. Do I see clearly *why* such a process gives the required result? To this question the student should be able to give an affirmative answer.

There is such a thing as *common sense*, and the use of it in solving practical business problems is a *sine qua non.* The answer of almost any question may be anticipated, at least approximately, previous to its solution. The common-sense student sees from the *conditions* of the question about what answer he may expect. In solving a problem in discount, for example, he knows whether the *present worth* will be nearest $3, $30, or $3000. I have often known "rule students" to hand in the most ridiculous answers to the simplest practical problems.

PROFIT AND LOSS.

ART. **75.** The price paid for an article, or the total expense of producing it, is its *cost ;* the amount received for an article by the vender is its *selling price.* It is evident, from this, that the *selling price* of the vender, or salesman, may be the *cost* of an article to the purchaser.

When an article is sold for more than its cost, there is a *profit*, or *gain ;* when it is sold for less than its cost, there is a *loss.* The actual gain or loss is the amount of this increase or decrease.

Profit or loss is generally computed as a given amount upon every hundred, or at a given rate per cent. The rate per cent. is the number of *hundredths of the cost* gained or lost.

Profit and Loss, though usually, are not always limited to transactions in money. When any quantity, whether it is money, or goods, or time, or distance, or any thing else, undergoes an increase or decrease, there is gain or loss, and it may be computed at a rate per cent.

ART. **76.** All the problems in Profit and Loss come under one or more of the four following cases, which correspond to the four cases of Percentage, already explained.

1. The cost and the per cent. of gain or loss being given, to find the *selling price.*

RULE.—*Multiply the cost by the rate per cent. of gain or loss expressed decimally ; the product will be the gain or loss. The cost increased by the gain or diminished by the loss will be the selling price.*

2. The cost and the selling price being given, to find the *per cent. of gain or loss.*

RULE.—*Divide the gain or loss by the* COST, *and express the quotient decimally.*

3. The actual gain or loss, and the per cent. of gain or loss being given, to find the *cost.*

RULE.—*Divide the gain or loss by the per cent. of gain or loss, and multiply the quotient by* 100.

4. The selling price and the per cent. of gain or loss being given, to find the *cost.*

RULE.—*Divide the selling price by* $1 *increased or diminished by the rate per cent. expressed decimally.*

Note.—Keep in mind that gain or loss is computed upon the COST.

Examples.

1. For how much per bbl. must I sell flour costing $4.50 per bbl., to gain 16⅔ per cent. ?

Explanation.—It must be sold for the cost plus 16⅔ per cent. of the cost (found according to Case I., Percentage) ; or, since 16⅔ per cent.=⅙, it must be sold for the cost plus ⅙ of the cost.

Remark.—When the given per cent. is a convenient part of 100, it is best to use the common fraction, instead of the given per cent.

2. A man offers a farm, for which he gave $3450, for 20 per cent. less than its cost. What is his price ?

Explanation.—He offers it for the cost minus 20 per cent. of the cost ; or, since 20 per cent.=⅕, he offers it for the cost minus ⅕ of the cost, or $2760.

3. How must I sell sugars that cost $7, $8.25, and $10.50 per cwt. to gain 12½ per cent. ? *Ans.* to last, $11.81¼.

4. Bought linen cloth for 45 cents, 50 cents, and 62½ cents per yard ; for what per yard must I sell it (being damaged) to lose 18 per cent. ? *Ans.* to last, 51¼ cts.

5. A merchant is selling cloth that cost $3.75 per yard for $5 ; what per cent. is his profit ? *Ans.* 33⅓%.

Explanation.—He gains $5.00 – $3.75 = $1.25 on each yard, or on $3.75, which (Case II. Percentage) is 33⅓ per cent. ;

or, since he gains $1.25 on $3.75, his gain is $\frac{125}{375}$ or $\frac{1}{3}$ of the cost, or $33\frac{1}{3}$ per cent.

6. A grocer sells coffee that cost 15 cents per lb. for 12 cents per lb.; what is his loss per cent.? *Ans.* 20%.

Remark.—The simple question in this problem is, what per cent. of 15 is 3?

7. A grocer sells tea costing $62\frac{1}{2}$ cents per lb. for 75 cents; sugar costing 9 cents for $12\frac{1}{2}$ cents; flour costing $5.20 for $5.75. What does he gain per cent. on each article?

Ans. to last, $10\frac{15}{26}$%.

8. Bought a horse for $130, paid for its keeping, two months, $6, and then sold it for $124; what per cent. was my loss? *Ans.* $8\frac{14}{17}$%.

9. A merchant made a profit of $156 by selling a quantity of silks at a gain of 12 per cent. What was the cost of the silks, and for how much were they sold? *Ans.* $1300 cost.

Explanation.—Since he gained 12 per cent., or $\frac{12}{100}$ of the cost, $156 must be $\frac{12}{100}$ of the cost, which (Case III. Percentage), is $1300; $1300+$156=$1456, selling price.

10. A grocer bought a lot of apples, and sold them at 30 per cent. profit, by which he gained $36.60. How much did they cost him, and for how much did he sell them?

Ans. Cost $122; sold for $158.60.

11. Sold a cargo of wheat for $16000, at a profit of 25 per cent. What was the cost of cargo? *Ans.* $12800.

Explanation.—$16000 is 25 per cent. *more* than what number? (Case IV. Percentage). Or thus: Since I gained 25 per cent. or $\frac{25}{100}=\frac{1}{4}$, I must have sold it for $\frac{5}{4}$ of the cost.

12. Gould & Brown sold a lot of goods for $16500, at a profit of $33\frac{1}{3}$ per cent. What did the goods cost them?

Ans. $12375.

13. Sold tea at 90 cents per lb., and gained 20 per cent. What per cent. should I have gained had I sold it for $1.00 per lb.? *Ans.* $33\frac{1}{3}$%.

Note.—This example involves Case IV. and Case II. of Percentage. First find the *cost* and then the gain per cent. on the *cost* by selling for $1.00 per lb.

14. Sold a lot of books for \$480, and lost 20 per cent.; for what should I have sold them to gain 20 per cent.?

Ans. \$720.

15. If tea, when sold at a loss of 25 per cent. brings \$1.25 per lb., what would be the gain or loss per cent. if sold for \$1.60 per lb.? *Ans.* Loss 4%.

16. A merchant marked a piece of carpeting 25 per cent. more than it cost him, but, anxious to effect a sale, and supposing he should still gain 5 per cent., sold it at a discount of 20 per cent. from his marked price. Did he gain or lose?

Ans. Neither.

Explanation.—Since the marked price was 125 per cent. of the cost, 20 per cent. of the marked price must be 20 per cent. of 125 per cent. of the cost, *or 25 per cent. of the cost.* 125 per cent.—25 per cent.=100 per cent., or *cost.*

Or thus:

Since the marked price was $\frac{1}{4}$ (25 per cent.) more than the cost, or $\frac{5}{4}$ of the cost, 20 per cent., or $\frac{1}{5}$ of the marked price must equal $\frac{1}{5}$ of $\frac{5}{4}=\frac{4}{4}$ of the cost.

17. My goods are marked to sell at retail at 40 per cent. above cost. I furnish my wholesale customers at 12 per cent. discount from the retail price. What per cent. profit do I make on goods sold at wholesale?

Illustration.—Suppose \$1.00 to be the basis of computation. We shall then have:

\$1.00	cost.	\$1.40	retail price.
1.40	retail price.	$.16\frac{4}{5}$	amount to be deducted.
$.16\frac{4}{5}$	12 per cent. of retail price.	$1.23\frac{1}{5}$	selling price.
		1.00	cost deducted.
		$.23\frac{1}{5}$	profit.

18. My retail price for broadcloth is \$4.75 per yard, by which I make a profit of $33\frac{1}{3}$ per cent. I sell a wholesale customer 100 yards at a discount of 30 per cent. from the retail price. What per cent. do I gain or lose, and what do I receive per yard? *Ans.* Lose $6\frac{2}{3}$%.

$\$3.32\frac{1}{2}$ per yard.

19. A merchant asked for a quantity of dried fruit 22 per cent. more than it cost him, but, being a little mouldy, he was

obliged to sell it for 10 per cent. less than his asking price. He gained $98 by the transaction. How much did the fruit cost? For how much did he sell it? What was his asking price?

Ans. to last, $1220.

20. I bought a horse of Mr. A for 15 per cent. less than it cost him, and sold it for 30 per cent. more than I paid for it. I gained $15 in the transaction. How much did the horse cost Mr. A? How much did it cost me? For what did I sell it?

Ans. to last, $65.

21. By selling Java coffee at 18 cents per pound I make a profit of 20 per cent., for how much must I sell it to make a profit of $16\frac{2}{3}$ per cent.? *Ans.* $17\frac{1}{2}$ cents.

22. The cost of purchasing and transporting a quantity of goods from New York to Chicago is 9 per cent. of the first cost of the goods. If a merchant in Chicago wishes to make a profit of 25 per cent. on the full cost of the goods, what per cent. gain on the *first cost* must he ask for them? What amount of goods must he purchase in New York to realize a profit of $3625 on the *first cost?* What would be the real profit on full cost? *Ans.* to the last, $2725.

23. What must be the asking price of cloth costing $3.29 per yard, that I may deduct $12\frac{1}{2}$ per cent. from it, and still gain $12\frac{1}{2}$ per cent. on the cost? *Ans.* $4.23.

24. I bought a lot of coffee at 12 cents per pound. Allowing that the coffee will fall short 5 per cent. in weighing it out, and that 10 per cent. of the sales will be in bad debts, for how much per pound must I sell it to make a clear gain of 14 per cent. on the cost? *Ans.* 16 cents.

25. What must be the asking price of raisins costing $7.364 per box, that I may fall 10 per cent. of it and still gain 10 per cent. on the cost, allowing 10 per cent. of sales to be in bad debts? *Ans.* $10.

Note.—Other problems in Profit and Loss, involving Interest, etc., will be given in miscellaneous examples.

COMMISSION AND BROKERAGE.

ART. 77. Money received for buying and selling goods or other property, collecting debts, or transacting other business of like nature for another person or party, is called *Commission.*

Commission is usually estimated at a certain per cent. of the amount of the purchase, sale, collection, or other business transacted.

A person who buys and sells goods, or transacts other business on commission, is called a *Commission Merchant, Agent,* or *Factor.*

When a person engaged in the Commission business lives in a foreign country, or in a different part of the country, he is called a *Correspondent* or *Consignee ;* goods shipped to such a person to be sold are called a *consignment,* and the person who sends the goods a *Consignor.*

The rate per cent. of commission, *or the rate of commission* as it is called, varies with the amount and nature of the business.

Brokerage is money received for buying and selling stocks, making exchanges of money, negotiating bills of credit, or transacting other like business. Like Commission, it is computed as a certain percentage of the amount of the money involved in the transaction. Brokerage upon stocks is usually computed upon their *par value.*

ART. 78. The problems in Commission and Brokerage come under one of the two following cases :

1. To find the commission or brokerage on any given sum at a given rate per cent.

RULE.—*Multiply the given sum by the given rate per cent. expressed decimally.*

2. When the given amount includes both the sum to be invested and the commission or brokerage.

RULE.—*Divide the given amount by $1, increased by the rate per cent. of commission and brokerage, expressed decimally; the quotient will be the sum to be invested.*

The commission or brokerage may be found by subtracting the investment from the given amount.

Examples.

1. A commission merchant in New Orleans purchased cotton for a manufacturer in Lowell to the amount of $16576. What is his commission at $2\frac{1}{2}$ per cent.? *Ans.* $414.40.

2. Paid a broker $\frac{1}{4}$ per cent. for exchanging $750 Ohio money for Eastern funds. How much was the brokerage? *Ans.* 1.87\frac{1}{2}$,

3. My agent charges me $25 for collecting $800. What is his rate of commission? *Ans.* $3\frac{1}{8}$%.

4. An architect charges $\frac{3}{8}$ per cent. for plans and specifications, and $1\frac{1}{2}$ per cent. for superintending a building which cost $32000. What is his fee? *Ans.* $600.

5. I collected 65 per cent. of a note of $87.50, and charged 5 per cent. commission. What is my commission and the sum paid over? *Ans.* to last, $54.03.

6. My agent in Baltimore has purchased goods for me to the amount of $1250, for which he charges a commission of $1\frac{3}{4}$ per cent. What sum must I remit to pay for goods and commission? *Ans.* 1271.87\frac{1}{2}$.

7. Sent to my agent in Cincinnati $765 to purchase a quantity of bacon; his commission is 2 per cent. on the purchase, which he is to deduct from the money sent. What is his commission, and what does he expend for bacon? *Ans.* to last, $750.

Remark.—The $765 sent includes the sum to be invested in bacon and the 2 per cent. commission on the money thus invested. For every 102 cents sent, he will lay out 100 cents for bacon; hence the $765 is $\frac{102}{100}$ of the amount invested. See Case IV. Percentage.

8. I have received $11200 from my correspondent in Boston with directions to purchase cotton, first deducting my commission, $2\frac{1}{2}$ per cent. What is my commission, and how much must I expend for cotton? *Ans.* to last, $10926.829.

9. My agent at Chicago writes that he has purchased for

me 4000 bushels of wheat at 80 cents a bushel, and wishes me to send him a check on New York, which he can sell to a broker for a premium of $\frac{3}{4}$ per cent. How large a check shall I send him, his commission being 3 per cent.?

Ans. $3271.464.

10. Field & Parsons sell for H. Johnson & Co. 3500 lbs. of butter at 20 cts. a lb., 2580 lbs. of cheese at 9 cts. per lb., at a commission of 5 per cent. They invest the balance in dry goods, after deducting their commission of $2\frac{1}{2}$ per cent. for purchasing. How many dollars worth of goods do Johnson & Co. receive? What is the entire commission of Field & Parsons?

Ans. to last, $863.99.

11. I received of Brown & Lincoln $560 in uncurrent money to purchase books. I pay a broker $3\frac{1}{2}$ per cent. for current funds, and invest the balance, after deducting my commission of 2 per cent. What do I pay for books, and what is my commission? *Ans.* to last, $10.596.

12. A broker bought 5 shares of R. R. stock at 35 per cent. discount, what is the brokerage at 5 per cent., the par value of each share being $100? *Ans.* $25.

INSURANCE.

Art. **79.** Insurance is a contract by which one party engages, for a stipulated sum, to insure another against a risk to which he is exposed.

The party who takes the risk is called the *Insurer* or *Underwriter*, and the party, protected by the insurance, the *Insured.*

The sum paid for obtaining the insurance is called the *Premium*, and the written contract is called the *Policy.*

Insurance is generally effected by a joint-stock company or by individuals who unite to insure each other, called a *Mutual Insurance Company.*

When the *insurer* agrees to pay the *insured* a certain sum of money if he is sick, it is called *Health Insurance.*

When the insurer agrees to pay to the heirs of the insured, or to some specified person, a certain sum in case of his death, it is called *Life Insurance.*

Insurance on *property* is either *fire* or *marine.*

Fire Insurance is a guarantied indemnity against the loss or damage of property by *fire.* It is generally effected for a year or term of years.

Marine Insurance is a guarantied indemnity against the loss or damage of property by the perils of transportation by water. Insurance on the property carried is called *Cargo Insurance ;* that on the vessel is called *Hull Insurance.*

In *Mutual Insurance Companies,* each person insured becomes a party to a certain extent in the losses of the concern. The person insured pays a small cash premium at the time the insurance is effected, and he also gives to the company a *premium-note,* upon which he is liable to be assessed to the amount of its face. After a sufficient sum has accumulated from the premiums no further assessments are made on the notes, and any surplus funds are distributed among the members of the company.

ART. **80.** Most of the problems in Insurance come under one of two cases.

1. When the amount insured and the rate of insurance are given to find the *Premium.*

RULE.—*Multiply the amount insured by the rate of Insurance expressed decimally.*

2. To find for what sum a policy must be taken out, at a given rate, to cover both property and premium.

RULE.—*Divide the sum for which the property is to be insured by* $1, *diminished by the rate of insurance expressed decimally.* (See Example 13.)

Examples.

1. What is the premiun for insuring goods valued at $4500 at $2\frac{1}{2}$ per cent. ? *Ans.* $112.50.

2. A hotel worth $15000 is insured for $\frac{2}{3}$ of its value at $\frac{3}{8}$ per cent. The policy and survey cost $1.50 ; what will be the premium ? *Ans.* $39.

3. An insurance company insured a block of buildings for \$350000 at $\frac{3}{5}$ per cent., but thinking the risk too great, they *re*insured \$150000 of it at $\frac{3}{4}$ per cent. in another company, and \$100000 of it at $\frac{5}{8}$ per cent. in another. How much premium did the company receive? How much did it pay to both the other companies? How much did it clear? What per cent. of premium did it really receive on the part not *reinsured?*

Ans. to last, $\frac{7}{20}$ per cent.

Note.—All property in one block, or in adjacent buildings, having communications, or on one vessel, is considered as *one risk*, and Insurance Companies seldom take more than \$10000 in one risk. Some companies of very large capital take \$20000, but small companies do not take more than from \$3000 to \$5000 in one risk.

4. A ship valued at \$40000 is insured for $\frac{3}{4}$ of its value at $1\frac{1}{2}$ per cent., and its cargo, valued at \$36000, at $\frac{4}{5}$ per cent. What is the cost of insurance? *Ans.* \$738.

5. A merchant paid \$1450 premium for the insurance of a cargo of cotton, shipped from New Orleans to Boston, the rate of insurance being $2\frac{1}{2}$ per cent. What was the value of the cargo? *Ans.* \$58000.

6. Paid \$7.20 for the insurance of a house at $\frac{3}{5}$ per cent. If the policy and survey cost \$1.50, for how much was the house insured? *Ans.* \$950.

7. I pay \$50 for an insurance of goods valued at \$32500, and shipped from New York to St. Louis. What was the rate of insurance? *Ans.* $\frac{2}{13}$%.

8. A house valued at \$1200 has been insured for $\frac{2}{3}$ of its value for 3 years at 1 per cent. per annum. Near the close of the third year it is destroyed by fire. What is the *actual loss* to the owner, no allowance being made for interest?

Note.—The insurance company must pay him \$800; but of this sum he has paid to the company \$24 premium; hence he actually receives but \$800−24=\$776.

9. My house was insured for \$45000 for 5 years The first year I paid \$1.50 for policy and survey, and $\frac{5}{8}$ per cent. premium; each succeeding year I paid $\frac{1}{2}$ per cent. premium.

What was the total cost of insurance? The house was burned during the fifth year; what was the actual loss of the *company*, no allowance being made for interest?

Ans. to last, $43817.25.

10. A merchant ships $31360 worth of wheat from Chicago to Buffalo. For what must he get it insured at 2 per cent. so as to *cover* both the value of the wheat and the premium paid for its insurance? *Ans.* $32000.

Explanation.—Since the policy is to cover both the value of the wheat and the premium, and, since the premium is 2 per cent., or $\frac{2}{100}$ of the amount covered by the policy, the value of the wheat must be $\frac{98}{100}$ (or 98 per cent.) of the sum insured. $31360 is $\frac{98}{100}$ (98 per cent.) of what? See Case III. Percentage.

11. For what must a cargo of R. R. iron worth $115200 be insured to cover both the value of the iron and premium, the rate of insurance being 4 per cent.? *Ans.* $120000.

12. A merchant shipped a cargo of flour worth $47880 from Chicago to San Francisco via New York. To insure it from Chicago to Buffalo he paid $1\frac{1}{2}$ per cent.; from Buffalo to New York $\frac{1}{4}$ per cent.; from New York to San Francisco $3\frac{1}{4}$ per cent. For what sum must it be insured to cover value of flour and premium for the voyage? *Ans.* $50400.

13. A policy covering property and premium is taken for $12045. What is the value of the property insured, the rate being $\frac{3}{8}$ per cent.? *Ans.* $12000.

Explanation.—Since the policy covers both property and premium, $12045 is $\frac{3}{8}$ per cent. *more* than the property. See Case IV. Percentage.

14. A merchant insures a cargo of goods for $81800, covering both the value of the goods and the premium. What is the value of the goods, the rate of insurance being $2\frac{1}{4}$ per cent.? *Ans.* $80000.

15. The owners of the steamer Florence have, for the past 20 years, paid 5 per cent. per annum for her insurance. She was sunk this morning. Have they gained or lost by having the steamer insured? *Ans.*

LIFE INSURANCE.

ART. **81.** Life Insurance is a contract by which the insurer agrees, for an annual premium, to pay to the heirs of him whose life is insured, or some person specified, a certain sum of money in case of his death during the time for which the insurance of his life is effected.

When the contract extends only a given number of years, it is called a *temporary insurance.*

The individual whose life is insured pays annually, during life, a certain percentage of the sum for which his life is insured. This sum is called an *Annual Premium*, and varies with the age of him whose life is insured.

The basis of the percentage is the average number of persons lives who have attained to the age of the applicant. This average extension of life, beyond a given age, is called *Expectation of Life.* Tables showing the expectation of life for every year of man's existence are deduced from life statistics, or, as they are commonly called, *Bills of Mortality.*

The annual premium must be such a sum as will, when put at interest, amount to the sum insured, *at the close of the expectation of life.* This sum is easily found upon the principle of Life Annuities.

Life Insurance Companies have tables showing the premium to be paid at any age to secure an annuity of $100, during the remainder of life. As the computations of Life Insurance are based upon these tables, it is unnecessary to add problems.

There are two tables showing the Expectation of Life. One, called the Carlisle Table, based upon Bills of Mortality prepared in England, is in general use in that country, and to a limited extent in this. The other, called the Wigglesworth Table, prepared by Dr. Wigglesworth, from data founded upon the mortality of this country, is used to a considerable extent here.

The Expectation of Life, according to the two tables named, is shown in the following

TABLE.

Age.	Expectation by C. Table.	Expectation by W. Table.	Age.	Expectation by C. Table.	Expectation by W. Table.	Age.	Expectation by C. Table.	Expectation by W. Table.	Age.	Expectation by C. Table.	Expectation by W. Table.
0	38.72	28.15	24	38.59	32.70	48	22.80	22.27	72	8.16	9.14
1	44.68	36.78	25	37.86	32.33	49	21.81	21.72	73	7.72	8.69
2	47.55	38.74	26	37.14	31.93	50	21.11	21.17	74	7.33	8.25
3	49.82	40.01	27	36.41	31.50	51	20.39	20.61	75	7.01	7.83
4	50.76	40.73	28	35.69	31.08	52	19.68	20.05	76	6.69	7.40
5	51.25	40.88	29	35.00	30.66	53	18.97	19.49	77	6.40	6.99
6	51.17	40.69	30	34.34	30.25	54	18.28	18.92	78	6.12	6.59
7	50.80	40.47	31	33.68	29.83	55	17.58	18.35	79	5.80	6.21
8	50.24	40.14	32	33.03	29.43	56	16.89	17.78	80	5.51	5.85
9	49.57	39.72	33	32.36	29.02	57	16.21	17.20	81	5.21	5.50
10	48.82	39.23	34	31.68	28.62	58	15.55	16.63	82	4.93	5.16
11	48.04	38.64	35	31.00	28.22	59	14.92	16.04	83	4.65	4.87
12	47.27	38.02	36	30.32	27.78	60	14.34	15.45	84	4.39	4.66
13	46.51	37.41	37	29.64	27.34	61	13.82	14.86	85	4.12	4.57
14	45.75	36.79	38	28.96	26.91	62	13.31	14.26	86	3.90	4.21
15	45.00	36.17	39	28.28	26.47	63	12.81	13.66	87	3.71	3.90
16	44.27	35.76	40	27.61	26.04	64	12.30	13.05	88	3.59	3.67
17	43.57	35.37	41	26.97	25.61	65	11.79	12.43	89	3.47	3.56
18	42.87	34.98	42	26.34	25.19	66	11.27	11.96	90	3.28	3.73
19	42.17	34.59	43	25.71	24.77	67	10.75	11.48	91	3.26	3.32
20	41.46	34.22	44	25.09	24.35	68	10.23	11.01	92	3.37	3.12
21	40.75	33.84	45	24.46	23.92	69	9.70	10.50	93	3.48	2.40
22	40.04	33.46	46	23.82	23.37	70	9.18	10.06	94	3.53	1.98
23	39.31	33.08	47	23.17	22.83	71	8.65	9.60	95	3.53	1.62

TAXES.

ART. **82.** *A Tax* is a sum of money assessed according to law upon the person or property of a citizen,* for the use of the nation, state, corporation, county or parish, society or company.

Taxes upon property are *direct* or *indirect,* according to the manner in which they are assessed.

A *direct tax* is assessed directly upon the taxable property (determined by law) of citizens, and is generally collected annually. Taxes are sometimes assessed at a certain per cent. of the property taxed ; but more commonly as a given number of *mills* on $1.

* The term citizen is used in its *general sense.*

Property, subject to taxation, is either *real* or *personal.* *Real Property* or *Real Estate* consists of lands, mills, houses, and other *fixed* property. All other property is called *personal.*

The value of taxable property is fixed either by the owner under oath, as in case of personal property, or by an officer chosen for the purpose, called an *Assessor.*

Indirect Taxes are assessed upon goods imported into the country, and are collected at their port of entry. They are called *customs* or *duties.*

Remark.—Duties are called *indirect taxes,* since, according to the tenets of most political economists, the duty, imposed upon imported goods and apparently paid by the importer, enhances the price of these goods in market, and is thus indirectly and really paid by the consumer. Other political economists, called *Protectionists,* hold that, in most instances, the protective duty really cheapens the price of goods. *Such* duties can hardly be called *taxes.*

A tax assessed upon the person of citizens is called a *poll* or *capitation* tax, since it is assessed at so much per head (*poll* or *caput*), without reference to property.

Note.—In some states poll-taxes are only collected for street or road purposes.

Examples.

1. The taxable property of the city of Cleveland for 1857 was $21648938. The taxes were assessed as follows :

For State purposes,	3.1 mills on a dollar.
" County purposes,	2.5 " " "
" Corporation purposes,	8. " " "

What was the amount of tax assessed for each purpose? How much will be collected, allowing 8 per cent. to be *uncollectible?* *Ans.* to last, $270871.51.

2. The taxable property of the city of B. for 1857 was $35500000 ; the assessment was 15 mills on a dollar. What was the total tax of the city? What tax was assessed upon each of the following citizens?

Mr. A	who paid tax on	$13560.
Mr. B	" " " "	9850.59.
Mr. C	" " " "	450.87.
Mr. D	" " " "	60850.
Mr. E	" " " "	119380.
Mr. F	" " " "	1000000.

ART. 83. The labor of making out a tax list may be lessened by using tables.

The following table will be found very convenient for such a purpose. One or two examples will illustrate the manner of using it. The table is easily formed for any number of mills on a dollar.

TABLE.

Rate of tax 15 mills on a dollar.

Prop.	Tax.	Prop.	Tax.	Prop.	Tax.	Prop.	Tax.	Prop.	Tax.
$ 1	$.015	$21	$.315	$41	$.615	$61	$ .915	$ 81	$1.215
2	.03	22	.33	42	.63	62	.93	82	1.23
3	.045	23	.345	43	.645	63	.945	83	1.245
4	.06	24	.36	44	.66	64	.96	84	1.26
5	.075	25	.375	45	.675	65	.975	85	1.275
6	.09	26	.39	46	.69	66	.99	86	1.29
7	.105	27	.405	47	.705	67	1.005	87	1.305
8	.12	28	.42	48	.72	68	1.02	88	1.32
9	.135	29	.435	49	.735	69	1.035	89	1.335
10	.15	30	.45	50	.75	70	1.05	90	1.35
11	.165	31	.465	51	.765	71	1.065	91	1.365
12	.18	32	.48	52	.78	72	1.08	92	1.38
13	.195	33	.495	53	.795	73	1.095	93	1.395
14	.21	34	.51	54	.81	74	1.11	94	1.41
15	.225	35	.525	55	.825	75	1.125	95	1.425
16	.24	36	.54	56	.84	76	1.14	96	1.44
17	.255	37	.555	57	.855	77	1.155	97	1.455
18	.27	38	.57	58	.87	78	1.17	98	1.47
19	.285	39	.585	59	.885	79	1.185	99	1.485
20	.30	40	.60	60	.90	80	1.20	100	1.50

Explanation of Table.—Suppose, for example, we wish to find the tax of Mr. A in the above example. $13560=$13000+$500+$60. The tax on $13000 is found from the tax of $13 (.195) by removing the decimal point *three* places to the right ($195.); the tax on $500 is found from the tax of $5 (.075) by removing the point *two* places to the right ($7.50); the tax on $60 is found in the table ($.90). $195.+$7.50+$.90=$203.40; tax on $13560. B's tax in Ex. 2 is found in the same manner. Thus: tax on $9=.135, tax on $9000=$135; tax on $8=.12, tax on $800=$12; tax on $50=.75; tax on 59 cents (found from tax of $59 by removing point two places to the *left*)=.0885=.09 nearly.

$135.
12.75
09

Tax on $9850.59=$147.84

3. Find from the above table the tax assessed upon

E. G.	who	paid	tax	on	$ 35867.50.
H. E. S.	"	"	"	"	115380.
A. K.	"	"	"	"	586789.99.
R. S.	"	"	"	"	480.48.

4. The cost of maintaining the Public Schools of the city of B for 1858 is estimated at $56000. The taxable property of the city is $22400000. How many mills tax on a dollar must be assessed for school purposes? Suppose the uncollectible tax will equal 10 per cent. of the tax assessed; how many mills on a dollar must in this case be assessed?

Ans. to last, $2\frac{7}{9}$ mills.

DUTIES OR CUSTOMS.

ART. 84. *Duties* or *Customs* are sums of money assessed by government upon imported goods.*

Duties upon goods are collected at their port of entry, by officers appointed by government and called *custom-house officers.* At each port of entry for foreign goods is a *custom-house,* where all custom business is done.

Duties are of two kinds, *specific* and *ad-valorem.*

Specific duties are assessed upon goods at a certain rate per tun, hogshead, bale, gallon, etc., without reference to their value.

Ad-valorem duties are a certain percentage of the cost of goods as shown by the *invoice.*

* In some countries duties are also assessed upon exported goods.

An Invoice or *Manifest* is a written account of the particulars of goods shipped or sent to a purchaser, consignee, factor, etc., with the actual cost or value of such goods made out in the currency of the place or country from whence imported.

The invoice is exhibited at the custom-house by the master of the vessel, or the owner or consignee.

When an invoice has not been received, the owner or consignee must testify to the fact under oath, and then the goods are entered by appraisement.

When the currency of a country has a depreciated value compared with that of the country into which they are imported, a consular certificate showing the amount of depreciation is attached to the invoice.

ART. **85.** In assessing *specific duties*, certain allowances are made, called draft, tare, leakage, breakage, etc., before the duties are estimated.

Draft is an allowance for waste. It must be deducted before other allowances are made.

Tare or *Tret* is an allowance for weight of box, cask, etc., containing the goods. It is generally computed at a given rate per box, cask, etc.

Leakage is an allowance for the waste of liquid.

Breakage is an allowance on liquors transported in bottles.

Gross Weight is the weight of goods before any allowances are made.

Net or *Neat Weight* is the real weight of goods after the allowances have been deducted.

Remark.—As specific duties in the United States were abolished by the tariff-bill of 1846, the examples given below will relate exclusively to *ad-valorem* duties. The rules governing the entry of vessels and goods are deemed too numerous and unimportant to merit more space.

Note.—In *ad-valorem* duties no allowances are made for draft, tare, or breakage.

Examples.

1. A portion of the cargo of the ship Europa from Liverpool to New York was invoiced as follows:

650 yds. Broadcloth,	cost 13s. sterling per yd.
1246 yds. Lace,	" 2s. " "
1200 yds, Coach Lace,	" 11d. " "
1950 yds. Ingrain Carpeting,	" 3s. " "
2560 yds. Drugget,	" 2s. 4d. " "

The duty on the broadcloth was 30 per cent.; on lace 25 per cent.; coach lace 25 per cent.; carpeting 30 per cent.; drugget 30 per cent. What was the amount of duty in our currency, allowing the pound sterling to be $4.84?

Ans. $1689.1358.

2. C. Hartwell & Co., of Baltimore, have imported from Havana

100 hogsheads of Molasses, 63 gals. each,	cost 25 cts. per gal.
50 hogsheads of Sugar, 500 lbs. each,	" 5 cts. per lb.
150 boxes of Oranges,	" $2.50 per box.
300 boxes of Cigars,	" $8 per box.
160 boxes of Bananas,	" $1.75 per box.

The leakage of molasses is 2 per cent.; duty on same 30 per cent.; duty on sugar 30 per cent.; on oranges 20 per cent.; on cigars 40 per cent.; on bananas 20 per cent. What was the duty on each article? What was the amount of duties?

Ans. $1900.05.

3. A wine merchant in New York imported from Havre

100 baskets Champagne,	at $13 per basket.
80 casks Madeira,	at $42 per cask.
56 casks Oporto,	at $45 "
50 casks Sherry,	at $25 "

If an allowance of 3 per cent. for leakage is made on the wine in casks, what will be the amount of duty at 40 per cent.? For what must the wine be sold per basket or cask to make a clear profit of 25 %? *Ans.* $3286.44 duty.

BANKRUPTCY.

Art. 86. *Bankruptcy* is a failure in business and an inability to pay indebtedness.

A Bankrupt or *insolvent* is a person who fails in business and has not means to pay all his debts.

An Assignment is the transfer of the property of a bankrupt to certain persons called *assignees*, in whom it is vested for the benefit of creditors.

It is the duty of assignees to convert the property into money and divide the proceeds *pro rata* among the creditors, after deducting expenses.

The entire property of an insolvent is called his *assets*; and the amount of his indebtedness his *liabilities*.

Ex. 1. A merchant failing in business owes A \$950, B \$2500, C \$1500, and D \$3050. His assets are \$6000, and the expense of settling will be \$800. What per cent. of his indebtedness can he pay? What dividend will each creditor receive?

A's claim,	\$ 950	\$ 950 × .65 = \$ 617.50	A's div.
B's "	2500	2500 × .65 = 1625.00	B's "
C's "	1500	1500 × .65 = 975.00	C's "
D's "	3050	3050 × .65 = 1982.50	D's "
Liabilities,	\$8000	Proof, \$5200.00	
Assets,	6000		
Expense of settling,	800		
Net proceeds,	\$5200		

5200.00 ÷ 8000 = .65, or 65 per cent.

Explanation.—Since his liabilities are \$8000 and the net proceeds of his assets \$5200, he can pay \$5200 on \$8000, or 65 per cent. of his liabilities. Hence each creditor can receive 65 per cent. of his claim.

Note.—It is more common to ascertain how much can be paid on a dollar. As 65 per cent. of \$1 is 65 *hundredths* of it, or 65 cents, the process is the same.

RULE.

Divide the net proceeds of the assets by the amount of

liabilities, and the quotient will be the per cent. of the indebtedness (or the number of cents on a dollar) *that can be paid.*

To find each creditor's dividend, multiply his claim by the per cent. thus found.

2. Best & Foster became embarrassed and failed in business. Their indebtedness was $65000. The firm had cash and goods convertible into cash, $12500; building and lot, $40000; bills collectible, $2100. If the expense of settling is 5 per cent. of the amount *distributed to creditors*, what per cent. of their indebtedness can they pay? What will C. Greene & Co. receive, whose claim is $25800? *Ans.* to first, 80 per cent.

Suggestion.—Divide assets by $1.05; the quotient will be net proceeds.

3. C. Smith & Co. have become insolvent. They owe A $3500, B $1500, C $1450, D $850, E $350, and F $450. Their effects (assets) amount to $4981.50. The charges of the assignees will be $2\frac{1}{2}$ per cent. of the amount distributed to creditors. What per cent. of their indebtedness can they pay? What will each creditor receive? *Ans.* to first, 60%.

STORAGE.

ART. **87.** Storage is the price charged for the safe keeping of goods in a store or warehouse.

There is no uniform method of computing storage. The Boards of Trade, or Chambers of Commerce of the different cities, adopt such rules and rates for storage as they deem equitable. The charges for storage are usually, however, a certain rate per month for each box, bale, cask, etc.

When goods are withdrawn before the close of the month no deduction is made, but storage is charged for the full month. After the first month, for a part of a month less than one half, no charge is made, but for a part greater than one half, charge is made for a month. In some cities all fractional parts of a month are considered full months.

If, however, goods are received and sold on account, as in the commission business, or are received and delivered at the pleasure of the consignor, an account is kept, showing the date and number of casks, etc., received, and the date and number sold or delivered. In computing the storage on such an account it is customary to average the time, and charge a certain rate per month of 30 days. If there is a fractional part of a barrel, etc., in the average, it is treated as in the case of parts of months above.

Examples.

1. What will be the storage of 150 barrels of flour at 4 cents per barrel from May 20 to June 6.

$$150 \times .04 = \$6. \quad Ans.$$

2. What will be the cost of storing salt at 2 cents per barrel, received and delivered as follows: June 6, 1858, 120 bbls.; June 16, 140 bbls.; June 26, 200 bbls.; July 5, 300 bbls; July 16, 180 bbls.; July 20, 160 bbls. All delivered Aug. 1.

Operation.

1858.		bbl.	d.	prod.
June 6.	Rec'd.	120	× 10 =	1200
" 16.	"	140		
		260	× 10 =	2600
" 26.	"	200		
		860	× 9 =	7740
July 5.	"	300		
		1160	× 10 =	11600
" 15.	"	180		
		1340	× 5 =	6700
" 20.	"	160		
		1500	× 11 =	16500
Aug. 1.	Deliv.	1500		
				30)46340

Bbls. chargeable for 1 month, $1544\frac{2}{3}$

$1545 \times .02 = \$30.90$, storage.

Explanation.—The storage of 120 bbls. for 10 d. is the same as the storage of 1200 barrels for 1 day; the storage of 260 for 10 days, the same as the storage of 2600 bbls. for 1 day, and so on. Hence the amount of storage is $1200+2600+7740+11600+6700+16500$ bbls. $=46340$ bbls. for 1 day $=4635$ ($\frac{2}{3}$ called 1 bbl.) bbls. for 1 month.

3. What will be the storage of flour at 5 cents per bbl. per month, received and delivered as follows?

Received July 1, 1858, 400 bbls.; July 15, 350 bbls.; July 26, 450 bbls. Delivered July 12, 200 bbls.; July 20, 400 bbls.; Aug. 1, 200 bbls.; and Aug. 8, 400 bbls.

Operation.

1858.				
July 1.	Rec'd.	400	× 11 =	4400
" 12.	Deliv.	200		
	Bal.	200	× 3 =	600
" 15.	Rec'd.	350		
	Bal.	550	× 5 =	2750
" 20.	Deliv.	400		
	Bal.	150	× 6 =	900
" 26.	Rec'd.	450		
	Bal.	600	× 6 =	3600
Aug. 1.	Deliv.	200		
	Bal.	400	× 7 =	2800
Aug. 8.	Deliv.	400		
			30)	1505.0
Bbls. chargeable 1 month,				502

$502 \times .05 = \$25.10$ *Ans.*

Explanation.—From July 1 to July 12, 400 bbls. were stored; from July 12 to July 15, 200 bbls.; from July 15 to July 20, 550 bbls.; from July 20 to July 26, 150 bbls.; from July 26 to Aug. 1, 600 bbls.; from Aug 1 to Aug. 8, 400 bbls.

RULE.

Commencing with the first date and ending with the last, multiply the number of barrels, or other articles in store, from each date to the one NEXT *following it, by the number of days between these dates. Divide the sum of the several products by* 30, *and the quotient will be the number of articles stored for one month, and this number multiplied by the rate of storage for each article will give the amount of storage charged.*

Remark.—The following form will give the student a very good idea of an Account of Storage. The form can be filled by the process used in solving Ex. 3.

4. Storage of goods on account of C. T. Wilder & Co.,

Chicago, Ill., at 5 cents a bbl. per month, by Hubby & Hughes, Cleveland, O.

RECEIVED. DELIVERED.

1858.		Bbls.	Balance on hand.	Days.	Products.	1858.		Bbls.
Jan.	1	350				Jan.	20	700
"	12	650				"	31	200
Feb.	5	500				Feb.	24	800
"	10	320				Mar.	20	350
"	28	440				"	25	700
Mar.	15	850				Apr.	5	400
"	30	200				"	8	100

What is the storage on the above account, closed April 12, 1858, and how many barrels are on hand?

ART. 88. Butchers and drovers sometimes hire their cattle pastured or fed on account, entering and withdrawing them as circumstances may require. The account is closed in the same manner as an account of storage.

Account of pasturage of cattle at 60 cents a head per week for Lewis & Vincent, Portsmouth, O., by John Goodwin, Wayne, tp.

RECEIVED. WITHDRAWN.

1858.		Head.	Balance on hand.	Days.	Products.	1858.		Head.
June	3	9				June	5	2
"	10	5				"	7	4
"	18	15				"	12	5
July	1	20				"	15	3
"	9	10				"	21	10
"	31	5				July	3	10
Aug.	3	12				"	12	10
"	16	13				"	20	6
"	31	10				"	28	2
Sept.	25	9				Aug.	7	5
"	30	3				"	13	15
Oct.	1	8				"	20	9
						Sept.	28	10
						Oct.	4	5
						"	8	10
						"	15	13

What is the average number of cattle pastured each week (7 days), and what is due John Goodwin? *Ans.* to last, $159.

GENERAL AVERAGE.

Art. 89. When, for the safety of a ship in distress, any destruction of property or expense is necessarily and voluntarily incurred, either by cutting away the masts, throwing goods overboard, or otherwise, all persons who have goods on board, or property in the ship, bear their proportion of the loss.

The method of apportioning the loss among the several interests, sacrificed or benefited by the sacrifice, is called *General Average*, and the property thus sacrificed is called *Jettison.*

In ascertaining the amount of *loss* to be averaged, not only the amount of goods thrown overboard is considered, but also all damages to the ship, cost of repairs, and expense of detention for making repairs, including the wages of officers and crew; also the expense of entering a harbor to avoid peril, or of setting afloat when stranded; also towage in case of being disabled, or salvage paid another vessel for affording relief, etc.

When the repairs made consist of new masts, rigging, etc., a deduction of $\frac{1}{3}$ of their cost is usually made, since they are considered better than the old.

In estimating the value of the three *contributing interests*—vessel, freight, and cargo—it is customary to value the cargo at the price it would have brought at its port of *destination.* It is sometimes valued at its *invoice* price at the port of *lading.*

As the wages of seamen, pilotage, etc., are paid out of the freight, a deduction is made from the gross freight for this purpose. The amount to be deducted is not determined in a uniform manner. According to some authorities, the gross freight less $\frac{1}{3}$ is the net freight, except in New York, where $\frac{1}{2}$ is deducted. The general practice, however, is to ascertain what sum will actually be left to the vessel as *net* freight, after paying seamen's wages, etc. Sometimes the vessel earns a net freight of $\frac{2}{3}$ the total amount, and sometimes the seamen's wages, etc., absorb the *whole* of a very low freight. Each case is estimated by its *attendant circumstances.*

The practical difficulty in General Average is to determine whether the loss is subject to a general average. In some cases the loss is borne by only a part of the contributory interests.

When either a part or the whole of the ship or cargo or both is insured, the insurers bear their proportion of the loss as found by average. (See Ex. 1.) In some instances the adjustment of the insurance becomes a very intricate problem.

RULE.

Divide the total loss subject to average by the sum of the values of the contributory interests, and multiply each interest by the percentage thus found.

Note.—The jettison must be included in the contributory interests, and bear its proportion of the loss.

Examples.

1. The ship Western World, in her passage from New York to Aspinwall was struck by a severe gale near the island of Cuba. After throwing overboard cargo amounting to $4650, she made the port of Havana. Here the cost of the necessary repairs of the vessel was $1800, and the cost of detention in port $450. The contributory interests were as follows: value of ship $35000; value of cargo $24000; net freight $4000. Of the cargo, $8500 was shipped by Terry & Wheeler; $7500 by Morse & Duty; $5000 by T. C. Hood & Co.; and $3000 by P. Kinney & Co. How ought the loss to be averaged?

Operation.

Vessel, ...	$35000	Jettison, . . .	$4650
Cargo, ...	24000	Repairs, less $\frac{1}{3}$, .	1200
Net freight, . . .	4000	Cost of detention,	450
Total contrib. interests,	$63000	Total loss, . .	$6300

6300.00÷63000=.10; loss 10 per cent.

$35000×.10=$3500, loss borne by ship.
24000×.10= 2400, " " " cargo.
4000×.10= 400, " " " freight.
8500×.10= 850, " " " Terry & Wheeler.
7500×.10= 750, " " " Morse & Duty.
5000×.10= 500, " " " T. C. Hood & Co.
3000×.10= 300, " " " P. Kinney & Co.

2. The steamship Asia sailed from Liverpool to Boston with a cargo as follows: shipped by T. S. Foot & Co. $45500; by C. S. Moore & Co. $10500; by T. Hope & Sons $7450; by C. White & Co. $12550. During a storm the captain was obliged to throw overboard cargo amounting to $8500, and the necessary repairs of the ship cost $2700. In addition to repairs, the charges for seamen's board, dockage, etc., were $500. How is the loss to be shared, the value of the ship being $40000, and the net freight $4000? *Ans.* Loss, 9%.

Remark.—The following examples will give the student some idea of Insurance as connected with General Average.

3. The schooner Michigan sailed from Chicago for Buffalo with the following cargo: 25000 bushels of wheat owned by Smith & Dewy; 18500 bushels of corn owned by Fisk & Hunter; 850 barrels of flour owned by T. Ford & Co. The schooner is insured in company A for $30000, which is $\frac{2}{3}$ of its value, at 3 per cent.; the wheat in company B for $22500 (invoice price) at 2 per cent.; the corn in company C for $9250 (invoice price) at $1\frac{1}{2}$ per cent.; and the flour in company D for $4250 (invoice price) at $2\frac{1}{2}$ per cent. The gross freight was $6000, and seamen's wages, etc., $\frac{1}{3}$ of the gross freight. During a severe storm the flour was thrown overboard. How is the loss to be borne? How is the payment of the sum for which the flour is insured to be adjusted?

Explanation.—By general average we find that the *average loss is 5 per cent.*, and that the schooner must sustain $2250 of the loss; the cargo $1800; and the freight $200. Insurance Company A must pay 5 per cent. of $30000=$1500; company B 5 per cent. of $22500=$1125; company C 5 per cent. of $9250=$462.50; and company D 5 per cent. of $4250=$212.50.

4. Suppose, in the above example, that when the schooner reached her dock in Buffalo the flour could have been sold for $6120; the wheat for $35780; the corn for $11100. How is the insurance to be adjusted?

INTEREST.

ART. **90.** Interest is the compensation allowed for the use of money or capital.

It arises from voluntary loans, from certain investments giving a periodical income, and from delay in payment of debts already due.

The *principal* is the sum loaned, or the debt on which interest is paid.

The *amount* is the principal and interest taken together.

The *rate of interest* is fixed by mutual agreement or by law; and is the ratio between the principal and interest for an assumed length of time, expressed by percentage; thus, "6 per cent. per annum," declares the interest for one year to be $\frac{6}{100}$ of the principal. In expressing the rate per cent., one year is generally assumed; though in discounting "short paper," a month is frequently used; as 1 per cent. per month.

Usury formerly was synonymous with *interest*, but now signifies *illegal interest*. England having abolished all usury laws, has no further use for that term. The practicability of voluntary contracts in loaning money, restricted only as other contracts are restricted, is gaining increased favor among intelligent political economists, and not the least among money *borrowers*. When the rate has not been previously agreed upon, a *legal rate* is desirable, to avoid contention or oppression. Government regulates all weights and measures, but not the prices of the articles weighed and measured. So it regulates the weight and fineness of coins, but it should not dictate the price paid for the use of them. The injustice of restricting the rate of interest may be seen by applying the principal to insurance companies. If the premium for insurance be restricted to a low rate, only the safest risks would be taken, those having greater risks could not be accommodated. So in restricting the rate of interest, only the rich and those who could offer the best securities would be able to borrow money. If the loan be made at higher than the legal rate, the rate must be raised still higher to cover the risk arising from illegality.

ART. 91. INTEREST may be *simple, annual,* or *compound.*

In *simple interest* the principal alone draws interest; which as it accrues remains unchanged until ultimate payment.

In *annual interest* the interest on the principal due at the end of each successive year becomes a new principal to draw simple interest until payment. When interest is made payable semi-annually or quarterly, the interest, if not paid, is convertible at those periods into the principal, as in annual interest.

In *compound interest* the entire amount due at regular intervals of time, both of principal and interest, is converted into one new principal. It is thus compounded annually, semi-annually, or quarterly.

Note.—The difference between simple, annual, and compound interest in their effect depends upon the time when interest money, if not paid, begins to draw interest. In general a debt should begin to draw interest as soon as it is due. The time when a debt of interest becomes due is conventional. In bank discounts it is payable in advance. In simple interest it is not considered due until the ultimate payment of the principal. In annual interest it is due after it has been accruing for one year, except the interest on interest, which is not due till ultimate payment. Compound interest supposes *all* interest, whether upon principal or interest, to be due at the end of equal successive intervals of time, generally of one year or six months. When the interest is considered due the *instant* it has accrued, and *all interest* is made to draw interest, it is called *instantaneous compound interest.* The actual difference between even *instantaneous* compound interest and simple interest is not so great as at first might be supposed. For 6% simple interest for one year will amount to more than $5\frac{4}{5}$% instantaneous compound interest.

SIMPLE INTEREST.

ART. **92.** Inasmuch as the *interest* varies directly as the *principal, rate per cent., and time*, these four terms bear such a relation to each other, that any three of them being given the fourth may be found. To find the *interest* is by far the most common problem, and may be obtained by the following

GENERAL RULE.

I. *Find the interest for one year by multiplying the principal by as many hundredths as are expressed in the rate per cent., then multiply by the number of years and fractional parts of years expressed in the given time.*

Note.—When the time is expressed in months and days, it is usual for convenience to regard each month as $\frac{1}{12}$, and each day as $\frac{1}{360}$ of the year. (See Art. 95).

Ex. What is the simple interest of $844.50 for 2 yrs. 3 mo. 6 da. at 7% ?

	$844.50
	.07
1 yr. =	$59.1150
2 yrs. =	$118.230
3 mo. = $\frac{1}{4}$	14.779
6 d. = $\frac{1}{60}$	.985
	$133.99 *Ans.*

Remark.—The multiplication may be performed by aliquot parts. The fractional parts of mills may be neglected when less than a half—otherwise, they should be counted as one.

The following rules may be found convenient in practice, and the pupil should become familiar with the *principle* of all, to apply that one which will give the result with the least work.

RULE II.—*Set down the entire number of months in the time as decimal hundredths, and one third of the number of days as decimal thousandths; multiply half the principal by this number. The result will be the interest at 6% per annum.*

For 4 per cent. subtract		$\frac{1}{3}$.	For 7 per cent. add			$\frac{1}{6}$.
" $4\frac{1}{2}$ "	"	$\frac{1}{4}$.	" 8	"	"	$\frac{1}{3}$.
" 5 "	"	$\frac{1}{6}$.	" 10	"	"	$\frac{2}{3}$.

Or in general, for other rates than 6%, increase or diminish the result obtained by the rule in the same ratio that the rate is increased or diminished.

Taking the last example, we have by this rule the following solution:

$\$422.25 \times 0.272 = \$114.852 =$ the interest at 6%.

Adding $\frac{1}{6}$, $\$133.99 =$ the interest at 7%.

RULE III.—*Take one per cent. of the principal for the interest for two months or sixty days; then by aliquot parts find the interest for the given time.*

Note.—It will be observed that the interest for 6 days may be found by removing the decimal point three places to the left. For any multiple of 6 days the result may be obtained by a simple multiplication.

This rule is convenient in cases of "short paper," as in bank discounts, which generally run 30, 60, or 90 days.

When not expressed, the rate is understood to be 6% per annum.

Ex. What is the interest of $420 for 30, 60, and 90 days, respectively, days of grace included?

60 d. 1%	=$4.20 (1)	Add (2) and (3)	=$2.31=int. 33 d.
30 d. take $\frac{1}{2}$ =	2.10 (2)	" (1) and (3)	= 4.41=int. 63 d.
3 d. take $\frac{1}{10}$ =	.21 (3)	" (1) (2) and (3)	= 6.51=int. 93 d.

By this analysis most examples in banking may be wrought mentally.

Examples.

ART. **93.** To be wrought by each of the three rules given above. Find the simple interest of

1. $120 for 1 yr. 2 mo. 12 d. at 6%? *Ans.* $8.64.
2. $340.50 for 2 yrs. 3 mo. 15 d. at 9%? *Ans.* $70.23.
3. $1000.25 for 1 yr. 9 mo. 3 d. at 10%? *Ans.* $175.86.
4. $25 for 3 mo. 3 da. at 12%? *Ans.* $.78.
5. $145.20 for 1 yr. 11 mo. 29 d. at 7%? *Ans.* $20.30.

6. $450 for 3 yrs. 2 mo. 21 d. at 8% ? *Ans.* $116.10.

7. If a man borrows $10000 at 6% interest, and loans it at 10%, what will be gain in 2 yrs. 3 d. ? *Ans.* $803.33.

8. A merchant bought 400 yards of cloth at $4 per yard, payable in 6 months, and immediately sold it at $4.10, giving a credit of 3 months, at the expiration of which term he anticipated the payment of his own paper, getting a discount off of 10% per annum. What did he gain by the transaction ?

9. A merchant bought 400 yards of cloth at $4 per yard, payable in 3 months, and after holding it for 15 days sold it at $4.25 per yard, receiving therefor a note payable in 4 months. When the purchase money became due, he had this note discounted at the bank to meet it. What did he gain by the transaction ?

10. Taking the conditions of the last example, what would he have gained if he had borrowed at 6% interest, until the maturity of the note he had received, sufficient to pay for the cloth, and why should there be any difference in the results ?

11. If I invest $1000 in wool, pay 5% for freight, and sell at 15% advance on cost price, giving 4 months credit, get this paper discounted at the bank at 6% interest, and repeat the operation every 15 days, investing all the proceeds each time, what shall I gain in 2 months ?

12. If a man borrows $1000 at 10% interest, and with it buys a note for $1100, maturing in 5 mo., but which not being paid when due runs 1 yr. 6 mo. beyond maturity, drawing 6% interest, will he gain or lose, and how much ?

Ans. He gains $7.33.

13. Jan. 1st. a man borrowed $10000 at 6% interest. Fifteen days after he lent $4500 for 8 mo. 15 d., without grace, at 10%. Feb. 1st, with the balance he purchased a note for $5650, due July 4, which not being paid at maturity was extended until the loan of $4500 became due, at the rate of 8% interest. Both notes having been then promptly paid, he immediately purchased a 7% State Bond of $10000, which, with its semi-annual interest, would mature Jan. 1st following, for which he paid 1% premium upon its par value, at the same

time loaning the balance at the rate of $1\frac{1}{2}\%$ per month. What was his profit for the year? *Ans.* \$249.49.

ART. **94**. To find the interest for days, counting 365 days for a year, the only strictly accurate

RULE.

Reduce the whole time to days, by which multiply the year's interest, and divide by 365. Or,

Reduce the actual number of days to months of 30 *days each, then find the interest by* Rule II, *subtracting from the result thus obtained* $\frac{1}{73}$ *part of itself.*

Examples.

1. Find the simple interest of \$1000 from April 1 to Dec. 1.

Solution.—$244 \times \$60 \div 365 =$ *Ans.* \$40.11.

2. Find the simple interest of \$125 from April 1 to Dec. 7.

Solution.—246 days $=$ 8 mo. 6 d. Then $\$125 \times .041 = \$5.125$, and $\$5.125 - \frac{5.125}{73} = \$5.055$, the interest required.

By the first rule we have the following equation: $246 \times \$7.50 \div 365 = \$5.055$.

3. Find the interest of \$1250 for 360 days at 6% per annum of 365 days.

Solution.—$\frac{6}{100}$ of $\$1250 = \$75$. Then $\$75 - \frac{5}{365}$ (or $\frac{1}{73}$) of $\$75 = \$73.97$.

4. Find the interest of \$1250 for 365 days at 6% per annum of 360 days.

Solution.—$\frac{6}{100}$ of $\$1250 = \$75$. Then $\$75 + \frac{5}{360}$ (or $\frac{1}{72}$) of $\$75 = \$76.04$.

5. What would be the difference between the accrued interest for 90 days on \$1000000 of 6% State Bonds, computed first in Ohio, counting 360 days for a year, then in New York, counting 365 days for a year? *Ans.* \$205.48.

Note.—In New York the interest for years and months is computed in the usual way without reducing to days, but for the odd days the interest is computed by the above rule.

6. A note for \$1000 runs from Jan. 1, 1856, to Jan. 25, 1858, with interest at 6%. What amount is due according to

the above rule? What amount is due computed as it would be in New York? What amount is due computed as it would be in Ohio?

COMPUTATION OF TIME IN INTEREST.

ART. 95. While most of the States have enacted rigid laws against taking usurious interest, they have left the *mode of computing legal interest* very indeterminate. Nearly all the rules in common use in this country are inaccurate and illegal, and have only been sustained by decisions based upon custom; but custom varies, and the legal decisions have not been uniform.

The difficulties attending this question, which has occasioned so much litigation and jeopardized so much capital, can be briefly stated.

The fundamental principle upon which lawful simple interest is computed is that the rate should be exactly proportionate to the term for which interest is paid. The time usually assumed for fixing the rate is one year, *e. g.*, 6 per cent. per annum; that is, when the time is one year, the interest should be $\frac{6}{100}$ of the principal; and when the time varies from one year, the proportion of interest should vary in exactly the same ratio. If, then, we assume that the year consists of 365 days (as that is regarded in law a civil year), it must be admissible, in computing the interest on a note running from Jan. 1, 1856, to Jan. 1, 1857, to add one day's interest to the interest for one year; for in the case proposed, February of a leap year intervening, the time was 366 days instead of 365, the legal civil year.

One year being the standard of reference in expressing the rate, all time in computing interest must be expressed in years or aliquot parts of the year. But the year has no *exact* natural or artificial subdivisions except the day, and the day is an aliquot part only as we *assume* the year to consist of a definite number of days. The number 360 being a multiple of more whole numbers than 365, for convenience in reckoning it would have been better to assume 360 days for the *nominal* year in fixing the rate, rather than 365. The *time* in expressing the rate is *arbitrary*, and as neither 360, 365, nor 366 is the exact number of days in all years, either civil or astronomical, would not the increased facility in computation, and the perfect accuracy in the result, warrant the change ?

The division of the year into twelfths, called months, is purely imaginary ; for no month, either lunar or calendar, was ever known which occupied just one-twelfth of a year. Manifestly, if we assume a year of 365 days as the standard for reference in expressing the rate, we never can introduce the denominations of months in any form whatsoever without inaccuracy, unless we involve in the calculation fractional parts of days, which would be as absurd as it would be difficult.

If, however, we assume a year of 360 days, we may have assumed months of 30 days. Then 6 per cent. per annum of 360 days would be 1 per cent. for 60 days, and all time being reduced to days or months of 30 days each, or years of 360 days each, the computation would be simple, rapid, and perfectly accurate. As it is, the law having accurately determined when a paper matures, however the time may be expressed in the paper, the only accurate rule for computing interest is to ascertain the actual number of days, and make each day's interest $\frac{1}{365}$ of the annual interest. Some banks are restricted by their charters in their discounts to " 6% per annum," but are allowed to compute by Rowlett's Tables. But Rowlett's rule " To find bank interest," makes all time reducible to days, and the interest for each $\frac{1}{360}$ of the year's interest, so that when the time in the note to be discounted reads " two months," the interest for $\frac{2}{12}$ of the year should never be taken except when February 29th of a leap year is included in the term, for in that case only will the " two months" contain just 60 days and no more. In all other cases, the interest should be 59, 61, or 62-360ths of the year's interest, according to the actual number of days contained in the time of the note. In Massachusetts and some other States interest computed on the supposition that 360 days make the year is regarded valid. But in New York each day's interest must be only $\frac{1}{365}$ of the year's interest.

ART. 96. RULES FOR COMPUTING THE DIFFERENCE OF TIME BETWEEN DATES.—Besides counting the exact number of days as referred to above, two rules are in common use.

RULE I.—*By compound subtraction, reckoning* 30 *days for a month.*

RULE II.—*By finding the number of entire calendar months from the first date, and counting the actual number of days left.*

Note.—By "calendar month" is meant the time from any day of one month to the corresponding day of the next month. If the days of the first month is a higher number than the greatest number of days in the last month, the calendar month ends with the last day. Thus from Oct. 31 to Nov. 30 is a calendar month.

From Aug. 20, 1854, to March 10, 1857, would be,
according to the 1st Rule, 2 yrs. 6 mo. 20 d.;
" " 2d Rule, 2 yrs. 6 mo. 18 d.

From Aug. 31, 1854, to March 10, 1857, would be,
according to the 1st Rule, 2 yrs. 6 mo. 9 d.
" " 2d Rule, 2 yrs. 6 mo. 10 d.

It will be observed that in these particular examples, though the actual difference of time in the two cases is 11 days, the result by the second rule shows only 8 days. A discrepancy of 2 days *may* also arise in the use of the first rule, for by it the time from Feb. 28, 1857, to March 2, 1857, would be 4 days, while the actual time is only 2 days. The first rule also shows no difference of time between March 31 and April 1. Each rule will give a result sometimes too large and sometimes too small.

The examples in this work, except those in Bank Discount, and those otherwise restricted, may be wrought by the second rule.

ART. 97. PROBLEMS IN WHICH THE INTEREST IS KNOWN.—Of the four quantities, the *principal, time, rate per cent., and interest,* to find either one of the first three, the remaining three being given, we have the following

GENERAL RULE.

Find the interest by the given conditions, assuming one dollar for the principal, one per cent. for the rate, or one year for the time, in place of the unknown quantity, as the case may be, by which divide the given interest, and multiply the assumed amount by the quotient.

Unity is assumed for convenience only in multiplication.

Note.—When the amount is given instead of the interest, to find the latter subtract the principal from the amount.

Examples.

1. What is the rate of interest if I receive $20.96 for the use of $126.75 for 2 yrs. 24 d.?

Solution.—At 1% I would have received $2.62, and since the given interest is *eight* times this, the rate should be *eight* times 1%.

2. What sum invested at 10% per annum will secure an income of $1000 semi-annually?

Solution.—One dollar thus invested would yield an income of 5 cents semi-annually, and since $1000 is 20,000 times 5 cents, the sum loaned should be 20,000 times one dollar.

3. In what time will $512.60 amount to $538.31 at 7% per annum?

Solution.—The interest of $512.60 in one year would amount to $35.88, and since the given interest is only $25.71, the required time would be $\frac{25.71}{35.88}$ of 1 year, which by reduction will be found to be 8 mo. 18 d.

Fractional days in the result may of course be neglected.

ART. 98. The same result may be obtained by making the statement in the form of a proportion, though it is better to work by analysis.

The above examples would be thus stated:

As $2.62 int. at 1% is to $20.96 given int., so is 1% the supposed rate to 8% the required rate.

Or, $2.62 : $20.96 : : 1% : 8%.

2. $0.05 : $1000 : : $1 : $20,000.

3. $35.88 : $25.71 : : 1 yr. : 8 mo. 18 d.

4. In what time will any sum double itself by simple interest at 5 per cent.?

Solution.—The required interest must be 100% of the principal, and as there is a gain of only 5% in one year, it will take as many years as 5 is contained times in 100.

Note.—To treble itself, the required interest must be 200% of the principal.

PRESENT WORTH.

ART. 99. Simple interest varies directly as the principal, time, and rate per cent. Either two of the latter terms remaining the same, *interest* varies as the other. The *principal* being given or fixed, the *amount*, consisting of the *sum* of principal and interest, or of a *constant* and *variable* quantity, can not vary as the time and rate per cent. But if the *time* and *rate per cent.* are constant quantities, the *interest* varies as the *principal*, and the *amount* being in this case the sum of two equally varying quantities, varies also as the principal. From this we see the truth of the following

PROPOSITION.—For the same time and rate per cent., whether the interest be simple or compound, the *amount* due varies as the principal.

The *Present Worth* of any debt is the sum or principal which at the current rate of interest will amount to that debt when it becomes due.

For example, $100 at 10% will amount in one year to $110. The *Present Worth* then of $110 due one year hence is $100.

The amount, rate, and time being given, to find the principal or *Present Worth*, we have the following

RULE.

Assuming any principal, determine the amount for the given rate and time, by which divide the given amount, and multiply the assumed principal by the quotient.

Note.—To render the multiplication easy, assume $1 or $100.

Remark.—The difference between the Present Worth and the Amount of the debt is called the Discount; and is really the interest on the Present Worth. For Bank Discount, see Art.

Examples.

1. What is the present worth and discount of a debt of $1000 due in 1 yr. 6 mo., the current rate of interest being 6 per cent.? *Ans.* Pres. Worth, $917.431; Dis., $82.569.

2. What sum must I put at interest at 10 per cent. to liquidate a debt of $3000 due 3 years hence?

3. A man can sell his farm for $5000 cash, or for $6000 payable in 2 years; if he accept the last offer, and receive instead its present worth at 8% interest, how much better would it be than the first offer? If he accept the first offer, and loan the $5000 at 8% interest, how much less would he receive at the end of the 2 years than if he accept the last? What is the present worth of that difference?

ANNUAL INTEREST.

ART. **100.** If a note reads "with interest payable annually," or "with annual interest," the interest may be collected at the close of each year; but, if not paid, the interest due draws only *simple interest* to the time of maturity, or until paid.

It is a principle in law, that money due or on interest always draws *simple interest,* unless a condition to the contrary is expressly stated. The condition, "with interest payable annually, applies to the interest which accrues on the *principal* or face of the note, and *not* to the interest on the *annual interest.*

If, when the annual interest is not paid at the close of each year, separate notes for the same, drawing simple interest, should be given, the sum of the amounts due on the several notes, including the original, would be the same as the amount due on the one note with annual interest unpaid till the time of maturity or settlement.

Ex. 1.

$500. CLEVELAND, May 10, 1850.

For value received, I promise to pay John Smith, or bearer, five hundred dollars, four years from date, with interest at 10 per cent., payable annually.

JAMES HOLT.

Nothing being paid till time of maturity, what will be the amount then due?

Operation.

Principal, ...		$500
Interest on the principal 1 yr.	=$50	
" " 4 yrs.	=	$200
Simple interest on $50 for 3 yrs.	=$15	
" " 2 yrs.	= 10	
" " 1 yr.	= 5	
" " 6 yrs.	=	30
Total amount due at maturity,		$730

Explanation.—At the close of the 1st year, $50 annual interest was due, but, being unpaid, draws *simple interest* to the time of maturity, or 3 years; at the close of the 2d year, $50 annual interest was again due, which, being unpaid, draws simple interest 2 years; at the close of the 3d year, $50 annual interest is again due, and draws simple interest 1 year; at the close of the 4th year, or time of maturity, $50 is again due, but, being paid, has no interest. Hence, the total interest due consists: 1. Of the annual interest ($50) multiplied by 4, the number of years to maturity. 2. Of the simple interest of the annual interest ($50) for 3 years, for 2 years, for 1 year, or for 3+2+1 years=6 years.

Note.—It will be noticed that the amount due consists of three parts: 1. Principal. 2. Total annual interest. 3. Simple interest on annual interest.

Ex. 2.

$1000. BUFFALO, Jan. 1, 1853.

For value received, I promise to pay Thos. Hunt, or order, May 7, 1858, one thousand dollars, with annual interest at 6 per cent. GEO. SWIFT.

Nothing being paid on the above note till time of maturity, what will be the amount then due ?

Operation.

Principal, ...		$1000
Interest on the prin. 1 yr., or annual interest,=$60		
" " 5 yrs. 4 mo. 6 da., the entire time of the note computed as in simple int.=		321
Simple interest on $60 for	4 yrs. 4 mo. 6 d.	
" "	3 " 4 " 6 "	
" "	2 " 4 " 6 "	
" "	1 " 4 " 6 "	
" "	4 " 6 "	
" "	11 yrs. 9 mo. =	42.30
Total amount due at maturity,	.	$1363.30

Note.—In this case, the amount due consists of *three parts* as in Ex. 1. The term "total annual interest" as used above, though nothing more than the simple interest on the principal, signifies that debt of interest which if not paid draws interest. As all interest is due at settlement, that which has accrued at the time of settlement, though for less than a year, as in the last example, may still be classed with "annual interest."

RULE.

Find the simple interest on the principal for the entire time, which will be the TOTAL *annual interest.*

Then find the SIMPLE *interest on the annual interest for one year, for a time equal to the* SUM *of the periods of time the several annual interests draw interest.*

The sum of the principal, total annual interest, and simple interest thus found, will be the amount due at maturity. Or,

On the annual interest due each year, compute SIMPLE INTEREST *till maturity, and to the sum of their several amounts add the principal.*

When the interest is payable semi-annually or quarterly,

each semi-annual or quarterly interest draws *simple* interest till paid.

Examples.

3. A note for $1200 is given to run 3 yrs. 3 mo. 12 d. with interest at 6 per cent., payable annually. Nothing being paid till maturity, what is then due? *Ans.* $1453.03.

4. Bought a city lot for $900, to be paid in 4 equal annual payments with annual interest. Nothing being paid, what is due 5 years from the date of the article or lease? What, 4 yrs. 7 mo. 9 d.? What, 10 years, interest payable semi-annually? *Ans.* to the last, $1593.90.

5.

$2000. CLEVELAND, March 15, 1853.

On the first day of January 1858, for value received, I promise to pay John F. Whitelaw, or order, two thousand dollars with annual interest. CHARLES L. CAMP.

What was due at maturity, no interest having been paid? What was due, supposing the annual interest to have been paid promptly?

COMPOUND INTEREST.

ART. **101.** In Compound Interest, as before stated, the entire amount due at regular intervals of time, whether principal or interest, is converted into one new principal. It may be thus compounded annually, semi-annually, or quarterly.

For illustration, consider $1 to draw interest at 6% and compounded annually.

	$1.
1st year's interest, ...	.06
Amount due forming a new principal,	1.06
2d year's interest, ...	.0636
Amount due forming a new principal,	1.1236
3d year's interest, ...	.067416
Amount due forming a new principal,	1.191016
4th year's interest, ...	.07146096
Amount due in four years, . . .	$1.26247696

Amount of $1 at Compound Interest in any number of years.

Yrs.	2 per cent.	2½ per cent.	3 per cent.	3½ per cent.	4 per cent.	4½ per cent.
1	1.0200 0000	1.0250 0000	1.0300 0000	1.0350 0000	1.0400 0000	1.0450 0000
2	1.0404 0000	1.0506 2500	1.0609 0000	1.0712 2500	1.0816 0000	1.0920 2500
3	1.0612 0800	1.0768 9062	1.0927 2700	1.1087 1787	1.1248 6400	1.1411 6612
4	1.0824 3216	1.1038 1289	1.1255 0881	1.1475 2300	1.1698 5856	1.1925 1860
5	1.1040 8080	1.1314 0821	1.1592 7407	1.1876 8631	1.2166 5290	1.2461 8194
6	1.1261 6242	1.1596 9342	1.1940 5230	1.2292 5533	1.2653 1902	1.3022 6012
7	1.1486 8567	1.1886 8575	1.2298 7387	1.2722 7926	1.3159 3178	1.3608 6183
8	1.1716 5938	1.2184 0290	1.2667 7008	1.3168 0904	1.3685 6905	1.4221 0061
9	1.1950 9257	1.2488 6297	1.3047 7318	1.3628 9735	1.4233 1181	1.4860 9514
10	1.2189 9442	1.2800 8454	1.3439 1638	1.4105 9876	1.4802 4428	1.5529 6942
11	1.2433 7431	1.3120 8666	1.3842 3387	1.4599 6972	1.5394 5406	1.6228 5305
12	1.2682 4179	1.3448 8882	1.4257 6089	1.5110 6866	1.6010 3222	1.6958 8143
13	1.2936 0663	1.3785 1104	1.4685 3371	1.5639 5606	1.6650 7351	1.7721 9610
14	1.3194 7876	1.4129 7382	1.5125 8972	1.6186 9452	1.7316 7645	1.8519 4492
15	1.3458 6834	1.4482 9817	1.5579 6742	1.6753 4883	1.8009 4351	1.9352 8244
16	1.3727 8570	1.4845 0562	1.6047 0644	1.7339 8601	1.8729 8125	2.0223 7015
17	1.4002 4142	1.5216 1826	1.6528 4763	1.7946 7555	1.9479 0050	2.1133 7681
18	1.4282 4625	1.5596 5872	1.7024 3306	1.8574 8920	2.0258 1652	2.2084 7877
19	1.4568 1117	1.5986 5019	1.7535 0605	1.9225 0132	2.1068 4918	2.3078 6031
20	1.4859 4740	1.6386 1644	1.8061 1123	1.9897 8886	2.1911 2314	2.4117 1402
21	1.5156 6634	1.6795 8185	1.8602 9457	2.0594 3147	2.2787 6807	2.5202 4116
22	1.5459 7967	1.7215 7140	1.9161 0341	2.1315 1158	2.3699 1879	2.6336 5201
23	1.5768 9926	1.7646 1068	1.9735 8651	2.2061 1448	2.4647 1555	2.7521 6635
24	1.6084 3725	1.8087 2595	2.0327 9411	2.2833 2849	2.5633 0417	2.8760 1383
25	1.6406 0599	1.8539 4410	2.0937 7793	2.3632 4498	2.6658 3633	3.0054 3446
26	1.6734 1811	1.9002 9270	2.1565 9127	2.4459 5856	2.7724 6979	3.1406 7901
27	1.7068 8648	1.9478 0002	2.2212 8901	2.5315 6711	2.8833 6858	3.2820 0956
28	1.7410 2421	1.9964 9502	2 2879 2768	2.6201 7196	2.9987 0332	3.4296 9999
29	1.7758 4469	2.0464 0739	2.3565 6551	2.7118 7798	3.1186 5145	3.5840 3649
30	1.8113 6158	2.0975 6758	2.4272 6247	2.8067 9370	3.2433 9751	3.7453 1813
31	1.8475 8882	2.1500 0677	2.5000 8035	2.9050 3148	3.3731 3341	3.9138 5745
32	1.8845 4059	2.2037 5694	2.5750 8276	3.0067 0759	3.5080 5875	4.0899 8104
33	1.9222 3140	2.2588 5086	2.6523 3524	3.1119 4235	3.6483 8110	4.2740 3018
34	1 9606 7603	2.3153 2213	2.7319 0530	3.2208 6033	3.7943 1634	4.4663 6154
35	1.9998 8955	2.3732 0519	2.8138 6245	3.3335 9045	3.9460 8899	4.6673 4781
36	2.0398 8734	2.4325 3532	2,8982 7833	3.4502 6611	4.1039 3255	4.8773 7846
37	2.0806 8509	2.4933 4870	2.9852 2668	3.5710 2543	4.2680 8986	5.0968 6049
38	2.1222 9879	2.5556 8242	3.0747 8348	3.6960 1132	4.4388 1345	5.3262 1921
39	2.1647 4477	2.6195 7448	3.1670 2698	3.8253 7171	4.6163 6599	5.5658 9908
40	2.2080 3966	2.6850 6384	3.2620 3779	3.9592 5972	4.8010 2063	5.8163 6454
41	2.2522 0046	2.7521 9043	3.3598 9893	4.0978 3381	4.9930 6145	6.0781 0094
42	2.2972 4447	2.8209 9520	3.4606 9589	4.2412 5799	5.1927 8391	6.3516 1548
43	2.3431 8936	2.8915 2008	3 5645 1677	4.3897 0202	5.4004 9527	6.6374 3818
44	2.3900 5314	2.9638 0808	3.6714 5227	4.5433 4160	5.6165 1508	6.9361 2290
45	2.4378 5421	3.0379 0328	3.7815 9584	4.7023 5855	5.8411 7568	7.2482 4843
46	2.4866 1129	3.1138 5086	3.8950 4372	4.8669 4110	6.0748 2271	7.5744 1961
47	2.5363 4351	3.1916 9713	4.0118 9503	5.0372 8404	6.3178 1562	7.9152 6849
48	2.5870 7039	3.2714 8956	4.1322 5188	5.2135 8898	6.5705 2824	8.2714 5557
49	2.6388 1179	3.3532 7680	4.2562 1944	5.3960 6459	6.8333 4987	8.6436 7107
50	2.6915 8803	3.4371 0872	4.3839 0602	5.5849 2686	7.1066 8335	9.0326 3627
51	2.7454 1979	3.5230 3644	4.5154 2320	5.7803 9930	7.3909 5068	9.4391 0490
52	2.8003 2819	3.6111 1235	4.6508 8590	5.9827 1327	7.6865 8871	9.8638 6463
53	2.8563 8475	3.7013 9016	4.7904 1247	6.1921 0824	7.9940 5226	10.3077 3853
54	2.9134 6144	3.7939 2491	4.9341 2485	6.4088 3202	8.3138 1435	10.7715 8677
55	2.9717 3067	3.8887 7303	5.0821 4859	6.6331 4114	8.6463 6692	11.2563 0817

Amount of $1 at Compound Interest in any number of years.

Yrs.	5 per cent.	6 per cent.	7 per cent.	8 per cent.	9 per cent.	10 per cent.
1	1.0500 000	1.0600 000	1.0700 000	1.0800 000	1.0900 000	1.1000 000
2	1.1025 000	1 1236 000	1.1449 000	1.1664 000	1.1881 000	1.2100 000
3	1.1576 250	1.1910 160	1.2250 430	1 2597 120	1.2950 290	1.3310 000
4	1.2155 063	1.2624 770	1.3107 960	1.3604 890	1.4115 816	1.4641 000
5	1.2762 816	1.3382 256	1.4025 517	1.4693 281	1.5386 240	1.6105 100
6	1.3400 956	1.4185 191	1.5007 304	1.5868 743	1.6771 001	1.7715 610
7	1.4071 004	1.5036 303	1.6057 815	1.7138 243	1.8280 391	1.9487 171
8	1.4774 554	1.5938 481	1.7181 862	1.8509 302	1.9925 626	2.1435 888
9	1.5513 282	1.6894 790	1.8384 592	1.9990 046	2.1718 933	2.3579 477
10	1.6288 946	1.7908 477	1.9671 514	2.1589 250	2.3673 637	2.5937 425
11	1.7103 394	1.8982 986	2.1048 520	2.3316 390	2.5804 264	2 8531 167
12	1.7958 563	2.0121 965	2.2521 916	2.5181 701	2.8126 648	3.1384 284
13	1.8856 491	2.1329 283	2.4098 450	2.7196 237	3.0658 046	3.4522 712
14	1.9799 316	2.2609 040	2.5785 342	2.9371 936	3.3417 270	3.7974 983
15	2.0789 282	2.3965 582	2.7590 315	3.1721 691	3.6424 825	4.1772 482
16	2.1828 746	2.5403 517	2.9521 638	3.4259 426	3.9703 059	4.5949 730
17	2.2920 183	2.6927 728	3.1588 152	3.7000 181	4.3276 334	5.0544 703
18	2.4066 192	2.8543 392	3.3799 323	3.9960 195	4.7171 204	5.5599 173
19	2.5269 502	3.0255 995	3.6165 275	4.3157 011	5.1416 613	6.1159 390
20	2.6532 977	3.2071 355	3.8696 845	4.6609 571	5.6044 108	6.7275 000
21	2.7859 626	3.3995 636	4.1405 624	5.0338 337	6.1088 077	7.4002 499
22	2.9252 607	3.6035 374	4.4304 017	5.4365 404	6.6586 004	8.1402 749
23	3.0715 238	3.8197 497	4.7405 299	5.8714 637	7.2578 745	8.9543 024
24	3.2250 999	4.0489 346	5.0723 670	6.3411 807	7.9110 832	9.8497 327
25	3.3863 54	4.2918 707	5.4274 326	6.8484 752	8.6230 807	10.8347 059
26	3.5556 727	4.5493 830	5.8073 529	7.3963 532	9.3991 579	11.9181 765
27	3.7334 563	4.8223 459	6.2138 676	7.9880 615	10.2450 821	13.1099 942
28	3.9201 291	5.1116 867	6.6488 384	8.6271 064	11.1671 395	14.4209 936
29	4.1161 356	5.4183 879	7.1142 571	9.3172 749	12.1721 821	15.8630 930
30	4.3219 424	5.7434 912	7.6122 550	10.0626 569	13.2676 785	17.4494 023
31	4.5380 395	6.0881 006	8.1451 129	10.8676 694	14.4617 695	19.1943 425
32	4.7649 415	6.4533 867	8.7152 708	11.7370 830	15.7633 288	21.1137 768
33	5.0031 885	6.8405 899	9.3253 398	12.6760 496	17.1820 284	23.2251 544
34	5.2533 480	7 2510 253	9.9781 135	13.6901 336	18.7284 109	25.5476 699
35	5.5160 154	7.6860 868	10.6765 815	14.7853 443	20.4139 679	28.1024 369
36	5.7918 161	8.1472 520	11.4239 422	15.9681 718	22.2512 250	30.9126 805
37	6.0814 069	8.6360 871	12.2236 181	17.2456 256	24.2538 353	34.0039 486
38	6.3854 773	9.1542 524	13.0792 714	18.6252 756	26.4366 805	37.4043 434
39	6.7047 512	9.7035 075	13.9948 204	20.1152 977	28.8159 817	41.1447 778
40	7.0399 887	10.2857 179	14.9744 578	21.7245 215	31.4094 200	45.2592 556
41	7.3919 882	10.9028 610	16.0226 699	23.4624 832	34.2362 679	49.7851 811
42	7.7615 876	11.5570 327	17.1442 568	25.3394 819	37.3175 320	54.7636 992
43	8.1496 669	12.2504 546	18.3443 548	27.3666 404	40.6761 098	60.2400 692
44	8.5571 503	12.9854 819	19.6284 596	29.5559 717	44.3369 597	66.2640 761
45	8.9850 078	13.7646 108	21.0024 518	31.9204 494	48.3272 861	72.8904 837
46	9.4342 582	14.5904 875	22.4726 234	34 4740 853	52.6767 419	80.1795 321
47	9.9059 711	15.4659 167	24.0457 070	37.2320 122	57.4176 486	88.1974 853
48	10.4012 697	16.3938 717	25.7289 065	40.2105 731	62.5852 370	97.0172 338
49	10.9213 331	17.3775 040	27.5299 300	43.4274 190	68 2179 083	106.7189 572
50	11.4673 998	18.4201 543	29.4570 251	46.9016 125	74.3575 201	117.3908 529
51	12.0407 698	19.5253 635	31.5190 168	50.6537 415	81.0496 969	129.1299 382
52	12.6428 083	20.6968 853	33.7253 480	54.7060 408	88.3441 696	142.0429 320
53	13 2749 487	21.9386 985	36.0861 224	59.0825 241	96.2951 449	156.2472 252
54	13.9386 961	23.2550 204	38.6121 509	63.8091 260	104.9617 079	171.8719 477
55	14.6356 309	24.6503 216	41.3150 015	68.9138 561	114.4082 616	189.0591 425

If compounded semi-annually, we should have the following result:

	$1.
Interest 1st six months, ...	.03
	1.03
Interest 2d six months, ...	.0309
	1.0609
Interest 3d six months, ...	.031827
	1.092727
Interest 4th six months, ...	.03278181
Amount in two years, ...	$1.12550881

We have seen heretofore that simple interest varies directly in the same ratio as the principal, time, and rate per cent. Compound interest likewise varies as the principal, but when the time or rate per cent. is increased, compound interest increases in a still greater ratio. *e. g.*

Doubling the principal doubles the compound interest.
Doubling the time *more* than doubles the compound interest.
Doubling the rate *more* than doubles the compound interest, as may be seen from the following figures:

When the interest of $100 is . . . . . $5.
The interest of $200 would be . . . . $10.
The compound interest of $100 for 2 years at 6% is $12.36
" " " " " " 4 years at 6% is $26.2477
" " " " " " 2 years at 5% is $10.25
" " " " " " 2 years at 10% is $21.

From the fact that compound interest (and therefore the compound amount) varies as the principal, the time and rate remaining the same, having ascertained the interest or amount for any one principal, the interest for any other may be found by a simple proportion. Tables have therefore been prepared giving the interest or amount of $1 for different intervals of time and at different rates per cent. The interest or amount for any given principal may then be found by simply multiplying the sum found in the table by the given principal. If the intervals are less than one year, as when the interest is to be compounded semi-annually or quarterly, tables computed with yearly intervals may still be used by reducing the rate per cent.

proportionably, and taking in the table the proper number of intervals.

For the *time* used in expressing *any rate* of interest is entirely arbitrary, and having fixed the ratio between the principal and interest at each compounding, the result depends upon the *number* of times the operation be repeated. Thus, if the interest be compounded a given number of times by adding to each respective amount 4% of itself, it matters not whether it be considered 4% per annum or 4% per minute, the result would be the same. If the interest is to be compounded quarterly, when the rate is said to be 8% per annum, 2% should be used at each compounding, though it would amount to more than 8% compounded annually.

Examples.

1. What is the compound interest and amount of $1000 for 5 yrs. at 6% per annum, payable annually?

Ans. $338.22 and $1338.22.

2. What is the compound amount of $2200 for 3 yrs. 2 mo. 12 d. at 6% per annum, payable annually?

Ans. $2651.67.

Note.—After having computed the compound amount for the number of *entire* intervals at the end of which the interest is payable or to be computed, compute the simple interest on that amount for any remaining time before the settlement.

3. What is the compound interest of $1400 for 10 yrs. 8 mo. at 8% per annum, payable quarterly.

Solution.—$2.29724447 × 1400 = $3216.1423 = the comp. amount for 10 yrs. 6 mo., and $3216.1423 × 1.01$\frac{1}{3}$ − $1400 = the comp. interest for 10 yrs. 8 mo. = $1859.024.

4. If the population of a city containing 10,000 inhabitants should increase 10% annually, what would it amount to in 10 years? *Ans.* 25,937.

5. If a farmer beginning with one bushel of wheat should sow his entire crop each successive year, and the increase each year should be 1900%, what would he have at the end of 5 years? *Ans.* 3,200,000 bushels.

6. If a banker's rate in loaning money is 12% per annum, and he reloans all his capital every two months, what must have been the rate at simple interest to realize the same amount at the end of one year? *Ans.* $12\frac{6}{10}$% nearly.
What, at the end of two years? *Ans.* $13\frac{4}{10}$% nearly.
What, at the end of eight years? *Ans.* $19\frac{3}{10}$% nearly.
What, at the end of fifteen years? *Ans.* 33% nearly.
What, at the end of twenty-five years? *Ans.* 74% nearly.

ART. **102.** In compound interest, as in simple interest, the four quantities, viz., principal, time, rate per cent., and interest or amount, bear such a relation to each other as that when any three of them are given, the fourth may be found. Hence four cases arise.

CASE I.

The principal, time, and rate being given, to find the compound interest and amount.

This case has already been presented, but the rule may be expressed in a more concise form.

RULE.—*Find from the table the amount of* \$1 *for the given number of entire intervals, or times of compounding, at the proper rate for each interval, and multiply it by the given principal. Taking this product for a new principal, find the amount at simple interest for any fractional interval, if any, remaining before settlement. This will be the compound amount, and the compound interest may be found by subtracting from it the given principal.*

CASE II.

The compound interest or amount, the time and rate being given, to find the principal.

RULE.—*Assume* \$1 *for the principal; compute for the given time and rate its compound interest or compound amount, by which divide the given compound interest or compound amount, observing always to divide interest by interest and amount by amount.* See Art. 97.

For illustration of *Present Worth* see Art. 99.

Examples.

1. What sum, in 17 yrs., at 6%, payable annually at compound interest, will amount to $1009.79? *Ans.* $375.

2. What sum, in 14 yrs., at 8%, payable semi-annually at compound interest, will amount to $10,795.34? *Ans.* $3600.

3. What principal will yield $3251.50 compound interest in 6 yrs. 2 mo. at 7%, payable semi-annually? *Ans.* $6150.

4. How much must a father, at the birth of his son, set apart for his benefit, so that with the interest at 7%, compounded semi-annually, it may amount to $10,000, when his son shall become 21 years of age? *Ans.* $2357 79.

5. What sum at 10%, payable quarterly, will produce $7197.22, compound interest, in 3 yrs. 6 mo. 9 d.? *Ans.* $17,280.

6. What is the present worth of $50,000, due 50 yrs. hence, at 9 per cent., payable annually? *Ans.* $672.43.

How much greater would be the present worth at simple interest?

CASE III.

The principal, time, and interest or amount being given, to find the rate. See Case IV.

CASE IV.

The principal, rate, and interest or amount being given, to find the time.

For the last two cases we have the following general

RULE.—*Divide the given amount by the principal; the quotient will be the compound amount of* $1 *at the given rate for the required time or for the given time at the required rate. By reference to the table, the rate heading the column in which this quotient is found opposite the given time or number of intervals, will be the required rate; and the number in the left hand column opposite the quotient under the given rate will be the required time or number of intervals.*

Examples.

1. At what rate will $7200 yield $12,665.02, compound interest in 15 yrs.? *Ans.* 7 per cent.

2. At what rates will any sum of money double itself by compound interest in 8, 10, 15 yrs. payable semi-annually?

Ans. $4\frac{1}{2}\%$, $3\frac{1}{2}\%$, $2\frac{1}{2}\%$, respectively.

3. In what time will $5428 amount to $27157.31 at 5%, payable annually? *Ans.* 33 yrs.

4. In what time will any sum of money triple itself by compound interest at 4%, 7%, 8%, 10%, payable quarterly?

Ans. 7 yrs., 4 yrs., $3\frac{1}{2}$ yrs., 3 yrs. nearly.

PARTIAL PAYMENTS.

ART. **103.** When partial payments are made on mercantile accounts which are past due, and on notes running *only for a year or less,* it is customary to use the

VERMONT RULE.

Compute the interest on the whole debt or obligation from the time it began to draw interest, and on each payment from the time it was made until the time of settlement, and deduct the amount of all the payments, including interest, from the amount of the debt and interest.

Note.—When a partial payment is made on a note or obligation *before* it is due, no part is applied to the discharge of the interest, but the whole is used to reduce the principal in accordance with the above rule.

$600. CLEVELAND, Nov. 18, 1856.

Ninety days after date, I promise to pay to the order of William Penn six hundred dollars, with interest, value received. WALTER JOHNSON.

Indorsements.—Nov. 30, $100; Dec. 10, $250; Dec. 20, $100; Jan. 2, $80.

What was due at maturity?

$600, with interest for 93 days, amounts to		$609.30
$100, " " " 81 " " "	$101.35	
$250, " " " 71 " " "	252.96	
$100, " " " 61 " " "	101.02	
$80, " " " 48 " " "	80.64	
Sum of payments, with their interest,		$535.97
Amount due at maturity, Feb. 19, 1857,		$73.33

The same result can be obtained more easily by the use of the following

RULE.

Multiply the amount due at first, and the balance of the principal due after deducting each payment, by the number of days that elapse between the several payments, add all the products, and divide the sum by 6000. The quotient will be the interest at 6 per cent.

Taking the same example as above.

$600 multiplied by 12=	7200
$500 " " 10=	5000
$250 " " 10=	2500
$150 " " 13=	1950
$70 " " 48=	3360
Sum =	20010
Which, divided by 6000, gives for the interest due	$3.33
This added to the balance of principal, gives	$73.33

When the principal does not draw interest, the last rule can not be used without some modification.

When the time of the note or obligation is more than one year, the following rule has been adopted by the courts of most of the States, and by the Supreme Court of the United States, and may therefore be called the

UNITED STATES RULE.

ART. **104.** *Apply the payment in the first place to the discharge of the interest then due; if the payment* exceeds *the interest, the surplus goes toward discharging the principal, and the subsequent interest is to be computed on the balance of principal remaining due.*

If the payment be less *than the interest, the surplus of interest must not be taken to augment the principal; but interest continues on the former principal until the period when the payments taken together equal or exceed the interest due, and then the surplus is to be applied toward discharging the principal, and interest is to be computed on the balance as aforesaid.*

This rule requires that the payment should in all cases be applied to the discharge of the interest first, then the principal.

Ex. 1. For value received, I promise to pay to the order of C. D. Stratton $1650 on demand, with interest at 7%.

J. O. SNYDER.

CLEVELAND, O., May 20, 1856.

Indorsements.—Sept. 1, 1856, $25; Oct. 14, 1856, $150; Mar. 20, 1857, $45; July 5, 1857, $300.

What was the amount due Nov. 11, 1857?

Solution.—Interest on $1650 from May 20, 1856, to Sept. 1, 1856, 3 mo. 12 d., at 7% per annum, ...	$32.725
The payment, $25, being less than the interest then due, neglecting the former work, find the interest on $1650 from May 20, 1856, to Oct. 14, 1856, 4 mo. 24 d.	46.20
	1650.
Amount due, Oct. 14, 1856, ...	1696.20
Sum of the two payments, $25 and $150, to be deducted, ...	175.
Balance due after the second payment, . . .	1521.20
Interest on $1521.20 from Oct. 14, 1856, to March 20, 1857 ($46.14), being more than the payment made, find the interest on $1521.20 from Oct. 14, 1856, to July 5, 1857, 8 mo. 21 d. . . .	77.201
	1598.401
Sum of the payments, $45 and $300, ...	345.
Balance due July 5, 1857, ...	1253.401
Interest on $1253.401 from July 5, 1857, to Nov. 11, 1857, 4 mo. 6d., ...	30.708
Balance due on settlement, Nov. 11, 1857, . . .	$1284.109

Note.—Frequently an estimate of the interest may be made *mentally* with sufficient accuracy to decide whether it be not more than the payment, whereby some labor may be saved.

2. A note of $1200 is dated June 10, 1854, on which,

Aug. 16, 1855, there was paid, . .	$100
Dec. 28, 1855, " " " . .	200
June 2, 1856, " " " . .	25
Dec. 29, 1856, " " " . .	25
June 1, 1857, " " " . .	25
Oct. 28, 1857, " " " . .	500

What is the amount due Dec. 10, 1857, the interest being 6%? *Ans.* $551.347.

3. BUFFALO, N. Y., April 10, 1852.

One year after date, I promise to pay to the order of James Johnson one thousand dollars, with interest, value received.

THEODORE LELAND.

Note.—The legal rate of interest in New York is 7%.

On the note were the following indorsements:

Nov. 10, 1853, rec'd	$ 80.50	Jan. 10, 1855, rec'd	$450.80
July 5, 1854, "	100.	Oct. 1, 1857, "	500.

What remained due Jan. 1, 1858? *Ans.* $170.146.

4. CHICAGO, July 15, 1854.

$650.

Two years from date, for value received, I promise to pay to the order of Peter Finney, six hundred and fifty dollars, with interest at 10%, payable annually. SILAS WARREN.

Mr. Warren paid on the above note, Sept. 15, 1856, $105; May 9, 1857, $250. What amount was due Sept. 24, 1858?

Note.—In cases like the last, the payments should be applied first to the discharge of the interest *on the annual interest*, then the *annual interest*, and finally the principal. The interest on the principal, which has not yet become *annual interest*, not being due, should not be cancelled by payments except it be at the final settlement of the note.

Solution.

First annual interest,		$65.
Interest on same from July 15, 1855, to Sept. 15, 1856,		7.583
Second annual interest,		65.
Interest on same from July 15, 1856, to Sept. 15, 1856,		1.083
		$138.666
First payment		105.
		33.666
Interest on $33.666 from Sept. 15, 1856, to May 9, 1857,		2.188
Original principal,		650.
		685.854
Second payment,		250.
New principal,		$435.854
Interest on $650 from July 15, 1856, to May 9, 1857, not due at time of payment,	$53.083	
Interest on $435.854 from May 9, to July 15,	7.990	
Third annual interest,		61.073
Interest on same from July 15, 1857, to Sept. 24, 1858,		7.278
Fourth annual interest,		43.585
Interest on same from July 15, 1858, to Sept. 24, 1858,		.835
Fifth annual interest, due at settlement,		8.354
Amount due Sept. 24, 1858,		$556.979

ART. **105.** Another rule for applying partial payments is in use among many business men, and has received the sanction of several legal decisions. This rule, because it is used by merchants, has been styled

THE MERCANTILE RULE.

Compute the interest on the principal or original debt for one year, and add it to the principal. Find the interest also on the payments made during the year, if any, from the time they were made to the end of the year. Deduct the sum of payments and interest from the amount of principal and interest for a new principal. Do the same for each succeeding year till the final settlement.

Note.—It will be observed that this is applying the Vermont Rule to each separate year, beginning with the date of the note, and making yearly *rests.* Sometimes these rests, or times of making a new principal in mercantile accounts, are made to come at the end of each civil year, sometimes once in six months, depending upon the custom of merchants in balancing their accounts. Bankers for the same reason have been allowed to make quarterly rests, carrying forward a new principal *every quarter*, at the time of balancing the ledger.

Ex. A note of $2000 is dated Feb. 1, 1850, on which were the following

Indorsements.—March 1, 1850, $200; July 1, 1850, $300; Oct. 1, 1850, $500; July 1, 1851, $100; Oct. 1, 1852, $200; Jan. 1, 1853, $600.

What was due July 1, 1853, the interest being 6%?

$2000 will amount, Feb. 1, 1851, to . . .		$2120
200 " " " " to .	$211	
300 " " " " to .	310.50	
500 " " " " to .	510	
Sum of payments and interest, ...		1031.50
New principal, ...		1088.50
$1088.50 will amount, Feb. 1, 1852, to . . .		1153.81
100 " " " " to . . .		103.50
New principal, ...		1050.31

[Carried over.]

[Brought over.]

$1050.31 will amount, Feb. 1, 1853, to . . .		1113.33
200 " " " " to	. $204	
600 " " " " to	. 603	. 807
New principal, ...		306.33
$306.33 will amount, July 1, 1853, to . . .		313.99

ART. **106.** MERITS OF THE RULES FOR PARTIAL PAYMENTS.—The method of computing interest when partial payments have been made is a subject that has given rise to much litigation. In many States the only law relating to it consists of *decisions* in particular cases, which, from the peculiar circumstances, do not always clearly indicate a principle that may be applied justly to other cases. The aim in legislative enactments appears to have been twofold, to avoid usury and the taking of compound interest. Now all interest is in effect compounded when it is paid, since it allows the lender to loan again and draw interest on interest, while, if not paid, the debtor has the use of the interest money without paying interest. No court ever objected to a man's paying interest as often as he chose, and the statutes generally allow a collection of legal interest as often as was agreed upon by the parties in the original contract. They also allow a collection of simple interest upon any interest money after it becomes due, if not paid. They also allow compounding at the legal rate as often as the debtor chooses, provided that the old obligation be cancelled and a new one given. Compound interest then is not of itself *illegal*, it is only certain forms of it.

The difficulty attending partial payments is in deciding whether they shall be applied to the debt of interest or principal. If applied to the debt of principal, there is only simple interest; if applied to the debt of interest, the practical effect is that of compound interest.

The Vermont Rule is the only one involving no compound interest. The objection to that rule, when the time is more than one year, may be seen in the fact that the payments may be no greater than the interest due at the time of the payment, and still if the payments are sufficiently frequent, and the note run sufficiently long, the entire debt of principal and interest may be discharged, and the holder of the note become indebted to the debtor. (See Ex. 1, page 143.) Both the Mercantile and the United States Rules involve compound interest, the former compounding it once a year, the latter as often as a payment is made which equals or exceeds the interest then due. When the payments occur at intervals of just one year, commencing with the date of the note, both rules give the same result. When they occur oftener than once a year, the Mercantile Rule is the more favorable to the debtor; when more than a year intervenes, the United States Rule is the more favorable. The Vermont Rule is usually more favorable than either, for by that there is no compound interest, and all the payments draw interest. By the use of the United States Rule an inducement is offered to defer payment as long as possible, and the longer payment be deferred, the greater the inducement to continue it. Strict justice to all parties, in all cases, would be to have the interest on the whole debt, whether of principal or interest, compounded instantaneously. This method, though desirable, can not at present be made practicable. See Note, page 118.

Examples.

1. A holds an obligation against B for $1000, which has run 25 years at 6% interest. At the expiration of each year a payment of $60 was made. What is the amount due, as computed by each of the rules given above?

By the United States Rule, B owes A $1000.
By the Mercantile Rule, B owes A $1000.
By the Vermont Rule, A owes B $80.

2. A note of $10000 runs 4 years at 8% interest, on which were made quarterly payments of $500. What was the amount due at the time of settlement?

By the Vermont Rule, $4000.
By the Mercantile Rule, $4322.30.
By the United States Rule, $4408.21.

Note.—It will be observed that generally the result obtained by the Mercantile Rule will be intermediate between those obtained by the other two.

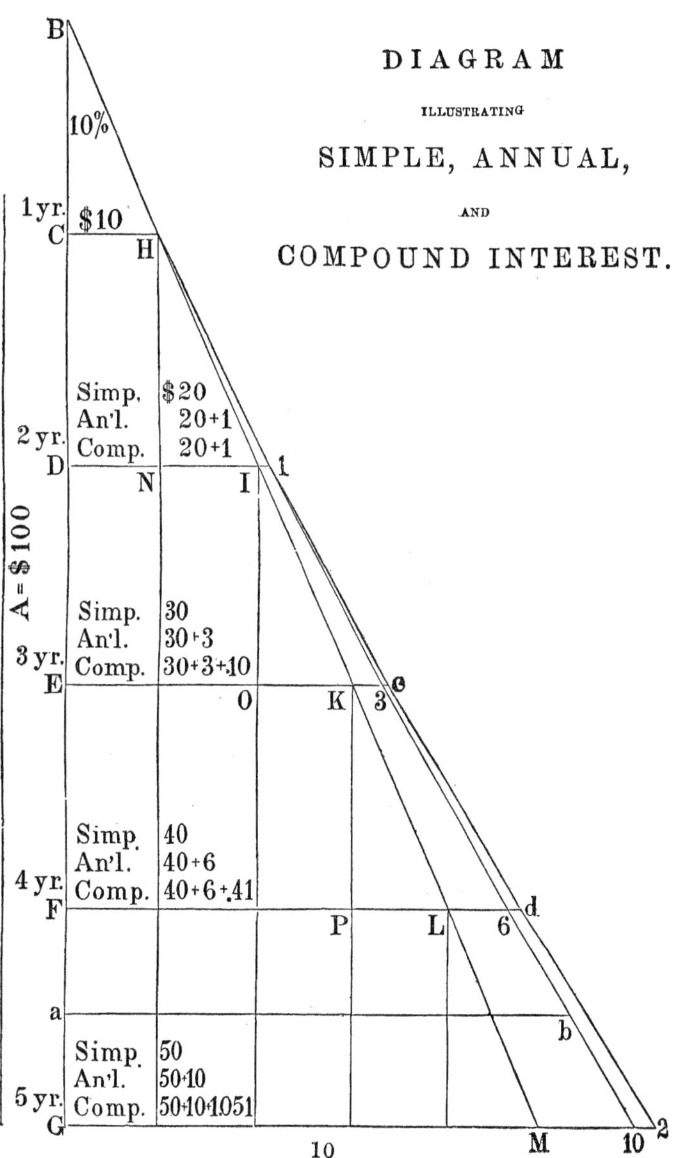
DIAGRAM
ILLUSTRATING
SIMPLE, ANNUAL,
AND
COMPOUND INTEREST.
B
10%
1 yr.
C
$10
H
Simp. $20
An'l. 20+1
2 yr.
Comp. 20+1
D
N
I
1
A = $100
Simp. 30
An'l. 30+3
3 yr.
Comp. 30+3+.10
E
O
K
3
c
Simp. 40
An'l. 40+6
4 yr.
Comp. 40+6+.41
F
P
L
6
d
a
b
Simp. 50
An'l. 50+10
5 yr.
Comp. 50+10+1.051
G
10
M
10
2

SIMPLE INTEREST.

ART. **107.** The relation between the principal, time, rate per cent., and interest, is exhibited to the eye in the diagram on the opposite page. Let the single line *A* (which for convenience is separated from the diagram, but which should be considered as extending horizontally to the left from *B*, *C*, *D*, etc., respectively,) represent the principal; the perpendicular line *BG* represent time with its divisions into years, at the points *C*, *D*, *E*, and *F*; and the horizontal lines *CH*, *DI*, *EK*, *FL*, and *GM* the accrued simple interest at the expiration of each successive year. As no ratio can be expressed between time and money, area can represent nothing in the diagram. As *rate per cent.* is nothing but the ratio between the principal and interest, *it* can only be represented by the degree of divergence of the lines *BC* and *BH*, by which the lines *CH*, *DI*, *EK*, and *FL* shall bear a proper relation to the line *A*. If the rate be 10% per annum, the line *CH* must be $\frac{10}{100}$ or $\frac{1}{10}$ of the line *A*, *DI* $\frac{2}{10}$, *EK* $\frac{3}{10}$, and so on. The line *BM* represents nothing but a limit to the lines representing interest for any time on the line *BG*.

$A+CH$, $A+DI$, $A+EK$, etc., represent the *amount* due each successive year at simple interest.

ART. **108.** ANNUAL INTEREST.

Simple and annual interest are the same for the first year. At this time in "annual interest," the accrued simple interest on the principal forms a new principal to draw simple interest till maturity. The same is true at the end of each following year. This increase of interest will be represented by the lines I_1, K_3, L_6, and M_{10}. The rate being 10%, I_1 must be $\frac{1}{10}$ of CH its principal; $K_3=\frac{2}{10}$ of $CH+\frac{1}{10}$ of $NI=\frac{3}{10}$ of CH; $L_6=\frac{3}{10}$ of $CH+\frac{2}{10}$ $NI+\frac{1}{10}$ of $OK=\frac{6}{10}$ of CH; and $M_{10}=\frac{4}{10}$ of $CH+\frac{3}{10}$ of $NI+\frac{2}{10}$ of $OK+\frac{1}{10}$ of $PL=\frac{10}{10}$ of $CH=CH$. It will be observed that the line B_{10} is not a straight line, but composed of straight lines, the *degree* of divergence from the line *BG* being increased at the end of each year; also that the numbers $_1$, $_3$, $_6$, $_{10}$, etc., are the sums of the several series $_1$;

$_1+_2$; $_1+_2+_3$; $_1+_2+_3+_4$, etc.; and also that they express the number of years that the simple yearly interest of the principal must draw interest to equal the interest on all the several amounts of annual interest. The line *ab*, though limited by the straight line $_6$, $_{10}$, is still a correct representation of the interest due at the end of $4\frac{1}{2}$ years with annual interest.

ART. 109. COMPOUND INTEREST.

Annual and compound interest are the same for two years. Then the interest which has accrued on the first annual interest becomes a part of the principal. In like manner all the interest at the end of each year becomes a part of the principal for the next year. The line $_1$, *c*, *d*, $_2$, limits the horizontal lines representing compound interest after the first two years. It should be separated from the line B_{10} at the point $_3$, a distance equal to $\frac{1}{10}$ of I_1. At the point $_6$, a distance equal to $_3c+\frac{1}{10}$ of Kc. At the point $_{10}$, equal to $_6d+\frac{1}{10}$ of Ld.

Or, comparing simple interest with compound, the line B_2 must begin to diverge from the line BM at the point H, and be separated from BM at the point I, a distance equal to $\frac{1}{10}$ of CH. At the point K, equal to the $I_1+\frac{1}{10}$ of D_1. At the point L, equal to $Kc+\frac{1}{10}$ of Ec. At the point M, equal to $Ld+\frac{1}{10}$ of Fd.

"PARTIAL PAYMENTS" ILLUSTRATED.

ART. 110. The *Diagrams* on the following pages illustrate the difference in the principle of the three foregoing rules for "Partial Payments."

The problem used in each diagram is the following:

A note for $1000 runs 4 years with interest at 6%.

In 1 yr. from date a payment of	$50	is made.
In $1\frac{1}{2}$ yrs. from date a payment of . . .	250	"
In 2 yrs. from date a payment of . . .	224	"
In 2 yrs. 8 mo. from date a payment of . .	20	"
In 2 yrs. 10 mo. from date a payment of. .	110	"

What was due at maturity?

In the illustration, time is measured horizontally by the distance between the perpendicular lines.

The horizontal base line in each figure separates principal from interest, the perpendicular lines above representing the former, and those below the latter. The perpendicular lines above are limited by a horizontal line which is more or less removed from the base line, as the payments are applied to increase or decrease the principal. The perpendicular lines below, representing interest, are limited by a line always diverging from the base line, the degree of divergence depending upon the rate per cent. and the size of the principal. When the entire interest is cancelled by any payment, the diverging line starts anew from the horizontal base line. The perpendicular distance between these two limiting lines at any time represents the amount of principal and interest due at that time.

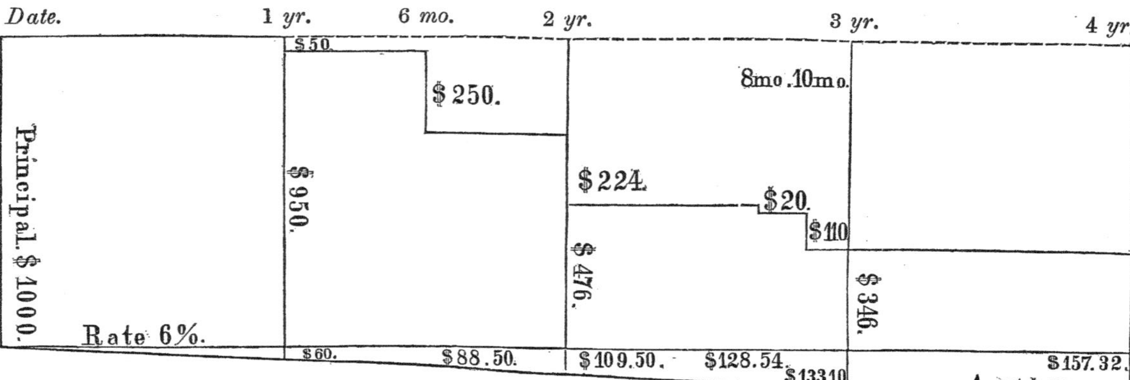

VERMONT RULE ILLUSTRATED.

The phraseology of the Vermont Rule requires that the principal draw interest entire by itself till maturity, and so of each separate payment. But manifestly the interest on any payment till maturity would just offset the interest on an equivalent amount of the principal for the same time. Therefore, to simplify the diagram, both are omitted, and the interest on the *balance* only of the principal, after deducting the payment, is represented.

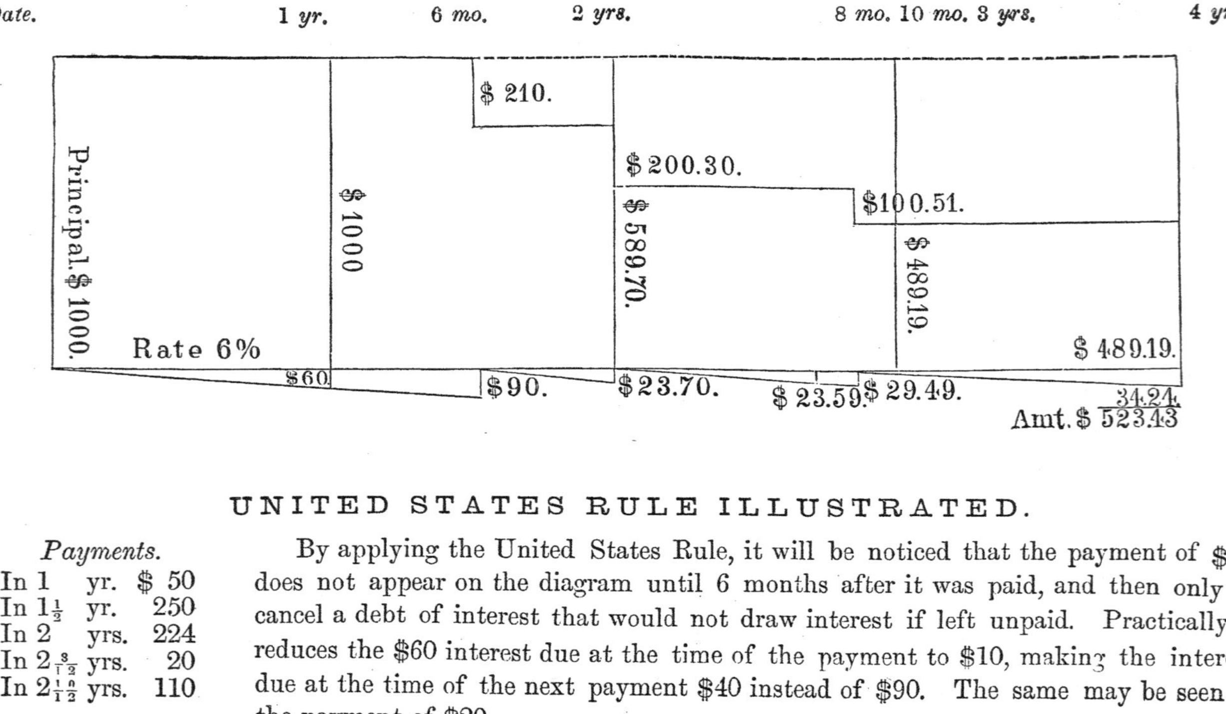

UNITED STATES RULE ILLUSTRATED.

Payments.

In 1	yr.	$ 50
In $1\frac{1}{2}$	yr.	250
In 2	yrs.	224
In $2\frac{8}{12}$	yrs.	20
In $2\frac{10}{12}$	yrs.	110

By applying the United States Rule, it will be noticed that the payment of $50 does not appear on the diagram until 6 months after it was paid, and then only to cancel a debt of interest that would not draw interest if left unpaid. Practically it reduces the $60 interest due at the time of the payment to $10, making the interest due at the time of the next payment $40 instead of $90. The same may be seen in the payment of $20.

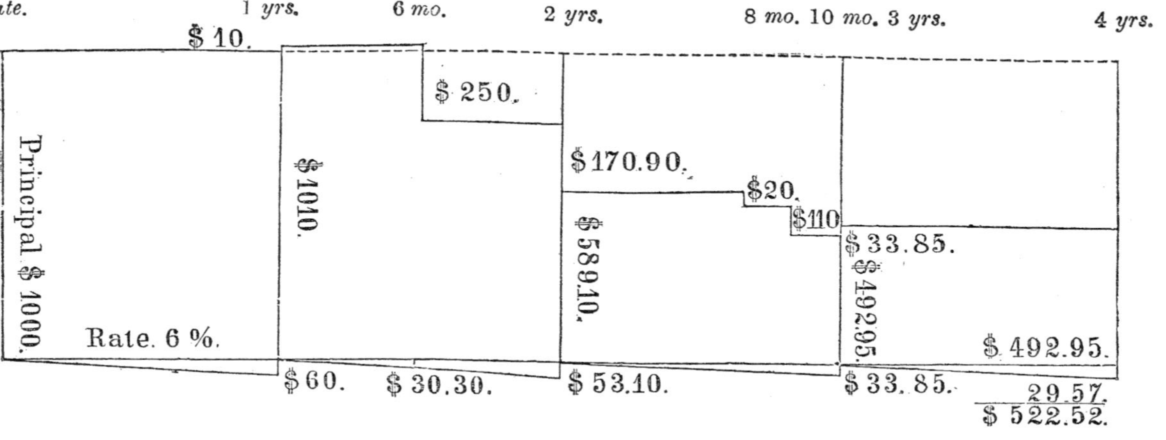

MERCANTILE RULE ILLUSTRATED.

In the Mercantile Rule, there is evidently a compounding of interest at the end of the first year, as the principal then becomes larger than at first. There is nevertheless a compounding of interest at the end of the 2d and 3d years, though by reason of the payments being larger, the principal is less. It is visible to the eye at the end of the 3d year. It will be observed that interest is compounded three times also in the use of the United States Rule, and would have been five times if the payments of $50 and $20 had equalled the interest then due. In fact, the loss of interest on these amounts till the next payment is a fair equivalent to compounding so much of the interest then due. Had the payments been more frequent, the amount due at maturity, by the United States Rule, would have been larger, as compared with the other rules, than in the present instance.

It is recommended to the pupil to study these diagrams till he becomes perfectly familiar with *the reason why* different rules give different results, and also to work other examples, drafting diagrams to correspond. With the use of proper mathematical instruments, tolerably accurate results may be obtained by drafting alone. Especially should the pupil notice that *rate per cent.* is the *ratio* between the principal and interest, and is represented in the diagram by the degree of divergence of the interest line from the horizontal base line. In the same diagram the less the principal, the less the divergence.

CURRENCY AND MONEY.

METALLIC CURRENCY.

ART. **111.** BARTER is simply exchanging one or more commodities for others, as giving one bushel of wheat for two bushels of corn.

MONEY is an instrument to facilitate exchanges, and, strictly speaking, should possess an intrinsic value equivalent to that for which it is exchanged.

Various articles have at different times and by different nations been used for this purpose, as shells, leather, corn, cattle, etc., but the precious metals, gold and silver, have been found to be most serviceable for the following reasons :

1st. They possess great value in small bulk.

2d. Their value remains quite uniform, changing only by slow degrees.

3d. They can be used or hoarded without much wear or decay.

4th. The pieces can be united or subdivided without loss of value.

5th. They are homogeneous in their structure, and easily identified.

Gold and silver, by being used as money, become the standard of reference for expressing the value of other commodities. The *price* of a commodity is usually its value expressed in the denominations of money.

When prices or obligations in debit and credit and barter are thus expressed, and business transacted without the intervention of *money*, we have what is called the "*money of account*." The denominations in the "money of account" may be even different from the denominations of the money in circulation, and if the denominations of both be the same, the values represented by them may be different. Still further, there may be a "money of account" where there is no money in actual use, in which case (as to a certain extent in all cases) *prices* are only expressions showing the *relative* value of commodities, and, like the terms used in the measure of arcs and angles, are indefinite until referred to other commodities, or to the same commodity of different amount. Gold and silver have an intrinsic value, depending upon their cost of production and uses. They derive a value from their capacity to facilitate exchanges, just as horses, mules, and railroads derive their value from facilitating transportation. Government can no more *create* a value to gold and silver than to sugar. It does, however, increase their value by coining them into pieces convenient for use, and declaring them legal tender in payment of debt. Coinage being only a certificate of value already existing in the metal, it is not necessarily the work of government, neither is legal tender a *necessary* element of even a metallic currency, as is seen in the coinage of copper and nickle. Coining gold and silver enhances their value in the same way that manufacturing steel enhances the value of the iron used, or as the brand of an official inspector renders certain articles of merchandise more salable. Making gold and silver coins legal tender increases their value because it increases their demand. For when other articles of value can not be used in liquidating indebtedness, these will always answer the purpose.

Money, by being legal tender, becomes naturally a standard of value for other property. But money itself is not an invariable measure of value, for the reason that its value, like that of other kinds of property, is affected by cost of production, supply, demand, etc. The debasement of coins by government is not here taken into the account. If gold alone were used as money and legal tender, its gradual change of value would be perceptible only as it caused an increase or decrease of prices. A diminution in value of gold would raise prices, and vice versa. But frequently gold and silver both are legal tender, as it was in the United States until A.D. 1853. In making both legal tender, it is necessary for government to establish their relative value. If the legal relative value be the actual commercial relative value, then both will circulate equally well, except so far as convenience may dictate. But as both are constantly changing in their commercial value, while the legal relative value remains the same, the metal that has the greatest commercial value will be used to make foreign purchases, while the cheaper metal will remain at home. It is a general principle in currency, that if several different articles be allowed to circulate as money, the cheaper will displace the dearer. If a thousand silver dollars will pay a larger debt in a foreign country than a hundred gold eagles, then silver will be shipped in payment.

By making silver legal tender for *small sums only*, its legal relative value, or mint valuation, may be considerably higher than its commercial or marketable value, and still the currency will not be burdened by its abundance, and gold will be retained for the reason that it will be demanded for the payment of those debts that are above the silver limit. Whenever both are legal tender for any amount, there must be frequent necessity for government to change the legal or nominal value. In A.D. 1853, silver coins in the United States were made "*legal tender for all sums not exceeding five dollars*," and its nominal value was made so great that it is not probable there will be need of another change for very many years, if ever. The same is true in England.

PAPER CURRENCY.

ART. **112.** Bank notes, certificates of deposit, checks, bills of exchange, etc., are in business *used as money*, but are not money. They are *representatives of money* when an *equivalent amount* of gold and silver is lying idle, and the paper takes its place in the circulation. Otherwise, they are *representatives of indebtedness* merely, and the man who receives them in payment of any debt has only given up one claim for another which may perhaps be more available. Bank notes, *actually representing gold or silver in store*, may be used with profit, for the reason that the coin lying in the vault is saved from wear, and the inconvenience and risk attending the transfer of large sums are to a great extent avoided. This is the case with the certificates of deposit that are used by the associated banks in New York in settling their balances at the "clearing house." It has been strongly advocated by some that a "gold-note currency" on such a basis might with many advantages be issued from the Sub-Treasury of the United States. Bullion banks might also be formed that would furnish the same kind of currency.

When gold or silver is received, it is an ultimate payment, for they are supposed to contain intrinsically an equivalent value. The policy of a paper currency, beyond an actual specie basis, is a question upon which intelligent political economists disagree. The use of certificates of deposit, checks, bills of exchange, etc., greatly facilitates the transaction of business and reduces the amount of metallic currency needed. To make them serviceable and reliable, however, they should not be issued as a basis of credit, or for procuring loans, but should arise from legitimate business transactions in which the drawee has previously become actually indebted for the amount of the bill.

Examples relating to Coins and Money of Account.

1. If a pound of sugar be worth a half a peck of wheat, what would be the price in wheat of 50 lbs. of sugar?

Ans. $6\frac{1}{4}$ bushels.

2. If a pound of sugar be worth 8 pounds of wheat or 10 yards of tape, how much tape can be bought for a pint of wheat, a bushel of wheat weighing 60 lbs.? *Ans.* $1\frac{1}{64}$ yds.

3. If an ounce of silver be worth 6400 ounces of iron, how many tons of iron can be bought with $3\frac{1}{2}$ pounds of silver?

Ans. $8\frac{2}{5}$ tons.

4. If the value of a bushel of wheat be represented by 1. what would be the value of 5 bush. 1 pk. 3 qts.?

Ans. $5\frac{11}{32}$.

5. Before the federal currency was established by Congress in 1786, and indeed for some time after, the denominations in the money of account in the United States colonies were pounds, shillings, and pence, as in England, while most of the *coin* in circulation consisted of Spanish silver dollars, their halves, quarters, and sixteenths. Owing to the scarcity of metallic currency, and the fact that the relative value of the money of account, compared with the silver dollar, had not been generally determined or agreed upon, remarkable fluctuations in the money of account arose, varying in different States, so that when it became necessary to fix their relative values, it was found that in the New England States £1 or 20 shillings $=3\frac{1}{3}$ Spanish dollars, while in New York and Ohio £1=only $2\frac{1}{2}$ Spanish dollars. How much below the New England standard was the money of account in Ohio? *Ans.* 25%.

6. Assuming the pound sterling of Old England to have been equal at that time to $4\frac{4}{9}$ Spanish dollars, as is stated by some, how much below that standard had the New England money of account depreciated? *Ans.* 25%.

7. Assuming the Spanish dollar to equal a ollar in federal currency, how much less in cents would an article cost in New

York whose price was 7 shillings, than in New England where the price was 6*s.* 6*d.* ? *Ans.* $20\frac{5}{6}$ cts.

8. Paper currency frequently occasions great fluctuations in the money of account. Continental money, when first issued, was very nearly par with silver. In 1778 its depreciation was as 6 to 1, in 1780 as 30 to 1, in 1781 as 1000 to 1. The money of account would, however, soon cease to follow such *extreme* fluctuations, but would adopt some other standard. Assuming the paper currency of Chicago to have depreciated the money of account 2% below that of New York city, how much more in New York funds would an article be worth in New York than in Chicago, the price in each place being $1000 ? *Ans.* $19.608.

9. In 1837 the fineness of the silver dollar United States coin was changed from $\frac{8924\frac{1}{3}}{10000}$ to $\frac{9}{10}$, but its weight, which was 416 grains, was so changed that the amount of pure silver in the coin remained the same as before. What was the weight after the change? *Ans.* $412\frac{1}{2}$ grs.

10. In 1853 the weight of the silver half-dollar was changed from $206\frac{1}{4}$ grains to 192 grains, the fineness remaining the same, viz., $\frac{9}{10}$. What is the value in new silver coin of the dollar coined before 1853 ? *Ans.* $107\frac{27}{64}$ cts.

11. From 1792 to 1834 the United States eagle weighed 270 grs., and was $\frac{11}{12}$ fine. Its weight was then reduced to 258 grs., its fineness remaining the same. In 1837 the fineness was reduced to $\frac{9}{10}$, the weight remaining the same, since which there has been no change. What is the present value of an eagle coined previous to 1834 ? *Ans.* \$$10.65\frac{115}{129}$.

12. Augustus Humbert, United States Assayer in California, under a legal provision of 1850, has issued fifty dollar pieces of gold, purporting on their face to be 887 thousandths fine and weighing 1310 grains each. Assuming them to be of full fineness and weight, what is their value in United States gold coinage ? *Ans.* \$$50.05\frac{115}{387}$.

In the above examples no account is made of the alloy.

13. If I take 20 lbs. of bullion of standard fineness to the mint to be coined, and pay a seigniorage of $\frac{1}{2}$%, what amount of money, in gold coin, should I receive ? *Ans.* $4442.79.

14. In A.D. 671 a pound sterling was equivalent to a pound Troy of silver. In the 14th century the same amount of silver was coined into £1 5*s.*, and a pound of gold into £15. After successive debasements for the profit of kings, a pound of silver now makes £3 11*s.* 2*d.*, and a pound of gold makes £50 9*s.* 5*d.* The average price of wheat in the 14th century was £1 for what now averages £2$\frac{1}{2}$. Prices of other staple commodities and wages have undergone a similar change. The conclusion is apparent, that though governments may depreciate the money of account, they can not force the sale of common merchandise at much less than its *value.* Though they may change the conditions of legal tender, so that 6 shillings worth of silver will pay a pound of debt, *new* contracts will recognize the change, and ultimately not be affected by it. Queen Elizabeth, using a pound of silver for coining £3 5*s.* for England, put no more than that into £8 for Ireland. What ought to have been the price of flour in Ireland for what in England cost £1? *Ans.* £2 9$\frac{3}{13}$ shillings.

15. James the Second manufactured four pennyworth of silver into £10, with which he paid off his soldiers. What per cent. of their just dues did they receive? *Ans.* $\frac{1}{6}$ per cent.

16. Suppose an estate to have been left, centuries ago, for the support of the dean of a cathedral and four choristers, the income then being £300 per year, out of which he was to pay each chorister £30. If the debasement of current coin has raised rents 250%, and the increased supply of the precious metals raised it 150% more, how do the relative salaries of the dean and choristers compare with what they were evidently designed to be by the testator?

Ans. The dean *should* receive 6 times what a chorister receives, but actually receives 46 times as much.

BANKS AND BANKING.

ART. **113.** BANKS are of four kinds. *Banks of Deposit*, *Banks of Discount*, *Banks of Issue*, and *Banks of Exchange.* The first two and the last may be established by individuals or associations, the other only by special authority from the State.

BANKS OF DEPOSIT.

ART. **114.** BANKS OF DEPOSIT are for the safe keeping of money.

A special deposit is made when the identical money is to be returned to the depositor, the bank being responsible only for the safe keeping; the loss, for instance, attending the failure of the banks whose notes are deposited being sustained by the depositor. In other cases, the *bank* or *banker* becomes indebted to the depositor, the banker being allowed to use the money as he pleases, but obligating himself to pay the depositor the whole or any part of the amount due him whenever it is demanded, if demanded during business hours. The improbability that all the depositors of a bank will call for the entire balance of their account at the same time, renders it safe for the banker to use a portion of the funds thus entrusted to him, in loaning to those who need the money but for a short time, and may therefore be relied upon for prompt payment. The interest money thus received is the banker's compensation for keeping the accounts of his depositors. Sometimes interest is paid by the banker for the deposit, but, as a general rule, that this interest may be refunded, there is a strong temptation to loan too large an amount "on call," or to seek largely paying investments, with doubtful securities, which is against the interest of both banker and depositor.

When the depositor usually has a large balance with his banker, there is an implied obligation with the banker to give such a customer or dealer the preference in "bank accommodation," if he offers equally good security.

The advantages to a business man in keeping a bank account are the following:

1st. If he has an honest prudent banker, his surplus funds are ordinarily safer than if kept by himself.

2d. The settlement of bills with checks drawn upon bankers is not only more convenient, but there is less liability of error, and if errors do occur, the vouchers, which should always be preserved, will aid in detecting them.

3d. He will lose less from counterfeit, broken, and uncurrent money, and will be relieved from frequent charges of paying out the same by throwing the responsibility upon his banker.

4th. By depositing his *Bills Receivable* and Drafts, he avoids much trouble and risk attending their collection. If by mistake, oversight, or neglect, drawers and endorsers are released from liability, the banker, by assuming the collection, becomes responsible for the consequences.

5th. It aids him in establishing his own credit, and learning the credit and responsibility of others with whom he wishes to do business.

The Bank of Hamburg is exclusively a *bank of deposit,* the silver in the vault always being equal to the amount of the deposits. This may be withdrawn at pleasure by the depositors, but the business is mostly done by checks, which have the effect merely of transferring the credits from one account to another. The expenses of the bank are met by a small percentage charged the depositors on the amount of business done. The currency of Hamburg being almost exclusively silver, exchanges are greatly facilitated through the means of this institution.

BANKS OF DISCOUNT.

ART. **115.** *Banks of Discount* are closely connected with *Banks of Deposit*, and, indeed, they generally exist together in the same institution. Their object is the loaning of money, the *discount* being the interest taken in advance. The capital may belong to one individual, or to a company forming a copartnership, or to a corporation organized by authority of the State. The securities usually taken are endorsed names, stocks, bonds, and business paper. The primary object of banks of discount being to grant temporary loans, where the business requires at some seasons more capital than can be profitably employed through the year, and to aid in preserving an equilibrium in such regular business as may be disturbed by irregularity of receipts and disbursements, it is unwise to depend upon such institutions for any portion of the permanent capital needed in business. Continued loans and renewals from a *bank of deposit* are very unreliable. For when the bank calls for payment to supply the withdrawal of deposits it will generally be found to be just the hardest time to pay.

BANKS OF ISSUE.

ART. **116.** *Banks of Issue* are those institutions that, by authority of the general government, put in circulation, to be used as money, their own notes, payable on demand in gold or silver coin. When payable at some future specified time, they are called *post notes.* Were banks of issue to retain in their vaults sufficient gold or silver to redeem all their circulating notes at once, there would be no profit to them from the circulation except so far as the notes should be lost or destroyed, and never presented for redemption, which has been found to amount, *extraordinary losses* excepted, to about one tenth of one per cent. per annum. If, on the other hand, they were loaned as money, and no actual capital kept idle to redeem them, the banker would receive the same revenue, until their redemption, as he would from an equivalent amount of capital furnished him in gold and silver. In short, his credit would at all times afford him as much working capital as his notes in circulation amount to.

The value of bank notes as currency depends upon the ease and certainty with which they may be converted into gold or silver coin. Hence the importance of rigid restrictions being imposed by government to insure a prompt and certain redemption. Without these the field is open to frauds, limited only by the intelligence and forbearance of the community.

The paper currency of our country is furnished by twenty-seven different States, each under somewhat different laws and regulations. In general, they can be classified under three different systems, *a specie basis, a safety fund, and the "free banking" principle.*

The *specie basis* requires a part, or all its capital, to be paid in coin, limits the amount of circulation in proportion to its capital paid in, and makes the assets of the bank, with perhaps the individual liability of the stockholders, furnish the means to redeem the circulating notes.

The "*safety fund*" system requires each of several banks to deposit, with a State officer or Board of Control, a certain percentage of its capital or circulation, which shall be safely invested as a "bank fund" to redeem the notes of any insolvent bank that may have contributed its due proportion for this purpose.

In "*free banking*" the circulating notes are secured by State stocks, to at least an equivalent amount at their marketable value. The stocks are deposited with an officer of State, for which he issues registered blank notes. These, when signed, are used as money by the banker, while he receives at the same time, the interest on the stocks deposited. If the bank fails to redeem, the stocks are sold, and the proceeds applied to the redemption.

BANKS OF EXCHANGE.

ART. **117.** Nearly all banks are Banks of Exchange, their legitimate business being the buying and selling of drafts, by which remittances and settlements of debt at distant places are made without the transmission of money. The operation of this department of banking will be more full explained under the subject of "EXCHANGE." Those bankers who deal exclusively in buying and selling gold, silver, and bank-notes, are called "*brokers*" or "*money brokers.*"

EXCHANGE.

ART. **118.** When a purchase is made a satisfactory equivalent is rendered by the purchaser in various ways. It may be by labor or services, or he may give other commodities in exchange, which last transaction is called *barter*. He may give gold and silver, which are also commodities of an equivalent value, but called money, because they are serviceable mainly in making other purchases, thereby facilitating several transactions in barter. Frequently, however, no equivalent is rendered; but an obligation merely on the part of the purchaser for a fixed amount is recognized by both purchaser and seller. This constitutes *debt* on the part of the purchaser, and *credit* on the part of the seller, and is expressed in the denominations of the "money of account." If now the debtor gives *a written obligation to pay*, in the form of a *due bill* or *promissory note*, this evidence of credit with the holder may he transferred as other property, and another become the creditor. In book-keeping, the account with the seller is closed, and "Bills Payable" receives the credit. Instead of giving his own promissory note, he may use those which he himself has received in the same way; as for example, bank notes which were issued expressly for this kind of circulation. When bank-notes, or certificates of deposit, are held as evidence of debt against a bank, the debt is collected by the return of these to the bank.

If it be an account current, and kept by a *pass-book*, it is subject to *drafts* or *checks*.

The facility with which business is transacted by means of *drafts* or other paper substitutes, for money, has given to the term *Exchange* a technical use, and now signifies *the method of making payments at distant places by the use of Drafts or Bills of Exchange, without the transmission of money.* The business is usually transacted through bankers, who buy the credits payable in distant places, and sell to those having payments to make in those places.

To illustrate, suppose the pork dealers of Cincinnati to send their pork to New York for sale, and receive therefor gold, which is returned to them by express. Suppose also the dry-goods' merchants of New York to send their goods to Cincinnati for sale, and receive therefor gold, which is returned to them by express. If the pork purchasers in New York had paid the dry-goods' merchants there, and the dry-goods' purchasers in Cincinnati had paid the pork dealers there, the whole business might have been closed without the risk and expense of transmitting gold either way. This would be done by the pork sellers drawing drafts or orders on the pork buyers, in favor of the dry-goods' buyers, who, having paid for these drafts, would forward them to the dry-goods' sellers in payment of their purchase. These drafts being presented to the pork buyers would be cashed, and thereby the debts arising in both cities liquidated without the transmission of any money. In making this system general, to include all kinds of trade in many different places, it would frequently be very difficult for those having bills of exchange to sell to find buyers, and *vice versa.* An exchange broker, or bank of exchange, will obviate this difficulty. They bring the buyers and sellers together, by buying bills with their own capital, and sending them forward for credit, then selling their own drafts drawn against this credit, in amounts to suit purchasers. If between any two places the amount of bills bought equal those sold, then no gold need be transmitted, and the difference between the buying and selling rate would be the commission charged by the broker for his services, use of his capital, and risk in buying such drafts as would not be honored.

PAR OF EXCHANGE.

ART. **119.** To understand the quotations of premium or discount in exchange, it is necessary to consider the currencies of the different places. Supposing gold, as a metal, to be so distributed as to have in all places a *uniform intrinsic value*, and gold coin to be the only currency, the *true par of exchange* between two countries *is the exact equivalent of gold in the standard coin of one country compared with the gold in the coin of the other.* If, however, gold is the standard of currency in one country, and silver in the other, the relative intrinsic values must be compared. This need be computed only when the coins and money of account in the two countries are different. Comparing the sovereign of England with the half eagle of America, for instance, we find the sovereign to weigh 123.3 grains, but only $916\frac{2}{3}$ thousandths of it pure gold. The half eagle weighs 129 grains and 900 thousandths pure gold. If we reduce the fineness of the sovereign to that of the half eagle, without changing its value, it must weigh $125\frac{583}{1000}$ grains. In this estimate the alloy is reckoned of no value. To ascertain the true equivalent we have this simple proportion, 129 grains : 125.583 grains : : \$5 : \$4.8675.

As the weight and fineness of the sovereigns coined previously to the present reign were somewhat less than the value, as derived above, the average value, as fixed by our mint, is \$4.84. A new Victoria sovereign, however, is worth $\$4.86\frac{3}{4}$. A pound sterling (£) is a denomination in the *money of account* only; the sovereign is a *coin* of an equivalent value. It follows from the above that exchange on London is *par* when a bill for £100 can be bought for \$486.75 in American gold.

The *common quotations* are based upon a *purely nominal value* of the pound sterling, viz.: $\$4.44\frac{4}{9}$, for that is not now its value in any other sense.

True value of the pound sterling, ... $4.8675
Nominal " " . . . . 4.4444+
Difference=9½% (nearly) of the nominal par, . .4230

When the *quotations* are 109½%, sterling exchange is really at par; when 110%, it is at a premium; when 109%, it is at a discount. Quotations are generally made on sterling bills drawn at 60 days' sight. As the cost of transmitting gold, including insurance, is about equal to the interest on the bill for 60 days, the time for the passage of both being the same, remittances often are made in these time drafts, for which the same is paid as for sovereigns of equivalent amount.

RULE FOR COMPUTING STERLING EXCHANGE.

ART. **120.** *To* $40 *add the premium on* $40, *at the quoted rate. By this sum multiply the amount of sterling exchange expressed in pounds, and divide the product by* 9. *The quotient will be the value in dollars.*

Example.

What will a bill for £224 5s. 6d. cost in New York when sterling exchange is par, quoted at 109½% or 9½% premium?

```
£224 5s. 6d.                 40
 43.8               9½%=   3.80
 179.2                     43.80
 672
896
  10.95
   1.095
9)9823.245
 $1091.47  Ans.
```

By comparing French coin with that of the United States, we find 20 francs Louis Napoleon equal to $3.84, or one dollar in gold equal to 5 francs and 21 centimes nearly, or $5\frac{21}{100}$ francs. The quotations of Paris exchange are usually made in this way, without involving percentage. If a bill of exchange for more than 521 francs can be bought for $100, Paris exchange is at a discount; if less, it is at a premium, and the quotations express the number of francs that can be thus bought.

The sum mentioned in a bill of exchange on a foreign country is usually expressed in the denominations of the money of account in the place where it is made payable. Computations in foreign exchange therefore require the use of tables of foreign money, including the comparative values of the coins or currencies in those countries.

NOMINAL EXCHANGE.

ART. **121**. In the United States, though the money of account be *nominally* the same, yet owing to the character of the paper money in circulation, the currencies, and hence the moneys of account of different states and cities, are essentially different. The relative value of paper money, as stated heretofore, depends upon the risk and cost of converting it into coin.

If, for example, in Buffalo, it costs $\frac{3}{8}$% to convert the usual paper currency into coin, the *true par of exchange* between that city and New York (where coin only, or its equivalent, is current) would be expressed by the nominal rate of $\frac{3}{8}$% premium, in favor of New York. For the same reason the currency of Chicago being redeemable in coin at still greater cost, exchange on New York may actually be at par when the nominal rate is 2% premium. This 2% no more expresses the *actual premium* than does the 9$\frac{1}{2}$% the actual premium of exchange on London. It is really the premium of New York currency over Chicago currency. The *true value* of the denominations in our money of account is represented by coin only, being established by the law regulating legal tender. Practically, however, by the use of a depreciated local currency, the money of account for that place is equally depreciated. Thus, goods bought in New York for $100, when sold in Chicago for $100 are sold for less than their cost, counting transportation and insurance nothing. *Prices,* however, will tend to *appreciate* as the value of the currency *depreciates,* so that the apparent loss by an unfavorable *nominal* exchange is, in general, compensated by increased prices. Inasmuch as *increasing the supply* of even a metallic currency depreciates its relative value, the *nominal* exchange between two places, using the same kind of currency, with the same mint standard, will be in favor of the place having the smallest amount of currency in proportion to its business wants, and therefore having the least depreciation. *The nominal exchange is then measured by the excess of the market price of bullion above the mint price, and is, so far, unfavorable.* A depreciation of metallic currency which affects the nominal exchange may also be occasioned by abrasion or wear of circulation, or by making only one of two metals legal tender where the other is in general circulation. It will be observed that, although this "exchange," which is merely nominal, almost universally enters into the quotations of exchange between different countries, it belongs rather to the exchange of currencies in the same country, and expresses the difference between the current and the standard moneys of that place.

Agio, meaning "difference," is the proper term to express this nominal exchange when considered alone. In the United States the expense of sending coin to and from New York, by the modern express companies, being so trifling, the premium on New York exchange must always be very nearly the same as on coin. The fluctuations in the *nominal rate* of exchange, or agio, where a depreciated paper currency is used, will be much greater than if the currency were coin or its equivalent, for the reason that the depreciation will be more variable. Sometimes the *scarcity* of such currency, compared with business wants, raises its current value temporarily to nearly par with coin. Just so far the nominal exchange disappears. *In* Bank notes that can be converted into coin at less expense than the usual local currency are, for that place, at a premium. Those costing more are at a discount, and are called *uncurrent.* Indeed, these notes, when removed from their native habitation, resemble bills of exchange on the places where they are redeemed, and are bought and sold at nearly the same rates as exchange.

COURSE OF EXCHANGE.

ART. **122.** Having ascertained the *par of exchange* we have a basis for computation. The *nominal exchange* modifies that computation, by showing the relative value of the metallic currency affected by scarcity and abundance or abrasion, and also the depreciation arising from the use of a paper currency not equivalent to coin, though bearing the same denomination in the money of account.

The course of exchange relates to the relative supply and demand for bills, or the relative amount of indebtedness between different countries or cities. If the debts and credits between two countries are equal, the *real exchange* is at par, if unequal it will fluctuate with the inequality. If New York owes London more than London owes New York, bills on London will be at a premium. The range of this course of exchange will be limited by the expense of transmitting coin or bullion, and the premium cannot for a long time exceed that expense. The *current*, or computed rate of exchange, includes both the *real* and *nominal* exchange, taking the *true par* for a basis. Within the United States it is reckoned by percentage. Between the United States and England it is reckoned also by percentage, but the *true par* is at a premium above an *assumed fictitious par.* So that an advance in quotation from 109 to 110 is not really 1%, that is, one on a hundred, but less, it being only 1 on 109½.

With other countries the current exchange is generally expressed by equivalents, thus \$1=5 francs 15 centimes, 1 marc banco=35½ cts. If the depreciation of Chicago currency be 1%, and the *real* exchange on New York ¼% premium, the *current* rate will be the *sum* of the nominal and real, viz.:

$1\frac{1}{4}\%$ premium. If, however, the real exchange be $\frac{1}{4}\%$ in favor of Chicago, the current rate will be equal to the difference, or $\frac{3}{4}\%$ premium.

The equilibrium in the course of exchange is only to a small extent restored by the shipment of coin or bullion, for the reason that almost always other articles of merchandise can be shipped with more profit, gold and silver bearing a nearly uniform value among all civilized nations. When, however, new productive mines are opened and worked, the metals depreciate in value in the mining country, in which case they become profitable articles of export to non-producing countries, until the depreciation becomes general. The unequal depreciation occasions a variation in the *nominal exchange* before the coin or bullion is shipped. The *transfer* of the metal would affect the *real exchange*, because it either pays or creates a debt.

"BALANCE OF TRADE."

ART. **123.** If a country, in her trade with other nations, buys more than she sells, so as to incur a debt, the payments of which, in bullion or coin, would reduce the amount of metallic currency below her proper proportion, as compared with the supply in other nations, she is said to "over-trade," and the "balance of trade" is against her. If the reverse be true, the balance of trade is in her favor. Some restrict the term "balance of trade" to the exchange of commodities other than gold or silver. But why should not gold be considered a staple article of export from California and Australia, as iron is from Sweden or lumber from Maine? It is not proposed here to discuss this subject in its bearing upon the *prosperity* of a country, but merely to offer a few suggestions to the student, in its relation to the subject of exchange. It is rather the *balance of payments* between separate countries, and the mode of estimating the amount, the direction, and means of liquidating it, that he should consider here. 1st. Although the direct commerce between two separate nations may be very unequal, yet the total amount of importations to any country are for the most part paid for by its exportations, through the agency of bills of exchange, drawn against the latter, and transmitted to other countries in payment of the former. Sometimes it is effected by a succession of bills drawn by bankers through intermediate points, or a more circuitous route, which gives rise to Circular Exchange and an Arbitration of Exchange. For example, a merchant in New York may remit to Hamburg by buying first a bill on Paris, and then by his agent another on London, and there a bill on Hamburg. Remittances to remote points are more frequently made by bankers' bills drawn on some commercial center, where other bankers are accustomed to keep an account, so that they may be easily negotiated, making the place thereby a kind of clearing-house. Thus, London has been styled "the clearing-house of the world." Nearly all our foreign trade is *settled* through England and France. In like manner, remittances between inland towns in the United States are made in drafts on New York. The course of exchange between London and New York does not arise alone from the commerce between the two cities, but from all that commerce that is settled for through those places. Thus, if we pay for our importations of tea with bills on London, our balance of payments with London is affected the same as if the tea came directly from London.

2d. So far as the commerce of any country is carried on by its own capital and labor, a large share of the excess of imports over the exports arises from the *profit* of the trade, which does not increase the *balance* of payments. If, for example, an American vessel leaves New York for Liverpool, with a cargo of wheat, valued at $10,000, which is sold there for $12,000, and that amount invested in manufactured goods, and taken to China and sold for $15,000, and that amount, with $5,000 cash invested in tea, which is brought home to New York, it is evident that, from that transaction, the importations exceed the exportations $10,000, one half of which represents the gross profit for the round trip, not including the enhanced value of the tea by being transported from China to New York.

3d. So far as *foreign* vessels, sustained by foreign capital and labor, transport our exports and imports, the difference between the two, as valued at our own ports, will show the balance of payments.

4th. Goods lost at sea have been entered at the Custom House whence they cleared as *exports*. But if the loss is sustained by the exporting country, they pay for nothing abroad, and foreign exchange is affected no more than if destroyed before shipment. If the loss be sustained by the country whither they were bound, exchange is affected the same as if they had reached their destination.

5th. When capitalists emigrate from one country to another, so far as they carry their capital, either in coin or goods, *with them*, the real exchange is not materially affected; but if they remove their capital through the agency of certificates of deposit, letters of credit, or their own bills of exchange, it becomes a debt of one country to the other, which, in the end, is generally paid in merchandise rather then money. This fact often affects sensibly the course of exchange between the east and west of the United States.

6th. The negotiation of bonds, stocks, and other loans in a foreign country creates a debt against that country, which, though nominally for money, is generally paid in merchandise. After this debt is paid, though the bonds are truly the evidence of debt against the country that issued them, yet, with the exception of the payment of the interest, the balance of payments and course of exchange are not affected till the maturity of the bonds.

7th. An excess of imports over exports, as shown by the Custom House returns, by no means prove that a country is in debt. Indeed, it is clear from what has been stated, that with every nation engaged in the carrying trade the imports will generally exceed the exports, and, so far as the latter pay for the former, the greater the excess the more profitable the commerce.

The *fluctuations* in the rate of exchange depend upon a variety of conditions, a few only of which have here been noticed. They cannot, to any great extent, be controlled by an arbitrary decree of bankers or merchants. Excepting when disturbed by a panic, or an unusual distrust in the credit of those who draw or accept bills of exchange, which gives it a fictitious value, the current rate represents the actual resultant of all the movements in trade and currency, whether traceable or not, and is, therefore, if properly analyzed, a better test of the condition of accounts between different countries and cities than any estimate that can be made, independent of it, based upon exports and imports and other Custom House data.

To understand the *current rate*, however, requires, as stated before, a thorough knowledge both of the *par of exchange* and the *nominal rate*, for frequently the fluctuations in the current rate are wholly due to the fluctuations in the nominal rate, which latter depends entirely upon the relative condition of the currency.

STATISTICS.

ART. **124.** To exhibit the truth of the foregoing principles, a few statistics have been compiled from reliable authorities.

Total imports to the United States, including bullion and specie, from 1790 to 1857, inclusive,					$7,658,722,496
Total exports for the same time,					6,860,004,549
Excess of imports for		68 yrs.	ending	1857,	798,717,947
"	"	7	"	"	36,363,971
"	"	30	"	1850,	250,438,055
"	"	31	"	1820,	511,915,921

The valuation of imports, as obtained from Custom House returns, owing to the *ad valorem* system of tariff, is, below their cost, generally estimated to average even 10%. It will be observed that allowing an undervalution of 1% will increase the *excess* of imports about 10%.

Excess of *imports* of bullion and specie for 30 years ending 1850, before the supply of gold from California, ...	$69.995.789
Excess of *exports* of bullion and specie for 7 years ending 1857, ...	269.797.168

From 1790 to 1820 the imports, including bullion and specie, exceeded the exports each year except in 1811 and 1813. From 1821 to 1857 the imports exceeded the exports each year except in 1821-5-7, 1830, 1840-2-3-4-7, 1851-5-6-7.

Total amount of public and corporation debt held in foreign countries against the United States in the form of bonds, stocks, &c., is generally estimated at, ...	$300,000,000
On which there is probably paid an annual dividend of about, ...	20,000,000

The average current rate of exchange on England at New York, for No. I bankers' bills, as quoted on the first of each month was, for—

1822 ..	12	1831 ..	$8\frac{3}{4}$	1840 ..	8	1849 ..	9
1823 ..	$7\frac{1}{2}$	1832 ..	9	1841 ..	$8\frac{1}{2}$	1850 ..	$9\frac{3}{4}$
1824 ..	9	1833 ..	8	1842 ..	$7\frac{1}{2}$	1851 ..	$10\frac{1}{3}$
1825 ..	$8\frac{1}{4}$	1834 ..	$3\frac{1}{2}$	1843 ..	$7\frac{1}{2}$	1852 ..	$10\frac{1}{8}$
1826 ..	10	1835 ..	$9\frac{3}{4}$	1844 ..	9	1853 ..	$9\frac{2}{3}$
1827 ..	$10\frac{3}{4}$	1836 ..	8	1845 ..	$9\frac{1}{2}$	1854 ..	$9\frac{1}{4}$
1828 ..	$10\frac{1}{2}$	1837 ..	$13\frac{1}{2}$	1846 ..	$8\frac{1}{2}$	1855 ..	$9\frac{1}{2}$
1829 ..	9	1838 ..	$8\frac{1}{4}$	1847 ..	7	1856 ..	$9\frac{1}{2}$
1830 ..	$7\frac{1}{4}$	1839 ..	$9\frac{1}{4}$	1848 ..	$9\frac{3}{4}$	1857 (to Sept.)	9

Average for the 9 years ending 1830, . . .	$9\frac{1}{3}$%
" " 10 " 1840, . . .	$8\frac{1}{2}$%
" " 10 " 1850, . . .	$8\frac{1}{2}$%
" " 7 " 1857, . . .	$9\frac{2}{3}$%

It will be perceived that the average rate of sterling exchange at New York, for the twenty years ending 1850, was 1% below par, or 1% in favor of New York; while, for the seven years following, it was above par, or in favor of England.

Of the $300,000,000 of gold deposited at the Mint and branches, and Assay Office at New York, for the six years ending 1855, about 94% per cent. was produced by California.

In San Francisco sight exchange on New York averages

about 3% premium, the currencies of both places having a metallic basis.

If we put 900 new sovereigns and 900 new shillings into average ordinary circulation, in 12 months time the former will be worth about 899 and the latter about 894.

In London, previous to the re-coinage in 1774, exchange was uniformly about 2% in favor of Paris, owing to the fact that the old coinage, by wear, had sunk below its standard weight about 2%, while the coinage of France was not thus degraded. As soon as the new coinage took the place of the old, exchange became par. Before the re-coinage, in the reign of William III, owing to the wear and clipping of the silver coins, the nominal exchange between England and Holland was 25% against England, while at the same time the *real* exchange was in her favor, as was shown upon the issue of the new coins.

EXAMPLES RELATING TO EXCHANGE.

ART. **125.** 1. What is the cost of a draft on New York for \$1250, the rate of exchange being $1\frac{1}{2}$% premium ?

Ans. \$1268.75.

2. What must be the face of a draft to cost \$1000, at $\frac{5}{8}$ per cent. premium ? *Ans.* \$993.79.

Remark.—For a strictly accurate solution assume, say \$1, for the face, and find *its* cost, then by it divide the given cost. Custom, however, allows, for small sums, the percentage to be computed on the cost instead of the face. By that rule the answer to the last question would be \$993.75. The approximation may be brought nearer by adding the premium on the premium, which, in this case, is $\frac{5}{8}$% of \$6.25=\$0.04 nearly.

3. What would be the proceeds of \$4000 invested in exchange on New Orleans, at a premium of $\frac{1}{2}$% ?

$\frac{1}{2}$% of \$4000=\$20, and $\frac{1}{2}$% of \$20=\$0.10.

\$4000−\$20+\$0.10=\$3980.10, *Ans.*

If the rate had been $\frac{1}{2}\%$ discount we should have had \$4000+\$20+\$0.10=\$4020.10.

4. What must be paid in New York for a draft on London for £1374 5*s.* 9*d.*, at 10% premium? *Ans.* \$6718.74.

5. What amount of sterling exchange can be bought for \$3122.25 the premium being $9\frac{3}{4}\%$? *Ans.* £640 1*s.* $11\frac{1}{4}d.$

Find by the rule the cost of £1, by which divide the given cost.

6. What will a draft on Paris for 12144.5 frcs. cost if \$1=5.35 frcs.? *Ans.* \$2270.

7. What will be the cost, at Milwaukie, of a bill on London for £1500, the quotation at New York being 110, the agio of Milwaukie current funds being 2% discount compared with those of New York, and the real exchange, or course of exchange, being $\frac{1}{4}\%$ in favor of New York? *Ans.* \$7498.33.

8. New York quotations of Paris exchange being 5.18 frcs., and the agio of Cincinnati current funds being $\frac{3}{4}\%$ discount compared with United States coin, what will a bill of 1000 frcs. cost at Cincinnati, if the purchaser buys coin and sends by express, at a charge of \$1.50 per thousand dollars, and buys the exchange in New York through a broker whose charges are $\frac{1}{2}\%$ for commission? *Ans.* \$195.75.

9. The money of account in Hamburg is of two kinds, each reckoned in marcs or marks, viz: *marks banco and marks current.* The former is the account kept at the bank where specie or bullion is deposited, and is generally the standard of reference in quotations of exchange. The latter is current in business, and is much depreciated, the agio of the two accounts being subject to slight variations. The par of exchange between Hamburg and London is 1 mark banco=1*s.* $5\frac{1}{2}d.$ Assuming £1=$\$4.86\frac{3}{4}$, what is the par of exchange between Hamburg and New York? *Ans.* 1 mark banco=$35\frac{1}{2}$ cts. nearly.

10. Assuming the quotations of $109\frac{1}{2}$ on London and $35\frac{1}{2}$ on Hamburg to represent the par of exchange, as they do very nearly, how much per cent. higher is Hamburg exchange than sterling exchange, when the quotations are 110 and 36.

Ans. .9518%.

11. Assuming the mark current at 1*s.* 2*d.* sterling, what is the agio between the two moneys of account at Hamburg?

Ans. The mark banco would be 25% premium.

It usually varies from 20 to 26% premium.

12. What would be the cost, at Chicago, of a bill on Hamburg for 10,000 marks banco, the banker in Chicago drawing direct, at New York quotations (37 cts. per mark), adding the current rate of exchange on New York ($1\frac{1}{2}$% premium), and 1% commission? *Ans.* $3792.50.

13. If the agio between New England paper currency and coin be $\frac{1}{4}$%, and between Illinois currency and coin 2%, what would it be if both circulated in equal proportions?

Ans. $1\frac{1}{8}$%.

14. If the currency in circulation in Cincinnati have an agio of $\frac{3}{4}$% compared with United States coin, what would be the ultimate effect of making Illinois currency "bankable" if its agio is 2%.

Ans. It would drive from circulation everything but Illinois currency or its equivalent, and depreciate the money of account $1\frac{1}{4}$%.

15. A banker in New York sends 1000 eagles to London, at a cost for freight and insurance of $\frac{3}{4}$%, which is paid in New York, and receives credit at the rate of £3 16*s.* 2*d.* per oz., and 3% per annum interest on the account. At the same time he sells a 60 days' sight bill drawn against the proceeds of the coin and the accrued interest, at the rate of $110\frac{1}{2}$%. Suppose the bill to be accepted on the day of the credit, and payable without grace, what profit does the banker receive in the transaction. *Ans.* $28.20.

16. At one time the laws of Spain rigidly restrained the exportation of the precious metals from that country, still they were secretly exported at a risk of about 2%. What, then, was the nominal exchange between that and other countries having a free-trade in bullion, arising from the depreciation occasioned by relative excess? *Ans.* About 2% against Spain.

17. If from the large increase of California gold, or excessive paper issues in the United States, the nominal exchange

between England and the United States should be 2% in favor of England, what should be the quotations of sterling exchange, other things being equal, to represent the balance of payments in equilibrium? *Ans.* $111\frac{1}{2}$%.

18. If the nominal exchange, at London, on Hamburg, be $16\frac{2}{3}$% discount, what would a London merchant make for his net profit, the cost of transportion, insurance, &c., being 5% on the purchase price, and payable at London, if he sells in Hamburg for £12,000 what cost in London £10,000?

Ans. He would lose £500.

19. If the currencies of England and the United States were in due proportion in amount compared with business wants, what would be the effect upon the "movement" of the precious metal between the two countries, if the United States should add to its currency a large issue of paper money or gold coinage, thereby raising prices and depreciating the relative value of money?

20. Why is any country better able to sustain an increase of importations compared with the exportations, when it arises from an excess of *specie* currency, than when it arises from an excess of *paper* currency?

Ans. Because nothing but metal will pay the balance, and in the one case we can afford to part with it, while in the other we cannot.

21. Suppose the circulating medium in San Francisco to be depreciated below the currency of New York $\frac{1}{2}$% in consequence of imperfect coinage, and the expense of transportation, including risk, be $\frac{1}{2}$% more, and the broker's commission in New York be $\frac{1}{4}$%, what does an exchange broker or gold exporter in San Francisco make, if he sells sight drafts on New York for 3% premium, and to make his exchange he is obliged to ship gold? *Ans.* $1\frac{3}{4}$%.

22. If a wheat merchant in Toledo buys wheat at $1.00 per bushel, and sends it to Buffalo for sale at 1.02\frac{1}{2}$ per bushel, the cost for transportation, insurance, and commission being $1\frac{1}{4}$%, what per cent. profit does he make, if, in view of the difference in value, or agio, of the currencies of the two places,

he is able to negotiate at $\frac{1}{2}$% premium the drafts drawn against the proceeds of the sale? *Ans.* $1\frac{3}{4}$%.

Remark.—In the last example the rates were made to correspond with those of the 21st, to show more clearly to the pupil that in general the same laws govern the movement of gold in large quantities as regulate the movements of wheat.

23. During the year ending June 30, 1857, our exports, including specie, to England, exceeded our imports from England $54,216,623; but in our trade with Cuba, Brazil, China, and France, our imports exceeded our exports, as follows: Cuba, $30,319,658; Brazil, $15,915,526; China, $3,961,802; France, $9,553,840. During the same time our total excess of exports of specie was $56,675,123, of which $46,821,211 went to England, and we will suppose, for this example and the one following, that the balance of excess went, in equal amounts, to the other four countries. Why did the specie go to England, when we were not in debt to her, and how was our debt to the other countries probably settled?

24. First, Suppose the last example to represent our entire foreign commerce and trade for that year, after a full settlement, and to include nothing else, and our due proportion of specie for currency to have been preserved by supply from California, and the Custom House value to be the exact exchangeable values of both importations and exportations, what was the balance of net profit as shown by the excess of imports? *Ans.* $5,534,203.

Second, What per cent. would that profit be on the entire exports to those countries which, for that year, specie included, were about $240 millions? *Ans.* About $2\frac{1}{4}$%.

Third, If the exports, as entered at the Custom House, not including specie, were $170,000,000, and the imports, as received, were entered $231,000,000, what was the balance of payments in specie, if the exports, being carried by American vessels, brought in the foreign market 10% advance on their Custom House valuation, and the imports were entered 5% below their cost? *Ans.* $56,157,895.

Actual balance of payments, $56,675,123.

Fourth, If our due proportion of currency required no increase of specie for the year 1857, and California, with other American mines, furnished for the market $49,000,000, how was our *balance of trade* for that year?

Ans. $7,675,123, against us.

Fifth, Suppose we had redeemed, during that year, of our foreign indebtedness in stocks and bonds, $10,000,000, what would then have been our balance of trade?

Ans. $2,324,877 in our favor.

BILLS OF EXCHANGE.

ART. **126.** *A bill of exchange* is an order or draft, made by one person upon a second, to pay a certain sum of money to a third, or to his order, or to the bearer. For example:

$1000. CLEVELAND, O., NOV. 6, 1858.

Sixty days after date, pay to the order of J. F. Whitelaw one thousand dollars, and place to the account of

To Messrs. SMITH & BROWN, ALBERT CLARK.
New York.

The person making the order is called the *drawer;* the person to whom the order is addressed is called the *drawee;* and the one to whom the amount is payable is called the *payee.* If the drawee accepts, by writing his name across the face of the bill, under the word "accepted," he then becomes an *acceptor*, and the instrument is then called an *acceptance.* If the payee writes his name upon the back of the instrument, he becomes an *indorser.* The person to whom it is afterward transferred by indorsement is called an *indorsee.*

Foreign bills are those which are drawn in one country but are payable in another.

Domestic or inland bills are those that are payable in the country where they are drawn.

The United States being separate sovereignties, are foreign to each other, and bills drawn in one payable in another, like the example given above, are *foreign bills,* though apparently *inland.*

Time bills are those requiring payment at a certain specified time after sight or after date. All others are payable on demand. When time bills are drawn "acceptance waived," they may be held till maturity before being presented to the drawee ; otherwise, they should be presented immediately for acceptance.

PROMISSORY NOTES.

ART. **127.** *A promissory note* is a written agreement by one party to pay to another a specified sum at a specified time. The one making the agreement or signing the note is called the *maker.* The person to whom the amount is payable is called the *payee,* and the owner of the note is called the *holder.* A *principal* is one directly responsible for the payment of a bill or note at maturity.

For different forms of notes, see examples under the subject of *Interest.*

A *joint and several note* is one signed by two or more distinct parties, in which case each one becomes liable as *maker* or *principal,* the same as if no others signed with him. Some of the features of a valid promissory note are the following:

A full consideration is implied from the nature of the instrument, but a want of consideration would be a valid defense on the part of the maker as against the payee, but not as against any other holder, into whose possession it may have come without a knowledge of such want of consideration, in which case he would be called an *innocent holder.*

It may be written with ink or pencil, or it may all be printed except the signature, which must always be in the hand-writing of the maker or his authorized agent. It should be an unqualified promise to pay in money, definite in amount, and independent of all contingencies. The amount should be expressed in the body of the note, in words, and should be relied on for accuracy rather than figures in the margin.

If the time is not definitely stated, it is payable on demand. If the place of payment is not specified it is payable at the place of business or residence of the maker.

In the settlement of bills of exchange and promissory notes, so far as their terms are subject to general law, as fixing the rate of legal interest and day of maturity for example, the law of the State where they are made payable should govern. If a note is not paid at maturity, it continues to draw the same interest as before, if it does not exceed the legalized rate ; but if no rate be mentioned, it draws simple interest at the legal rate till paid.

NEGOTIABLE PAPER.

ART. **128.** Bank notes, checks, certificates of deposit, bills of exchange, and promissory notes, when properly drawn, are negotiable, except when made payable by the terms of the contract, to one person only. If the amount is payable to "bearer," or is subject to the "order" of the payee, they are negotiable. But if neither the word "bearer" nor "order" appears in the instrument, but simply the name of the payee, it is not negotiable, and the payee cannot give full title to a third party; for the account, as between the maker and payee, would still be subject to a garnishee process from other creditors of the payee.

In the negotiation of paper the transfer may be made *by delivery* or *by indorsement.* If payable to "bearer," or to the payee "or bearer," as are bank notes and most checks, the transfer is by delivery. If payable "to the order of" the payee, or to the payee "or order," the transfer is by indorsement.

If the payee simply writes his name across the back of the paper it is an *indorsement in blank*, and is afterward negotiable by delivery. But if above this indorsement it be made payable to the order of another person, called an *indorsee*, it is an *indorsement in full*, and is then negotiable only by the indorsement of the indorsee. By repeating this kind of indorsement there may be several indorsees. When the indorsement is in blank, any legal holder is allowed to write that above it, which will make it an indorsement in full. A *qualified* indorsement is one that affects the liability of the indorser, but not the negotiability of the paper, as when made "*without recourse*."

LIABILITY OF PARTIES CONNECTED WITH NEGOTIABLE PAPER.

ART. **129.** Bank notes designed to circulate as money, checks, and other paper negotiable by delivery, may be legally retained by an *innocent holder*, who receives them in good faith for a valuable consideration, though the party from whom they were received obtained them fraudulently.

Bank notes are a good tender if not objected to at the time of payment, unless it should appear afterward that they were, at the time of payment, worthless, or of less value than represented, as when counterfeit, altered, spurious, broken, or uncurrent. Any unreasonable delay to return them, after the discovery is made, whereby the payer loses the opportunity or means of indemnity, would throw the loss upon the payee or holder, on account of the neglect.

If a person receives a check on a bank, it is his duty to present it for payment at the bank during *the same or the next day at the furthest;* otherwise he holds it at his own risk, the loss being his if the bank fails meantime, provided that the funds were there to meet the check before the failure. If he lives at a distance from the bank he must send it for collection by mail, or otherwise, during the same or next day. If the check passes through the hands of several persons, each one is allowed one day, and his liability, so far as above described, ceases with the succeeding day. Bank drafts, or "bankers' exchange," from their service in making remittances to distant points, may be used to fulfill that mission, but should not be allowed to lie still or circulate as money beyond the reasonable expectation of the drawer.

When the holder of a check gets it certified as good by a bank on which it is drawn, the drawer is released though the bank fail to pay.

As between the maker and payee of a note the maker is allowed any defense that would be allowed in any other debt between the two. But as between the maker and indorsee, or other holder, no defense can be set up, except it be shown that the holder had knowledge, at the time of the note's coming into his possession, of a just ground of defense between the maker and payee. If, however, the note came into the possession of the holder, after it became due, the claim of the holder would be subject to all the equities in favor of the maker that existed at maturity, or that had arisen after maturity.

On a promissory note the maker is *principal*, and is directly responsible to any bona fide holder. The indorsers are responsible in the order of their indorsements, that is, each one to all those who follow, on condition of their being duly notified of non-payment, as explained hereafter. The liability of those who indorse as guarantors is not so easily discharged by a failure to give prompt notice of non-payment.

A bill of exchange involves no direct liability until presented for acceptance. If acceptance be refused by the drawee, the drawer immediately becomes principal, and is bound to redeem the draft from the holder without delay, though it be a time draft, and the time not yet expired. If the bill be accepted, the acceptor becomes principal, the same as the maker of a promissory note, in which case the drawer sustains practically the position of first indorser, in case of non-payment on the part of the acceptor. The liability of indorsers on bills is the same as of those on promissory notes. That liability, however, may be avoided in both cases by their writing over their indorsements "without recourse," or other words of equivalent signification, except so far as to warrant that the bill or note is genuine, that is, not forged or fictitious, a liability which attaches not only to all indorsers, but to all who negotiate the paper by delivery, as owners, or even as agents, unless that agency, with the name of the principal, be distinctly stated at the time of the transfer.

Indorsers are also released from liability, if they are not duly notified of non-acceptance or non-payment, the paper having been duly presented.

If a man lends his name and credit by making a note or accepting a bill of exchange for the accommodation of another party, it is called an *accommodation paper*. He thereby becomes liable to any bona fide holder, to the same extent as if he had received a full consideration, except to the person for whose accommodation the credit was given. But for his indemnity for payment he has a valid claim on the party accommodated.

PRESENTMENT, PROTEST, AND NOTICE.

ART. **130.** The limits of this work will not allow the detail of all the particulars necessary to be observed by the holder of a bill or note, in making a proper demand for payment, and, in case of non-payment, in properly notifying the indorsers, so that they may not be released from liability. The importance of the subject demands the careful study of those who deal in negotiable paper, or who undertake the collection of it for others. Business men, unless thoroughly posted, had better intrust their collections with some responsible banker. A few brief rules only will be given.

There should be no unnecessary delay in presenting for payment any paper payable on presentation, and for acceptance all time drafts (unless drawn "acceptance waived"), especially if the time of maturity is to be determined by the time of sight or presentment.

When the time is definitely fixed by the date of the instrument or of the acceptance, it must be presented for payment on the *exact day of maturity*, as regulated by the law of the State where it is made payable. A protest on any other day would be of no avail.

The paper itself must be presented by the holder personally to the acceptor or maker, or their authorized agent, at the place where it is made payable, during reasonable business hours. If no such person or agent is found with funds to meet it, the paper may be treated as dishonored. In case of non-acceptance or non-payment the paper should be protested, and the drawer and indorsers notified.

"A *protest* is a solemn declaration on behalf of the holder, drawn up by an official person, against any loss to be sustained by the non-acceptance or non-payment of a bill." This protest should be made by a notary public, who should also *personally* make due presentment or demand, and should *on the same day*, or, at furthest, *the next day*, send written notices of protest to the parties to be notified. If the residence of all the indorsers be not known, and all the notices be sent under one cover to the last indorser, he is allowed only one day to forward the notices to antecedent indorsers. So also for each of the others. Sundays and legally recognized holidays are excepted. Notices to parties residing in the same town must be delivered in person or by a messenger. Notices to all others must be sent by mail. If an indorser writes over his name "waiving demand and notice," a protest is not necessary to retain his liability.

DAYS OF GRACE AND TIME OF MATURITY.

ART. **131.** It may be observed here that each of the United States makes its own laws in regard to negotiable paper, and probably the laws of no two States agree in all respects. The laws of that State are applied in which the paper is made payable, though it be drawn in another. For a valuable compend upon this whole subject the student is referred to a "Manual for Notaries Public," published by J. Smith Homans, New York.

As a general law in the United States the day of maturity for all negotiable time-paper does not come till three days after the expiration of the time mentioned in the instrument, except when the time is limited by the expression "without grace." These days are called *days of grace*, but they give the maker no special advantage, for interest is allowed on those days the same as others, and no presentment need be made till the last day of grace.

If the last day of grace falls on Sunday, or any legally recognized holiday, the paper is payable on the preceding day.

Bills drawn at sight are sometimes allowed grace and sometimes not. The statutes of different States, so far as they exist, do not agree, and in the absence of special statutes the custom is not uniform. In New York, commercial bills, drawn at sight, are payable *without grace*, and all paper in which either the maker, drawer, or drawee is a bank or banker, is also payable without grace.

If the time be expressed in months, calendar months are always to be understood. For example, three months from January 31, without grace, would be April 30; including grace, May 3.

If the time be expressed in days, the time of maturity may be found by taking the remaining number of days in the month of the date, and as many days of the following months separately as will equal the given number of days plus three. The number of days in the last month will be the date of the month on which the paper matures.

For example, a note dated August 20, 1858, payable ninety days from date, would mature November 21, 1858.

Solution.—$11+30+31+21=93$.

Or, to the day of the date add the time of the note plus three, from which subtract consecutively the number of days of each following month, beginning with the month of the date, until the remainder be smaller than the number of days in the next month. The remainder will be the date of maturity.

Solution.—$20+93=113$, and $113-31-30-31=21$.

Or, if the time be 30, 60, or 90 days, call each 30 days a calendar month, and correct by subtracting 1 for each month passed over containing 31 days, and adding 1 or 2, according as it is a leap year or not, if the last day of February be included.

Thus, 90 days from January 10, 1856, would be, counting three calendar months, April 13, including grace.

Now, from 13 subtract 1 for January and 1 for March, and add 1 for February, and we have April 12, for the result. The last rule is convenient for bank paper, which usually runs 30, 60, or 90 days.

It is evident from the above rules that the day of the date should be excluded from the calculation.

The following fact may be worth remembering by those who get "accommodations" at bank.

A paper having 60 days to run will mature on the same day of the week as that on which it was made. Having 30 days to run, it will mature 2 days *earlier* in the week, and having 90 days to run will mature 2 days *later* in the week.

PROOF.

$33 = 7 \times 5 - 2$
$63 = 7 \times 9$
$93 = 7 \times 13 + 2$

DISCOUNTING NOTES.

ART. **132.** In negotiating promissory notes and time-bills of exchange their estimated value depends upon three considerations, viz.

1st. The responsibility and promptness of the maker.

2d. The relative value of the currency, used in the purchase, compared with that of the payment of the obligation at maturity.

3d. The market rate of interest.

The range of the first consideration is from A No. 1 to worthless.

The range of the second, in the United States, is generally within 2%.

The range of the third may be said to be between 3 and 20% per annum.

In view of the first, a man may make a bad bargain in buying a note having sixty days to run, if he pay for it but 10 cents on a dollar. The United States may perhaps borrow money at 4% per annum, when individual States would have to pay 5 or 6%, and railroad companies 10 or 15%. A corresponding difference is found in promissory notes made by individuals and business firms.

The purchase of a draft on New York, payable in *coin*, with Illinois paper currency, which is convertible into coin at a cost, say, of 1%, will illustrate the force of the second consideration.

In regard to the third, the *market*, or *ruling rate of interest*, depends mainly upon the *rate of profit* with which capital can otherwise be employed. New countries, rapidly developing, furnish profitable investments, and therefore sustain a high rate of interest. Sudden expansions and contractions of currency *temporarily* affect the rate, causing it to fall with the expansion and rise with the contraction, but a *continued* increase in the supply of money stimulates prices, awakens enterprise, and increases the profits in business and speculation, thereby *raising* the rate of interest proportionably.

The *rate of interest* does not express the *value of money*, but only the value of the *use* of it for a limited time, or rather, it expresses the value of the use of the *capital* or *credit* measured by money. *Money*, from its nature, is always *cheap* when *prices* are *dear*, and *vice versa ;* for as money measures the value of other commodities, so the comparative price of the standard articles of commerce measures the relative value of money. Generally, when money is cheap, interest is high. For many years money has been cheaper in the United States than in England, but during the whole time the rate of interest has ruled higher. In the early history of California money was exceedingly cheap, but the rate of interest remarkably high. The current rate of interest is also made higher from the effect of unwise usury laws, and laws under which the collection of valid claims can be enforced only after a protracted, uncertain, and expensive prosecution.

There are many other causes that occasion remarkable fluctuations in the market rate of interest, as war, commercial revulsions, &c. Unlimited confidence in business encourages a high rate of interest, while excessive caution and distrust cause it to decline.

As a general rule, the market rate of interest, like the price of exchange, is not subject to arbitrary control, but is the resultant of sundry contributing causes; and whatever legislation is necessary should be expended on the *cause* rather than on the *effect*.

BANK DISCOUNT.

Art. **133.** The banks of the United States are usually restricted by charter in their rates of discount, but being allowed, in the interior, to deal in time-drafts or bills on New York, payable in coin, and being allowed frequently to pay out paper currency of less value than coin in purchasing such drafts, they are enabled by this and other means to realize more than the nominal, legally restricted rate of interest. It is not proposed in this work to discuss the policy of bank charters with special privileges and special restrictions, nor any other question of *policy*, but merely to furnish to the student and inexperienced business man the fundamental principles upon which money and negotiable paper do rest and should rest.

It may, however, be taken for granted, that although banks, railroad companies, &c., may have been established for "the accommodation of the people," yet so long as they are controlled by *human nature*, and the profits go into the pockets of *individuals*, corporations no more than individuals can be expected to furnish "accommodations" without their being paid for. As a general rule, a business man may expect accommodations from a bank only so far as he makes it for the interest of the bank to grant them.

The interest which is charged on notes discounted at a bank is generally paid in advance, and is computed upon the amount due on the note at maturity. The difference between the interest and face of the note is the *proceeds*, which is received by the customer.

Thus the proceeds of a note for $2000, having 63 days to run, including grace, would be, at 6% interest, $2000 − $21 = $1979.

If "business paper," drawing interest, is discounted, the amount due at maturity, *including interest*, is taken as the face of the note upon which the *bank discount* is computed. It will be observed that *bank discount* exceeds the "*true discount*," as heretofore explained; for while the latter is the interest on the *present worth* or principal, the former is the interest on the *amount* of principal and interest, and the excess is equal to the interest on the *true discount* for the given time. The *ratio* of this excess will also increase as the time is lengthened, so that, other considerations remaining the same, the longer the time the more profit to the bank. If the note run $16\frac{2}{3}$ years, the bank discount, at 6%, would absorb the whole note, and the proceeds would be nothing. Frequent renewals, so far as the matter of interest is concerned, are unfavorable to the bank. The reason for the custom among banks of discounting only "short paper," as it is called, is two-fold.

First, A large portion of the capital invested in discounts is based upon deposits, which are subject to "call," and their own "circulation," which must be redeemed on presentation. In case of unusual demands for redemption, or withdrawal of deposits, the early maturity of Bills Discounted is their main reliance.

Secondly, The risk arising from the varying circumstances of the makers and indorsers is lessened by shortening the time.

If, however, bills of exchange are discounted, payable in a better currency than that used in the discount, or for which a charge is made for collection, the shorter the time the greater the pecuniary profit.

In considering the percentage of profit in "bank discount" with frequent renewals, there is a partial offset in favor of the banker by his being able to compound the interest at each renewal. But this advantage is very small if we consider its effect for one year only (See Note, page 118), at which time *simple* interest, if paid, may also be compounded by re-loaning.

Comparing simple interest with "bank discount," including the advantage from compounding the interest, we obtain the following result:

Bank discount at 6% on paper,

Renewed	once in	12	mos.,	is equivalent to	6.383%	simple interest.
"	"	6	"	"	6.281%	"
"	"	4	"	"	6.248%	"
"	"	3	"	"	6.232%	"
"	"	2	"	"	6.216%	"
"	"	1	"	"	6.200%	"
"	every instant			"	6.182%	"

From the above we see that the excess of bank discount over true discount, as affecting the *rate* of interest received, when the time is less than a year, *can be* but trifling, being for 6% always less than $\frac{4}{10}$%.

BANKERS' ACCOUNT CURRENT.

ART. **134.** Bankers frequently receive and pay interest on the account current with their correspondents and depositors, paying interest on the deposits and receiving interest on the over-drafts. A settlement occurs once in 3, 6, or 12 months, as custom or special agreement may dictate, at which time the balance of interest is entered to the debit or credit of the account as the case may be, after which *it* draws interest the same as other items in the account. The principle involved in this kind of interest account forms the basis of the "MERCANTILE RULE" in Partial Payments, as given in this work.

The process of computing the interest on such accounts is made easy by the use of the following

RULE.—*Divide the sum of all the daily balances by* 6 *and*

the quotient, after pointing three places for decimals, will be the interest required.

Remark.—It is evident that each daily balance draws interest one day. The interest, then, of the sum of daily balances for one day is all that is required.

Note 1st.—If the daily balance remains the same for several days, instead of setting down the amount as many times as there are days, use the product of the balance into the number of days.

Note 2d.—If the balances are sometimes debit and sometimes credit, take the difference between their sums before dividing.

Note 3d.—The above rule gives the interest at 6%. To find the interest at 4% divide by 9 instead of 6. For 3%, divide by 12. In general, the divisor for any rate may be found by dividing 36 by the rate. Or, having found the interest at 6%, the interest for any other rate may be found by aliquot parts.

Note 4th.—If a different rate of interest is to be charged on the over-drafts or debit entries, the footings of the daily balances should be divided by their appropriate divisors before subtraction.

The following abbreviated form will serve to illustrate the foregoing rule :

Account Current.			Daily Balances.		Total Daily Balances.	
1859	Dr.	Cr.	Dr.	Cr.	Dr.	Cr.
July 1		$500		500		500
2	$200	100		400		400
3	75			325 × 17	=	5525
20		500		825 × 10	=	8250
30	1000		175	× 5	=875	
Aug. 4		375		200 × 10	=	2000
14	125	250		325 × 30	=	9750
Sept. 13		125		450 × 10	=	4500
23		1000		1450 × 8	=	11600
		Int. 4.63				42525
Bal.	1454.63					875
	2854.63	2854.63			9)	41.650
Oct. 1	By Bal.	$1454.63			Int. at 4%	$4.63

RULES FOR DETECTING ERRORS IN TRIAL BALANCES

ART. **135.** The first rule of the book-keeper should be *to make no error*, but as all are fallible a few suggestions may not come amiss.

1st. If the error is found to be in one figure only it is probably an error of footing or copying.

2d. If it involves several figures it may have arisen from the omission of an entire entry or the entering of the same twice.

3d. If it be divisible by 2, without a remainder, it may have arisen by posting an item to the wrong side of the account, in which case the item would be half of the apparent error.

4th. If the error be divisible by 9, without a remainder, it may have arisen from transposition, three cases of which may be easily detected by rules founded on the peculiar property of the number 9. They are—

First. When two figures are made to exchange places with each other, the orders in notation remaining the same: *e. g.*, 372 made to read 327, or 732, or 273.

Second. When two or more figures are made to change their places in notation, their arrangement in respect to each other remaining the same: *e. g.*, $4275 made to read $42750, or $42.75, or $427.50.

Third. When *two* significant figures are made to change position both with respect to themselves and also the orders of notation: *e. g.*, $14 made to read $0.41.

To detect the first and second cases of transposition *divide the amount of the error in the trial balance successively by* 9, 99, 999, 9999, *&c., so far as possible without a remainder, rejecting all ciphers at the right of the last significant figure in the error.*

The quotients that contain but one digit figure will express the difference between the two digit figures transposed, which will be adjacent to each other if the divisor contained but one 9, separated by one other figure if it contained two 9s, by two other figures if it contained three 9s, and so on.

Those quotients, which contain two or more figures will express the *number* itself, which is transposed in notation simply, the arrangement of the significant figures remaining the same. In either case the *order* of the last *significant* figure in the error will be the lowest order of the figures transposed. The orders of the other figures can be easily determined by referring to the error and applying the principles of notation.

To detect the *third* case, divide the error in the balance by as many 9s as is possible so as to give only a single figure in the quotient, and then the remainder in the same way, rejecting all ciphers at the right of the last significant figure in both dividends, after which there should be no remainder.

The first quotient will be the figure filling both the highest and lowest order in the transposition ; the second quotient will be the other figure.

Note.—If the error of the trial-balance be not divisible by 9 it cannot be the result of transposition alone. But whenever the error becomes so reduced as to be divisible by 9 without a remainder, a transposition being then possible, the above tests should be given.

To illustrate the application of the foregoing rules, four examples are given below, each one representing a balance-sheet taken from the ledger, but erroneous, from the fact that the footings of the Dr. and Cr. columns do not agree.

Dr.	Cr.	Dr.	Cr.	Dr.	Cr.	Dr.	Cr.
25	34	184	74	100	22	184	22
100	981	24.50	10.25	320.60	36.40	23.50	185
87.50	73	30	200.75	400.90	20	126	71
300	90	20.40	80	10	31.20	81.44	137.80
18.40	92	120	110	10.44	10	326	323
7	93.50	100	50	495	800	3.51	6.44
94	12	90.60	33	450	200	74.25	100
81.50	310	75	25	100.16	120.50	353	40
144	86.24	201.75	40	30	200.10	25	10
63	122.22	8.25	30	20.10	10	350	290
922.40	11.84	75	333.92	8	49.50	24	35.99
1,842.80	1,905.80	855.25	929.50	1,945.20	1,499.70	1,570.70	1.221.23
63		74.25			445.50		349.47

The "errors" 63, 7425, 4455, and 34947 being each divisible by 9, transposition is possible. Taking the first example, we have 63÷9=7. As this is the only division we can perform, we conclude the transposition can occur only in those amounts where the digit figures expressing the units and tens of dollars differ by 7. In the Dr. column there are three numbers answering these conditions, and in the Cr. column two, viz.: $18.40, $7, $81.50, $981 and $92. The transposition could not have occurred in the third number for the footing is already too small. If, then, either of the other numbers had been transposed from $81.40, $70, $918, and $29 respectively, the error is accounted for, a question easily settled by reference to the ledger. In the second example, we have 7425÷9=825 and 7425÷99=75. The quotients containing two or more figures in the transposition must be in *notation* simply. By reference to the Dr. and Cr. columns it will be observed that these quotients occur four times in the former and once in the latter, viz.: $0.75, 201.75, $8.25, $75, and $200.75. The transposition could not have occurred in the second number without displacing other significant figures, nor in the fourth, because the Dr. footing is already too small, nor in the fifth, because the Cr. footing is already too large. The only two numbers to be compared, therefore, are the first and third, which, perhaps, should have been $75 or $82.50, either of which would account for the error.

In the third example we have 4455÷9=495, 4455÷99 =45. Here the transposition must be in notation simply, and may be found in one of two places only, viz.: $495 and $450.

In the fourth example we have 34947÷9=3883, 34947÷99=353, 34947÷9999=3, with a remainder 495, which ÷99 =5. We omit the division by 999, because the remainder is not divisible by 99 without a remainder. For the same reason we omitted it in the third example. In this case there could be no transposition in the notation of 3883, because the number does not occur. There may have been a transposition of $353 from $3.53, or the figure 3 and 5 may somewhere have been made to change places with respect to themselves and notation also ; as, when $0.53 had been made to read $350.

Remark.—In the use of these rules in practice, not only the balances of the ledger accounts as they appear on the balance sheet should be examined, but also all the separate postings, as a transposition there will equally affect the final balance.

STOCKS AND BONDS.

ART. **136.** *Capital* is a term applied to the property invested, by an individual or company, in trade, manufactures, railroads, banking, &c. The capital of an incorporated company is generally called its *capital stock,* and is divided into equal parts of convenient size called *shares :* the persons owning one or more of these shares being called *stockholders.*

The management of such companies is generally vested in officers and directors, who are elected by the stockholders, each stockholder being entitled to as many votes as the number of shares he holds.

It not unfrequently happens that the capital stock considerably exceeds the actual capital paid in, which occurs when it is made payable in installments, and is called in only as the wants of the company demand. The profits which are distributed among the stockholders are called *dividends,* and when "declared" are a certain per cent. of the *par value* of the shares.

Certificates of stock are issued by the company, signed by the proper officers, indicating the size and number of shares each stockholder is entitled to. These are transferable, and may be bought and sold like any other property.

When their *marketable value* equals their *nominal value* they are said to be *at par.* When they sell for more than their nominal value or face they are *above par,* or at a premium ; when for less, they are *below par,* or at a discount.

Quotations of their marketable value are generally made by a *percentage* of their *par value.*

When States, cities, railroad companies, and other corporations borrow large amounts of money, instead of giving common promissory notes, they issue *bonds,* in denominations of convenient size, payable at a specified time, with interest usually payable semi-annually.

When issued by governments these bonds are frequently called *government stocks* or *State stocks,* but the terms should be carefully distinguished from the *capital stock* of business corporations.

To these bonds are attached what are called *coupons**, each of which is a due bill for the interest on the bond to which it is attached, representing the amount of the periodical dividend or interest, and the time of payment, which coupons are severally *cut off* and presented for payment as they become due.

These bonds and coupons are signed by the proper officers, and, like certificates of capital stock, are negotiable by delivery, being made payable "to bearer." The loan is made by the sale of the bonds, with coupons attached, but they are rarely negotiated at par. Their value depends upon the degree of certainty of their being paid at maturity, and the market rate of interest compared with the rate drawn by the bond.

Treasury notes are also issued by the United States government for the purpose of effecting temporary loans, which more nearly resemble bank notes, and are made payable with interest, but without coupoı

Consols is a term abbreviated from the expression "consolidated annuities," the British government having at various times borrowed money at different rates of interest, and payable at different times, consolidated the stock or bonds thus issued, by issuing new stock drawing interest at three per cent. per annum, payable semi-annually, and redeemable only at the option of the government, becoming practically *perpetual annuities.* With the proceeds of this the old stock was redeemed. The quotations of these three per cent. perpetual annuities or

* Coupon, pronounced koo-pong′.

consols, indicate pretty accurately the state of the money market, as they form a staple credit and become a standard for reference.

Examples.

ART. **137.** 1. A person buys 25 shares, par value $100 each, in the Illinois Central Railroad, at a discount of 12% per cent. To what did they amount?

2. What will be the cost of $15,000 of Ohio State Bonds, at a discount of $2\frac{1}{2}$%?

3. Bought 40 shares ($100 each) of New York and Erie Railroad stock, at a discount of 3%, and sold the same at a discount of $37\frac{1}{2}$%. How much did I lose in the transaction?

4. If the New York Central Railroad Company declares an annual dividend of 14%, what will a stockholder receive who owns 240 shares ($100 each)?

5. How many shares of canal stock, of $100 each, at 14% discount, can be bought for $1020? How much would be gained by selling them at $33\frac{1}{3}$% discount?

6. If the capital stock of a bank be $500,000, what amount is necessary to declare a dividend of $5\frac{1}{2}$%?

7. A person owns 20 shares ($100 each) of bank stock, and receives a dividend of $150; what was the rate of dividend?

8. A certain stockholder draws $270 when a dividend of 9% is declared; what is the amount of his stock?

9. Bought stock at 4 per cent. discount, and sold the same at 5% premium, and gained $450. How many shares of $100 each were transferred?

10. A broker paid $9748.50 for bank stock, at a discount of 3%. How many shares of $50 each did he purchase?

11. Which is the better investment, railroad stock paying a semi-annual dividend of 4%, bought at a discount of 25%, or money loaned at 10% interest, payable annually?

Ans. Railroad stock by $\frac{2}{3}$%, besides the use, each year, of one semi-annual dividend for six months.

12. Bought bank stock, paying 12% dividend, at a discount of 20%. What per cent. interest did the investment pay?

13. When the annual dividend of railroad stock is 15%, and the interest of money is 10%, at what premium ought the railroad stock to sell? *Ans.* 50%.

14. At what per cent. discount must I buy bank stock, paying 6%, that the investment may pay 9%. *Ans.* $33\frac{1}{3}$%.

15. If the C. & E. RR. Co. declare a dividend of 15% per annum, what is the value of its stock, money being worth 8%?

16. The free banking law of New York requires that the stocks deposited with the superintendent, as security for bank-note circulation, shall be made equal to stock producing an interest of 6% per annum. What amount of circulating notes could a bank receive on a five per cent. stock?

Ans. $83\frac{1}{3}$% of the par value of the stock.

What on a 7% stock? *Ans.* $116\frac{2}{3}$%.

17. In January, 1848, the total amount of British consols was £378,019,855. What was the amount of interest paid on them semi-annually? *Ans.* £5,670,297$\frac{33}{40}$.

18. The debt of Great Britain and Ireland, in round numbers, is £780,000,000, and the annual revenue £56,000,000. Supposing the annual interest to average $3\frac{1}{2}$%, what per cent. of the revenue is needed to pay the interest on the debt?

19. In July, 1859, forty-five New York Fire Insurance Companies (out of fifty), on a capital of $8,712,000, divided among the stockholders, as a semi-annual dividend, $679,950. Compared with railroad stock paying 5% semi-annually, which would yield the greater income, railroad stock bought at 65% or insurance stock at par?

20. A man subscribed $20,000 stock in a mining company, the capital stock of which is $500,000, but only 20% paid in. A cash dividend of 2% on the par value is declared and a dividend of 10% to be credited to the stockholders as an installment on their unpaid stock. What is the amount of cash he receives, and what is the balance due on his subscription?

21. I buy 100 shares of $100 each in a railroad company, the capital stock being $3,000,000. The first year they declare a cash dividend of 10%. The second year they increase their stock by declaring a stock dividend of 10%. The third

year they divide among their stockholders the same amount as in the first year. What would be the per cent. of the last dividend? *Ans.* $9\frac{1}{11}$ per cent.

How much more would they need to declare a dividend of 10%, the same as in the first year? *Ans.* $30,000.

22. If the paid up stock in a railroad company be worth 100%, and a stock dividend of 10% be made to the stockholders, what would be the value of the stock after the dividend?

Ans. $90\frac{10}{11}$ per cent.

23. If the net earnings of a bank with $200,000 capital be sufficient to pay an annual dividend of 10%, and reserve $4000 as a surplus to provide for future losses, and it pay 6% on its net earnings to the State in lieu of taxes, what would be the rate of taxation on its capital?

Ans. $\frac{72}{100}$ per cent.

NEW RULE FOR FINDING THE VALUE OF A BOND.

ART. **138.** Most of the problems respecting stocks and bonds, and brokerage in money and exchange, can be solved by the application of the ordinary principles of percentage, without special rules. One problem, however, not unfrequently arises, more complicated, to the solution of which the attention of the student is now directed.

To find the present value of a bond having several years to run, with interest payable semi-annually, in order to realize from the dividends and final payment an equivalent to a given rate per cent. per annum on the investment, use the following

RULE.—1st. *Taking a single dividend or semi-annual interest on the bond for a principal, compute the simple interest on it at the proposed rate, for one-fourth as many years as would be the product of the number of semi-annual dividends into the number less one. To this interest add the sum of the several amounts of semi-annual interest, and the face of the bond, setting this sum down for a* DIVIDEND.

2d. *Suppose another bond, differing from the given bond only in its rate of interest being the same as the proposed rate for investment. Proceed with this as with the other, and use the result for a* DIVISOR.

The quotient, after division, will express, decimally, the rate per cent. of the par value equal to the present value.

Ex. 1. What should I pay for a bond for $1000 due in 10 years, with interest at 5%, payable semi-annually, in order to make it a 10% investment?

Solution.

Interest on $25 at 10%, for $\frac{20\times10}{4}$ years, . .	$237.50
Total amount of semi-annual dividends $=\$25\times20=$	500
Face of the bond, ...	1000
Dividend, ...	1737.50
Interest on $50 at 10% for $\frac{20\times10}{4}$ years, . .	475
Total amount of semi-annual dividends $=\$50\times20=$	1000
Face of the bond, ...	1000
Divisor, ...	2475

$\$1737.50\div\$2475=.70202.$

$\$1000\times.70202=\$702.02$, the present value of the bond.

REMARK.—A *strictly accurate* solution of the above problem requires the aid of logarithms, and the operation is tedious. The above rule is simple and brief, and gives a result sufficiently approximate for all practical purposes. The question involves compound interest, the interest on the investment being supposed to be compounded annually, while the interest on the dividends is compounded at the proposed rate at the end of each year. Though annual interest gives a result somewhat less than compound interest, yet if two problems be wrought, first by annual interest and then by compound, the *ratio* between the results by the first operation will not differ essentially from the *ratio* by the second. This principle forms the basis of the rule given above. The work of computing the "annual interest," or rather semi-annual interest, is much shortened by incorporating in the rule an expression for *the sum of the arithmetical series* of years, during which a single dividend would draw interest. The approximation to strict accuracy is furthermore increased by treating the *supposed* bond or investment the same as the one given, so far as that its interest should be payable semi-annually instead of annually, as proposed in the conditions of the problem.

The answer given to the above example in PRICE'S STOCK TABLES, computed by logarithms, is 70% instead of $70\frac{1}{5}\%$, as given by the above rule.

If the rate per cent. to be realized be the same as the rate of interest on the bond, the *present value*, by the above rule, would be the *par value*. By *Price's Stock Tables* it would be at a premium; if 7%, and running 50 years, the premium would be $1\frac{69}{100}$ per cent.

Ex. 2. Money being worth 10% per annum, what is the present value of a 7% bond, interest payable semi-annually, running 20 years? *Ans.* $76\frac{06}{100}$ per cent.

By Price's Stock Tables. " $75\frac{95}{100}$ "

Note.—As the *ratio* only is sought, any convenient amount may be assumed for the face of the bond.

Ex. 3. In 1813 the United States government borrowed $16,000,000, selling their bonds to run 12 years, at 6% interest, payable semi-annually, at 12% discount. At what discount should the purchasers have taken them, to realize on their investment an average annual interest of 8%?

Ans. $14\frac{386}{1501}\%$.

REMARK.—It is manifest that, if a corporation sells in New York its bonds, drawing 7% interest, for less than par value, it is borrowing money at a higher rate of interest than the legal rate, and the contract under the general law of that State, regulating interest, becomes tainted with usury. But for the accommodation of corporations, and the security of capitalists investing in such bonds, it was enacted by the Legislature of New York, in 1850, that "no corporation shall hereafter interpose the defense of usury in any action." With this restriction upon them, corporations can negotiate their bonds more readily and at better rates than without such restriction. A large class of individual borrowers desire a similar legal prohibition for a like accommodation.

EQUATION OF PAYMENTS.

ART. **139.** *Equation of payments* is the process of finding the mean or average time for the payment of several sums of money due at different dates. The mean or average time sought is called the *equated time.*

The common methods of finding the equated time are based upon the principle that money kept *after* it is due is counterbalanced by an equal sum of money paid the same length of time *before* it is due.

This principle obviously depends upon another which may be expressed as follows: The payment of $100 down, and $100 in two years without interest *is equivalent* to the payment of $212 in two years, without interest, the rate of interest being 6 per cent.; or to express the same abstractly, the *use* of any sum of money is worth its *interest* for the time it is used.

ART. **140.** To find the equated time for the payment of several sums of money with different terms of credit.

Ex. 1. A owes B $1200, of which $300 is due in 4 months, $400 in 6 months and $500 in 12 months. What is the equated time for the payment of the whole sum?

FIRST METHOD.

$$\begin{array}{rl} 300\times\ 4 &= 1200 \\ 400\times\ 6 &= 2400 \\ 500\times 12 &= 6000 \\ \hline 1200 &)9600 \\ & \overline{8} \text{ mos. } \textit{Ans.} \end{array}$$

Explanation.—Suppose the sums to be paid respectively, 4 months, 6 months, and 12 months before due. The *amount* to be paid will be $300—its discount for 4 months; $400—its discount for 6 months; and $500—its discount for 12 months. The interest or discount of $300 for 4 months equals the discount of $1 for 1200 months; the discount of $400 for 6 months equals the discount of \$1 for 2400 months; the discount of \$500 for 12 months equals the discount of \$1 for 6000 months; or, the discount on the whole sum equals the discount of \$1 for 1200 +2400+6000=9600 months. Now, the discount of \$1 for 9600 months equals the discount of \$1200 for one-twelve hundredths of 9600 months=8 months, the equated time.

RULE.—*Multiply each payment or debt by its time of credit, and divide the sum of the* PRODUCTS *by the sum of the* PAYMENTS.

Note.—1. By the term discount, as used above, is meant mercantile discount or *simple interest.*

2. If we suppose all the sums to be paid in 12 months, the time upon which the last debt becomes due, the amount to be paid will be \$300+its interest for 8 months, \$400+its interest for 6 months, and \$500, or \$1200+the interest of \$1 for 4800 months. It is plain the debts will be cancelled by paying \$1200 *four* months *before* the last debt is due; or, which is the same thing, eight months *after* the first debt is due.

For convenience we have commenced at first date and discounted.

SECOND METHOD.

Discount on	\$300 for 4	months,	at 6%	=\$ 6.00
"	400 for 6	"	"	= 12.00
"	500 for 12	"	"	= 30.00
Discount on \$1200				=\$48.00

\$12=Discount of \$1200 for 2 months
6= " 1200 for 1 "
48÷6=8. *Ans.* 8 months.

Explanation.—The interest of \$1200, or the sum of the payments, being \$6 a month, A is entitled to the use of \$1200 as many months as \$6 is contained times in \$48=8. Hence, 8 months is the equated time.

RULE.—*Find the interest of each payment, or debt, for its term of credit, and divide the amount of interest thus found by the interest of the sum of payments for one month or one day.*

Note.—As the result will be the same for any rate of interest, take that rate which is most convenient.

ART. **141.** That the equated time obtained by both of the above methods is correct, will appear from the following proofs:

First Proof.—By paying the $1200 at the close of 8 months A *gains* the use of $300 for 4 months=$6 interest, and $400 for 2 months=$4 interest, and *loses* the use of $500 for 4 months=$10 interest. Hence, A gains $6+$4=$10 interest, and loses $10 interest. On the other hand B *loses* $6 +4=$10 interest, and *gains* $10 interest.

Second Proof.—If neither payment should be made till the last debt is due A would then owe B $300+its interest for 8 months=$300+$12=$312; $400+its interest for 6 months =$400+$12=$412; and $500 without interest: that is, A would owe B in 12 months $312+$412+$500=$1224. Now, the present worth of $1224, four months before it is due, is $1200. Hence, A's paying B $1200 at the close of eight months is the same as his paying him $1224 in 12 months, or $300 in 4 months, $400 in 6 months, and $500 in 12 months.

Third Proof.—If A should pay each debt when it is due, and B lend the money received to C, at the time A's last payment is due C would owe B $24 interest. If A should pay the *sum* of the debts, or $1200, at the equated time (8 months), and B lend as before, he would also receive from C $24 interest. Hence, the amount of interest is the same in either case, and 8 months is an equitable time for the payment of the debts.

The correctness of the above methods is called in question by a number of good authors. I can account for this only by the well known fact that a specious error, well authenticated and often repeated, sometimes passes current among good scholars, without being submitted to the rigid test of examination. The following is the common method of demonstrating the incorrectness of the above methods of finding the equated time:

"If I owe a man $200, $100 of which is now due, and the other hundred in two years, the equated time is not *one* year. For in deferring the payment of the first $100 one year I ought to pay the *amount* of $100 for the time, which is $106; but for the \$100 which I pay one year before it is due, I ought to pay the *present worth* of \$100, which is \$94.35$\frac{51}{53}$; and \$106 + \$94.35$\frac{51}{53}$ = \$200.33$\frac{51}{53}$; whereas by the mercantile method I only pay \$200."

This argument is fallacious. For *if* I ought to pay the present worth (\$94.33$\frac{51}{56}$) of the \$100, I pay one year before it is due, I ought *not* to pay the amount (\$106) of the \$100 I pay one year after it is due. The \$6 interest in this amount is not due until the close of the two years. I ought to pay \$100 + the present worth of \$6 due in one year, which is \$5.66$\frac{2}{53}$; and \$100 + \$5.66$\frac{2}{53}$ + \$94.33$\frac{51}{53}$ = \$200.

The mistake is in considering the sums of money payable at different times as *separate* from each other; whereas, by the very nature of the problem of finding a *common time* of payment, they must be regarded as parts of the *same contract*. Suppose, for example, I buy a horse, and agree to pay \$100 in one hour, and \$100 in two years, without interest. Failing to pay the \$100 due in one hour until the close of one year, which I then pay *without interest*, how much must I pay at the close of the second year? Evidently \$106 (if the legal rate is 6), since I paid at the close of one year only the principal (\$100), leaving the interest (\$6) unpaid, which cannot draw interest. Now, in finding the equated time for the payment of several debts due at different dates, the question is to find a time for the payment of the several *principals without interest*. Instead of paying the *amount* of \$100 in the problem proposed, the principal alone is paid.

The following is given by these authors as the "only accurate rule:"

"*Find the present worth of each of the given amounts due; then find in what time the sum of these present worths will amount to the sum of all the payments.*"

The inaccuracy of this "accurate rule," tested by the logic of its authors, will appear from the following:

The equated time for the payment of \$200, \$100 of which is now due, and the other \$100 due in two years, as found by this rule, is 11.32075 months. Now, the amount of \$100 for

11.32075 months, at 6 per cent., is $105.660387; the present worth of the other $100, due in 12.67925 months, is $94.03832, and $105.660387+94.03832=$199.698707, whereas it ought be $200.

It is also evident that the equated time, as found by this "accurate" rule, will not be the same for all rates of interest. At 50 per cent. the equated time of the above example is 8 months, and the error, by the above test, $8.33⅓; at 100 per cent. it is 6 months, with an error of $10.

This supposed accurate rule is based upon the principle that the amount to be paid on a debt due at a future date, without interest, *at any time previous to this date*, is the *present worth* of the debt at any prior date, plus the interest of the present worth up to date of payment. The incorrectness of this principle is easily shown. Suppose I owe a man $100, due in two years, without interest; how much ought I to pay in one year?

The present worth of $100, due in two years (at 6 per cent.), is $89.2857, and the interest on this sum for one year is $5.3571; hence the sum to be paid is $89.2857+$5.3571=$94.6428. The true amount to be paid, however, is the present worth of $100, due in one year, which is $94.339.

In finding the equated time for the payment of a bill of goods or of an account current, the exact number of days between the different dates is used. The pupil may commence with the first dates or with the last. In commencing with the first dates, each item, except the first, is subject to *discount;* if the last date is taken, each item, except the last, draws *interest.*

Ex. 2. A merchant sold goods to one of his customers, at different dates, as by the statement annexed. What is the average time for the payment of the same?

June 16, 1858,	a bill	amounting	to	$500,	no credit.
" 30,	"	"	"	220	"
July 30,	"	"	"	300	"
Aug. 15,	"	"	"	250	"
Sept. 1,	"	"	"	112	"
Oct. 1,	"	"	"	100	"

OPERATION BY FIRST METHOD.

			days.	days.
June 16,	1858,	$500 ×	00=	
" 30,	"	220 ×	14=	3080
July 30,	"	300 ×	44=	13200
Aug. 15,	"	250 ×	60=	15000
Sept. 1,	"	112 ×	77=	8624
Oct. 1,	"	100 ×	107=	10700
		1482		50604 | 34 days.
				4446
				6144
				5928

Counting forward 34 days from June 16, the date of the first bill, we have July 20, the equated time for the payment of the above bills.

Note.—A little reflection will make it evident that the above example is similar to one requiring the equated time for the payment of $500 cash ; $220 due in 14 days ; $300 due in 44 days ; $250 due in 60 days ; $112 due in 77 days ; and $100 due in 107 days. The average date of *purchase* of several bills is found in the same manner.

OPERATION BY SECOND METHOD.

				days.	dis.
June 16,	1853,	$500	for	00=	
" 30,	"	220	"	14=	$ .51
July 30,	"	300	"	44=	2.20
Aug. 15,	"	250	"	60=	2.50
Sept. 1,	"	112	"	77=	1.44
Oct. 1,	"	100	"	107=	1.78
		$1482			$8.43

$14.82 dis. for 60 days.
.247 " 1 day.

.247) 8.430 (34 *Ans.* 34 days.
7.41
1.020
.988
32

Counting forward 34 days from June 16, we have July 20, the equated time.

Note.—As the result will be the same for any rate of interest (discount), it is generally most convenient to compute the interest at 6 per cent. When the time is in days, as in the second example, the interest is readily found *by removing the point, or separatrix, two places to the left, and taking such aliquot parts of the result as the given days are of 60 days.*

Suppose, for example, we wish to find the interest of \$230.60 for 39 days. Since $39=30+6+3$, the interest for 39 days will be the sum of $\frac{1}{2}$, $\frac{1}{10}$ and $\frac{1}{20}$ of the interest for 60 days.

Thus:	Interest for 60 days		=\$2.306
	" " 30 "	($\frac{1}{2}$) =	1.153
	" " 6 "	($\frac{1}{10}$) =	.231
	" " 3 "	($\frac{1}{20}$) =	.115
	" " 39 "		=\$1.50

Note.—2. If the equated time contains a fraction greater than $\frac{1}{2}$ add 1 to the number of days; if less than $\frac{1}{2}$ disregard it.

Examples.

3. I owe \$450, due in 6 months; \$300, due in 8 months; \$125 due in 10 months; and \$100, due in 12 months. What is the equated time for payment? *Ans.* $7\frac{29}{39}$ months.

4. Bought a farm for \$3500; $\frac{1}{2}$ of it is to be paid down, $\frac{1}{5}$ of it in 8 months, $\frac{1}{5}$ in 12 months, and the remainder in 15 months, without interest. What is the equated time for the payment of the whole? *Ans.* $5\frac{1}{2}$ months.

5. A merchant owes a bank \$1500, of which \$300 is due in 30 days, \$250 in 45 days, \$350 in 60 days, \$450 in 80 days, and \$150 in 90 days. What is the equated time for the payment of the whole? *Ans.* 61 days.

6. Bought of Ivison & Phinney the following bills of goods:

June 3, 1858,	a bill	amounting	to	\$300
July 1,	"	"	"	220
" 20,	"	"	"	400
Aug. 15,	"	"	"	330
Sept. 13,	"	"	"	240

What is the *average date* of purchase? *Ans.* July 22.

7. A merchant has charged on his ledger \$120, due May 15, 1858; \$90, due July 3, 1858; \$75, due Aug. 30, 1858; \$60, due Sept. 10, 1858; \$160, due Oct. 18, 1858; \$150, due

Dec. 20, 1858. What is the equated time for the payment of these accounts? *Ans.* Sept. 10.

ART. **142.** To find the equated time for the payment of several sales, made at different dates, and for different terms of credit.

Ex. 1. James Russell bought of Fink, Hall & Co., several bills of goods, as below stated:

April 3,	1858, a bill of	$220,	on 3	months' credit.
May 1,	" "	125,	on 5	" "
" 15,	" "	200,	on 6	" "
June 24,	" "	140,	on 8	" "
July 1,	" "	190,	on 9	" "

What is the equated time of payment?

Operation.

```
                                days.    days.
Due, July  3, 1858, $220 ×  00=
 "   Oct.  1,   "     125 ×  90=  11250
 "   Nov. 15,   "     200 × 135=  27000
 "   Feb. 24, 1859,   140 × 236=  33040
 "   April 1,   "     190 × 272=  51680
                      875       )122970(141 nearly.
                                 875
                                 3547
                                 3500
                                  470
```

The equated time for the payment of the above bills is 141 days from July 3, which is Nov. 21.

METHOD BY DISCOUNT.

```
                                      dis.
Due, July  3, 1858, $220 for  00=
 "   Oct.  1,   "     125 for  90=$ 1.88
 "   Nov. 15,   "     200 for 135=  4.50
 "   Feb. 24, 1859,   140 for 236=  5.51
 "   April 1,   "     190 for 272=  8.61
                    $875   .1458 )$20.5000(141 days.
                     8.75          1458
                  (1/60).1458       5920
                                    5832
                                     880
```

141 days from July 3, is Nov. 21, the equated time as above.

Explanation.—The bill of $220 falls due 3 months from April 3, which is July 3; the bill of $125 falls due 5 months from May 1, which is Oct. 1, and so on: the *time of maturity* of each bill being found by adding its term of credit to its date of purchase. The *average* time of maturity is the equated time for the payment of the bills.

RULE.—*First find the* MATURITY *of each bill* (*or the time when it falls due*) *and then proceed as in the previous case. The equated time is found by counting forward from the date of the first amount falling due.*

Notes.—1. The bill having the earliest *date* does not always fall *due* first. It sometimes happens that the term of credit of the first bill is longer than that of the succeeding bills. It is most convenient to arrange the statement of maturity so that the bill *maturing* first shall stand first.

2. The equated time for the payment of several bills may be found by commencing at *the last date and finding how long each bill draws interest.* Thus, the last example may be equated as follows:

			days.	days.
Due, April 1, 1859,	$190 ×	00 =		
" Feb. 24, "	140 ×	36 =	5040	
" Nov. 15, 1858,	200 ×	137 =	27400	
" Oct. 1, "	125 ×	182 =	22750	
" July 2, "	220 ×	273 =	60060	
	875		)115250(132 nearly.	

```
875 )115250(132 nearly.
      875
      2775
      2625
       1500
```

The equated time is 132 days previous to April 1, 1859, which is Nov. 20, 1858. The difference of *one* day between the results of the two methods is due to the fractional parts of days being omitted.

Examples.

2. T. W. Cook & Co. sold to Murray & Co. several bills of goods, as shown in the statement annexed. What is the average time of maturity?

April 15, 1857, a bill amounting to $450, on 5 months' credit.
June 16, " " " 560, on 2 " "
July 31, " " " 180, on 6 " "
Sept. 19, " " " 760, on 5 " "

Ans. Nov. 19.

3. Bought goods of Smith & Moore, at sundry times, and on different terms of credit, as follows ?

Dec.	18, 1857,	a bill of	$375.50,	on 6 months' credit.
Jan.	10, 1858,	"	290.60,	on 6 " "
March	13, "	"	800.00,	on 8 " "
April	30, "	"	650.80,	on 7 " "
June	15, "	"	460.25,	on 4 " "

What is the equated time for the payment of the whole ?

Ans. Oct. 8, 1858.

4. O. Blake & Co. sold goods to J. B. Foster, at sundry times, and on different terms of credit, as follows :

Sept.	30, 1858,	a bill of	$ 80.75,	on 4 months' credit.
Nov.	3, "	"	150.00,	on 5 " "
Jan.	1, 1859,	"	30.80,	on 6 " "
March	10, "	"	40.50,	on 5 " "
April	25, "	"	60.30,	on 4 " "

How much will balance the account June 2, 1859 ?

Ans. $364.04.

Note.—The equated time for the payment of the above account is May 5, 1859 ; hence the several bills above are equivalent to a bill of $362.35 due May 5. It is evident that the $362.35 should draw interest from May 5 to June 2, the time of settlement. When it is required to know the amount due at any date *previous* to the equated time, the *present worth** of the sum of the several bills must be found.

5. A merchant sold to one of his customers several bills of goods, as follows :

May	9, 1857,	a bill of	$340	on 4 months' credit.
June	6, "	"	400	on 3 " "
July	8, "	"	345	on 5 " "
Aug.	30, "	"	130	on 5 " "
Sept.	30, "	"	240	on 6 " "

How much money will balance the account Jan 1, 1858 ?

Ans. $1466.40.

6. J. D. Stuart bought of Geo. A. Davis & Co. several bills of goods, as follows :

* The mercantile method of finding the present worth in such cases is to deduct *interest* for the time.

March 3, 1850,	a bill of	$250, on 3	months' credit.
April 15,	" "	180, on 4	" "
June 20,	" "	325, on 3	" "
Aug. 10,	" "	80, on 3	" "
Sept. 1,	" "	100, on 4	" "

What is the equated time of payment, and how much money would balance the account July 1, 1850?

Ans. Aug. 30; $925.65.

7. Purchased goods of a merchant at sundry times and on different terms of credit, as follows:

Nov. 9, 1857,	a bill of	$ 20.00 on 5	months' credit.
" 30,	" "	50.60 on 3	" "
Dec. 31,	" "	90.00 on 4	" "
Feb. 1, 1858,	"	120.00 on 3	" "

What is the average date of *purchase*, and what the average time of *maturity*? *Ans.* to first Jan. 4, 1858.

8. A merchant sold goods to one of his customers, as stated below:

April 6, 1857,	a bill of	$450, on 4	months' credit.
May 12,	" "	600	" "
June 20,	" "	750	" "
Aug. 1,	" "	300	" "

When must a note for the whole be made payable?

Note.—When the sales have the *same* term of credit, as in the above example, it is most convenient to find *first the average date of purchase.* The equated time of payment is then readily found by adding the common term of credit to this average date of purchase. The average date of purchase in the above example is 54 days from April 6, which is May 30; the equated time of payment is 4 months from May 30, which is Sept. 30.

The days of grace generally allowed may be added to the equated time.

9. Sold John Smith, on a credit of 90 days, the following bills of goods:

Jan. 10, 1858,	a bill of	$20.
April, 12,	" "	45.
May 27,	" "	60.
June 30,	" "	75.

What is the equated time of payment? *Ans.* July 13, 1858.

10. Purchased goods of Stratton & Co, at different dates, and on a credit of 6 months, as below stated :

Oct. 12,	1858,	a bill of	$460	on 6 months'	credit.
" 30,	"	"	95	"	"
Dec. 1,	"	"	180	"	"
" 25,	"	"	390	"	"
Jan. 20,	"	"	410	"	"

How much money will balance the account July 1, 1858 ?

Ans. $1542.907.

ART. **143.** To find what extension should be granted to the balance of a debt, partial payments having been made before the debt was due.

Ex. A owed B $1200, due in 6 months, but to accomodate him paid $400 in 2 months. When ought the balance to be paid ? *Ans.* in 8 months.

Explanation.—Since A paid B $400 four months *before* it was due, B, at the close of the 6 months, owed A the interest of $1 for 400×4 months$=1600$ months. To balance this interest due A, he can keep the $800 unpaid $\frac{1}{800}$ of 1600 months $=2$ months after the debt is due.

Ex. 2. Singer & Morton sold Wm. Williams, June 10, 1858, goods to the amount of $1300, on 6 months credit. Aug. 20, Mr. Williams paid $200 ; Sept. 18, $250 ; Oct. 30, $350. When, in equity, ought the balance to be paid ?

Operation.

		days.		
200	×	112	=	22400
250	×	83	=	20750
350	×	41	=	14350
$800				57500

$57500\div500=115$

The balance ought to be paid 115 days from Dec. 10, 1858, which is April 4, 1859.

RULE.—*Multiply each payment by the time it was paid before due, and divide the sum of the products by the balance unpaid.*

3. A sold B, July 1, 1858, goods to the amount of $1500, on a credit of 90 days. Aug. 5, B paid $400 ; Sept. 3, $600; Sept. 15, $300. When ought B to pay the balance.

Ans. April 26, 1859.

4. A merchant sells a customer to the amount of $600, $\frac{1}{2}$ of which is to be paid in 3 months, $\frac{1}{3}$ in 4 months, and the balance in 7 months. The customer pays $\frac{1}{2}$ down. How long may he keep, in equity, the remainder? *Ans.* $7\frac{2}{3}$ months.

5. A owes B $600, payable in 6 months. At the close of 3 months he wishes to make a payment so as to extend the time of the balance to one year. How great a payment must B make? *Ans.* $400.

Explanation.—B wishes to pay such a sum of money three months *before* it is due, as will extend another sum 6 months *after* it is due. It is evident the sum *paid* must be twice as great as the sum *extended.* Divide $600 into two parts, which shall be to each other as 2 to 1.

6. A owes B $1000, payable in 6 months. At the close of 2 months A pays B $1200, and B gives A his note for the balance. When ought the note to be dated?

Ans. 24 months back.

Explanation.—Since B paid A $1200 four months before the $1000 was due, A, at the close of the 6 months, owed B the interest of $1200 for 4 months, or $1 for 4800 months. It is evident that a note for the balance, $1200—$1000=$200, must be dated $\frac{1}{200}$ of 4800 months, or 24 months *previous* to the time the $1000 was due.

7. July 10, 1858, A paid B $600; Sept. 12, 1858, B paid A $800. When ought A to pay the balance?

Explanation.—Sept. 12, B owed A $600+its interest for 64 days. He paid A $600+$200. Hence, A is entitled to the use of the balance ($200) until its interest equals the interest of $600 for 64 days, or 192 days. 192 days from Sept. 12, 1858, is March 23, 1859.

8. July 10, 1858, A paid B $800; Sept. 12, 1858, B paid A $600. What should be the date of a note for the balance?

Explanation.—Sept. 12, B owed A $800+its interest for 64 days. He paid A but $600. Hence, he owes A the balance ($200) and the interest of $800 for 64 days, or the interest of $200 for 256 days. A note for the balance must therefore be dated 256 days *previous* to Sept. 12, 1858, which is Dec. 30, 1857.

Remark.—The above eight examples, if well understood, will aid the student in equating accounts which contain both *debits and credits.*.

EQUATION OF ACCOUNTS.

ART. **144.** Equation of accounts (also called "Averaging of Accounts," and "Compound Equation of Payments") is the process of finding the equated time for the payment of the balance of an account that contains both *debits* and *credits.*

Since the debit and credit sides of an account are respectively equivalent to the sum of their several items, due at the *equated time* (See Note, page 213), the *first step* in equating accounts is to find the time when each side of the account becomes due.

This may be found by equating each side of the account, *without any reference to the other*, commencing either at the *first* or the *last* date of each, or by using the *first* or *last* date of the account as a common *starting-point* for both sides.

The solution of the following example will sufficiently illustrate these two methods of equating the debit and credit sides of an account.

Note.—In the following solution we have commenced at the first date and discounted:

Ex. 1.

Dr. Fisk, Hull & Co. in account with Jas. Russell. *Cr.*

1858.			Time of credit.	1858.		
April 3	To Mdse.	$220	3 mo.	July 1	By Cash.	$200
May 1	"	125	5 "	Oct. 3	"	150
" 15	"	200	6 "	Dec. 20	"	300
June 24	"	140	8 "			
July 1	"	190	9 "			

FIRST METHOD.

Debits.

Due,		
July 3, 1858,	$220 × 00=	
Oct. 1, "	125 × 90=	11250
Nov. 15, "	200 × 135=	27000
Feb. 24, 1859,	140 × 236=	33040
April 1, "	190 × 272=	51680
	$875	)122970
		141 ds.

Debits are due 141 days from July 3, which is Nov. 21.

Credits.

Due,		
July 1, 1858,	$200 × 00=	
Oct. 3, "	150 × 94=	14100
Dec. 20, "	300 × 172=	51600
	$650	)65700
		101 ds.

Credits are due 101 days from July 1, which is Oct. 10.

The above account thus equated will stand as follows :

Dr.	*Cr.*
Due, Nov. 21, 1858, $875.	Due, Oct. 10, 1858, $650.

Or thus :

Debits.

Due,		
July 3, 1858,	$220 × 2=	440
Oct. 1, "	125 × 92=	11500
Nov. 15, "	200 × 137=	27400
Feb. 24, 1859,	140 × 238=	33320
April 1, "	190 × 274=	52060
	$875	)124720
		143 ds.

Debits due 143 days from July 1, which is Nov. 21.

Credits.

Due,		
July 1, 1858,	$200 × 00=	
Oct. 3, "	150 × 94=	14100
Dec. 20, "	300 × 172=	51600
	$650	)65700
		101 ds.

Credits due 101 days from July 1, which is Oct. 10.

The account thus equated stands as before :

Dr.	*Cr.*
Due, Nov. 21, $875.	Due, Oct. 10, $1650.

Note.—In the above operation, we start from the earliest date upon which any item of either side of the account *becomes due.*

The next step is to find when the balance of the account, as thus equated, becomes due.

Debits, ...	$875	650
Credits, . . .	650	42
Balance, . . .	$225	1300
Difference in time 42 days.		2600
		225)27300
		121 days.

Or thus, by Discount:

$6.50	$4.55÷.0375 (dis. of $225 for 1 day)=121 days.
3.25 Dis. for 30 days.	
1.30 " 12 "	
$4.55 Dis. for 42 days.	

Balance is due 121 days from Nov. 21, 1858, which is March 22, 1859.

Explanation.—Assume the account settled Nov. 21, the *latest* date. The credit side of the account has been due from Oct. 10 to Nov. 12, or 42 days. Nov. 21, the credit side is equal to $650, and the interest of the same 42 days. That the debit side of the account may be increased by an equal amount of interest, it is evident that the balance of the account must remain unpaid 121 days, or the 121 days must be counted *forward* from Nov. 21.

Or thus:

The above account may be stated as follows: Oct. 10, 1858, James Russell paid Fisk, Hull & Co. $650; Nov. 21, 1858, Fisk, Hull & Co. paid James Russell $875. Now, since F., H. & Co. had the use of $650 for 42 days, J. H. is entitled to the use of $225 (the balance) until its interest equals the interest of $650 for 42 days, which is 121 days. 121 days from Nov. 21, 1858, is March 21, 1859.

Proof.

Dr.		*Cr.*	
Due Nov. 21, . .	$875	Due, Oct. 10, . .	$650
Int. to March 21, 1859,	17.65	Int. to March 21, 1859,	17.65
	$892.65	Balance, ...	225.
			$892.65

2. Suppose the debit and credit side of the above account, when equated, to stand as follows:

Dr.	*Cr.*
Due, Nov. 21, 1858, $650.	Due, Oct. 10, 1858, $875.

What is the equated time for the payment of the balance?

Credits, ...	$875	875
Debits, ...	650	42
Balance, ...	$225	225)36750(163 days.
Difference in time, 42 days.		225
		1425
		1350
		750
		675

Balance due 163 days *previous* to Nov. 21, 1858, which is June 11, 1858.

Explanation.—Suppose the account settled Nov. 21. The credit side is equal to $875, and its interest from Oct. 10 to Nov. 21, or 42 days. That the debit side of the account may be increased by an equal amount of interest, the balance of the account must be regarded as due 163 days *previous* to Nov. 21, or June 11.

Or thus :

Oct. 10, 1858, James Russell paid Fisk, Hull & Co. $875; Nov. 21, 1858, F., H. & Co. paid J. R. $650. Since F., H. & Co. had the use of $875 for 42 days, J. H. is entitled to the interest of $225 (the balance) for 163 days. Hence, the balance must be regarded as due 163 days *previous* to Nov. 21. The simple question is: How long must $225 be on interest to equal the interest of $875 for 42 days?

Note.—If Fisk, Hull & Co. should wish to give their note for the balance, it is evident the note must be dated June 11, 1858.

RULE.

First find the equated time for each side of the account without any reference to the other. Then multiply the side of the account which falls due FIRST *by the number of days between the dates of equated time, and divide the product by the balance of the account. The quotient will be the number of days to be counted* FORWARD *from the* LATEST DATE *when the* SMALLER *side of the account falls due* FIRST; *and* BACKWARD *when the* LARGER *side falls due* FIRST.

NOTE.—Some authors give the following *rule:*—Multiply the *smaller* side of the account by the number of days between the dates of equated time, and divide the product by the balance of the account. The quotient will be the time for consideration. From the equated date of the *larger* side, count FORWARD when that side becomes due *last*, but BACKWARD when it becomes due *first.*

ANOTHER METHOD.

ART. **145.** The equated time for the payment of the balance of an account may be found *directly* without first averaging the debit and credit items, by the following method:

Due,				Due,			
July 3, 1858,	$220 ×	2 =	440	July 1, 1858,	$200 ×	0 =	
Oct. 1, "	125 ×	92 =	11500	Oct. 3, "	150 ×	94 =	14100
Nov. 15, "	200 ×	137 =	27400	Dec. 20, "	300 ×	172 =	51600
Feb. 24, 1859,	140 ×	238 =	33320		$650		65700
April 1, "	190 ×	274 =	52060				
	$875		124720				
	650		65700				
	$225		59020				

59020÷225=262.

262 days from July 1, 1858, is March 21, 1858.

Explanation.—We assume July 1, 1858 (the earliest date upon which any item becomes due), as the time upon which *all* the items of the account becomes due. The interest of the debit items, from this assumed date of maturity to the time they respectively become due, equals the interest of $1 for 124720 days; the interest of the credit items equals the interest of $1 for 65700 days. Hence, the balance of interest in favor of the debit side equals the interest of $1 for 59020 days, or $225 for $\frac{1}{225}$ of 59020 days=262 days. Since the balance of items is also in favor of the debit side, it is evident it can remain unpaid 262 days without interest, or will become due 262 days from July 1, 1858, which is March 21, 1859. If the balance of items had been on the credit side it would have been due 262 days *previous* to July 1, 1858.

RULE.

Assume the earliest date upon which any item of the account becomes due to be the time of maturity for all the items.

Multiply each item by the number of days intervening between this assumed date and the date upon which it becomes due, and find the sum of these products on each side of the ac-

count. Then divide the DIFFERENCE *between the sums of the debit and credit products by the balance of the account; the quotient will be the time for consideration.*

When the difference of products and the balance of the account fall on the SAME *side count* FORWARD; *when on* OPPOSITE *sides count* BACKWARD.

Note.—The *latest* date may be used as a starting-point.

Examples.

3. A has with B an account, which, when each side is equated, stands as follows:

Dr.	*Cr.*
Due, June 5, $1285.	Due, June 24, $1080.

What is the equated time of payment for the balance?

Ans. Feb. 25.

4. C has with D an account, the debit and credit sides of which, when equated, are as follows:

Dr.	*Cr.*
Due, Jan. 7, $325	Due Jan. 11, $1090.

What must be the date of a note for the balance?

Ans. Jan. 13.

5. What is the equated time for the payment of the balance of an account, which, when the two sides are equated, stands as follows:

Dr.	*Cr.*
Due, July 12, $450.	Due, Sept. 1, $800.

Ans. Nov. 6.

6. At what time will the balance of the following account commence drawing interest?

Cr.	*Dr.*
Due, Oct. 15, $1260	Due, Nov. 20, $900.

Ans. July 17.

7. What is the equated time for the payment of the balance of the following account, the merchandise items having a credit of 4 months?

Dr. R. Bill & Co. in account with Orvil Blake. *Cr.*

1858.				1859.			
May 1	To Mdse.	$850	70	Jan. 1	By Cash.	$500	00
June 6	"	340	75	Jan. 19	"	440	00
July 3	"	180	25	Feb. 1	"	100	00
Aug. 13	"	500	00	Feb. 15	"	980	00
20	"	340	40				
30	"	80	00				

Ans. 808 days back of Jan. 28, 1859.

Note.—In finding the equated time, when the cents are less than 50 reject them; when more, add $1. The work will be sufficiently accurate.

8. When will the balance of the following account commence drawing interest, allowing that each item was due from date? What will balance the account Oct. 1?

Dr. A in account with B. *Cr.*

1858.				1858.			
July 10	To Mdse.	$120	00	Aug. 20	By Cash.	$350	00
" 30	"	450	00	Sept. 25	" Mdse.	250	00
Aug. 30	"	380	00	Oct. 3	" Cash.	950	00
Sept. 9	"	560	00				
" 30	"	400	00				

Ans. to first, Dec. 12.

Remark.—Since the balance of the above account commences to draw interest at the *equated time* of the account, it is evident that the *cash value* of this balance, at any date *subsequent* to the equated time of the account, may be found *by adding to the balance its interest up to date;* and at any date *previous* to the equated time, *by deducting from the balance its interest for the intervening time.* By mercantile custom interest is deducted (as in the last case) instead of finding the *true present worth,* when money is paid before it is due.

9. When will the balance of the following account commence drawing interest? What will be the *cash value* of the balance, Jan. 1, 1859? Credit of 90 days on merchandise items.

Dr. B in account with C. *Cr.*

1858.				1858.			
Aug. 18	To Mdse.	$ 50	00	Oct. 7	By Cash.	$200	00
Sept. 15	"	140	00	" 30	"	100	00
" 30	"	80	00	Dec. 1	"	400	00
Oct. 8	"	200	00		"		
Nov. 1	"	350	00		"		

CASH BALANCE.

Art. **146.** When an account current is settled *by cash,* it is not necessary to find the equated time as in the preceding article. The *true or cash* balance of an account at a particular date may be found directly as follows:

Ex. 1.

Dr. Dr. Murray & Co. in account with Jones & Sons. *Cr.*

1859.			1859.		
April 10	To Mdse.	$150	April 12	By Cash.	$250
" 30	"	400	May 1	"	180
May 16	"	90	June 7	"	400
" 24	"	100	" 25	"	564
June 1	"	300			
" 10	"	340			
" 26	"	200			

What will be the true balance of the above account July 1, 1859, the time of settlement, allowing that each item draws interest from its date, at 6 per cent.?

Operation.

Debits. Due,	Days.		*Credits.* Due,		
April 10,	$150 × 82 =	12300	April 12,	$250 × 80 =	20000
" 30,	400 × 62 =	24800	May 1,	180 × 61 =	10980
May 16,	90 × 46 =	4140	June 7,	400 × 24 =	9600
" 24,	100 × 38 =	3800	" 25,	564 × 6 =	3384
June 1,	300 × 30 =	9000		$1394	6)43964
" 10,	340 × 21 =	7140			7.327
" 26,	200 × 5 =	1000			
	$1580	6)62180			
		$10.364			

Sum of debit items,	$1580	Int. of debit items,	$10.364
" credit "	1394	" credit "	7.327
Balance of items,	$186	Balance of interest,	$3.037

True balance, July 1, $186+$3.04=$189.04.

Explanation.—Since each item of the debit side of the account was on interest from its date to the time of settlement, the total interest of the several debit items equals the interest of $1 for 62180 days, which is $10.364. (The interest of $1 for 6 days is 1 mill; hence, the interest of $1 for 62180 days is found by dividing 62180 by 6, and pointing off three decimal places.) The total interest of the several credit items equals the interest of $1 for 43964 days, which is $7.327. Now, instead of increasing each side of the account by its interest, and then finding the balance, this same result may be obtained by finding separately the balance of items and the balance of interests. If the two balances fall on the same side of the account, it is evident the *true balance* will be their *sum;* if on different sides, their *difference.*

METHOD BY INTEREST.

Due,			Days.	Int.	Due,			Days.	Int.
April	10,	$150	for 82=	$2.05	April	12,	$250	for 80=	$3.333
"	30,	400	for 62=	4.133	May	1,	180	for 61=	1.83
May	16,	90	for 46=	.69	June	7,	400	for 24=	1.60
"	24,	100	for 38=	.634	"	25,	564	for 6=	.564
June	1,	300	for 30=	1.50			$1394		$7.327
"	10,	340	for 21=	1.19					
"	26,	200	for 5=	.17					
		$1580		$10.367					

Balance of items =$1580 −$1394 =$186.
" of interest=$10.367−$7.327= $3.04.
True balance, =$186 +$3.04 =$189.04.

Note.—The "method by interest" will generally be found most convenient either for finding the equated time for the payment of the balance of accounts, or in finding the cash balance.

The above account, when balanced by interest, may be presented as follows:

Dr. Murray & Co. in account with Jones & Sons. *Cr.*

1859.		Am't.	Ds.	Int	1859.		$250.00	Ds.	Int.
April 10	To Mdse.	$150.00	82	$2.05	April 12	By Cash.	180.00	80	$3.333
" 30	"	400.00	62	4.133	May 1	"	400.00	61	1.83
May 16	"	90.00	46	.69	June 7	"	564.00	24	1.60
" 24	"	100.00	38	.634	" 25	"	189.04	6	.564
June 1	"	300.00	30	1.50	July 1	bal. acc't.			$7.327
" 10	"	340.00	21	1.19					
" 26	"	200.00	5	.17					
July 1	bal. by int.	3.04		$10.367					
		$1583.04					$1583.04		

Errors excepted. Portsmouth, July 1, 1859. Jones & Son.

RULE.

Multiply each item of the account by the number of days intervening between the date on which it becomes due and the time of settlement. Divide the sums of the debit and credit products respectively by 6 : *the quotient will be the interest of the two sides of the account, at* 6 *per cent., expressed in* MILLS. *Find the balance of items and also the balance of interests.*

When the two balances fall on the SAME *side of the account, the cash balance will be their* SUM ; *when on opposite sides, their* DIFFERENCE.

Or,

Find the interest of each item from the date on which it becomes due to the time of settlement The difference between the sums of interests on the debit and credit sides of the account will be the BALANCE OF INTEREST.

When the balance of interest falls on the same side as the balance of items, the cash balance will be their SUM ; *when on opposite sides, their* DIFFERENCE.

2. The following account was settled July 1, 1857. What was the cash balance, interest being computed on each item from date at 7% ?

Dr. James Kehoe in account with J. Smith. *Cr.*

1857.			Ds.	Int. or prods.	1858.			Ds.	Int. or prods.
Jan. 7	To bal. of acc't.	$120.00			April 1	By cash.	$140.00		
" 15	" mdse.	96.75			" 30	" "	50.00		
" 24	" bills payable	130.50			May 20	" order on T. S.	140.00		
Feb. 27	" mdse.	200.80			" 31	" cash.	450.00		
March 7	" "	80.00			June 11	" Mdse.	500.00		
May 10	" "	300.00							
June 9	" "	240.75							

Ans.

3. What was due on the following account, Jan. 1, 1858, interest 6 per cent., and a credit of 90 days being allowed on each merchandise item?

Dr. John Scott in account with Geo. Fields. *Cr.*

1857.				Days.	Int. or products.	1857.				Days.	Int. or product.
July 3	To Mdse.	$104	85			Aug. 12	By Mdse.	$300	00		
" 16	"	340	60			" 25	" "	116	80		
" 31	"	67	50			Sept. 15	" "	339	75		
Sept. 13	"	236	80			Oct. 13	" Cash.	50	00		
" 20	"	90	38			Nov. 1	" "	148	75		
" 27	"	60	84								
Oct. 1	"	360	40								

Ans. $307.492.

4. What would have been the true balance of the above account Jan. 1, 1858, at 7 per cent., no credit being allowed on merchandise items? *Ans.* $316.563.

ACCOUNT OF SALES.

ART. **147.** An *account* of *sales* is a statement of the quantity and price of goods sold, the charges incurred in the sales, and the net proceeds, which a commission merchant or consignee makes to his employer or consignor.

The *net proceeds* is the sum to which the employer is entitled after all charges are deducted. The net proceeds are due as cash at the equated time of the different sales.

The following examples will give a fuller idea of an account of sales.

1. Account of sales of grain for Fisk, Cook & Co.

Date.		Purchaser.	Description.	Bush.	Price.	$
1858.						
Jan.	30	M. B. Gilbert.	Wheat, white.	250	$ .95	237.50
Feb.	3	Crest & Fisk.	Wheat, med.	1000	.88	880.00
"	16	Wheeler&Co.	Corn.	2000	.55	1100.00
"	28	C. A. Davis.	Oats.	1500	.37½	562.50
March	20	T. C. Skinner.	Wheat, Ky. white.	750	1.00	750.00
April	9	Talcott & Co.	Wheat, red.	1450	.85	1232.50
"	28	J. B. Howard.	Corn.	1300	.58	754.00
May	7	T. Benton.	"	450	.60	270.00
"	30	F. Hart.	Wheat, med.	955	.90	859.50
						$6646.00

Charges.

	Commission $2\frac{1}{2}$ per cent. on $6646,	$166.15	
May 30—	Freight on 955 bushels wheat, .	47.75	
	Drayage and sacks, . . .	51.00	
	Advertising in "Tribune," .	7.50	
			$272.40
	Net proceeds to credit of F. C. & Co.,		$6373.60

Errors excepted.

New York, June 1, 1858. SMITH & JONES.

2. Sales 544 barrels flour, for account of P. Rhodes & Son, Navarre, O., by Bryant & Stratton, Cleveland, O.

1858.		Monroe Extra.	Granite Mills.	Fine.						
July 2	P. Anderson.	400				8^{30}	3,320			
" "	"			19		5^{00}	95			
" 5	Morgan & Co.		125			7^{50}	937	50		
	Charges :	400	125	19					4,352	50
June 15	Trans. Boat "Kent."	400	125	19	=544 bls.	16	87	04		
	Less am't de	duc	ted	for	damage					
	on boat.						10			
							77	04		
	Storage.					3	16	32		
	Insurance.						10	88		
	Commission	on	43	52^{50}		$2\frac{1}{2}\%$	108	81		
									213	05
	Proceeds to	cre	dit	as	cash, Jul	y 10	1858.		4,139	45
									4,352	50

Cleveland, O., July 12, 1858. (Signed) BRYANT & STRATTON.

3. What will be due P. Rhodes & Son on the above account January 1, 1859?

4. Sales, 100 barrels linseed oil, for account of Robert Miller, Warren, O., by Bryant & Stratton, Cleveland, O.

1855.		Bls.	Gals.					
May 14	Cash.	10	403	95	382	85		
" "	Gaylord & Co.	30	1,200	92	1,104			
" 15	Cash.	5	201½	95	191	43		
" 18	"	55	2,200	90	1,980			
		100	4,004½				3,658	28
	Charges:							
" 13	Tr., Boat Cuyahoga.	100		37^{2}	37	50		
	Storage.			8¢	8			
	Fire Insurance.			1¼%	9	14		
	Cooperage.			2½%	2	50		
	Com. on 3658^{28}				91	46		
							148	60
	Net proceeds due as cash May 18, 1855.						3,509	68

Cleveland, O., (Signed) Bryant & Stratton.
May 24, 1855.

5. Sales of provisions for account of M. Fisher & Co., Cincinnati, O., by James & Co., St. Paul, Min.

1858.		Boxs & kegs.	Bls.	Pieces.		Pounds.			
Feb. 7	Wheeler & Co.			29	Hams, plain.	1450	8¢		
" 22	"			42	" sugar cured.	2300	10½¢		
Mar. 6	"			18	Shoulders, plain.	846	7½¢		
" 15	Altram & Co.		25		Mess pork, No. 2.		16^{50}		
Apr. 3	E. Miller.	15			Kegs butter, W. R.	840	16¢		
" "	"	80			Cheese.	4200	6¼¢		
" 10	Wheeler & Co.			150	Bacon sides.	2432	7½¢		
May 2	Altram & Co.		15		Mess pork, No. 2.		16^{50}		
" 5	Geo. Singer.			37	Shoulders (city).	2512	7¾¢		
		95	40	276		14,580			

Charges.

Feb. 1—Freight of 13,040, at 70¢. per 100.
April 2— " 5,040, " 68¢. "
Storage, 5^{50}. Cooperage, 3^{20}=880.
Fire Insurance, at ½% on $.
Commissions, " 2½% " $.
Net proceeds as cash, due ——

St. Paul's, Minnesota, Janes & Co.
May 15, 1858.

ANNUITIES.

ART. **148.** An *Annuity* (*L. annus,* a year) is a fixed sum of money payable annually, or at the end of equal periods of time, to continue for a given number of years, for life, or forever.

A certain Annuity, or an *Annuity certain,* is one that is payable for a definite length of time.

A contingent Annuity is one that is payable for an uncertain length of time; as during the life of one or more persons.

A perpetual Annuity, or an *Annuity in perpetuity,* is one that continues forever.

A deferred Annuity, or an *Annuity in reversion* (whether certain, contingent, or perpetual) is one that begins at a future time; as at the death of a certain person.

An *immediate Annuity,* or an *Annuity in possession,* is one that begins at once.

An Annuity *forborne,* or *in arrears,* is one whose payments have not been made when due.

The *amount,* or *final value,* of an annuity is the sum of the amounts of all its payments, at compound interest, from the time each is due, to the end of the annuity.

The *present value* of an annuity, at compound interest, is the sum of the present values of all its payments; or the present worth of its final value. The present value, put out at compound interest, will amount, at the time of the expiration of the annuity, to its final value.

The subject of annuities is one of great practical importance in the affairs of life. Its principal applications are leases, life-estates, rents, dowers, reversions, life-insurance, etc. The problems are readily solved by means of tables which give the present and final values of $1 for a given number of years at the ordinary rates of interest. A complete discussion of the principles upon which these tables are computed would require too much space.

Art. 149. A Table,

Showing the present value, and also the amount, or final value, of an annuity of $1, for any number of years not exceeding fifty:

Years.	Present value of an Annuity of $1. 4 per cent.	5 per cent.	6 per cent.	7 per cent.	Years.	Final value of an Annuity of $1. 4 per cent	5 per cent.	6 per cent.	7 per cent.
1	0.961 538	0.952 381	0.943 396	0.934 579	1	1.000 000	1.000 000	1.000 000	1.000 000
2	1.886 095	1.859 410	1.833 393	1.808 017	2	2.040 000	2.050 000	2.060 000	2.070 000
3	2.775 091	2.723 248	2.673 012	2.624 314	3	3.121 600	3.152 500	3.183 500	3.214 900
4	3.629 895	3.545 951	3.465 106	3.387 207	4	4.246 464	4.310 125	4.374 616	4.439 943
5	4.451 822	4.329 477	4.212 364	4.100 195	5	5.416 323	5.525 631	5.637 093	5.750 739
6	5.242 137	5.075 692	4.917 324	4.766 537	6	6.632 975	6.801 913	6.975 319	7.153 291
7	6.002 055	5.786 373	5.582 381	5.389 286	7	7.898 294	8.142 008	8.393 838	8.654 021
8	6.732 745	6.463 213	6.209 744	5.971 295	8	9.214 226	9.549 109	9.897 468	10.259 803
9	7.435 332	7.107 822	6.801 692	6.515 223	9	10.582 795	11.026 564	11.491 316	11.977 989
10	8.110 896	7.721 735	7.360 087	7.023 577	10	12.006 107	12.577 893	13.180 795	13.816 448
11	8.760 477	8.306 414	7.886 875	7.498 669	11	13.486 351	14.206 787	14.971 643	15.783 599
12	9.385 074	8.863 252	8.383 844	7.942 671	12	15.025 805	15.917 127	16.869 941	17.888 451
13	9.985 648	9.393 573	8.852 683	8.357 635	13	16.626 838	17.712 983	18.882 138	20.140 643
14	10.563 123	9.898 641	9.294 984	8.745 452	14	18.291 911	19.598 632	21.015 066	22.550 488
15	11.118 387	10.379 658	9.712 249	9.107 898	15	20.023 588	21.578 564	23.275 970	25.129 022
16	11.652 296	10.837 770	10.105 895	9.446 632	16	21.824 531	23.657 492	25.670 528	27.888 054
17	12.165 669	11.274 066	10.477 260	9.763 206	17	23.697 512	25.840 366	28.212 880	30.840 217
18	12.659 297	11.689 587	10.827 603	10.059 070	18	25.645 413	28.132 385	30.905 653	33.999 033
19	13.133 939	12.085 321	11.158 116	10.335 578	19	27.671 229	30.539 004	33.759 992	37.378 965
20	13.590 326	12.462 210	11.469 421	10.593 997	20	29.778 079	33.065 954	36.785 591	40.995 492
21	14.029 160	12.821 153	11.764 077	10.835 527	21	31.969 202	35.719 252	39.992 727	44.865 177
22	14.451 115	13.163 003	12.041 582	11.061 241	22	34.247 970	38.505 214	43.392 290	49.005 739
23	14.856 842	13.488 574	12.303 379	11.272 187	23	36.617 889	41.430 475	46.995 828	53.436 141
24	15.246 963	13.798 642	12.550 358	11.469 334	24	39.082 604	44.501 999	50.815 577	58.176 671
25	15.622 080	14.093 945	12.783 356	11.653 583	25	41.645 908	47.727 099	54.864 512	63.249 030
26	15.982 769	14.375 185	13.003 166	11.825 779	26	44.311 745	51.113 454	59.156 383	68.676 470
27	16.329 586	14.643 034	13.210 534	11.986 709	27	47.084 214	54.669 126	63.705 766	74.483 823
28	16.663 063	14.898 127	13.406 164	12.137 111	28	49.967 583	58.402 583	68.528 112	80.697 691
29	16.983 715	15.141 074	13.590 721	12.277 674	29	52.966 286	62.322 712	73.639 798	87.346 529
30	17.292 033	15.372 451	13.764 831	12.409 041	30	56.084 938	66.438 848	79.058 186	94.460 786
31	17.588 494	15.592 811	13.929 086	12.531 814	31	59.328 335	70.760 790	84.801 677	102.073 041
32	17.873 552	15.802 667	14.084 043	12.646 555	32	62.701 469	75.298 829	90.889 778	110.218 154
33	18.147 646	16.002 549	14.230 230	12.753 790	33	66.209 527	80.063 771	97.343 165	118.933 425
34	18.411 198	16.192 204	14.368 141	12.854 069	34	69.857 909	85.066 959	104.183 755	128.258 765
35	18.664 613	16.374 194	14.498 246	12.947 672	35	73.652 225	90.320 307	111.434 780	138.236 878
36	18.908 282	16.546 852	14.620 987	13.035 208	36	77.598 314	95.836 323	119.120 867	148.913 460
37	19.142 579	16.711 287	14.736 780	13.117 017	37	81.702 246	101.628 139	127.268 119	160.337 400
38	19.367 864	16.867 893	14.846 019	13.193 473	38	85.970 336	107.709 546	135.904 206	172.561 020
39	19.584 485	17.017 041	14.949 075	13.264 928	39	90.409 150	114.095 023	145.058 458	185.640 292
40	19.792 774	17.159 086	15.046 297	13.331 709	40	95.025 516	120.799 774	154.761 966	199.635 112
41	19.993 052	17.294 368	15.138 016	13.394 120	41	99.826 536	127.839 763	165.047 684	214.609 570
42	20.185 627	17.423 208	15.224 543	13.452 449	42	104.819 598	135.231 751	175.950 645	230.632 24[illegible]
43	20.370 795	17.545 912	15.306 173	13.506 962	43	110.012 382	142.993 339	187.507 577	247.776 496
44	20.548 841	17.662 773	15.383 182	13.557 908	44	115.412 877	151.143 006	199.758 032	266.120 851
45	20.720 040	17.774 070	15.455 832	13.605 522	45	121.029 392	159.700 156	212.743 514	285.749 311
46	20.884 654	17.880 067	15.524 370	13.650 020	46	126.870 568	168.685 164	226.508 125	306.751 763
47	21.042 936	17.981 016	15.589 028	13.691 608	47	132.945 390	178.119 422	241.098 612	329.224 [illegible]
48	21.195 131	18.077 158	15.650 027	13.730 474	48	139.263 206	188.025 393	256.564 529	353.270 [illegible]
49	21.341 472	18.168 722	15.707 572	13.766 799	49	145.833 734	198.426 663	272.958 401	378.999 00[illegible]
50	21.482 185	18.255 925	15.761 861	13.800 746	50	152.667 084	209.347 976	290.335 905	406.528 929

ART. **150.** To find the amount, or final value, of an annuity certain, at compound interest, in arrears, or forborne.

Ex. 1. Suppose a rental of $500 a year to remain unpaid 8 years; what is the amount due, at 5 per cent. compound interest? *Ans.* $47745.545.

Operation.

$9.549109, amount of $1 for 8 years. (See Table).
500
$47.745.545; " $500 '

RULE.—*Multiply the amount, or final value, of an annuity of* $1, *for the given rate and time, by the given annuity.*

Note.—When the annuity draws *simple interest*, the amount is found as in *annual interest.*

Ex. 2. Find the final value of an annuity of $150, running 12 years at 4 per cent. compound interest.

Ans. $2253.87+.

Ex. 3. An annuity of $200 has been in arrears 15 years; what is the amount due, at 6 per cent. compound interest?

Ans. $4655.194.

ART. **151.** To find the present value of an *annuity certain.*

Ex. 1. What is the present value of an annuity of $120, to continue 25 years, at 6 per cent.? *Ans.* $1534.

Operation.

$12.783356, present value of $1. (See Table.)
120
$1534.002720 " $120.

RULE.—*Multiply the present value of* $1, *as an annuity for the given rate and time, by the given annuity.*

Note.—Since the present value of an annuity is the *present worth* of its *amount*, or final value, the present value of an annuity may also be found by first finding the amount, and then the present worth of this amount.

Ex. 2. What is the present value of an annuity of $650, to continue 15 years, at 5 per cent.? *Ans.* $6746.7777.

Ex. 3. What is the present worth of a leasehold of $1200, payable annually for 50 years, at 6 per cent. ?

Ans. $18914.23.

Ex. 4. A widow is entitled to $140 a year, payable semi-annually, for 18 years ; what is the present value of her interest, at 10 per cent compound interest ? *Ans.* $1158.80.

Ex. 5. I wish to purchase an annuity which shall secure to my ward, at 4 per cent. compound interest, $250 a year for 14 years. What must I deposit in the annuity office ?

Ans. $2640.78.

ART. **152.** To find the present value of a *perpetuity.*

Ex. 1. What is the present value of a perpetual leasehold of $1200 a year, at 5 per cent. ? *Ans.* $24000.

Operation.

$1200.00÷.05=$24000, present value.

Explanation.—The present value must evidently be a principal which yields an annual interest of $1200, at 5 per cent.

RULE.—*Divide the given annuity by the interest of* $1, *for one year.*

Ex. 2. What is the present value of the perpetual lease of $4800 a year, at 8 per cent. interest ? *Ans.* $60000.

Ex. 3. What is the present value of a perpetual leasehold of $1600 a year, payable semi-annually, at 6 per cent. interest per annum ? *Ans.* $27066⅔.

Suggestion.—When an annuity is payable semi-annually, or quarterly, interest must be allowed on the half-yearly or quarterly payments to the close of the year. The annuity in the last example is $1624.

Ex. 4. The ground rent of an estate yields an annual income of $2400, payable quarterly, at 4 per cent. per annum. What is the value of the estate ? *Ans.* $60900.

ART. **153.** To find the present value of a certain annuity *in reversion.*

Ex. 1. What is the present value of an annuity of $250, deferred 12 years and to continue 10 years, allowing 6 per cent. compound interest ? *Ans.* $914.43+.

Operation.

\$12.041582—present worth of	\$1	for 22 yrs.	
8.383844 "	"	12 yrs.	
\$3.657738 "	"	10 yrs. deferred 12 yrs.	
250			
\$914.434500 "	\$250	"	"

Explanation.—The present worth of an annuity of \$1 for 22 years must be equal to its present worth for 12 years, *plus* its present worth for the 10 succeeding years. Hence the present worth of an annuity of \$1 for 10 years deferred 12 years must equal its present worth for 22 years, *minus* its present worth for 12 years. The present worth of \$250 is evidently 250 times the present worth of \$1.

RULE.—*Find from the table the present value of an annuity of* \$1, *commencing at once and continuing till the* TERMINATION *of the annuity, and also till the reversion* COMMENCES. *Multiply the differences of these present values by the given annuity.*

Note.—If the annuity is *perpetual*, the present worth of \$1, commencing at once, is found according to the last article.

Ex. 2. What is the present value of a leasehold of \$1800, deferred 10 years and to run 20 years, at 5 per cent. compound interest? *Ans.* \$13771.2888.

Ex. 3. A lease, whose rental is \$1000 a year, is left to two sons. The elder is to receive the rent for 9 years and the youngest for the 12 years succeeding. What is the present value of each son's interest, allowing 6 per cent. compound interest? *Ans.* to last, \$4962.385.

Ex. 4. What is the present value of a perpetuity of \$900, to commence in 30 years, allowing 4 per cent. compound interest? *Ans.* \$6937.17.

ART. **154.** To find the annuity, the present or final value, time and rate being given.

Ex. 1. An annuity running 20 years, at 7 per cent. compound interest, is worth \$15,000; what is the annuity?

Ans. \$1415.89.

Operation.

$$\$15000 \div \$10.593997 = 1415.89.$$

Explanation.—Since $10.593997, at 7 per cent. compound interest for 20 years, yields an annuity of $1, $15000 will yield an annuity equal to $15000÷10.593997.

RULE.—*Divide the present or final value of the given annuity by the present or final value of an annuity of* $1, *for the given rate and time.*

Ex. 2. An annuity in arrears for 8 years, at 5 per cent. compound interest, amounts to $47745.545; what is the annuity? *Ans.* $500.

Ex. 3. A yearly pension, unpaid for 12 years, at 6 per cent. compound interest, amounted to $1591.7127; what was the pension? *Ans.* $100.

Ex. 4. The present value of a lease, running 25 years, at 6 per cent. compound interest, is $15340.037; what is the annual income? *Ans.* $1200.

CONTINGENT ANNUITIES.

ART. **155.** When the annuity is to cease with the life of a certain person or persons, it becomes necessary to ascertain the *probability* of the person or persons, upon the continuance of whose life the annuity depends, surviving a given period. The measure of this probability is called *Expectation of Life*, and has already been noticed under Life Insurance.

In computing contingent annuities, the expectation of life of the person or persons named, as shown in Bills of Mortality, is taken as the *time* of the annuity. It can then be computed as an annuity certain.

A table, showing the present value of an annuity of $1, to continue during the life of an individual, is called a *Table of Life Annuities.*

ART. **156.** To find the present value of a life annuity.

Ex. 1. What is the present value of a life pension of $150, the age of the pensionary being 75 years ; interest, 5 per cent. ? *Ans.* $748.35.

Operation.

$4.989—	value of annuity of $1.		
150			
$748.350	"	"	$150.

Rule.—*Multiply the present value of a life annuity of* $1, *as shown in the table, by the given annuity.*

Ex. 2. Suppose a person 60 years of age is to receive an annual salary of $600 during life. What is the present value of such income, at 6 per cent., compound interest ? *Ans.* $4982.40.

Ex. 3. What must be paid for a life annuity of $560 a year, by a person aged 55 years, at 5 per cent., compound interest ? *Ans.* $5794.32.

Art. **157.** To find how large a life annuity can be bought for a given sum, by a person of a given age.

Ex. 1. How large a life annuity can be purchased for $2400, by a person aged $65 years, at 7 per cent. *Ans.* $350.51.

Operation.

$$2400.000 \div 6.847 = 350.51.$$

Rule.—*Divide the given sum by the present value of an annuity of* $1 *for the given age and rate.*

Note.—This is the reverse of the preceding article.

Ex. 2. How large a pension, at 6 per cent., compound interest, can be bought for $1600, the age of the pensionary being 50 years ?

Ex. 3. How large an annuity can be bought for $3000, by a person aged 25 ; interest, 5 per cent. ? *Ans.* 190.15.

ALLIGATION.

ART. 158. In various kinds of business, it is sometimes convenient or necessary to mix articles of different values or qualities, thus forming a compound whose value or quality differs from that of its ingredients. This process is called ALLIGATION (*L. ad*, to, and *ligatus*, bound); a name suggested by the method of solving some of its problems by joining or *binding* together the terms.

The various problems in Alligation may be divided into two classes, commonly called *Alligation Medial* and *Alligation Alternate.*

ALLIGATION MEDIAL.

ART. 169. *Alligation Medial* teaches the method of finding the average value or quality of a mixture, the value or quality, and also the quantity, of whose ingredients are known.

Ex. 1. A farmer mixed together 50 bushels of oats, at 40 cents per bushel; 30 bushels of barley, at 50 cents per bushel; and 25 bushels of corn, at 60 cents per bushel. What was a bushel of the mixture worth?

OPERATION.

Cts.	Cts.
$40\times 50=$	2000
$50\times 30=$	1500
$60\times 25=$	1500
105	)5000
	$47\frac{13}{21}$

Explanation.—Since the value of 50 bushels of oats, at 40 cents a bushel, is 2000 cents; of 30 bushels of barley, at 50 cents a bushel, 1500 cents; and 25 bushels of corn, at 60 cents a bushel, 1500 cents; the value of the mixture is 2000 cents + 1500 cents + 1500 cents = 5000 cents. But the mixture contains 50 bushels + 30 bushels + 25 bushels = 105 bushels. Hence, the value of 1 bushel of the mixture is $\frac{1}{105}$ of 5000 cents $=47\frac{13}{21}$ cents.

Ex. 2. A goldsmith melted together 12 oz. of gold, 20

carats fine; 6 oz., 18 carats fine; and 10 oz., 16 carats fine. What was the quality of the mixture? *Ans.* $18\frac{1}{7}$ carats.

OPERATION.

Carats.		Carats.
20 × 12	=	240
18 × 6	=	108
16 × 10	=	160
28	)	508
		$18\frac{1}{7}$

Explanation.—Since a carat of gold is the *twenty-fourth* part of the mass regarded as a *unit* (here an oz.), 12 oz. of gold, each oz. containing 20 carats of pure gold, contain 12 times 20 carats =240 carats; 6 oz. of gold, each containing 18 carats, contain 108 carats; 10 oz. of gold, each containing 16 carats, contain 160 carats. Hence, 12 oz.+6 oz.+10 oz.=28 oz. of mixture contain 240 carats + 108 carats + 160 carats = 508 carats, and 1 oz. of the mixture must, therefore, contain $\frac{1}{28}$ of 508 carats=$18\frac{1}{7}$ carats.

Note.—The regarding of a carat as a unit of measure of the pure gold in a given mass is not essential to the explanation of the above solution. For, suppose the comparative qualities of the above varieties of gold, represented respectively by the numbers 20, 18, and 16. Now, as these numbers represent the *comparative qualities* of the three varieties of gold, it is clear they must contain a *common unit of quality*. The number 20 denotes that the quality of the first variety contains this common union of quality 20 times; and, hence, 20 is the measure of its quality. But the effect of 12 oz. in determining the *quality of a mixture* is 12 times as great as the effect of 1 oz.; hence, 12×20 or 240, is the *effective quality* of 12 oz. of gold, if the quality of 1 oz. is 20.

RULE.

Multiply the value or quality of each article by the number of articles, and divide the sum of the products by the sum of the articles. The quotient will be the average value or quality of the mixture.

Ex. 3. A grocer mixed 15 lbs. of coffee, at 18 cents a pound; 35 lbs., at 16 cents a pound; and 40 lbs., at 14 cents a pound. What is a pound of the mixture worth? *Ans.* $15\frac{4}{9}$ cents.

Ex. 4. A grocer mixed 25 gallons of wine, at 90 cents a

gallon; 40 gallons of brandy, at 75 cents a gallon; and 10 gallons of water without price. What is a gallon of the mixture worth? *Ans.* 70 cents.

ALLIGATION ALTERNATE.

ART. **160.** *Alligation Alternate* teaches the method of finding in what proportion several simple ingredients, whose values or qualities are known, must be taken to form a mixture of a given mean value or quality.

Sometimes the quantity of one or more of the ingredients is given, and it is required to find what amount of the other ingredients must be taken.

Sometimes the quantity of the *mixture* is given, and the relative amount of ingredients is required.

We shall give the solution of examples involving the last two conditions, but omit special rules.

Ex. 1. A grocer has coffees worth 10 and 15 cents a pound. In what proportion must they be taken that the mixture may be sold for 13 cents a pound?

Solution.—By selling the mixture for 13 cents a pound, he will gain 3 cents on each pound of the coffee worth 10 cents, and will lose 2 cents on each pound of the coffee worth 15 cents. Hence, to counterbalance the gain of 3 cents on 1 pound of the first kind, he must use $1\frac{1}{2}$ ($3 \div 2$) pounds of the second kind. The proportion, therefore, must be 1 lb., worth 10 cents, to $1\frac{1}{2}$ lbs., worth 15 cents.

Ex. 2. A grocer has sugars worth 7, 10, and 12 cents a pound. In what proportion must they be taken to make a mixture worth 9 cents a pound?

Solution.—On each pound of sugar worth 7 cents there is a gain of 2 cents, and on each pound of sugar worth 10 cents there is a loss of 1 cent. He must, therefore, take 2 pounds of the second that the loss may counterbalance the gain on 1 pound of the first. On each pound of sugar worth 12 cents there is a loss of 3 cents. To counterbalance this loss $1\frac{1}{2}$ ($3 \div 2$) pounds more of the first kind must be taken. Hence, the proportion is $1+1\frac{1}{2}=2\frac{1}{2}$ lbs. worth 7 cents, to 2 lbs. worth 10 cents, to 1 lb. worth 12 cents.

Ex. 3. A grocer has four kinds of tea, worth respectively 50, 60, 70, and 90 cents a pound. In what proportion must they be taken to make a mixture worth 80 cents a pound?

Solution.—On a pound of the first kind there is a gain of 30 cents; on a pound of the second, a gain of 20 cents; on a pound of the third, a gain of 10 cents; and, hence, on a pound of each of these three kinds a gain of $30+20+10=60$ cents. On 1 pound of the fourth kind there is a loss of 10 cents; and, hence, to counterbalance the 60 cents gain, 6 pounds of the fourth kind must be taken. The proportion is, therefore, 1 lb. of the first kind, to 1 lb. of the second, to 1 lb. of the third, to 6 pounds of the fourth or multiples of these numbers.

Ex. 4. A farmer has oats worth 40 cents a bushel; corn, worth 50 cents; rye, worth 70 cents; and wheat, worth 90 cents. How must they be mixed that the mixture may be worth 60 cents?

Solution.—On each bushel of oats there is a gain of 20 cents; on each bushel of wheat a loss of 30 cents. Hence, he must take $1\frac{1}{2}$ bushel of oats to 1 bushel of wheat. On each bushel of corn there is a gain of 10 cents; on each bushel of rye, a loss of 10 cents. Hence, he must take 1 bushel of corn to 1 of rye. Proportion, $1\frac{1}{2}$, 1, 1, 1.

Note.—In the above solutions, it will be observed *that the ingredients are combined, two and two, in such quantities as to make gains and losses* EQUAL.

METHOD BY LINKING.

3d Example above.

		Ans.,		or Ans.	Verifications.	
80	50	- - 10	÷10=	1	$10\times50=$ 500	$1\times50=$ 50
	60	- - 10		1	$10\times60=$ 600	$1\times60=$ 60
	70	- - 10		1	$10\times70=$ 700	$1\times70=$ 70
	90	$30+20+10=60$		6	$60\times90=$5400	$6\times90=$540
					90)7200	9)720
					80	80

4th Example.

		Ans.,		or Ans.	Verifications.	
60	40	30	÷10=	3	30 × 40 = 1200	3 × 40 = 120
	50	10		1	10 × 50 = 500	1 × 50 = 50
	70	10		1	10 × 70 = 700	1 × 70 = 70
	90	20		2	20 × 90 = 1800	2 × 90 = 180
					70)4200	7)420
					60	60

Or thus :

		Ans.,		or Ans.	Verifications.	
60	40	10	÷10=	1	10 × 40 = 400	1 × 40 = 40
	50	30		3	30 × 50 = 1500	3 × 50 = 150
	70	20		2	20 × 70 = 1400	2 × 70 = 140
	90	10		1	10 × 90 = 900	1 × 90 = 90
					70)4200	7)420
					60	60

RULE.

Write the values or qualities of the ingredients in a column, and the value or quality of the mixture at the left hand. Link each number in the column that is LESS *than the value or quality of the mixture with one that is* GREATER, *or the reverse.*

Then find the difference between the value or quality of the mixture and that of each ingredient, and place the same opposite the number with which it is connected. The number, or the sum of the numbers, opposite the value or quality of each ingredient, will denote the amount of the same to be taken.

Remark.—Since equi-multiples of quantities have the same relation to each other as the quantities themselves, it follows that any equi-multiples of these numbers will also satisfy the conditions of the problem.

Ex. 5. A merchant has teas worth 60, 75, 80, and 100 cents per lb. How much of each kind must he take to make a mixture worth 85 cents per lb. ? *Ans.* 1, 1, 1, 2.

Ex. 6. A wine-merchant wishes to mix wine worth $1.20 and $1.40 per gallon, with water. How much of each kind must he use to make a mixture worth $1.00 per gallon ?

Ex. 7. A goldsmith wishes to combine gold 22 carats fine ; 19 carats fine ; 18 carats fine ; and 17 carats fine. In what proportion must they be united that the compound may be 20 carats fine?

Ex. 8. A farmer wishes to mix 60 bushels of corn, at 60 cents a bushel, with rye, at 75 cents; barley, at 50 cents; and oats at 45 cents. What quantity of rye, barley, and oats must be taken that the mixture may be worth 65 cents a bushel?

OPERATION.

$$65\left|\begin{array}{l}45\\50\\60\\75\end{array}\right. \begin{array}{r}-\quad-\quad 10\\-\quad-\quad 10\\-\quad-\quad 10\\20+15+5=40\end{array}\left.\vphantom{\begin{array}{l}1\\1\\1\\1\end{array}}\right\}\times 6=\left\{\begin{array}{r}\text{Ans.}\\60\\60\\60\\240\end{array}\right.$$

Explanation.—Since the amount of corn to be taken is 6 times the amount found—10 bushels—the quantity of oats, barley, and rye, must be increased in the same ration: *i. e.*, be multiplied by 6.

Ex. 8. A grocer wishes to mix 100 pounds of coffee, worth 12 cents, with coffee worth 15, 10, and 8 cents. What quantities must he take that the mixture may be worth 11 cents a pound?

10. A wine-merchant wishes to fill a cask containing 36 gallons with a mixture of wines worth $1.00, $1.20, $1.50, and $1.60 per gallon. How many gallons of each kind must he take that the mixture may be worth $1.40 per gallon?

Operation.

Or thus:

$$140\left|\begin{array}{l}100\\120\\150\\160\end{array}\right. \begin{array}{r}-\ 20\\-\ 10\\-\ 20\\-\ 40\\\hline 90\end{array}\ \times\tfrac{2}{5}=\left\{\begin{array}{r}\text{Ans.}\\8\\4\\8\\16\end{array}\right. \qquad \left.\begin{array}{r}20\\10\\20\\40\end{array}\right\}\div 10=\left.\begin{array}{r}2\\1\\2\\4\\\hline 9\end{array}\right\}\times 4=\begin{array}{r}\text{Ans.}\\8\\4\\8\\16\\\hline 36\end{array}$$

$36\div 90=\frac{2}{5}$ $\qquad$ $36\div 9=4$

Explanation.—Since, in the first case, the amount required—36 gallons—is $\frac{2}{5}$ of the amount obtained by mixing 20 gallons of the first kind, 10 gallons of the second, 20 gallons of the third, and 40 of the fourth, it is evident that $\frac{2}{5}$ of the quantity of each ingredient must be taken. In the second case, the amount required is 4 times the amount obtained;

and, hence, the quantity of each ingredient must be multiplied by 4.

Ex. 11. A trader wishes to fill 10 casks, each containing 28 gallons, with a mixture of brandy, rum, and water. If the brandy is worth 80 cents a gallon, and the rum 95 cents, how many gallons of each must be taken that the mixture may be worth 75 cents?

PARTNERSHIP.

ART. **161.** *Partnership* is the association of two or more persons, for the purpose of carrying on business at their joint expense.

Each person thus associated is called a *partner*; and the several partners, in their associated capacity, are called a *company*, *firm*, or *house*.

The money or property invested by such a company in business is called their *capital*, or *joint-stock*, or *stock in trade*.

The profits and losses of the business are sometimes shared by the several partners in proportion to their stock in trade; or more correctly, in proportion to the use or *interest* of their stock in trade. When the stock of the several partners is invested for the same length of time the *interest* of the stock is proportioned to the *stock itself*; and, hence, the profits and losses in this case are shared in proportion to the *stock* of the several partners.

Sometimes one or more of the partners furnish the capital, and the other or others contribute their services.

The profit or loss to be shared is called a *dividend*.

The duration of a partnership is limited by contract, or is left indefinite, subject to be dissolved by mutual consent and agreement.

When a company is dissolved, either by the limitations of the contract or by mutual agreement, the adjustment of the accounts of the company, and the division of effects, is called a *partnership settlement*.

Note.—Although partnership settlements fall properly within the province of book-keeping, we have added a few examples to illustrate the manner of closing such accounts.

ART **162.** When the capital of the several partners is invested for the same length of time, to find each partner's share of the profit or loss.

Ex. 1. A, B, and C enter into partnership in the lumber business for 3 years. A put in $2400; B, 3600; C, $600. At the time of the dissolution of the firm the net profits were $4000. What is each partner's share of the profits?

FIRST METHOD.

A's stock, \$2400 $=\frac{2400}{12000}=\frac{1}{5}$ of entire stock.
B's " 3600 $=\frac{3600}{12000}=\frac{3}{10}$ " "
C's " 6000 $=\frac{6000}{12000}=\frac{1}{2}$ " "
Entire stock, \$12000

Hence, A's share of profits $=\frac{1}{5}$ of \$4000 = \$ 800
B's " " $=\frac{3}{10}$ of \$4000 = 1200
C's " " $=\frac{1}{2}$ of \$4000 = 2000
Entire profits, ... \$4000

Explanation.—Since A's stock equals $\frac{1}{5}$, B's $\frac{3}{10}$, and C's $\frac{1}{2}$ of the entire stock, A would be entitled to $\frac{1}{5}$, B to $\frac{3}{10}$, and C to $\frac{1}{2}$ of the entire profits.

SECOND METHOD.

A's stock, \$2400
B's " 3600
C's " 6000
Entire stock, \$12000
" profits, \$4000

$\frac{4000}{12000}=\frac{1}{3}$. Hence, profits $=\frac{1}{3}$ of stock.
A's share of profits $=\frac{1}{3}$ of \$2400 = \$ 800
B's " " $=\frac{1}{3}$ of \$3600 = 1200
C's " " $=\frac{1}{3}$ of \$6000 = 2000
Entire profits, ... \$4000

Explanation.—Since the entire profits equal $\frac{1}{3}$ of the entire stock, each partner's share of the profits must equal $\frac{1}{3}$ of his stock.

THIRD METHOD.

$4000÷$12000=.33⅓. Hence the profits=33⅓ per cent. of the stock.

A's share of profits	=$2400×.33⅓=	$ 800
B's " "	= 3600×.33⅓=	1200
C's " "	= 6000×.33⅓=	2000
Entire profits, . .		$4000

FOURTH METHOD.

$12000 : $2400 : : $4000 : $ 800, A's profits.
$12000 : $3600 : : $4000 : $1200, B's "
$12000 : $6000 : : $4000 : $2000, C's "
$4000, Entire profits.

RULE.—*First find* WHAT PART *of the entire stock each partner has contributed, then take the* SAME PART *of the total profits or loss for each partner's share of the same.*

Or,

First find WHAT PART *of the entire stock the total profits or loss may be; then take the* SAME PART *of each partner's stock for his share of the profits or loss.*

Or,

Find what per cent. of the entire stock the total profits or loss may be; then multiply each partner's stock by the rate per cent. expressed decimally.

Or,

Form the proportion, as the whole stock is to each partner's stock, so is the whole profit or loss to each partner's profit or loss.

Ex. 2. A, B, and C traded in company. A put in $8000; B, $4500; and C, $3500. Their profits were $6400. What is each partner's share of the profits? *Ans.* C's $1400.

Ex. 3. A and B, in trading for three years, make a profit of $4800. A invested ⅗ as much stock as B. What is each man's share of profit? *Ans.* B's $3000.

Ex. 4. Two drovers, A and B, have been operating in company in buying and selling sheep. A made purchases to the amount of $6780, and paid expenses amounting to $274.12. B made purchases to the amount of $3840, and paid expenses amounting to $312. The sheep were sold by A for $10,482. How much was made or lost? How will A and B settle, the profits or losses to be shared equally?

Ex. 5. C and D agree to perform a certain piece of work for government, for which they are to receive $4680, provided it passes inspection as No. 1. If it pass as No. 2, 15 per cent. is to be deducted; as No. 3, 20 per cent. is to be deducted.

The result of the inspection was as follows:

1st division,	which is	$\frac{3}{8}$	of contract,	is	No. 1.
2d	"	" $\frac{1}{8}$	"		No. 3.
2d	"	" $\frac{1}{2}$	"		No. 2.

C has advanced, for the prosecution of the work, $1328; B has advanced $987.45. Neither has received anything from government, and all the money advanced has been used. How much have they gained, and what is each man's share?

ART. **163.** When the capital is invested for different periods of time, to find each partner's share of the profits or loss.

Ex. 1. A, B, and C traded in company. When they commenced business, A put in $4000; B, $3000; and C, $5000. At the close of the first year A put in $3000 more, and C took out $1000. At the close of the second year B put in $2000. At the close of the third year they dissolve partnership, and the net profits of the firm are found to be $2100. What is each partner's share of the gain?

Operation.

A had in	$4000 × 1 = $ 4000 " $7000 × 2 = $14000	$4000 + $14000 = $18000.
B "	$3000 × 2 = $ 6000 " $5000 × 1 = $ 5000	$6000 + $ 5000 = $11000.
C "	$5000 × 1 = $ 5000 " $4000 × 2 = $ 8000	$5000 + $ 8000 = $13000.

A, B, and C, together, had in $42000 for one year.

Hence, A's share of gain $=\frac{18000}{42000}$ or $\frac{3}{7}$ of $2100 = $900
" B's " $=\frac{11000}{42000}$ or $\frac{11}{42}$ of $2100 = $550
" C's " $=\frac{13000}{42000}$ or $\frac{13}{42}$ of $2100 = $650
Entire profits, ... $2100

Explanation.—Since A had in \$4000 for 1 year, and \$7000 for 2 years=\$14000 for 1 year, A had in trade the same as \$4000+\$14000=\$18000 for 1 year; and, since B had in \$3000 for 2 years=6000 for 1 year, and \$5000 for 1 year, B had in trade the same as \$6000+\$5000=\$11000 for 1 year; and since C had in \$5000 for 1 year, and \$4000 for 2 years=\$8000 for 1 year, C had in trade the same as \$5000+\$8000=\$13000 for 1 year. Hence, A, B, and C, together, had in trade the same as \$18000+\$1100+\$13000=\$42000 for 1 year.

Note.—The remaining portion of the solution may be in accordance with either of the *four preceding rules;* for the *time* the stock of the several partners is invested is now the same—one year—A's stock being \$18000; B's, \$11000; and C's, \$13000.

BY INTEREST.

		Years.	Int.	Int.
A had in	\$4000 for	1=	\$240.00	=\$1080.00
"	\$7000 for	2=	\$840.00	
B "	\$3000 for	2=	\$360.00	=\$ 660.00
"	\$5000 for	1=	\$300.00	
C "	\$5000 for	1=	\$300.00	=\$ 780.00
"	\$4000 for	2=	\$480.00	
Total interest of entire stock, at 6%=				\$2520.00

Hence, A's share of profits $=\frac{1080}{2520}$ or $\frac{3}{7}$ of \$2100=900
" B's " $=\frac{660}{2520}$ or $\frac{11}{42}$ of \$2100=550
" C's " $=\frac{780}{2520}$ or $\frac{13}{42}$ of \$2100=650

Note.—Since like parts of two numbers have the same ratio as the numbers themselves, it is evident the interest may be computed at any per cent. It is also evident, from the same principle, that the interest of the stock may be regarded as the stock itself; and, hence, when the interest is obtained, the remaining portion of the solution may be in accordance with either of the *four preceding rules.*

RULE.—*Multiply each partner's stock by the time it was invested, and regard the product as his stock in trade, and the* SUM *of the products as the entire stock in trade, and then proceed according to either of the four preceding rules.*

Or,

Find the interest of each partner's stock for the time it was invested, and regard the interest thus found as his stock in trade, and the SUM *of the interests as the entire stock in trade, and then proceed in accordance with either of the four preceding rules.*

Ex. 2. A and B entered into partnership Jan. 1, 1858. A put in $4500, and B, $5500. July 1, 1858, B put in $1500 more. Oct. 1, 1858, A took out $500. Jan. 1, 1859, each put in $1500. July 1, 1859, they dissolved partnership, and found they had lost $846. What is each partner's share of the loss? *Ans.* A's $342.
B's $504.

Ex. 3. A, B, and C hired a pasture for 6 months, for $245. A put in 40 sheep; B, 50 sheep; C, 80 sheep. At the close of 3 months A put in 20 more; at the close of 4 months B took out 20; and at the close of 5 months C took out 60. How much ought each to pay? *Ans.* A $75.
B $65.
C $105.

Ex. 4. A and B enter into a partnership for 3 years. A put in $10000, and B, $2500. B is to do the business, and his services are to be regarded as worth the use of $7500, the difference between his and A's stock. At the close of the first year A increased his stock to $18000. At the close of the 3 years the partnership closed, and a net gain found of $9500. What is each partner's share of the gain? *Ans.* A's $5750.
B s $3750.

DUODECIMALS.

ART. **164.** *A Duodecimal* (Latin *duodecim, twelve*) is a number whose scale is 12; hence, 12 units of any order make one unit of the next higher order.

This system of numbers is used by artificers in finding the contents of surfaces and solids. For this purpose the foot is divided into 12 equal parts called inches or *primes*, marked ′; the inch or prime is divided into 12 equal parts called *seconds*, marked ″, &c. The accents used to mark the different orders are called *indices*.

TABLE.

12 fourths (⁗)	make	1 third (‴)
12 thirds	"	1 second (″)
12 seconds	"	1 inch or prime (′)
12 inches or primes	"	1 foot (ft.)

Note.—Duodecimals may be added and subtracted like Denominate Numbers.

MULTIPLICATION OF DUODECIMALS.

ART. **165.** To multiply one duodecimal by another.

Ex. 1. How many square feet in a board 9 ft. 5 in. long, and 2 ft. 8 in. wide?

Operation.

9 ft.	5′	
2 ft.	8′	
6	3′	4″
18	10′	
25 sq.ft.	1′	4″

Explanation.—Since $8' = \frac{8}{12}$ of a foot, and $5' = \frac{5}{12}$, $8' \times 5' = \frac{8}{12} \times \frac{5}{12} = \frac{40}{144} = 40'' = 3'\ 4''$. Write 4″ in seconds order. Again, since $8' = \frac{8}{12}$, 9 ft. × 8′ = 9 ft. × $\frac{8}{12} = \frac{72}{12} = 72'$ and $72' + 3'$ (above) $= 75' = 6$ sq. ft. 3′. Hence 9 ft. 5′ × 8′ = 6 sq. ft. 3′ 4″. Again 5′ or $\frac{5}{12} \times 2$ ft. $= \frac{10}{12}$ $= 10'$ and 9 ft. × 2 ft. = 18 sq. ft. Hence 9 ft. 5′ × 2 ft. = 18 sq. ft. 10′. Adding these two products, the total product is 25 sq. ft. 1′ 4″.

It will be observed that the denomination of the product of any two denominations is denoted by the *sum of their indices;* thus $5' \times 8'' = 40'''$, $6'' \times 4'' = 24''''$, &c.

In the above process, the notations of feet, primes, &c., are used for convenience. The multiplier is, however, really an abstract number.

RULE.

Write the Multiplicand under the Multiplier, placing ft. under ft., primes under primes, &c.

Beginning at the lowest order, multiply each order of the multiplicand by each order of the multiplier, adding their indices to ascertain the denomination of the product, and carrying one for every twelve from a lower order to the next higher.

Add the several partial products for the product required.

Examples.

2. Multiply 12 ft. 8′ by 4 ft. 10′. *Ans.* 61 sq. ft. 2′ 8″.
3. Multiply 4 ft. 6′ 4″ by 8 ft. 8′. *Ans.* 39 sq. ft. 2′ 10″ 8‴
4. Multiply 10 ft. 6′ 6″ by 4′ 8″.
5. How many square feet in a board 12 ft. 9 in. long and 11′ 4″ wide? *Ans.* 12 sq. ft. 2′ 6″.
6. How many cubic inches in a block 2 ft. 9′ long, 1 ft. 8′ wide, and 2 ft. 4′ high?
7. Required the solid contents of a block 4 ft. 4′ long, 2 ft. 3′ wide, and 10′ high.
8. How many square feet in 60 boards, each board being 15 ft. 4′ long, and 1 ft. 2′ wide?
9. Divide 10 sq. ft. 2′ 10″ by 5 ft. 7′. *Ans.* 1 ft. 10′.

Remark.—By observing that division is the reverse of multiplication, the following process will be readily understood. The divisor is placed at the right of the dividend for convenience.

DIVIDEND.	DIVISOR.
10 sq. ft. 2′ 10″	5 ft. 7′
5 7′	1 ft. 10′, *Quotient.*
4 7′ 10″	
4 7′ 10″	

10. Divide 62 sq. ft. 11″ 3‴ by 8 ft. 6′ 9″. *Ans.* 7 ft. 3′.

INVOLUTION.

ART. **166.** *Involution* is the method of finding the powers of numbers or quantities.

The power of a number (except the *first*) is the product obtained by multiplying the number by itself one or more times.

The *first* power of a number is the number itself. It is also called the *root.*

The *second* power, or *square,* is the product of the number multiplied by itself *once.*

The *third* power, or *cube,* is the product of the number multiplied by itself *twice.*

The different powers derive their names from the number of times the number is taken as a factor. Thus, the first power contains the number as a factor *once;* the second power, *twice;* the third power, *three times,* &c.

The *index* or *exponent* of a power is a small figure placed at the right and a little above the number, to show the *degree* of the power, or how many times the number is taken as a factor.

The 0 power of any number or quantity results from dividing the number by itself and is equal to unity or 1. Thus, $6^0=1$, $25^0=1$, $50^0=1$, &c.

The following table will illustrate the above definitions and remarks.

$5^0(5\div5)=1$, the 0 power of 5.

$5^1=5$, the first power or root of 5.

$5^2=5\times5=25$, the second power or square of 5.

$5^3=5\times5\times5=125$, the third power or cube of 5.
$5^4=5\times5\times5\times5=625$, the fourth power of 5.
$5^5=5\times5\times5\times5\times5=3125$, the fifth power of 5.

Remark.—The *second* power of a number is called its *square*, because the area of a geometrical square is obtained by multiplying the number of linear units in one of its sides by itself once. The *third* power is called the *cube*, because the solid contents of a geometrical cube is obtained by multiplying the number of linear units in one of its sides by itself twice.

Ex. 1. What is the cube or third power of 24?

Operation.

```
   24, 1st power.
   24
   --
   96
  48
  ---
  576, 2d power.
   24
 ----
 2304
1152
-----
13824, 3d power.
```

It is evident from the definition that the cube of a number is obtained by multiplying the number by itself twice, or by taking it three times as a factor.

Rule.—*Multiply the number by itself as many times as there are units in the exponent of the power,* less one. *The last product will be the required power.*

Note.—The power of a fraction, either common or decimal, is found in the same manner.

Examples.

2. What is the square of 204? *Ans.* 41616.
3. What is the 4th power of 25?
4. What is the cube of $\frac{4}{5}$? *Ans.* $\frac{64}{125}$.
5. What is the square of 2.5?
6. What is the 4th power of .04? *Ans.* .00000256.
7. What is the 5th power of $\frac{1}{2}$?
8. What is the 9th power of 12?

Suggestion.—Since the product of two or more powers of a given number is the power denoted *by the sum of their ex-*

ponents, the 9th power of 12 may be found by multiplying the the 3d power by itself *twice* ; thus, $12^3 \times 12^3 \times 12^3 = 12^9$.

9. What is the 4th power of $2\frac{1}{2}$? *Ans.* $39\frac{1}{16}$.
10. What is the 3d power of 2.04?
11. What is the value of 15^4?
12. What is the value of $(\frac{2}{3})^5$? *Ans.* $\frac{32}{243}$.
13. What is the value of 201^3?
14. What is the value of $.001^5$?
15. What is the square of $9\frac{1}{4}$? *Ans.* $85\frac{9}{16}$.

EVOLUTION.

ART. **167.** *Evolution* is the method of finding the roots of numbers or quantities.

Evolution is the reverse of *involution.* In the latter, the *root* is given to find the *power.* In the former, the *power* is given to find the *root.*

The *root* of a number is such a number as multiplied by itself a certain number of times, will produce the given number.

The *first* root of a number is the number itself. It is also called the *first* power.

The *second,* or *square root* of a number is that number which, multiplied by itself *once,* will produce the given number.

The *third,* or *cube root* must be multiplied by itself *twice* to produce the given number.

The different roots take their names from the number of times they are taken as factors to produce the given number. The first root is taken *once* as a factor ; the second or square root, *twice;* the third or cube root, *three times,* &c.

A root of a number may be defined to be a *factor* which taken a certain number of times, will produce the given number.

The root of a number is usually indicated by the *radical sign* $\sqrt{}$ placed before it, with the *index* of the root written above it.

Thus, $\sqrt[3]{64}$ shows that the 3d root of 64 is to be taken; $\sqrt[4]{81}$, the 4th root of 81; $\sqrt[1]{15}$, the 1st root of 15, &c.

The index is usually omitted in case of the second or square root. Thus, $\sqrt{64}$ or $\sqrt[2]{64}$ equally indicates the square root of 64.

The root of a number may also be indicated by a fractional exponent, placed on the right of the number. Thus $16^{\frac{1}{2}}$ indicates the square root of 16; $81^{\frac{1}{4}}$, the fourth root of 81.

$12^{\frac{2}{3}}$ denotes that the cube root of the square of 12 is to be taken.

A number may be either the perfect or imperfect power of a required root. 25 is a perfect square, but an imperfect cube. The *exact* root of an imperfect power can not be extracted and is called a *surd*. Prime numbers are imperfect powers of all their roots, except the *first*.

SQUARE ROOT.

ART. **168.** *The Square Root* of a number is a number which multiplied by itself will produce the given number. Thus the square root of 16 is 4, since $4\times4=16$.

The process of finding the square root of a number is best understood by observing the manner in which the square of a number is formed, and the relation which the orders of the square bear to those of the root.

The first nine numbers are:

1, 2, 3, 4, 5, 6, 7, 8, 9,

and their squares

1, 4, 9, 16, 25, 36, 49, 64, 81.

From which it is seen that the square of any number composed of one order of figures, can not contain more than two orders.

Conversely, that the square root of any number composed of one or *two* orders is composed of but *one* order.

It will further be seen that the numbers in the second line above are the only perfect squares found below 100, and that the square root of any number between any two of these consecutive perfect squares is between the two corresponding roots above. Thus, 75 is not a perfect square and its square root is between 8 and 9.

The first nine numbers expressed by *tens* are,

10, 20, 30, 40, 50, 60, 70, 80, 90,

and their squares,

100, 400, 900, 1600, 2500, 3600, 4900, 6400, 8100.

From which it is seen that the square of *tens* gives no order below *hundreds* or above *thousands.* In the same manner it may be shown *that the square of any number must contain at least twice as many orders, less one, as the number squared.* If the left hand figure of the number squared is more than *three*, the square will always contain *just twice as many orders as the root.* Thus, the square of 456 contains six orders.

Again, every number may be regarded as composed of tens and units. Thus, 65 is composed 6 tens and 5 units, that is $60+5=65$; 365, of 36 tens and 5 units, that is $365=360+5$.

Hence $(65)^2=(60)^2+2\times60\times5+(5)^2=3600+600+25=4225$, and $(365)^2=(360)^2+2\times360\times5+(5)^2=129600+3600+25=133225$.

In like manner it may be shown that *the square of any number is equal to the square of the tens plus twice the product of tens by units plus the square of units.*

The two principles, above, determine the process of extracting the square root of a number.

Ex. 1. What is the square root of 4225?

Operation.

```
          4̇22̇5|65
          36
6×2=12  5)62 5
          62 5
```

Explanation.—Since 4225 is composed of four orders, its root will be composed of but two; and since the square of units is composed of units and tens, and the square of tens, of hundreds and thousands, we separate the number into periods of two figures each, by placing a dot over units and another over hundreds.

Now 42 must contain the square of the ten's figure of the root. The greatest perfect square in 42 is 36, the square root of which is 6. Hence 6 is the ten's figure of the root. Subtracting the square of the ten's figure of the root from 42 hundreds, we have 6 hundreds for a remainder, to which, if the 25 units be added, we shall have 625, which is composed of *twice the product of the tens of the root by the units* (*to be found*) *plus the square of the units.*

Now the product of tens by units gives no order below tens, hence 62 tens must contain *twice the product of the tens by the units.* It may contain more, since the square of *units* may give *tens.*

If 62 tens be divided by 2×6 tens, or 12 tens, the quotient, 5, will be the *unit figure of the root.* By placing 5, the unit figure, at the right of 12 tens, and multiplying the result, 125, by 5, the product will be twice the tens by the units, plus the square of the units.

Ex. 2. What is the square root of 133225?

```
                 13̇32̇25̇(365, Ans.
    3×3=          9
    3×2=6      6)43 2
   66×6=          39 6
   36×2=72     5)362 5
  725×5=         362 5.
```

RULE.

1. *Separate the given number into periods of two figures each, commencing at units.*

2. *Find the greatest perfect square in the left hand period and place its root on the right as the highest order of the root.*

3. *Subtract the square of the root figure from the left hand period, and to the remainder annex the next period for a dividend.*

4. *Double the part of the root already found for a trial divisor, and see how many times it is contained in the dividend, exclusive of the right hand figure, and write the quotient as the next divisor of the root, and also at the right of the trial divisor.*

5. *Multiply the divisor thus formed by the figure of the root last found, and subtract the product from the dividend.*

6. *To this remainder annex the next period for the next dividend, and divide the same by twice the root already found, and continue in this manner until all the periods are used.*

Notes.—1. The left hand period often contains but one figure.

2. Twice the root already found is called the *trial divisor*, since the quotient may not be the next figure of the root. The quotient may be too large, in which case it must be made less. The true divisor is the trial divisor with the figure of the root found annexed.

3. When any dividend exclusive of its right hand figure is not large enough to contain its trial divisor, place a cipher for the next figure of the root, and double the root thus formed for a new trial divisor, and form a new dividend by bringing down the next period.

4. When there is a remainder after all the periods are used, annex a period of two ciphers, and thus continue the operation until the requisite number of decimal places is obtained. In this case, there will be a remainder, how far soever the operation be continued, since the square of no one of the nine digits ends with a *cipher*.

5. The square root of a common fraction may be found by taking the root of both terms, when they are perfect squares. When both terms of a fraction are not perfect squares, and can not be changed to perfect squares, the root of the fraction can not be exactly found. The approximate root, however, may be found by multiplying the numerator of the fraction by the denominator, and extracting the root of the product, and dividing the result by the denominator. By extracting the root to decimal places the error may be further lessened.

6. In finding the square root of a decimal or a mixed decimal, commence separating into periods at the order of units for the whole number, and at the order of *tenths* for the decimal. If there be an *odd* number of decimal places, annex a cipher.

7. Mixed numbers must first be reduced to improper fractions or to mixed decimals.

3. What is the square root of 32041 ? *Ans.* 179.
4. What is the square root of 492804 ? *Ans.* 702.
5. What is the square root of 94249 ? *Ans.* 307
6. What is the square root of 2 ? *Ans.* 1.414+.
7. What is the square root of 62.8 ?

```
                       6̇2.80(7.924, Ans.
       7×7=            49
       7×2=14 .9)13.80
    14.9×.9=           13.41
     7.9×.2= 15.8 2).3900
  15.82×.02=             .3164
   7.92×2=15.84 4).073600
15.844×.004=             .063376
                         .010224.
```

8. What is the square root of .0625 ? *Ans.* .25.
9. What is the square root of 57600 ? *Ans.* 240.
10. What is the square root of 176.89 ?
11. What is the square root of $\frac{25}{256}$? *Ans.* $\frac{5}{16}$.
12. What is the square root of $\frac{625}{2304}$? *Ans.* $\frac{25}{48}$.
13. What is the square root of $30\frac{1}{4}$? *Ans.* $5\frac{1}{2}$.
14. What is the square root of $69\frac{4}{9}$? *Ans.* $8\frac{1}{3}$.

THE RIGHT-ANGLED TRIANGLE.

ART. **169.** An *angle* is the divergence of two lines meeting at a common point.

Angles are divided into three classes ; *acute, obtuse,* and *right.*

The annexed figures illustrate the three kinds of angles.

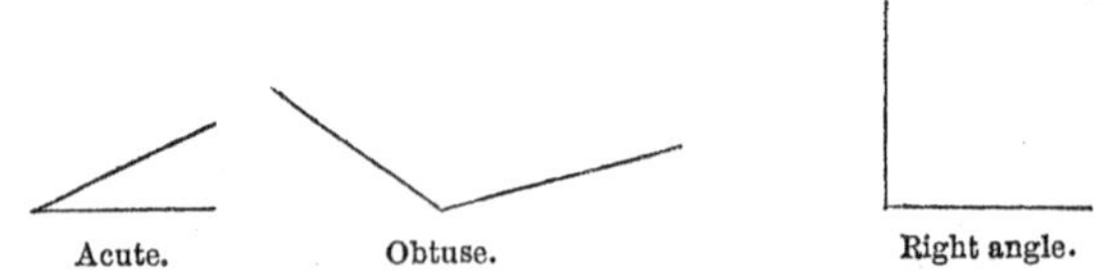

A triangle is a figure bounded by three straight lines. It also contains, as its name indicates, three angles.

A right-angled triangle contains a right angle.

The side opposite the right angle is called the *hypotenuse.*

The other two sides are called the *base* and *perpendicular.*

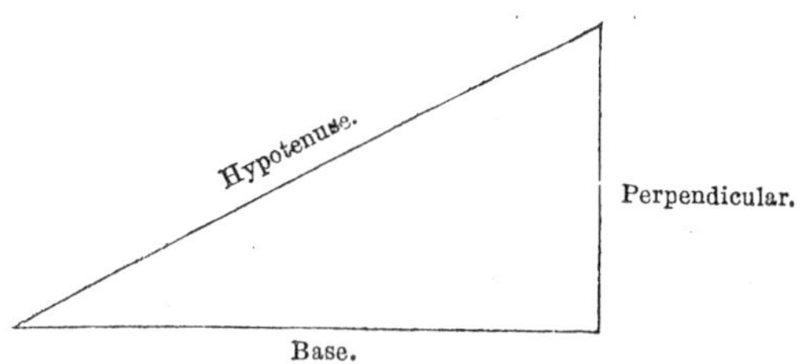

It is an established theorem *that the square of the hypotenuse of a right-angled triangle is equal to the sum of the squares of the other two sides.*

The annexed figure illustrates this theorem and the following rules.

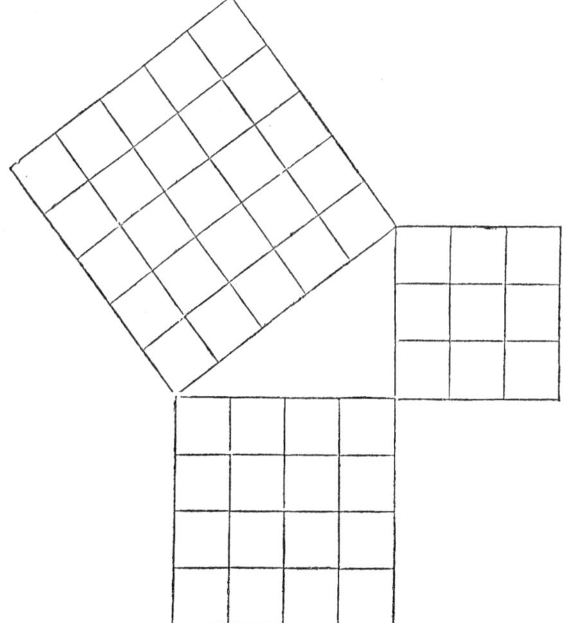

RULE 1.—*Extract the square root of the* SUM *of the square of the base and the square of the perpendicular ; the result will be the* HYPOTENUSE.

RULE 2.—*Extract the square root of the* DIFFERENCE *between the square of the hypotenuse and the square of the given side; the result will be the other side required.*

Examples.

1. What is the hypotenuse of a right-angled triangle whose base is 36 ft. and perpendicular 45 ft.? *Ans.* 57.6 ft.

2. If the hypotenuse of a right-angled triangle is 65 feet, and the base 52 feet, what is the perpendicular?
Ans. 39 feet.

3. The hypotenuse of a right-angled triangle is 80 feet, and the perpendicular 48 feet, what is the base?
Ans. 64 feet.

4. Two ships start from the same point at the same time. In six days, one has sailed 500 miles due east, and the other 400 miles due north. What is their distance apart?

5. How far from the base of a building must a ladder 100 feet in length be placed so as to reach a window 60 feet from the ground? *Ans.* 80 feet.

6. A room is 32 feet long and 24 feet wide; what is the distance betweon the opposite corners? *Ans.* 40 ft.

7. A boy in flying his kite let out 500 feet of string and then found that the distance from where he stood to a point directly under the kite was 400 feet; how high was the kite?
Ans. 300 feet.

CUBE ROOT.

ART. **170.** *The Cube Root* of a number is a number which multiplied by itself twice, will produce the given number. Thus, the cube root of 64 is 4, since $4\times4\times4=64$.

The process of finding the cube root of a number is best understood, as in square root, by involving a number, and thus ascertaining the law of the formation of the power.

The first nine numbers are,

1, 2, 3, 4, 5, 6, 7, 8, 9,

and their cubes,

1, 8, 27, 64, 125, 216, 343, 512, 729.

From which it is seen that the cube of any number composed of one order of figures may contain one, two, or three orders.

Conversely, the cube root of any number composed of one, two, or three orders, is composed of but one order.

The numbers in the second line above are the only perfect cubes below 1000.

Again, $10^3=1000$ and $90^3=729000$. From which it is seen that the cube of *tens* gives no order below *thousands*, or above *hundreds of thousands*. In the same manner it may be shown *that the cube of any number must contain at least three times as many orders, less two, as the number cubed.* Thus the cube of any number composed of four orders must contain either ten, eleven, or twelve figures.

Let us now involve a number composed of two orders—tens and units—to the third power, and observe the law of formation.

$54^3 = 50^3+3\times50^2\times4+3\times50\times4^2+4^3 = 125000+30000+2400+64=157464.$

By using algebraic symbols, it may be rigidly shown that what is true of the above number, is true of any number composed of tens and units; that is,

The cube of any number composed of tens and units is equal to the cube of the tens, plus three times the product of the square of the tens by the units, plus three times the product of the tens by the square of the units, plus the cube of the units.

Let us now proceed to determine a process by which the cube root of a number may be found.

Ex. 1. What is the cube root of 157465 ?

$$\begin{array}{r} 54 \\ 54 \\ \hline 216 \\ 270 \\ \hline 2916 \\ 54 \\ \hline 11664 \\ 14580 \\ \hline 157464 \end{array} \qquad \begin{array}{rl} & 157\dot{4}6\dot{4}4 \,|\, 54 \\ 5^3= & 125 \qquad |\, 4 \\ \hline 5^2\times3=75 & |324 \\ 54^3= & 157464 \end{array}$$

Explanation.—Since 157464 is composed of six orders, the root will be composed of two, and since the cube of tens give no order below thousands, we separate the number into periods of three figures each by placing a dot over units, and another over thousands. Now, according to principles above explained, 157 must contain *the cube of the ten's figure of the root.* The greatest cube in 157 is 125, the cube root of which is 5. Place 5 for the ten's figure of the root. Subtract the cube of 5 from 157, and annex 4 of the next period to the remainder, giving 324. Now *three times the product of the square of the tens by the units* must be found in 324, since the square of tens gives no order below *hundreds.*

Square 5 tens and multiply the result by 3 for a trial divisor to find the next root figure. Place the quotient below the order in the root. It may be too large, since *three times the product of the tens by the square of the units* may give orders above tens, thus forming a part of 324, cube 54, and since the result is not greater than 157464, place 4 for the unit's figure of the root.

Ex. 2. What is the cube root of 34328125 ?

33	32		$\dot{3}4\dot{3}28\dot{1}2\dot{5}$	325
33	32	$3^3=$	27	35
99	64	$3^2\times3=$	27)73	
99	96	$32^3=$	32768	
1089	1024	$32^2\times3=$	3072)15601	
33	32	$325^3=$	34328125.	
3267	2048			
3267	3072			
35937	32768			

RULE.

1. *Separate the given numbers into periods of three figures each, commencing at units.*

2. *Find the greatest perfect cube in the left hand period, and place its root on the right as the highest order of the root.*

3. *Subtract the cube of the root figure from the left hand period, and to the remainder annex the first figure of the next period for a dividend.*

4. *Take three times the square of the root figure now found for a trial divisor, and place the number of times it is contained in the dividend, for the next figure of the root. Cube the root now found, and if the result is less than the first two periods of the given number, bring down the first figure of the next period for a new dividend; if, however, the cube is greater than the first two periods, diminish the last root figure by* 1.

5. *Take three times the square of the root now found for a new trial divisor, and place the number of times it is contained in the new dividend for the third figure of the root. Cube the three figures of the root, and subtract the result from the first three periods of the given number. Continue the operation in a similar manner until all the periods are used.*

Notes.—1. When any dividend is not large enough to contain its trial divisor, place a cipher for the next figure of the root, and take three times the square of the root thus formed for a new trial divisor. Form a new dividend by bringing down the remaining two figures of the period, and the first figure of the next period.

2. When there is a remainder after all the periods are used, annex periods of ciphers and continue the operation until the requisite number of decimal places is obtained.

3. Extract the cube root of both terms of a common fraction, when they are perfect powers; otherwise multiply the numerator by the square of the denominator, and divide the root of the product by the denominator. The result will be the root with an error, less than one divided by the denominator.

4. In extracting the cube root of decimals or mixed decimals, ciphers must be added, to fill the periods.

Examples.

1. What is the cube root of 912673? *Ans.* 97.
2. What is the cube root of 128024064? *Ans.* 504.
3. What is the cube root of 48228544? *Ans.* 364.
4. What is the cube root of 3048625? *Ans.* 145.
5. What is the cube root of $39\frac{38}{125}$? *Ans.* $3\frac{2}{5}$.

6. What is the cube root of .000097336 ? *Ans.* .046.
7. What is the cube root of $11\frac{25}{64}$? *Ans.* $2\frac{1}{4}$?
8. What is the cube root of $\frac{216}{42875}$? *Ans.* $\frac{6}{35}$.
9. What is the cube root of 14 ? *Ans.* 2.42+.
10. What is the cube root of .015625 ? *Ans.* .25.

ARITHMETICAL PROGRESSION.

ART. **171.** When several numbers are so arranged as to increase or decrease in regular order by a common difference, they are said to be in arithmetical progression.

When they increase by the *addition* of a constant number, it is called an *ascending series, e. g.*, 1, 3, 5, 7, 9, 11, 13, &c.

When they decrease by the *subtraction* of a constant number, it is called a *descending series, e. g.*, 19, 16, 13, 10, &c.

The numbers are called *terms*, the first and last being called *extremes*, and the intermediate terms the *means.*

In arithmetical progression there are five quantities so related to each other, that any three of them being given, the remaining two may be found. This fact gives rise to twenty different cases or problems, only six of which will here be given.

These five quantities in the formulas expressing their relation, are represented as follows :

a = The first term.
l = The last term.
d = The common difference.
n = The number of terms.
s = The sum of all the terms.

FORMULAS.

(1), a, d and n being given, $l=a\pm(n-1)d$.
(2), a, n " l " " $d=\frac{l-a}{n-1}$.
(3), a, d " l " " $n=\frac{l-a}{d}+1$.
(4), a, n " l " " $s=\frac{1}{2}n(a+l)$.
(5), d, n " s " " $a=\frac{s}{n}\mp\frac{(n-1)d}{2}$.
(6), a, d " n " " $s=\frac{1}{2}n[2a\pm(n-1)d]$.

The interpretation of these formulas for those not familiar with algebraic expressions, will furnish the following rules. The student will be able to select the proper rule for any particular case by noting carefully which three of the five quantities are given, and which is required.

(1). The first term, common difference, and number of terms being given to find the last term.

RULE.—*Multiply the common difference by the number of terms, less one, and add the product to the first term, if the series be* ASCENDING, *but subtract it from it, if the series be* DESCENDING.

(2). The first term, number of terms, and last term being given to find the common difference.

RULE.—*Divide the difference of the extremes by the number of terms, less one.*

(3). The first term, common difference, and last term being given to find the number of terms.

RULE.—*Divide the difference of the extremes by the common difference, and add 1 to the quotient.*

(4). The first term, number of terms, and last term being given to find the sum of all the terms.

RULE.—*Multiply half the sum of the extremes by the number of terms.*

(5). The common difference, number of terms, and sum of all the terms being given to find the first term.

RULE.—*Divide the sum of the terms by the number of terms; subtract from the quotient, if the series be ascending, otherwise add to it half the product of the common difference into the number of terms, less one.*

(6). The first term, common difference, and number of terms being given to find the sum of all the terms.

RULE.—*Add to twice the first term, if the series be ascending; otherwise subtract from it the product of the common difference into the number of terms, less one; multiply the sum or difference by half the number of terms.*

Examples.

1. A laborer agreed to dig a well 100 feet deep, for which he was to receive 1 cent for the first foot, 5 cents for the second and so on increasing the price 4 cents per foot for the entire depth. What would he get for the last foot?

Ans. $3.97.

2. If a man begin by lifting 200 lbs., and make equal additions to the weight daily for a year of 365 days, what must be the daily additions to reach 800 lbs. at the end of the year?

Ans. $1\frac{59}{91}$ lbs.

Secondly. With what weight must he begin, so that the daily additions may be two pounds? *Ans.* 72 lbs.

Thirdly. If he begin with 200 lbs., and add $1\frac{1}{2}$ lbs. daily, how many days would it require to reach 800 lbs.

Ans. 401 days.

3. How many strokes does the hammer of a clock make in 12 hours? *Ans.* 78.

4. If 100 stakes be set in a straight line 10 feet apart, how much twine will it require to connect the first one in the line with each of the others separately? *Ans.* 49500 feet.

5. A man agreed to contribute for a benevolent object one cent the first day, two cents the second day, three cents the third day, and so on through the year of 365 days. What was the amount of his donation? *Ans.* $667.95.

6. A note was given for $1000, with interest payable annually, at 7%. Nothing having been paid for ten years, how much did the total amount of interest due exceed the simple interest of the principal? See Art. 100. *Ans.* $220.50.

7. If a note for $2000, drawing interest at 6% per annum, run 10 yrs. 3 mo. 9 d. with nothing paid, how much would the condition of making the "interest payable semi-annually" increase the amount due? *Ans.* $361.80.

GEOMETRICAL PROGRESSION.

ART. **172.** A *geometrical progression* is such a series of numbers, that each term after the first shall be the product of the preceding term and a constant multiplier, called the *common ratio.*

The progression is *ascending* or *descending,* according as the ratio is greater or less than unity.

In geometrical progression, as in arithmetical progression, there are five quantities so related to each other, that any three of them being given the remaining two may be found. Of the twenty cases arising therefrom only four will here be noticed.

In the formulas expressing the relation of the five quantities referred to above, they are represented as follows:

$a =$ The first term.
$l =$ The last term.
$r =$ The common ratio.
$n =$ The number of terms.
$s =$ The sum of all the terms.

FORMULAS.

(1,) a, r and n being given, $l = a\,r^{n-1}$.
(2,) l, r and n " " $a = \frac{l}{r^{n-1}}$.
(3,) a, l and r " " $s = \frac{r\,l - a}{r-1}$.
(4,) a, r and n " " $s = \frac{a(r^n - 1)}{r-1}$.

These formulas are equivalent to the following rules:

(1.) The first term, common ratio, and number of terms being given to find the last term.

RULE.—*Raise the common ratio to a power whose degree is one less than the number of terms, and multiply it by the first term.*

(2.) The last term, common ratio, and number of terms being given to find the first term.

RULE.—*Raise the common ratio to a power whose degree is one less than the number of terms, and divide the last term by it.*

(3.) The first term, last term, and common ratio being given to find the sum of all the terms.

RULE.—*From the product of the last term into the ratio, subtract the first term; then divide the remainder by the ratio less one.*

(4.) The first term, common ratio, and number of terms being given to find the sum of all the terms.

RULE.—*From the power of the ratio whose degree is the number of terms, subtract one; divide the remainder by the common ratio less one, and multiply the quotient by the first term.*

REMARK.—It is sometimes convenient in working problems to transpose a descending series so as to make it ascending, the last term of the first series becoming the first term in the new. In that case the new ratio would be the *reciprocal* of the old, *i. e.*, unity divided by that ratio, *e. g.*, $\frac{1}{3}$ would become 3, $\frac{1}{4}$ would become 4, and so on.

Infinite Series.

ART. 173. If the number of terms in a descending geometrical series be infinite, the last term will be 0.

It does not, however, follow that, because the number of terms is infinite, the sum of those terms must be infinite, for if we apply formula (3) making the last term 0, we shall find *the sum of an infinite decreasing series to be the first term divided by the difference between the common ratio and unity*,

$$s = \frac{a}{1-r}.$$

Examples.

1. A man offered to purchase 10 cows, paying for the first 5 cents, for the second 15 cents, and so on tripling the amount for each succeeding cow. What would the last one cost him, and what would the whole cost him?

Ans. The last would cost $984.15.
" " whole " $1476.20.

2. If the first term be 100, the common ratio 1.06, and the number of terms 5, what is the last term? *Ans.* 126.2477.

NOTE.—As the principles of arithmetical progression may be applied with advantage to the computation of annual interest, so may those of geometrical progression in computing compound interest. When thus applied the principal is the first term, the amount the last term, the number of regular intervals, at the end of which the interest is to be compounded, one less than the number of terms, and the amount of one dollar for one of those intervals the common ratio. To find the different powers of the ratio, the table on pages 132 and 133 may be used, the number in the column of years indicating the degree of the power; *e. g.*, the 50th power of $1.03\frac{1}{2}$ is 5.58492686.

3. What is the amount of $100 for 50 years at 10 % compound interest? *Ans.* $11739.09.

4. If a man beginning at the age of 21, at the end of each year puts $100 at compound interest, what will these sums amount to when he is 50 years old? *Ans.* $7363.98.

5. A gentleman offered for sale a lot of ten acres on the following terms: one mill for the first acre, one cent for the second, one dime for the third, and so on in geometrical progression. What was his price for the whole?

Ans. $1111111.111.

6. What is the sum of the series $\frac{3}{10}$, $\frac{3}{100}$, $\frac{3}{1000}$, &c., or .333, &c., carried to infinity? *Ans.* $\frac{1}{3}$.

7. What common fraction is equivalent to the repetend .7777, &c.? *Ans.* $\frac{7}{9}$.

8. At 12 o'clock the hour and minute hands of a clock are together. In what time will they be together again?

SOLUTION.—When the minute hand has performed one entire revolution around the face of the clock, the hour hand will be $\frac{1}{12}$ of a revolution in advance. When the minute hand shall have gone over this $\frac{1}{12}$, the hour hand will still be $\frac{1}{12}$ of that twelfth in advance, or $\frac{1}{144}$ of an entire revolution. When the minute hand shall have reached that point, the hour hand will be $\frac{1}{12}$ of $\frac{1}{144}$ in advance, and so the comparison of their relative position may be supposed to be made an infinite number of times. It is evident that for the minute hand to overtake the hour hand, it must perform as many revolutions (and hence take as many hours) as would be the sum of the series 1, $\frac{1}{12}$, $\frac{1}{144}$, $\frac{1}{1728}$, &c., continued to infinity equal to $1\frac{1}{11}$ hours. With the above reasoning one might almost believe that the hour hand would always be ahead, but as a matter of fact we know that the minute hand does overtake and pass the hour hand, and therefore at some point the distance between the two must be nothing. Farthermore, as the series above represents the successive distances apart in their actual progress, we have from this case conclusive proof that the last term of an infinite decreasing geometrical series is *absolutely nothing.*

9. If an ivory ball is let fall upon a marble slab, from a height of 10 feet, and it rebounds 9 feet, falling again it rebounds 8.1 feet, and so continues always rebounding $\frac{9}{10}$ of the distance through which it fell last, will it ever come to rest, and if so, through what space will it have passed?

Ans. It would pass through 190 feet.

10. If the banking law of Illinois allows the State Auditor to issue to any banker depositing State Stocks, 90 per cent. of the par value of those stocks in circulating bank notes, without farther restriction, what is the amount of Stocks a banker could so put on deposit with only $10000 Cash Capital, if he continue to re-invest the bank notes for other Stocks both at par, until he should have nothing to re-invest? If the Stocks draw 6 % interest, what dividend does he realize on his capital?

Ans. to the first $100.000.
" " second 60 % per annum.

MENSURATION.

Art. **174.** A *point* has neither length, breadth, nor thickness, but position only.

A *line* has length without breadth or thickness, and may be straight or curved.

A *surface* has length and breadth without thickness, and may be plain or curved.

A *solid* has length, breadth, and thickness.

An *angle* is the divergence of two straight lines from a common point. When the divergence is equal to that made by a straight line and one perpendicular to it, it is called a *right angle*, and its measure is 90 degrees (90°). A less divergence forms an *acute* angle, and a greater an *obtuse* angle.

The *area* of a figure is its quantity of surface, and is measured by the product of the linear dimensions of length and breadth, which will give the number of square units of the same denomination covering an equivalent surface.

REMARK.—The only difficulty then in computing the area of any figure is to find the linear dimensions of its average length and breadth, or those of another figure known to be of equal area. Take for example the "quadrature of the circle." It can easily be proven that the area of a circle is equal to the area of a rectilinear figure, with a length equal to the circumference of the circle, and a breadth equal to half the radius; but as our system of notation will not express the exact length of the radius for a given circumference, nor the exact length of the circumference for a given radius, the problem will not admit of an *exact* solution, though the approximation may be carried to an indefinite extent.

The *solidity* or *volume* of a *solid* or *body* is the quantity of space which it occupies, and is measured by the product of the three linear dimensions of length, breadth, and thickness, which will give the number of cubic units of the same denomination occupying an equivalent space.

A *rectilinear figure*, or *polygon*, is a plane figure bounded by straight lines. A polygon of three sides is called a triangle, of four sides a quadrilateral, of five a pentagon, of six a hexagon, and so on.

A *regular polygon* is one whose sides and angles are equal.

A *trapezium* is a quadrilateral which has no two sides parallel.

A *trapezoid* is a quadrilateral which has only two sides parallel.

A *parallelogram* is a quadrilateral whose opposite sides are equal and parallel.

The *altitude* of a parallelogram or trapezoid is the perpendicular distance between the parallel sides.

A *rectangle* is a right-angled parallelogram.

A *square* is an equilateral rectangle.

A *rhombus* is an equilateral parallelogram with only its opposite angles equal.

A *rhomboid* is a parallelogram neither equilateral nor equiangular.

Similar figures are those whose corresponding angles are equal, and the sides about the equal angles proportional.

The areas of similar figures are to each other as the *squares* of their corresponding linear dimensions, and the volumes of similar solids are to each other as the *cubes* of their corresponding linear dimensions.

TRIANGLES.

ART. **175.** In computing the area of a triangle, either side may be assumed as the *base*, and the *altitude* will be the perpendicular let fall from the vertex of the angle opposite upon the base, or base produced if necessary.

To find the area of a triangle.

RULE.—*Multiply the base by half the altitude, and the product will be the area;* or

Take half the sum of the three sides, and from this subtract each side separately; then multiply together the half sum and the three remainders, and the square root of the product will be the area.

Examples.

1. How many square yards in a piece of ground of triangular shape, one side measuring 50 yards, and the shortest distance from this side to the opposite angle being 24 yards?
Ans. 600 sq. yds.

2. The three sides of a triangle measure respectively 10, 12, and 14 feet; what is the area? *Ans.* 58.7878 sq. ft.

3. How much greater would be the area if we double the linear dimensions in the last example! *Ans.* Four times.

4. What should be the dimensions of a triangle similar to the one proposed in example 1, to make the area 5400 sq. yards instead of 600? *Ans.* The base 150 yds.
The altitude 72 yds.

5. If one side of a field containing 50 acres is 50 rods,

what must be the length of the corresponding side of a field of similar shape to contain $112\frac{1}{2}$ acres? *Ans.* 75 rods.

6. The area of a certain triangular field is $3\frac{3}{4}$ acres, and one of its sides is $37\frac{1}{2}$ rods long; what is the length of a perpendicular from the opposite corner? *Ans.* 32 rods.

7. What is the side of a square containing the same area as a triangle whose base is 36.1 feet, and altitude 5 feet?

Ans. $9\frac{1}{2}$ feet.

QUADRILATERALS, PENTAGONS, &c.

ART. 176. (1.) To find the area of any quadrilateral having two sides parallel.

RULE.—*Multiply half the sum of the two parallel sides by the altitude, or perpendicular distance between those sides, and the product will be the area.*

NOTE.—This rule is equally applicable to the square, rectangle, rhombus, rhomboid, and trapezoid. If the parallel sides are equal, the half sum would be equal to one of them.

(2.) To find the area of a regular polygon.

RULE.—*Multiply the sum of the sides or perimeter by half the perpendicular let fall from the center upon one of its sides.*

Or,

Multiply the square of one of the sides by the appropriate number as given in the following

TABLE.

Triangle,	.433013	Octagon,	4.828427
Square,	1.000000	Nonagon,	6.181824
Pentagon,	1.720477	Decagon,	7.694209
Hexagon,	2.598076	Undecagon,	9.365640
Heptagon,	3.633912	Dodecagon,	11.196152

(3.) To find the area of an irregular polygon of four or more sides.

RULE.—*Divide the figure into triangles by diagonals connecting some one angular point with each of the others; compute the area of each triangle, and their sum will be the area required.*

18

Examples.

1. How many square feet in a board 14 feet long and 10 inches wide? *Ans.* $11\frac{2}{3}$ sq. ft.

2. How many square feet in a board 14 feet long, it being 15 inches wide at one end, and 9 inches at the other?

Ans. 14 sq. ft.

3. If the same board be cut in two in the middle, making each piece 7 feet long, how much more would one piece contain than the other? *Ans.* $1\frac{3}{4}$ sq. ft.

4. If the parallel sides of a trapezoid are 48 and 52 feet, and the perpendicular breadth 17 feet, what is the area?

Ans. 850 sq. ft.

5. What is the area of a regular decagon, one of its sides being 10 feet, and the perpendicular let fall from the center upon one of the sides being 15.3884 feet?

Ans. 769.420 sq. ft.

6. What is the area of a regular pentagon, one of its sides being 20 rods? *Ans.* 688.191 sq. rods.

7. What must be the side of a regular octagonal field to contain 3 acres, 2 roods, 14 rods, 19 yards? *Ans.* 60 yards.

8. The sides of a certain trapezium measure 10, 12, 14, and 16 rods respectively, and the diagonal which forms a triangle with the first two sides named 18 rods, what is the area?

Ans. 1 acre 3.9 rods.

9. How much more fencing will it require to enclose an acre in the form of a square than in the form of a hexagon?

Ans. 3.51 rods.

CIRCLES.

ART. **177.** The ratio between the diameter and circumference is an important number in problems relating to the circle, and its approximate value should be retained in the memory. That ratio is very nearly equivalent to the fraction $\frac{355}{113}$, which may easily be remembered from its containing the first three odd numbers each repeated, and found in their natural order, if we read the denominator first. If expressed decimally, and the approximation be carried to thirty places, we have the following, 3.141592653589793238462643383 28.

(1.) To find the circumference of a circle whose diameter is known.

RULE.—*Multiply the diameter by* $\frac{355}{113}$ *or* 3.1416.

(2.) To find the diameter, the circumference being known.

RULE.—*Divide the circumference by* $\frac{355}{113}$ *or* 3.1416.

(3.) To find the area of a circle, the diameter being known.

RULE.—*Multiply the square of half the diameter by* $\frac{355}{113}$ *or* 3.1416.

(4.) To find the area of a circle, the circumference being known.

RULE.—*Divide the square of half the circumference by* $\frac{355}{113}$ *or* 3.1416.

(5.) To find the area of a circle, the circumference and diameter both being known.

RULE.—*Multiply the circumference by one fourth of the diameter.* See Art. 174, Remark.

(6.) To find the diameter or circumference of a circle, the area being known.

RULE.—*Divide the area by* $\frac{355}{113}$ *or* 3.1416, *the square root of the quotient will be equal to half the diameter; and the diameter multiplied by* $\frac{355}{113}$ *or* 3.1416, *will equal the circumference.*

(7.) To find the side of the largest square that can be inscribed in a circle.

RULE.—*Multiply the radius by the square root of two* ($\sqrt{2}$).

(8.) To find the side of the largest equilateral triangle that can be inscribed in a circle.

RULE.—*Multiply the radius by the square root of three* ($\sqrt{3}$).

Note.—The side of an inscribed hexagon is equal to the radius.

Examples.

1. Suppose the earth to be distant from the sun 95 millions of miles, and to revolve in a circular orbit, how far does it move in an hour? *Ans.* 68093 miles.

2. What is the diameter of a peach which measures 12 inches in circumference? *Ans.* 3.82 inches.

3. What must be the inside measure of a square box to exactly contain a globe 56 inches in circumference? *Ans.* 17.825+ in. sq.

4. If a horse be tied to a stake in a meadow, with a halter 20 feet long, upon how many square yards can he feed? *Ans.* 139.626+.

5. If a circular fish pond is to be laid out containing just half an acre, what must be the radius or length of the cord needed to describe the circle? *Ans.* 27.75 yds.

6. What is the area of a ring formed by two circles whose diameters are 9 and 13 inches? *Ans.* 69.1152 sq. in.

7. How large a square stick may be hewn from a piece of round timber 100 inches in circumference? *Ans.* 22.5 in. sq.

ELLIPSE.

ART. **178.** To find the area of an ellipse the two diameters being given.

RULE.—*Multiply the two diameters together, then multiply one fourth of this product by* $\frac{355}{113}$ *or* 3.1416.

Examples.

1. What is the area of an ellipse whose two diameters are 18 and 24 feet? *Ans.* 339.2928 sq. ft.

2. What is the area of an ellipse whose longest diameter is 20 feet, and shortest 15 feet? *Ans.* 235.62 sq. ft.

MENSURATION OF SOLIDS.

PRISMS AND CYLINDERS.

ART. **179.** A *prism* is a solid whose sides or faces are parallelograms and whose ends or bases are equal and parallel polygons. A prism is triangular, quadrangular, pentagonal, &c., according as its bases are triangles, squares, or pentagons, &c.

A *parallelopiped* is a prism whose bases are parallelograms.

A *cylinder* is a solid resembling a prism, but having, instead of polygons, for its bases, equal parallel circles or other figures more or less elliptical; its surface otherwise being uniformly curved instead of being made up of several plane faces.

The *lateral* or *convex surface* of a prism or cylinder does not include the two ends or bases.

A solid is said to be *right* when its axis or general direction is at right angles with the base; otherwise it is *oblique*.

To find the entire surface of a right prism or right cylinder.

RULE.—*Multiply the perimeter or circumference of the base by the height, and to the product add the area of the two bases.*

To find the solidity of a prism or cylinder.

RULE.—*Multiply the area of the base by the perpendicular height.*

NOTE.—In this case it matters not whether the solid be *right* or *oblique*.

Examples.

1. What is the extent of surface of a rignt cylinaer 10 feet long, the diameter of the base being 2 feet?

Ans. 69.1152 sq. ft.

2. What is the solidity of a triangular prism whose perpendicular height is 150 feet, the sides of the base being 60, 80, and 100 feet? *Ans.* 360000 cu. ft.

PYRAMIDS AND CONES.

ART. **180.** A *pyramid* is a solid whose base is a polygon, and whose sides are triangles meeting in a common point called the *vertex*.

A *right cone* is a solid resembling a pyramid, but having a curved surface, a circular base, and its vertex always equally distant from all points in the circumference of the base.

A pyramid is *regular* when besides being right, its base is a regular polygon.

The *altitude* or *height* of a pyramid, or of a cone, is the perpendicular distance from the vertex to the plane of the base.

The *slant height* of a regular pyramid or cone is the shortest distance from the vertex to the boundary of the base.

The *frustum* of a pyramid or cone is that part that remains after cutting off the top by a plane parallel to the base.

(1.) To find the entire surface of a regular pyramid, or of a cone.

Rule.—*Multiply the perimeter or the circumference of the base by half of the slant height, and to the product add the area of the base.*

(2.) To find the solidity of any pyramid or cone.

Rule.—*Multiply the area of the base by one third of the altitude.*

(3.) To find the entire surface of a frustum of a right pyramid, or of a cone.

Rule.—*Multiply the sum of the perimeters, or of the circumferences of the two ends by half of the slant height, and to the product add the areas of the two ends.*

(4.) To find the solidity of the frustum of any pyramid, or of a cone.

Rule.—*Multiply the areas of the two bases together, and extract the square root of the product. This root will be the the area of a base which is a mean between the other two. Take the sum of the areas of the three bases, and multiply it by one third of the altitude; the product will be the solidity.*

Examples.

1. What is the entire surface of a right cone, the diameter of the base, and the slant height being each 40 feet? What its solidity? *Ans.* Entire surface 3769.92 sq. ft.
Solidity 14510.42 cu. ft.

2. What are the contents of a stick of round timber whose length is 20 feet, the diameter of the larger end being 12 inches, and of the smaller end 6 inches?

Ans. $9\frac{1}{6}$ cu. ft. nearly.

SPHERES.

Art. 181. A *sphere* is a solid bounded by a curved surface, all the points of which are equally distant from a point within called the center.

The *diameter* or *axis* of a sphere is a line passing through the center, and terminated each way by the surface.

The *radius* is a line extending from the center to the surface, and is equal to half the diameter.

(1.) To find the surface of a sphere.

RULE.—*Multiply the diameter by the circumference.* Or, *Multiply the square of the diameter by* $\frac{355}{113}$ *or* 3.1416.

(2.) To find the solidity of a sphere.

RULE.—*Multiply the cube of the diameter by* $\frac{355}{113}$ *or* 3.1416, *and take one sixth of the product.* Or,

Multiply the area of the surface by one sixth of the diameter.

Examples.

1. How many square miles on the surface of the earth, it being 7912 miles in diameter? *Ans.* 196663355.7504 sq. m.

2. What are the solid contents of a globe whose diameter is 10 inches? *Ans.* 523.6 cu. in.

3. The surface of a certain sphere is 1648 square feet; what is the surface of another whose diameter is three times as great? *Ans.* 14832 sq. ft.

4. What is the diameter of a sphere containing $\frac{8}{27}$ of the solidity of another sphere $7\frac{1}{2}$ feet in diameter? *Ans.* 5 ft.

GAUGING.

ART. 182. Gauging is the art of measuring the capacity of casks and vessels of any form. In commerce, most of the gauging is done by the use of technical rules and instruments, which give only an approximate result; perfect accuracy by a long process being less desirable than a tolerable approximation requiring but little skill and labor.

To gauge accurately use the following general

RULE.—*Having taken the necessary linear measurements, compute by the rules under* MENSURATION *heretofore given, the volume of the inside of the cask or vessel in cubic inches. Divide this by* 2150.42 *for the measurement in bushels, by* 282 *for beer gallons, by* 231 *for wine gallons.*

PARTNERSHIP SETTLEMENTS.

ART. **183.** The true basis of all partnership settlements is the original agreement or contract between the parties.

To avoid misapprehension and difficulty, such agreements should be explicit and comprehensive on all essential points; for, although the legal construction of such instruments aims at the "intent of the contracting parties," it is best to save the necessity of such construction, by putting the *intent* in the plainest possible English.

The following points should be embraced in a partnership contract:

1. The amount, time of investment, and continuation of each partner's capital.
2. The proportionate amount to be drawn by each partner for his private use.
3. The basis of gain or loss, and each partner's proportion thereof.
4. The limitation of copartnership.

Other points may be added, according to the necessities of the case; but great care is necessary to avoid defeating the purposes of the contract by verbosity and ambiguity of terms. The object of a partnership settlement is to ascertain the relations in which the partners stand to the business and each other. Such settlements should be effected at least as often as once every year.

The dissolution of a copartnership may be effected by the expiration of the terms of copartnership—the decease of one of the partners—the breaking out of a war between the two countries of which the partners are citizens—or the mutual consent of the partners themselves.

After a partnership has been dissolved, and proper notice given, one member of the firm can not bind the others by drawing or accepting drafts, or by making promissory notes, even for previously existing debts of the firm ; and although the partner drawing the same was authorized to settle the partnership affairs.

If a partnership be formed for a single purpose or transaction, it ceases as soon as the business is completed, and a settlement should be immediately effected between the partners.

Either partner may dissolve the partnership at any time, by giving notice to his copartners ; even though it was understood and agreed at commencing, that the partnership should continue for a longer and definite period. But the partner thus dissolving his connection with the firm, will subject himself to a claim of damages for breach of contract.

When notice of dissolution is given, and also of the appointment of one of the partners to settle up the business, a settlement made by a debtor of the firm with one of the other partners, without the knowledge and consent of the partner so appointed, would be fraudulent and void.

The almost endless variety of conditions which affect partnership settlement, renders it extremely difficult to give general rules and illustrations, which will cover all cases. The following examples, however, will be found both practical and important.

CASE I.

ART. **184**. The investment and the resources and liabilities at closing, being given to find the net gain or loss.

RULE.

Subtract the sum of the liabilities (including the investment) from the sum of the resources, and the difference will be the net gain; or (if the liabilities are the larger) subtract the sum of the resources from the sum of the liabilities, and the difference will be the net loss.

Ex. 1. A and B are partners. At the close of one year's business, an inventory is taken showing the condition of affairs to be as follows, viz. : Cash on hand $3278. Merchandise in store valued at $1500. Five shares City Bank Stock $500.

House and lot valued at $4000. The firm owe on their notes $2000, and to Wm. Brown on account, $1200. A invested $2426, B invested $2872. What is the net gain? *Ans.* $780.

Operation.

Resources.		*Liabilities.*	
Cash	$3278	Firms' Notes	$2000
Merchandise	1500	Due Wm Brown	1200
City Bank Stock	500	A invested	2426
House and Lot	4000	B do.	2872
	9278		$8498
	8498		
Net Gain	$780		

Ex. 2. C, D, and E are partners. After conducting business one year they have the following resources and liabilities: Cash on hand $4860. Mill and fixtures valued at $6924. Bills Receivable $896. Brown & Co. owe $2000. Ten shares R. R. Stock $1000. The firm owe on notes outstanding $6400. C invested $4500. D invested $3800. E invested $3600. What is the net loss? *Ans.* $2620.

CASE II.

ART. **185.** The investment, the resources and liabilities at closing, and the proportion in which the partners share the gains or losses being given to find each partner's interest in the concern at closing.

RULE.

Find the net gain or net loss by Rule under Case I. Then, if there is a gain, add each partner's share of gain to his investment and subtract the amount he owes the firm. Or, if there is a loss, find each partner's share of loss and subtract it from his investment; also subtract any amount that the partner owes the firm, as before.

Ex. 1. A and B are partners. A is to share $\frac{2}{5}$ of the gain or loss, and B $\frac{3}{5}$. At the close of business the following is shown to be the condition of their affairs, viz.: Cash on hand $2680. Bills Receivable on hand $3620. Five shares United States Stock valued at $520. House and lot valued at $6000.

Sturgis & Co. owe on account $1800. The firm owe on notes outstanding $2840. They owe G. P. Carey on account $890. A invested $4610. B invested $4860.

What is A's interest in the concern? *Ans.* A $5178.
" " B's " " " B $5712.

Operation.

Resources.		*Liabilities.*	
Cash on hand	$2680	Notes unpaid	$2840
Bills Receivable	3620	Due G. P. Carey	890
U. S. Stock	520	A invested	4610
House and Lot	6000	B do.	4860
Sturgis & Co. owe	1800		
	14620		$13200
	13200		
Net Gain	$1420		

5)1420 Net Gain,
284 $\frac{1}{5}$ " "
3
$852 B's $\frac{3}{5}$ " "
$568 A's $\frac{2}{5}$ " "

Proof.

Cash	$2680	Bills Payable		$2840
Bills Receivable	3620	G. P. Carey		890
U. S. Stock	520	A invested	4610	
		" $\frac{2}{5}$ Net Gain	568	
House and Lot	6000	" present interest in concern		5178
Sturgis & Co.	1800	B invested	4860	
		" $\frac{3}{5}$ Net Gain	852	
		" present interest in concern		5712
Total Resources	$14620	Total Liabilities		$14620

Note.—In the following examples the resources are supposed to be brought in at their actual cash value. No interest is allowed on the partners' accounts unless so specified.

Ex. 2. C, D, and E are partners. To share the gains or losses each one third. The resources and liabilities at the close of the year are found to be as follows, viz.: Money doposited in City Bank $8460. Copper Mine Stock valued at $10240.

Bills Receivable on hand \$6420. Fulton Bank Stock on hand valued at \$3826. Block of buildings and Lot valued at \$35000. Hall & Co. owe on account \$1344. L. M. Howard owes on account \$960. The firm owe on their notes unredeemed \$5680. To Mason & Austin on account \$1700. C invested \$18420. D invested \$18460. E invested \$18432. What is each partner's present interest in the concern?

Ans. C \$19606, D \$19646, E \$19618.

Ex. 3. F, G, H, and I are partners. They share the gains or losses as follows, viz.: F and G $\frac{3}{12}$ each, H $\frac{4}{12}$ and I $\frac{2}{12}$. At the close of business the resources are Cash \$4628, Merchandise \$12620, Real Estate \$5000, Bank Stock \$3000, Wheat and Corn \$2800, Horses and Harness \$500, Lumber \$520, Money deposited in Globe Bank \$8620. F has drawn from the business \$450, H has drawn \$180. The liabilities of the concern are, Notes unredeemed \$4600, Due Simon Good on account \$800, Due S. S. Packard on account \$1200. F invested \$6682. G invested \$6682. H invested \$8908. I invested \$4454. What is each partner's interest in the concern?

Ans. F \$7480, G \$7930, H \$10392, I \$5286.

Ex. 4. J, K, L, M, and N are partners. The gain or loss is to be divided as follows: J $\frac{5}{15}$, K $\frac{4}{15}$, L $\frac{3}{15}$, M $\frac{2}{15}$, N $\frac{1}{15}$, Upon examination the following is found to be the condition of affairs at the close of business, viz.: Notes on hand against other persons \$12680, Ohio State Stocks \$8420, New York State Stock \$6000, City Bank Stock \$2800, Bonds and Mortgages \$9460, Deposit in Ocean Bank \$6742, Attica Bank owes the firm \$4286, Brown & Bros. owe \$1520, Interest on Notes, and Bonds and Mortgages in the hands of the firm \$688. Office Furniture on hand valued at \$824. The liabilities of the concern are as follows, viz.: Notes and Acceptances outstanding \$5486, Interest due on firm's Notes and Acceptances \$280, Bal. favor Trader's Bank \$2626, Bal. favor of Fulton Bank \$1500, N invested \$2287, M invested \$4575, K invested \$9150, L invested \$6861, J invested \$11455. What has been the Net Gain? What is J's interest in the concern? K's? L's? M's? N's?

Ans. Net Gain $10200. J's interest $14855. K's interest $11870. L's interest $8901. M's interest $5935. N's interest $2967.

Ex. 5. There are four partners in a concern, O, P, Q, and R. Each partner to share $\frac{1}{4}$ of the gains or losses. At dissolution there is Cash on hand $6820, Bills Receivable $8922, Croton Water Stock $4500, Deposit in Bank Commerce $3860. O has drawn from the concern $860, P has drawn $575, Q has drawn $630, R has drawn $452. The liabilities are: Notes and Acceptances outstanding $3680, Bal. in favor of Smith & Co. $1264, in favor of Hall & Reed $860, Geo. Carey $575. O invested $5590, P invested $5322, Q invested $5540, R invested $5228. What has been the net gain or loss? What is each partner's interest in the business?

Ans. Net Loss $1440. O's interest $4370. P's $4387. Q's $4550. R's $4416.

CASE III.

ART. **186.** The resources, the liabilities (except the investment), and the net gain or loss being given, to find the net capital at commencing.

RULE.

When the resources are larger than the liabilities, deduct the given liabilities from the given resources (the difference will be the present worth of firm), and from this remainder deduct the net gain, or add the net loss. Or,

When the liabilities are greater than the resources, deduct the resources from the liabilities (the difference will be the net insolvency of firm), and deduct this remainder from the net loss.

Note 1.—The liabilities can never exceed the resources at closing when there is a capital at commencing and a net gain during business.

Note 2.—In the following examples it is supposed that the whole investment is made at the time of commencing business, and that it remains undisturbed until the date of partnership settlement.

Ex. 1. A and B are partners. A invested $\frac{2}{5}$ and B $\frac{3}{5}$ of the capital. They are to share equally in gains or losses. At the close of business the resources are: Cash \$6800, Bills Receivable \$4700, Merchandise \$6400, Real Estate \$5000, Bank Stock \$900, Steamboat Stock \$9000. A has drawn from the business \$365, B has drawn \$526. The liabilities are: Firm's Notes unredeemed \$4680, Bal. favor of S. S. Packard \$620, J. T. Calkins \$476, R. H. Hoadley \$326. The net gain during business has been \$2644. What was the firm worth at commencing? What was each partner worth?

Ans. Firm \$24945. A \$9978. B \$14967.

Operation.

Cash	\$6800	Bills Payable		\$4680
Bills Receiv.	4700	S. S. Packard		620
Merchandise	6400	J. T. Calkins		476
Real Estate	5000	R. H. Hoadley		326
Bank Stock	900			\$6102
Steam Bt. Stock	9000	33691	Resources	
A is charged	365	6102	Liabilities	
B "	526	27589	Present worth of firm	
	\$33691	2644	Net Gain	
		5)24945	Net Cap. at com.	
		4989		
		2		
		9978	A's $\frac{2}{5}$ of the Cap. at com.	
		14967	B's $\frac{3}{5}$ " " "	

Proof.

Cash	\$6800	Bills Payable		\$4680
Bills Receiv.	4700	S. S. Packard		620
Merchandise	6400	J. T. Calkins		476
Real Estate	5000	R. H. Hoadley		326
Bank Stock	900	A's Cap. at com.	9978	
Steam Bt. Stock	9000	" $\frac{1}{2}$ Net Gain	1322	
A is charged	365	" Present worth .		. 11300
B "	526	B's Cap. at com.	14967	
		" $\frac{1}{2}$ Net Gain	1322	
		" Present worth .		. 16289
	\$33691			\$33691

Ex. 2. C, D, and E are partners. C invested $\frac{1}{8}$, D $\frac{3}{8}$, and E $\frac{4}{8}$, to share the gain or losses equally. At the close of business the resources are found to be: Wheat on hand valued at $2600, Corn on hand $3200, Flour $1600, Mill and Fixtures $8000. The firm owe Digby V. Bell $2600, to J. H. Goldsmith $1500, and on their Notes unredeemed $949. The net loss in the business has been $633. What was the net capital of the firm at commencing? What was each partner's net capital?

Ans. Firm $10984. C $1373. D $4119. E $5492.

Ex. 3. There are four partners engaged in business as a firm, F, G, H, and I. They have been unfortunate, the net loss being $15320. On examination the resources are found to be as follows, viz.: Live Cattle on hand valued at $9680, Packed Beef valued at $12600, Empty Barrels on hand valued at $500, Deposit in Drovers' Bank $2500. The firm owe on their Notes and Acceptances $22600, Warren P. Spencer on account $4000, J. C. Bryant on account $6000. The partners invested in equal amounts and are to share the gains or losses in the same proportion. What was the investment of the firm? What was each partner's investment?

Ans. Firm $8000. F $2000. G $2000. H. $2000. I $2000.

CASE IV.

ART. **187.** *When the firm commence insolvent.*

The resources and liabilities at closing, and the net gain or loss being given, to find the net insolvency at commencing.

RULE.

When the liabilities are greater than the resources at closing, deduct the given resources from the given liabilities, and to this remainder add the net gain or from it subtract the net loss. Or,

When the resources are larger than the liabilities at closing, deduct the liabilities from the resources, and deduct this remainder from the net gain.

Ex. 1. A and B are partners. They commence business insolvent. The proportion of their insolvency is A $\frac{3}{4}$, B $\frac{1}{4}$.

The gains or losses are to be equally divided. At the close of business the resources are, Cash on hand $3246, Lumber on hand valued at $6428, Timber and Logs valued at $3272, Bills Receivable $1800. The firm owe on their Notes and Acceptances $9400, to E. R. Felton on account $3684, to H. W. Ellsworth on account $2160. The net gain during business has been $1568. What was the net insolvency of the firm at commencing? What was each partner's net insolvency at commencing?

Ans. Firm's $2066. A's $1549.50. B's $516 50.

Operation.

Cash on hand	$3246	Bills Payable	$9400
Lumber "	6428	E. R. Felton	3684
Timber and Logs on h.	3272	H. W. Ellsworth	2160
Bills Receivable "	1800		
	$14746		$15244

	$15244 Liabilities
4)2066 Net Insolv. at com.	14746 Resources
516.50 B's $\frac{1}{4}$ " "	498 Pres. Net Insolv. of firm
3	1568 Net Gain
$1549.50 A's $\frac{3}{4}$ " "	2066 Insolv. of firm at com.

Proof.

Cash		$3246	Bills Payable	$9400.00
Lumber		6428	E. R. Felton	3684.00
Timber and Logs		3272	H. W. Ellsworth	2160.00
Bills Receivable		1800	B's $\frac{1}{2}$ Net Gain 784.00	
A's Insolv. at com.	1549.50		" Ins. at com. 516.50	
" $\frac{1}{2}$ Net Gain	784		" Net Capital	26750.00
" Net Insolvency . .		765.50		
Tot. Resources of firm		$15511.50	Tot. Liab. of firm	$15511.50

Remark.—In the foregoing example the partners were both insolvent at commencing business. The business was profitable, and B's share of the gain was more than his insolvency at commencing, so that he ends with a *net capital.* A is still insolvent, but to a less amount than when he commenced.

Ex. 2. C, D, E, and F are partners, commencing with equal insolvency, the gains or losses to be shared as follows, viz.: C $\frac{3}{12}$, D $\frac{4}{12}$, E $\frac{2}{12}$, F $\frac{3}{12}$. Two years having passed an inventory is taken, showing the following condition of affairs: 20000 lbs. Cheese on hand @ 8 cents, $1600; 40000 lbs. Butter @ 18 cents, $7200; 2000 bush. Potatoes @ 40 cents, $800; 3000 bush. Wheat @ 90 cents, $2700. The firm owe on their Notes and Acceptances $8628. They owe E. B. Rockwell on account $3242. They owe W. H. Clark on account $4563. There has been a *net loss* during the business of $528. What was the net insolvency of the firm at commencing? What was the net insolvency of each partner? What is the net insolvency of each partner at closing?

Ans. Insolvency of firm at com. $3605. Insolvency of each partner $901.25. Insolvency of firm at closing $4133. C $769.25. D $725.25. E $813.25. F $769.25.

Ex. 3. G, H, I, J, and K formed themselves into a copartnership for the purpose of carrying on the building and masonry business. The firm to assume the liabilities of the partners. The proportion in which the partners are insolvent at commencing is as follows, viz.: G $\frac{2}{20}$, H $\frac{3}{20}$, I $\frac{4}{20}$, J $\frac{5}{20}$, and K $\frac{6}{20}$. The gains or losses are to be divided in the proportion of their insolvency. At the close of business the following is the condition of affairs: Deposit in City Bank $5428, Bonds and Mortgages Rec. $3826, Notes and Drafts $6294. J. C. Bryant owes on account $4466, Brick and Stone on hand valued at $3688. The firm owe on their Notes and Acceptances $18000. They owe Baldwin & Co. $3620. The Net Gain has been $5622. What was the net insolvency of firm at commencing? What was the insolvency of each partner? What is the net capital of firm at closing? Of each partner?

Ans. Insolvency of firm at commencing $3540. Of G $354, H $531, I $708, J $885, K $1062.
Net capital of firm at closing $——
Of G $——, H $——, I $——, J——, K $——

MISCELLANEOUS.

1. D. V. Bell, J. H. Goldsmith, E. G. Folsom, and J. C. Bryant, are partners. The two former furnish the capital, and the two latter are to bear the expenses of conducting the business, each one half. The profits or losses are to be distributed as follows: Bell $\frac{7}{20}$, Goldsmith $\frac{6}{20}$, Folsom $\frac{4}{20}$, and Bryant $\frac{3}{20}$. Bell advanced at commencing business $18423. Goldsmith advanced $13142. At the close of the year it is ascertained that the profits have exceeded the losses (not including expenses) $6823.80. The expense account has an excess of debits of $2412.08. Bell has drawn out during business $426. Folsom has drawn out $2342.13. What is each partner's interest in the concern at the close of the year?

Note.—In the above example Mr. Goldsmith was allowed to draw a large amount from the business, and by consent of the other partners was not to pay interest upon it. Interest is not to be taken into account in solving this and the following examples unless it is so specified.

2. S. S. Packard, J. T. Calkins, and E. B. Rockwell are partners, to share the gains or losses equally. At the close of one year the following is the result of the business: Cash on hand $8920, Bills Receiv. $6273, Merchandise $5682, Bank Stock $896, Mr. Packard has drawn from the concern $672.43, Mr. Calkins $2471.04, Mr. Rockwell $1896.06. Bills Payable outstanding $5957.95. Packard invested $7420, Calkins invested $6812, Rockwell invested $4635. What has been the gain or loss? What is each partner's present interest in the concern?

3. R. W. Hoadley, H. W. Ellsworth, and H. C. Spencer are partners. They invest in equal amounts, and share gains and losses equally. At the expiration of two years they have Cash on hand $7242, R. R. Stock $4860, Real Estate $4673, Produce $2921. They have Bills Payable outstanding $2326.41. During business Mr. Ellsworth has withdrawn from the concern $924, and Mr. Spencer has advanced to the

concern $1138. The total losses have been $754.25, the total gains $3269.54. What is each partner's share of gain or loss? What was each worth at commencing? What is each partner's interest in the concern at closing?

4. R. C. Spencer, W. H. Clark, L. Fairbanks, and C. E. Wilber have been associated in business during the past three years. The books have remained unclosed to this date.

R. C. S. invested at commencement of business				$6824.00
W. H. C.	"	"	"	5982.00
L. F.	"	"	"	7126.00
C. E. W.	"	"	"	4998.00.

They are to share equally in gains or losses. Since the books were opened the partners have made the following additional investments: R. C. S. $2128.40, W. H. C. $684.12, L. F. $1242.78, C. E. W. $946.64. The partners have each drawn from the concern the following amounts: R. C. S. $8126 42, W. H. C. $5274.18, L. F. $8232.64, C. E. W. $3178.26. There are no resources or liabilities at this date except such as are shown by the partners' accounts. Has the business been prosperous or adverse? If a dissolution now take place, how shall the partners settle with each other?

5. G. B. Collins, A. H. Redington, and Alonzo Gaston were partners in a manufacturing business, commencing July 1st, 1856. At that date G. B. C. put into the concern $1600, A. H. R. put in $4000, A. G. made no investment, but was to superintend the business. They were to share equally in gains or losses. Six per cent. interest to be allowed on each side of the partners' accounts. The books are not closed until July 1st, 1858, when the following statement is rendered by the bookkeeper: G. B. C. has drawn from the concern at different times to the amount of $14760, the average date at which it was drawn, being September 12th, 1857. A. H. R. has drawn $11380, average date January 22d, 1858. A. G. has drawn $16240, average date May 16th, 1857. G. B. C.'s total investment has been $2982, average date August 17th, 1857. A. H. R.'s total investment $6824, average date October 9th, 1856. A. G.'s total investment $1528, average date April 24th, 1858.

Cash on hand $628, Cash in Bank $2892, Bills Receivable on hand $5462, Real Estate $7586, Manufactured Articles $4327, Personal Accounts $1523, R. R. Stocks $837, Bills Payable unredeemed $6248, Balance due on personal accounts $4895.

What has been the net gain or loss of the firm? What is each partner's present interest in the concern?

A. H. R. proposes to retire from the business, and the other partners agree to give him $900 more than the books show to be due him. How much will he receive?

6. A of New York, and B of Ohio, enter into an arrangement to buy and sell Cattle, and share equally in gains and losses; B to make the purchases, and A to effect most of the sales. A forwarded to B a draft of $8000, B made purchases to the amount of $13682.24. B has forwarded cattle to A during the season, from which he has made sales to the amount of $9241.18. B has made sales to the amount of $2836.24. A has paid out for expenses $364.16. B has paid out for expenses $239.14. At the close of the season B has on hand a number of cattle the cost of which was $2327.34. A has a quantity on hand which are estimated to be worth, in the New York market, $3123.42. The parties now propose to dissolve the copartnership, each taking the stock he has in his possession at the figures given above, and the balance in their accounts, if any, to be paid in cash. What has been the gain or loss? What is each partner's share of gain or loss? What is the cash balance to be paid, and which partner is to receive it?

7. C and D make a contract with government to do a certain piece of work, which is divided into three sections, for which they are to receive as follows, provided the work all pass as No. 1 on being inspected: for Section 1, $1842, for Section 2, $1275, for Section 3, $1563. If any portion of the work pass as No. 2 on inspection, 15 per cent. will be deducted from the original estimate; if any portion as No. 3, 20 per cent. will be deducted. The following is the result of the inspection:

Section 1, passes as No. 1. Section 2, as No. 3, and Section 3, as No. 2.

C has drawn from government $728.42. D has drawn $1226.14. D has made disbursements to the amount of $1342.25. C has made disbursements on the work to the amount of $987.45. What has been the gain or loss? How much is due C? How much is due D?

8. Two persons, E and F, enter into business under an agreement that E shall draw from the concern weekly $5 more than F. Subsequently F lends E $260 from his private funds, with the understanding that they were then to draw an equal sum weekly until the loan be liquidated. How long will it take?

9. Three mechanics are partners. They agree that each shall pay $2.25 per day for all working days that he is absent from the business. At the close of the year it is found that A has lost 44 days, B 28 days, C 12 days. How will the partners adjust the matter between them?

10. A, B, and C enter into a copartnership, each investing $5000. A is worth to the business $1500 a year; B $1200; C $1000. At the end of two months B draws out $500, and A adds to his capital $1000. At the end of five months, C withdraws $300. They close up their business at the end of a year, and find that a net profit has been realized of $3500. What proportion of this gain belongs to each partner, if money is worth 7 per cent. per annum?

11. Again: A, B, and C are partners, each investing at the commencement of business $5000, and each being of equal value to the business. They draw from and add to the capital, as before, and at the end of the year ascertain their gain to be, as before, $3500. How will the gain be equitably divided? And should the value of money, as in the former case, have any effect on the adjustment of gains?

12. Again: A, B, and C are partners, investing as in the former two instances, with the understanding that C shall conduct the business, for which he is to receive a commission of 25 per cent. on the net gain. The additions and withdrawals the same as above, and also the gain. How much of the gain should each have?

13. There are five partners in a concern, sharing the gains or losses equally. The liabilities of the firm have been canceled, after which the remaining effects were appropriated by the partners without regard to the proper proportion that each should take. The following is the condition of the partners' accounts, as they now stand. A invested $5680, and has drawn from the concern $4700. B invested $4780, and has drawn $4400. C invested $4980, and has drawn $4600. D invested $3984, and has drawn $3300. E invested $5600, and has drawn $5346. How will the partners settle with each other?

14. A and B are partners. They have Cash and Collectable Paper on hand to the amount of $5280.11. A has drawn from the concern $2446.80, B has drawn $905.98. A put into the concern $3127.25, B put in $448.75. The firm owe on Paper and Book Debts $4005.48. What is each partner's present interest in the concern, if they share equally in gains and losses?

15. S. S. Guthrie and H. C. Walker purchased a vessel on joint account, for which they paid $8400, Mr. G. taking one third interest and Mr. W. two thirds.

During the season G. paid for supplies, repairs and sundry expenses $956.00
And received Cash from freight and passage receipts 2686.40
W. paid for repairs, supplies, &c. 1548.26
And received Cash from freight and passage receipts 4862.48

At the close of the season they sell the vessel for $9000, receiving one half in Cash, and the purchaser's Note for one half.

W. agrees to take this Note, to apply on his account, at 2% discount, which G. assents to; and then the $4500 Cash is properly divided between the two partners; how much is taken by each?

16. Alonzo Gaston and G. B. Collins take a contract of A. H. Redington to sink an aqueduct of a certain width 50 rods in length, and if it average 10 feet deep, they are to receive for constructing the same $26 per rod. If on measure-

ment it average less than 10 feet, 3% will be deducted for the first 6 inches, 5% for the second 6 inches, 9% for the third 6 inches.

A. G. has paid out for wages and material $158

G. B. C. " " " $536

A. H. R. has advanced $488, of which A. G. received $242.18, G. B. C. received $245.82. The average depth was to be ascertained by measurement at the end of every five rods, which resulted as follows:

	ft.	in.		ft.	in.
End of 1st five rods	10	4	End of 6th five rods	7	10
" 2d "	10	9	" 7th "	8	4
" 3d "	9	8	" 8th "	7	9
" 4th "	9	4	" 9th "	9	7
" 5th "	8	3	" 10th "	8	8

What has been the gain or loss? How much is due from A. H. R.? How will Mr. Gaston and Mr. Collins settle with each other?

17. A and B contracted with Russell & Co. to erect a Steam Flouring Mill for $11000. Not wishing to be burdened with the salary of a bookkeeper, it was arranged that each partner should keep a strict account of all his receipts and expenditures, and report at the completion of the contract, at which time they would have a general settlement. On the fulfillment of the contract they find their affairs standing as follows, viz.: A has paid out for building material and wages $2862.48. He has received from Russell & Co. at different times to the amount of $1324.08. B has paid out for building material and wages $4788.04. He has received from Russell & Co. $5024.44. There is due the hands for wages $410.

What has been the profit? How much is due from Russell & Co.? And how much of it should be paid to A? How much to B?

18. E. C. Bradford, Joseph Dawson, and E. Young have been doing business together as partners, with the understanding that Mr. B. should receive a salary of $1200, for managing the concern, the other partners' time not to be required in the business. Interest to be allowed on both sides of each part-

ner's account. The profits or losses to be divided equally between them. Mr. B. invested January 1, 1860, $6000, May 2, $350, October 12, $500. He drew out February 8, $250, April 4, $380, July 5, $620, November 20, $782. Mr. D. invested January 1, $5400, June 12, 860, $280, October 3, $365, December 18, $428. He drew out March 2, $468, May 21, $428, August 3, $542, September 15, $247, December 19, $388. Mr. Y. invested January 1, $4896, May 9, $356, July 2, $428. He drew out March 13, $355, June 3, $126, August 9, $281, October 6, $126, December 24, $439. On December 31, 1860, one year from the day of commencing business, the resources and liabilities (not including the partners' accounts) are as follows, viz.:

Cash on hand	$5680
Bills Receivable on hand	4366
Real Estate "	5200
Bank Stock "	5388
	$20634
Bills Payable unredeemed	$1298.40

What is the net capital of the firm at closing? What is each partner's interest in the concern at closing?

19. The following "Statement," taken from a single entry ledger, in part, the balance being made up from inventories and estimates shows the present condition of the affairs of the firm of A & B.

RESOURCES TAKEN FROM THE LEDGER.

John Smith owes	$460.00
Wm. Brown "	680.00
Geo. Carey "	1260.00
Wm. Dudley "	870.00
Geo. Bryant "	260.00
Amos Dean "	890.00
A has drawn from the concern	2400.00
B " " "	1261.00

LIABILITIES TAKEN FROM THE LEDGER.

Due Baldwin & Co., on account	$546.00
A invested	11600.00
B "	13742.00

RESOURCES NOT SHOWN ON LEDGER, TAKEN FROM INVENTORIES AND ESTIMATES.

Merchandise on hand, per Inv.	$9685.00
Notes and Drafts on hand, per B. B. (Face) . .	5672.00
Store Fixtures on hand	384.00
Horses, Carriages, and Harnesses	865.00
Stable and Feed	1262.00
City Bank Stock	892.00
House and Lot valued at	6000.00
C. C. & C. R. R. Stock valued at	1820.00
Rent paid in advance	600.00

LIABILITIES NOT SHOWN ON LEDGER.

Firm's Notes and Acceptances outstanding (Face)	$3826.00
Mortgage on House and Lot	500.00

ADDITIONAL ITEMS OF RESOURCE AND LIABILITY.

The interest upon the Notes and Drafts that are on hand, computed up to this date, is	$694.00
The interest upon the Notes and Drafts that the firm owe, computed to this date, is	148.00

A was to share $\frac{2}{5}$ of the gain or loss, and B $\frac{3}{5}$. What was the firm worth at commencing business? What is the firm worth at the close of business? What has been the net gain or net loss of firm? What is each partner's interest in the concern at closing?

20. Wm. H. Kinne and Edward Rice are partners in the Stone business. They have a Stone Yard, and buy and sell that material. Their books are kept by single entry. The books run four years before they are closed. An Inventory is taken and a Statement made up at the close of the first year. At the close of the second year, the party having charge of the books neglects to do this. At the close of the third year, the Inventory and Statement are made up, showing the result of two years' business. The Statement and Inventory are made up again at the close of the fourth year.

The profits or losses of the first year are to be divided as follows, viz.: Wm. H. Kinne $\frac{2}{3}$, Edward Rice $\frac{1}{3}$.

At the commencement of the second year J. G. Ranney is admitted as a partner, the three partners to be equally interested in gains or losses.

The following Statements were made out at the close of the first, third, and fourth years.

1856 to 1857. 1st year's business.

	Resources.	*Liabilities.*
Cash on hand	$1260.11	
W. H. Kinne—paid him	786.49	
Stone on hand	430.66	
Balances on Ledger	6945.00	
Edward Rice—advanced by him		$2675.44
Gains		6746.82
	$9422.26	$9422.26

1857—1858 to 1859. 2d and 3d years' business.

Edward Rice—paid him	$2675.44	
" " advanced last year		$2675.44
" " paid him	829.58	
W. H. Kinne " "	2947.73	
J. G. Ranney " "	1535.39	
Balances on Ledger	7039.67	
" " " last year		6945.00
Gains		5407.37
	$15027.81	$15027.81

1859 to 1860. 4th years' business.

Edward Rice—paid him	$1014.47	
Wm. H. Kinne " "	1543.16	
J. G. Ranney " "	557.95	
Balances on Ledger	10137.06	
" " " last year		$7039.67
Stone on hand	981.49	
Gains		7194.46
	$14234.13	$14234.13

The above Statements are given precisely as they were made up by one of the partners who handed them to us for adjustment. The student will please exercise his skill in producing the best form of Statement for showing clearly and conclusively each of the answers to the following questions.

How much is the firm worth at the close of each year, and what does the property consist of? What is each partner's nterest in the concern at the close of each year?

SUPPLEMENT.

RATES OF INTEREST AND STATUTE LIMITATIONS IN THE UNITED STATES.

STATES.	Legal rate.	Allowed by contract.	PENALTY FOR USURY.	Statute Limitations. Open Acc't.	Notes.	Judgments.
	%	%		yrs.	yrs.	yrs.
Alabama	8		Forfeiture of entire interest............	3	6	20
Arkansas.......	6	10	Usurious contracts void..............	3	5	10
California.......	10	18		1	4	5
Connecticut.....	6		Forfeiture of entire interest...........	6	6	17
Delaware.......	6		" " principal..........	3	6	
Florida.........	6	8	Forfeiture entire interest..............	5	5	
Georgia.........	7		" excess of interest...........	4	6	20
Illinois.........	6	10	" entire interest..............	5	5	20
Indiana.........	6		Usurious interest recoverable..........	6	20	20
Iowa...........	6	10	" " "		5	20
Kentucky.......	6		" excess void.................	1	5	15
Louisiana.......	5	8	Forfeiture of entire interest...........	3	5	
Maine..........	6		Usurious excess void.................	6	6	20
Maryland.......	6		Forfeit of usury.....................	3	3	12
Massachusetts...	6		Forfeit 3 fold usurious interest taken.....	6	6	
Michigan.......	7	10	Usurious excess void.................	6	6	
Minnesota.......	7	Free			6	10
Mississippi......	6	10	Forfeiture of interest.................	3	6	7
Missouri........	6	10	Forfeit entire interest.................	5	10	20
New Hampshire..	6		Forft. 3 fold usurious interest taken.....	6	6	20
New Jersey.....	6		Contract void........................	6	16	16
New York......	7		* Con. void. Fine not over $100, and imprisonment not over 6 mos., or both...	6	6	20
North Carolina...	6		Forfeit double the debt...............	3	3	
Ohio...........	6		Usurious excess void.................	6	15	
Pennsylvania....	6		Forfeit entire principal and interest......	6	6	20
Rhode Island....	6		Usurious excess void.................	6	6	20
South Carolina...	7		Forfeit entire interest.................	4	4	
Tennessee.......	6	10	Fine, at least $10.....................	3	6	16
Texas..........	8	12	Forfeit entire interest.................	2	4	
Vermont........	6		Usurious excess void.................	6	6	8
Virginia........	6		Contract void........................	5	5	20
Wisconsin......	7	12	Forfeit entire debt....................	6	6	

* Corporations excepted.

EXCHANGE TABLES.

[COMPILED MAINLY FROM TATE'S MODERN CAMBIST, AND THE BANKERS' MAGAZINE.]

GREAT BRITAIN.

MONEY OF ACCOUNT.—1 pound=12 shillings=240 pence, called *Sterling* money, to distinguish it from Colonial money, and other moneys of the Continent having the same denominations.

PAR OF EXCHANGE.—1 sovereign=£1=4.86\frac{2}{3}$.*

FRANCE.

MONEY OF ACCOUNT.—1 franc=100 centimes. Formerly livres and sous were used; 81 livres=80 frcs., and 1 sou=5 centimes.

PAR OF EXCHANGE.—20 francs gold=15s. 10$\frac{1}{4}$d. sterling=$3.84. Or, $1=5 frcs. 21 centimes, or £1=25 frcs. 22 centimes.

AMSTERDAM.

MONEY OF ACCOUNT.—6 florins or guilders=600 centimes=120 stivers=240 grotes Flemish=20 schillings Flemish=2$\frac{2}{5}$ rix dollars.

PAR OF EXCHANGE.—12 florins 9 centimes=£1=4.86\frac{2}{3}$. Or, 1 florin=$0.40. In the U. S. the quotations of exchange on Amsterdam are so many cents per florin or guilder.

BELGIUM.

MONEY OF ACCOUNT.—The official money of account is kept in francs and centimes the same as in France. But in mercantile accounts and exchange it is generally in florins and centimes, as in Amsterdam—the denominations of schillings and grotes being sometimes used in London Exchange.

* This value of the pound sterling is $\frac{1}{12}$ of a cent lower than that given on page 164, as here the weight of the sovereign is taken to be 123$\frac{171}{623}$ grains instead of 123$\frac{3}{10}$ grains, as assumed there.

Par of Exchange.—The fixed relative value of the franc to the florin is 47¼ centimes of a florin=1 franc. 25 frcs. 22 centimes=12 florins 9 centimes=40 schillings 3 grotes=£1=$4.86⅔.

HAMBURG.

Money of Account.—There are two standards in Hamburg, the one Banco and the other currency—the former being from 20 to 26% higher than the latter, varying with the market price of fine silver. The former is used in wholesale business and in exchanges, and is nominal; while the latter is used in the smaller trade, and is represented by coins in circulation. The Cologne mark weight, of the Hamburg standard, is 3608 grains Troy; and this weight of fine silver is *assumed* to be divided into 27¾ marks banco, but is *coined* into 34 marks current. The denominations in the two valuations being the same, the terms *banco* and *current* are used to distinguish the standard. 1 mark=16 schillings=192 pfennings. 3 marks, or 48 schillings, are called in exchange a rix dollar.

Par of Exchange.—13 marks 10½ schil. *banco* =£1=$4.86⅔.
16 " 12 " *current*=£1=$4.86⅔.
Or, 1 mark banco=35$\frac{6}{10}$ cents. In the U. S. the quotations of exchange on Hamburg are so many cents per mark banco.

PRUSSIA.

Money of Account.—1 Prussian dollar=30 silver groschen.

Par of Exchange.—1 Cologne mark weight of fine silver is coined into 14 dollars; hence, 6 Prussian dollars 27 silver groschen=£1=$4.86⅔.

RUSSIA.

Money of Account.—1 ruble=100 copecs. 100 silver rubles=350 paper or bank rubles—the latter being the money of account, previously to July, 1839.

Par of Exchange.—1 silver ruble=37½d. sterling. At Odessa the rate of exchange on London is still generally made in paper rubles, in which the par of exchange is 2240 paper rubles=£100 sterling.

FRANKFORT-ON-THE-MAINE.

Money of Account.—1 rix dollar=90 kreuzers=$1\frac{1}{2}$ florins=$22\frac{1}{2}$ batzen=360 hellers. The Prussian money is used for the payment of duties in Frankfort, and in all the States of the German Customs-Union—the value of 1 Prussian dollar being fixed at 105 kreuzers. There are two moneys of account at Frankfort, viz., Reichsgeld or 24 Guldenfuss, and Wechselzahlung. Reichsgeld is called 24 Guldenfuss or florin-foot, from the Cologne mark weight of fine silver being valued at 24 of these florins. Wechselzahlung, or exchange reckoning, is deduced from the estimation of the carolin at 9 florins 12 kreuzers in Wechselzahlung, the value of the same being 11 florins in 24 Guldenfuss, from which 46 rix-dollars W. Z.=55 rix dollars in 24 G.F.

Par of Exchange.—148.2 batzen W. Z.=£1=$4.86\frac{2}{3}.

1 rix-dollar in 24 Guldenfuss=30.47 pence sterling.
" Wechselzahlung=36.43 "

AUSTRIA.

Money of Account.—1 florin=60 kreuzers. A rix-dollar is $1\frac{1}{2}$ florins or 90 kreuzers, and is a nominal money used in exchanges but not in accounts. The value of the money of account is that called Convention, or 20 Guldenfuss, in which the Cologne mark weight of fine silver is supposed to be coined into 20 florins, a standard only $\frac{4}{11}$% above the Wechselzahlung of Frankfort. The currency of Austria is of both paper and metal. The paper money, called Wiener-wahrung, or Vienna value, is at a fixed discount of 60%: by which 100 florins in cash are equal to 250 florins in W. W. Bills upon Vienna are generally directed to be paid in effective—that is, in cash—sometimes mentioning the kind (as 20 kreuzer-pieces, for example), to guard against their being paid in paper money of the depreciated value.

Par of Exchange.—9 florins 50 kreuzers=£1=$4.86\frac{2}{3}.

1 rix-dollar in 20 Guldenfuss=36.56 pence sterling.

VENICE AND MILAN.

Money of Account.—1 lira Austriaca=100 centisimi=20 soldi Austriaci. The lira has the same value as the 20 kreuzer-piece, or the third of an Austrian florin.

Par of Exchange.—29 lire 52 cent.=£1, or 1 lira=$8\frac{1}{8}$d.

TUSCANY.

MONEY OF ACCOUNT.—1 lira Toscana=100 centisimi=20 soldi di Lira, a little below the Venetian standard.

PAR OF EXCHANGE.—30.69 lire=£1, or 1 lira=$7\frac{82}{100}$d.

BREMEN.

MONEY OF ACCOUNT.—5 schwaren=1 grote; 72 grotes=1 rix-dollar. The rix-dollar is valued, in gold, from the old French and German Louis d'or, at the rate of 5 rix-dollars to 1 Louis d'or.

PAR OF EXCHANGE.—1 rix-dollar=3s. 3.4d. sterling=$0.79\frac{7}{8}$. In the U. S. the quotations of exchange on Bremen are so many cents per rix-dollar.

CANADA.

MONEY OF ACCOUNT.—1 pound=20 shillings=240 pence=4 dollars=400 cents. The decimal system of dollars and cents has been recently introduced.

PAR OF EXCHANGE.—The Canadian pound (£), as represented by their paper currency, has been considered equivalent to four dollars U. S. currency. But the recent silver coinage, furnished that province by England, is $3\frac{2}{3}$% below the silver coinage of the U. S. in value, their 20 cent-piece being worth only $0.1927; and as the U. S. silver coinage is somewhat below par, taking the gold coinage for the standard, we may conclude that the par of exchange between Canada and the United States will soon be 104 cents Canada currency=$1, or 100 cents U. S. currency.

UNITED STATES.

PAR OF EXCHANGE.—Gold, or its equivalent, being the currency of New York city, and paper money being extensively used throughout the States, the par of exchange on New York city, for the year 1860, is very nearly as follows:

New England States,	$\frac{1}{8}$% prem.	Ohio, Ky., and Ind.,	$\frac{1}{2}$% prem.
New York State,	$\frac{3}{8}$% "	Detroit, - -	$\frac{1}{2}$% "
Baltimore, - -	Par.	Interior Michigan,	$1\frac{1}{2}$% "
Philadelphia, -	"	Iowa, Ill., and Wis.,	$1\frac{1}{2}$% "
Pittsburg "par funds,"	"	Missouri, - -	1 % "
" "currency,"	$\frac{1}{2}$% prem.	New Orleans, -	Par.

FOREIGN COINS.

Their Weight, Fineness, and Value, as Assayed at the United States Mint.

Remark.—The basis of valuation of the silver coins is $1.21 per ounce of *standard* fineness, which is the present mint price.

Gold Coins.

Country.	Denomination.	Weight.	Fineness.	Value.
		Oz. dec.	*Thous.*	*D. C. M.*
Australia	Pound of 1852	0.281	916.5	5.32.0
Australia	Pound of 1855	0.257	916.5	4.85.0
Austria	Ducat	0.112	986	2.28.0
Austria	Sovereign	0.363	900	6.77.0
Belgium	Twenty-five francs	0.254	899	4.72.0
Bolivia	Doubloon	0.867	870	15.58.0
Brazil	20,000 reis	0.575	917.5	10.90.5
Central America	Two escudors	0.209	853.5	3.66.0
Chili	Old doubloon	0.867	870	15.57.0
Chili	Ten pesos	0.492	900	9.15.3
Denmark	Ten thaler	0.427	895	7.90.0
Ecuador	Four escudors	0.433	844	7.60.0
England	Pound, or sovereign, new	0.256.7	916.5	4.86.3
England	Pound, average	0.256	915.5	4.84.8
France	Twenty francs, new	0.207.5	899.5	3.86.0
France	Twenty francs, average	0.207	899	3.84.5
Germany, North	Ten thaler	0.427	895	7.90.0
Germany, North	Ten thaler, Prussian	0.427	903	8.00.0
Germany, South	Ducat	0.112	986	2.28.3
Greece	Twenty drachms	0.185	900	3.45.0
Hindostan	Mohur	0.374	916	7.08.0
Mexico	Doubloon, average	0.867.5	866	15.53.4
Naples	Six ducati, new	0.245	996	5.04.0
Netherlands	Ten guilders	0.215	899	3.99.0
New Grenada	Old doubloon, Bogota	0.868	870	15.61.7
New Grenada	Old doubloon, Popayan	0.867	858	15.39.0
New Grenada	Ten pesos, new	0.525	891.5	9.67.5
Peru	Old doubloon	0.867	868	15.56.0
Portugal	Gold crown	0.308	912	5.81.3
Rome	2½ Scudi, new	0.140	900	2.60.0
Russia	Five roubles	0.210	916	3.97.6
Sardinia	Same as France	....	....	......
Spain	100 reals	0.268	896	4.96.3
Sweden	Ducat	0.111	975	2.26.7
Turkey	100 piastres	0.231	915	4.37.4
Tuscany	Sequin	0.112	999	2.30.0

The above shows the intrinsic relative value, as compared with the amount of fine gold in the U. S. coin. The price paid at the mint would be ½% less.

Silver Coins.

Country.	Denomination.	Weight.	Fineness.	Value.
		Oz. dec.	*Thous.*	*D.C.M.*
Austria	Rix-dollar	0 902	833	1.01.3
Austria	Scudo of six lire	0.836	902	1.01.5
Austria	20 kreutzer	0.215	582	16.8
Belgium	Five francs	0.803	897	96.8
Bolivia	Dollar	0.871	900.5	1.05.4
Bolivia	Half dollar, 1830	0.433	670	38.5
Bolivia	Quarter dollar, 1830	0.216	670	19.2
Brazil	2,000 reis	0.820	918.5	1.01.3
Central America	Dollar	0.866	850	97.3
Chili	Old dollar	0.864	908	1.04.7
Chili	New dollar	0.801	900.5	97.0
Denmark	Two rigsdaler	0.927	877	1.09.4
England	Shilling, new	0.182.5	924.5	22.7
England	Shilling, average	0.178	925	22.2
France	Five francs, average	0.800	900	96.8
Germany, North	Thaler	0.712	750	71.7
Germany, South	Gulden, or florin	0.340	900	41.2
Germany, North & South	2 thaler, or 3½ guld	1.192	900	1.44.3
Greece	Five drachms	0.719	900	86.9
Hindostan	Rupee	0.374	916	46.0
Japan	Itzebu	0.279	991	37.0
Mexico	Dollar, average	0.866	901	1.04.9
Naples	Scudo	0.884	830	98.8
Netherlands	2½ guilder	0.804	944	1.02.3
Norway	Specie-daler	0.927	877	1.09.4
New Grenada	Dollar of 1857	0.803	896	96.8
Peru	Old dollar	0.866	901	1.04.9
Peru	Old dollar of 1855	0.766	909	93.6
Peru	Half dollar, 1835–'38	0.433	650	37.7
Portugal	Silver crown	0.950	912	1.16.6
Rome	Scudo	0.864	900	1.04.7
Russia	Rouble	0.667	875	78.4
Sardinia	Five lire	0.800	900	96.8
Spain	New pistareen	0.166	899	20.1
Sweden	Rix-dollar	1.092	750	1.10.1
Switzerland	Two francs	0.323	899	39.0
Turkey	Twenty piastres	0.770	830	86.5
Tuscany	Florin	0.220	925	27.4

LINEAR, OR LONG MEASURE.

This measure is used to define distances in any direction

TABLE.

12 inches	(*in.*) make	1 foot	*ft.*
3 feet	"	1 yard	*yd.*
$5\frac{1}{2}$ yards	"	1 rod	*rd.*
40 rods	"	1 furlong	*fur.*
8 furlongs	"	1 statute mile	*mi.*

EQUIVALENTS.

mi.	*fur.*	*rd.*	*yd.*	*ft.*	*in.*
1 =	8 =	320 =	1760 =	5280 =	63360
	1 =	40 =	220 =	660 =	7920
		1 =	$5\frac{1}{2}$ =	$16\frac{1}{2}$ =	198
			1 =	3 =	36
				1 =	12

Scale of Units:—12, 3, $5\frac{1}{2}$, 40, 8.

ALSO:

3 barleycorns	make	1 inch	..*used by shoemakers.*
4 inches	"	1 hand	.. " *to measure horses.*
6 feet	"	1 fathom	.. " *to measure depths at sea*
1.15 statute miles	"	1 geographic mile	.. " " *distances* "
3 geographic miles	"	1 league.	
60 " "	"	1 degree.	
$69\frac{1}{5}$ statute "	"	1 degree.	
360 degrees	"	the circumference of the earth.	

SQUARE MEASURE.

This measure is used to compute surfaces or areas.

TABLE.

144 square inches	(*sq. in.*) make	1 square foot	*sq. ft.*
9 square feet	"	1 square yard	*sq. yd.*
$30\frac{1}{4}$ square yards	"	1 square rod	*sq. rd.*
40 square rods	"	1 rood	*R.*
4 roods	"	1 acre	*A.*
640 acres	"	1 square mile	*sq. mi.*

EQUIVALENTS.

sq. mi.	*A.*	*R.*	*sq. rd.*	*sq. yd.*	*sq. ft.*	*sq. in.*
1 =	640 =	2560 =	102400 =	3097600 =	27878400 =	4014489600
	1 =	4 =	160 =	4840 =	43560 =	6272640
		1 =	40 =	1210 =	10890 =	1568160
			1 =	$30\frac{1}{4}$ =	$272\frac{1}{4}$ =	39204
				1 =	9 =	1296
					1 =	144

Scale of Units:—144, 9, $30\frac{1}{4}$, 40, 4, 640.

SURVEYORS' MEASURE.

This measure is used to compute land distances and areas. A Gunter's chain, which is the measure used by surveyors, is four rods in length, and consists of 100 *links.*

TABLE OF LINEAR DISTANCES.

7.92 inches (*in.*)	make	1 link.... *l.*
25 links	"	1 rod..... *rd.*
4 rods, or 66 feet,	"	1 chain... *ch.*
80 chains	"	1 mile.... *mi.*

EQUIVALENTS.

mi.		*ch.*		*rd.*		*l.*		*in.*
1	=	80	=	320	=	8000	=	63360
		1	=	4	=	100	=	792
				1	=	25	=	198
						1	=	7.92

SCALE OF UNITS:—7.92, 25, 4, 80.

TABLE OF AREAS.

625 square links (*sq. l.*)	make	1 pole........ *P.*
16 poles	"	1 square chain. *sq. ch.*
10 square chains	"	1 acre........ *A.*
640 acres	"	1 square mile.. *sq. mi.*
36 square miles (6 miles square)	"	1 township.... *Tp.*

EQUIVALENTS.

Tp.		*sq. mi.*		*A.*		*sq. ch.*		*P.*		*sq. l.*
1	=	36	=	23040	=	230400	=	3686400	=	2304000000
		1	=	640	=	6400	=	102400	=	64000000
				1	=	10	=	160	=	10000
						1	=	16	=	1000
								1	=	625

SCALE OF UNITS:—625, 16, 10, 640, 36.

CUBIC MEASURE.

This measure is used to compute the contents of solid substances; it is sometimes called "solid" measure.

TABLE.

1728 cubic inches (*cu. in.*)	make	1 cubic foot.... *cu. ft.*
27 cubic feet	"	1 cubic yard... *cu. yd.*
16 cord feet	"	1 cord foot..... *cd. ft.*
8 cord feet, or 128 cubic feet	"	1 cord of wood.. *cd.*
24¾ cubic feet	"	1 perch........ *Pch.*

LIQUID MEASURE.

This measure is used for measuring liquids; such as liquors, molasses, water, etc.

TABLE.

4 gills (*gi.*)	make	1 pint.......... *pt.*
2 pints	"	1 quart......... *qt.*
4 quarts	"	1 gallon........ *gal.*
$31\frac{1}{2}$ gallons	"	1 barrel........ *bbl.*
2 barrels	"	1 hogshead...... *hhd.*

EQUIVALENTS.

hhd.		*bbl.*		*gal.*		*qt.*		*pt.*		*gi.*
1	=	2	=	63	=	252	=	504	=	2016
		1	=	$31\frac{1}{2}$	=	126	=	252	=	1008
				1	=	4	=	8	=	32
						1	=	2	=	8
								1	=	4

SCALE OF UNITS:—4, 2, 4, $31\frac{1}{2}$, 2.

ALSO,

36 gallons	make	1 barrel of ale, beer, or milk.
54 "	"	1 hogshead " "
42 "	"	1 tierce.
2 hogsheads	"	1 pipe, or butt.
2 pipes	"	1 tun.

DRY MEASURE.

Used for measuring articles not liquid; as grain, fruit, salt, etc.

TABLE.

2 pints (*pt.*)	make	1 quart...... *qt.*
8 quarts	"	1 peck....... *pk.*
4 pecks	"	1 bushel...... *bu.*
36 bushels	"	1 chaldron... *ch.*

EQUIVALENTS.

ch.		*bu.*		*pk.*		*qt.*		*pt.*
1	=	36	=	144	=	1152	=	2304
		1	=	4	=	32	=	64
				1	=	8	=	16
						1	=	2

SCALE OF UNITS:—2, 8, 4, 36.

AVOIRDUPOIS WEIGHT.

Used to weigh all coarse articles; as hay, grain, groceries, wares, etc., and all metals, except gold and silver.

TABLE.

16 drams (*dr.*)	make	1 ounce.......... *oz.*
16 ounces	"	1 pound.......... *lb.*
25 pounds	"	1 quarter........ *qr.*
4 quarters	"	1 hundred weight. *cwt.*
20 hundred weight	"	1 Ton............ *T.*

EQUIVALENTS.

T.		cwt.		qr.		lb.		oz.		dr.
1	=	20	=	80	=	2000	=	32000	=	512000
		1	=	4	=	100	=	1600	=	25600
				1	=	25	=	400	=	6400
						1	=	16	=	256
								1	=	16

SCALE OF UNITS:—16, 16, 25, 4, 20.

TROY WEIGHT.

For weighing gold, silver, jewels, and liquors.

TABLE.

24 grains (*gr.*)	make	1 pennyweight.. *pwt.*
20 pennyweights	"	1 ounce........ *oz.*
12 ounces	"	1 pound........ *lb.*

EQUIVALENTS.

lb.		oz.		pwt.		gr.
1	=	12	=	240	=	5760
		1	=	20	=	480
				1	=	24

SCALE OF UNITS:—24, 20, 12.

APOTHECARIES' WEIGHT.

Used by apothecaries and physicians in mixing medicines.

TABLE.

20 grains (*gr.*)	make	1 scruple.... ℈
3 scruples	"	1 dram...... ʒ
8 drams	"	1 ounce..... ℥
12 ounces	"	1 pound..... ℔

EQUIVALENTS.

℔		℥		ʒ		℈		gr.
1	=	12	=	96	=	288	=	5760
		1	=	8	=	24	=	480
				1	=	3	=	60
						1	=	20

SCALE OF UNITS:—20, 3, 8, 12.

TIME MEASURE.

Used to denote the passage of time.

TABLE.

60 seconds (*sec.*)	make	1 minute.... *m.*
60 minutes	"	1 hour...... *hr.*
24 hours	"	1 day....... *da.*
7 days	"	1 week..... *wk.*
365$\frac{1}{4}$ days	"	1 year...... *yr.*
100 years	"	1 century.... *C.*

EQUIVALENTS.

yr.		*wk.*		*da.*		*hr.*		*min.*		*sec.*
1	=	52	=	$365\frac{1}{4}$	=	8766	=	525960	=	31557600
		1	=	7	=	168	=	10080	=	604800
				1	=	24	=	1440	=	86400
						1	=	60	=	3600
								1	=	60

Note.—It is customary to reckon 4 weeks to the month, and 12 months to the year, but as this only approximates the truth we have omitted it. Twelve *calendar* months make a year, but these months are not of regular length, as the following table will show:—

1. January	has	31	days.	7. July	has	31	days.
2. February	"	28	"	8. August	"	31	"
3. March	"	31	"	9. September	"	30	"
4. April	"	30	"	10. October	"	31	"
5. May	"	31	"	11. November	"	30	"
6. June	"	30	"	12. December	"	31	"

The year, as indicated above, would consist of 365 days. This is the length of the common year. Once in four years, however, one day is added to February, making 366 days; and thus, each year averages $365\frac{1}{4}$ days. The longest year is called Bissextile, or Leap year. The leap years are all exactly divisible by 4.

CIRCULAR MEASURE

Is used to determine localities, by estimating latitude and longitude; also, to measure the motions of the heavenly bodies, and computing differences of time. All circles, of whatever dimensions, are supposed to be divided into the same number of parts—as quadrants, signs, degrees, etc. It will, therefore, be evident, that there can be no "fixed" dimensions of the units named.

TABLE.

60 seconds (″)	make	1 minute.... ′
60 minutes	"	1 degree.... °
30 degrees	"	1 sign...... *S.*
12 signs, or 360 degrees	"	1 circle..... *C.*

EQUIVALENTS.

C.		*S.*		°		′		″
1	=	12	=	360	=	21600	=	1296000
		1	=	30	=	1800	=	108000
				1	=	60	=	3600
						1	=	60

SCALE OF UNITS:—60, 60, 30, 12.

MISCELLANEOUS TABLE.

12 units	make	1	dozen.
12 dozen	"	1	gross.
12 gross	"	1	great gross.
20 things	"	1	score
100 pounds	"	1	quintal of fish.
196 pounds	"	1	barrel of flour.
200 pounds	"	1	barrel of pork.
18 inches	"	1	cubit.
22 inches (nearly)	"	1	sacred cubit.
14 pounds of iron or lead	"	1	stone.
21½ stones	"	1	pig.
8 pigs	"	1	fother.

BOOKS AND PAPER.

Names of different sizes of paper made by machinery.

Double imperial,	32 by 44	inches.	Imperial,	22 by 32	inches.
Double Super Royal,	27 by 42	"	Super Royal,	21 by 27	"
Double medium,	23 by 26	"	Royal,	19 by 24	"
"	24 by 37½	"	Medium,	18½ by 23½	"
"	25 by 38	"	Demy,	17 by 22	"
Royal and Half,	25 by 29	"	Folio Post,	16 by 21	"
Imperial and Half,	26 by 32	"	Foolscap,	14 by 17	"

Crown, 15 by 20 inches.

A sheet	folded in	2	leaves is called	a folio.
"	"	4	"	a quarto, or 4to.
"	"	8	"	an Octavo, or 8vo.
"	"	12	"	a 12mo.
"	"	18	"	an 18mo.
"	"	24	"	an 24mo.
"	"	32	"	a 32mo.

In estimating the size of the leaves, as above, the double medium sheet is taken as a standard.

24 sheets	make	1	quire.
20 quires	"	1	ream.
2 reams	"	1	bundle.
5 bundles	"	1	bale.

PRACTICAL HINTS FOR FARMERS.

1. MEASURING GRAIN.—By the United States standard, 2150 cubic inches make a bushel. Now, as a cubic foot contains 1728 cubic inches, a bushel is to a cubic foot as 2150 to 1728; or, for practical purposes, as 4 to 5. Therefore, to convert cubic feet to bushels, it is necessary only to multiply by $\frac{4}{5}$. EXAMPLE.—How much grain will a bin hold which is 10 feet long, 4 feet wide, and 4 feet deep? *Solution*.—10 × 4 × 4 = 160 cubic feet. 160 × $\frac{4}{5}$ = 128, the number of bushels.

To measure grain on the floor.—Make the pile in form of a pyramid or cone, and multiply the area of the base by one-third the height. To find the area of the base, multiply the square of its diameter by the decimal .7854. EXAMPLE.—A conical pile of grain is 8 feet in diameter, and 4 feet high, how many bushels does it contain? *Solution*.—The square of 8 is 64; and 64 × .7854 × $\frac{4}{3}$ = 83.776, the number of cubic feet. Therefore,
83.776 × $\frac{4}{5}$ = 67.02 bushels. *Answer*.

2. TO ASCERTAIN THE QUANTITY OF LUMBER IN A LOG.—Multiply the diameter in *inches* at the small end by one-half the number of inches, and this product by the length of the log in *feet*, which last product divide by 12. EXAMPLE.—How many feet of lumber can be made from a log which is 36 inches in diameter and 10 feet long? *Solution*.—36 × 18 = 648; 648 × 10 = 6480; 6480 ÷ 12 = 540. *Ans*.

3. TO ASCERTAIN THE CAPACITY OF A CISTERN OR WELL.—Multiply the square of the diameter in inches by the decimal .7854, and this product by the depth in inches; divide this product by 231, and the quotient will be the contents in gallons. EXAMPLE.—What is the capacity of a cistern which is 12 feet deep and 6 feet in diameter? *Solution*.—The square of 72, the diameter in inches, is 5184; 5184 × .7854 = 4071.51; 4071.51 × 144 = 586297.44, the number of cubic inches in the cistern. There are 231 cubic inches in a gallon, therefore, 586297.44 ÷ 231 = 2538 +, gallons. To reduce the number of gallons to barrels, divide, by $31\frac{1}{2}$.

4. TO ASCERTAIN THE WEIGHT OF CATTLE BY MEASUREMENT.—Multiply the girth in feet, by the distance from the bone of the tail immediately over the hinder part of the buttock, to the fore part of the shoulder-blade; and this product by 31, when the animal measures *more than 7 and less than 9 feet in girth*; by 23, when *less than 7 and more than 5*; by 16, when *less than 5 and more than 3*; and by 11, when *less than 3*. EXAMPLE.—What is the weight of an ox whose measurements are as follows; girth, 7 feet 5 inches; length, 5 feet 6 inches?
Solution.—$5\frac{1}{2} \times 7\frac{5}{12} = 40\frac{57}{72}$; $40\frac{57}{72} \times 31 = 1264 +$. *Ans*.

A deduction of one pound in 20 must be made for half-fatted cattle, and also for cows that have had calves. It is understood, of course, that such standard will at best, give only the *approximate* weight.

5. MEASURING LAND.—To find the number of acres of land in a rectangular field, multiply the length by the breadth, and divide the product by 160, if the measurement is made in rods, or by 43560 if made in feet. EXAMPLE.—How many acres in a field which is 100 rods in length, by 75 rods in width? *Solution*.—100 × 75 = 7500; 7500 ÷ 160 = $46\frac{14}{16}$. *Answer*. To find the contents of a triangular piece of land, having a rectangular corner, multiply the two shorter sides together, and take one-half the product.

6. MEASUREMENT OF HAY.—10 cubic yards of meadow hay, weigh a ton. When the hay is taken out of old, or the lower part of large stacks, 8 or 9 cubic yards will make a ton. 10 or 12 cubic yards of clover, when dry, make a ton.

Hay stored in barns, requires from 300 to 400 cubic feet to make a ton, if it be of medium coarseness, and greater or less quantity, varying from 300 to 500 solid feet, according to its quality.

TABLES OF
MONEY, WEIGHT, AND MEASURE,
OF THE
PRINCIPAL COMMERCIAL COUNTRIES IN THE WORLD.

WE are indebted to the Publishers of "WEBSTER'S COUNTING HOUSE DICTIONARY" for the use of the following admirably arranged Tables, which will be found of great value for reference. The tables have been prepared with much care and may be relied upon as correct.

GREAT BRITAIN.

(*Principal Commercial City*, LONDON.)

Money.

The national Currency of Great Britain is called *Sterling Money*—thus we say, so many pounds sterling. The Pound Sterling is represented by a gold coin called a *Sovereign*, and its custom-house value in the United States is fixed by law at $4.84. The *intrinsic* value of the *Sovereign* varies somewhat, depending on the date of the coinage. Victoria sovereigns are worth the most, as being of the latest coinage; those of William IV. or George III. less, as more worn. The commercial value of the pound sterling varies, like merchandise, according to demand; $4.84 is that on which duties are charged. Thus if you buy a bill of goods in London of £100, on which the duty in this country is 25 per cent., and import them, you pay at the Custom house 25 per cent. on $484, or $121. What is called the *par* value of the pound sterling in the United States is $4.44 4-9. The *par* value of the pound in London, in American currency, is $4.80. The difference between the *par* value of the pound sterling in this country ($4.44 4-9) and the actual value to us here, at the time, of a pound sterling in London, is called the Exchange. Thus, if exchange on London, in New York, is 9 per cent., a pound sterling is worth $4.44 4-9, and 9 per cent. added, or $4.84. If 7 per cent., of course, less; if 10 per cent., more.

Freight bills for goods by ship are payable at $4.80 the pound, which is 8 per cent. on $4.44 4-9. Exchange on London is usually 7 to 10 per cent. in New York, i. e. a pound sterling in London is worth $4.44 4-9 and 7 to 10 per cent. additional, in New York, nearly.

In the following Tables we give the pound at $4.84, it being understood that its commercial value is sometimes higher and sometimes lower.

4 farthings, *qr.*	=	1 penny, *d.*
12 pence	=	1 shilling, *s.*
20 shillings	=	1 pound, *£.*
A sovereign	=	20 shillings.
A guinea	=	21 "
A crown	=	5 "
A groat	=	4 pence.

The farthing is an imaginary coin; the penny, copper; the sixpence, shilling, and crown, silver; sovereign and guinea, gold.

The English Tables of Weights, Measures, Time, &c., are the same essentially as the American.

The value of the Pound Sterling in the following Tables is put at $4.84.

AUSTRIA.

(*Chief Commercial City*, VIENNA.)

Money. In Silver.

fl.	krt.			£	s.	d.		$	c.	m.
10	0	.. ..	=	1	0	0	=	4	84	0
0	30	.. ..	=	0	1	0	=	0	24	2
0	2½	.. ..	=	0	0	1	=	0	02	0 2-12
7	0	.. ..	=	0	13	6	=	3	26	7
4	40	or ducat ..	=	0	9	4	=	2	25	8 8-12
1	0	silver florin	=	0	2	0	=	0	48	4
2	0	or 1 dollar	=	0	4	0	=	0	96	8
0	20	or 1 zwanziger	=	0	0	8	=	0	16	1 4-12

1 florin is equal to 60 kreutzers.

Paper currency is depreciated now from 25 to 35 per cent.

Weights and Measures.

AUSTRIAN.		ENGLISH.
100 commercial lbs.	=	123.6 lbs. avoirdp.
1 staro	=	2.34 Winch. bush.
1 polonick ..	=	0.861 ditto
1 eimer	=	15 wine gallons
1 barile	=	173½ ditto
1 ell woolen measure	=	26.6 in.
1 ell silk.. ..	=	25.2 in.

Or more particularly—

Weight.

AUSTRIAN.		ENGLISH.
100 commercial lbs.	=	123.6 lbs. avoirdp.
1 lb.	=	4 vindlinge
1 vindlingo ..	=	4 unzen
1 unzen	=	2 loth
1 loth	=	4 quintl.
1 stone	=	20 lbs.
1 sanno	=	275 lbs.

Measure.

1 foot	=	12¼ inches
1 mult	=	4⅓ miles

Grain.

64 monsel	=	1 metz
30 metz	=	1 muth
1 muth	=	50⅓ bush. Eng.

BAVARIA AND BADEN.

(*Principal Commercial City*, AUGSBURG.)

Money.

fl.	krt.			£	s.	d.		$	c.	m.
12	0	at par	=	1	0	0	=	4	84	0
0	36	.. ..	=	0	1	0	=	0	24	2
0	3	.. ..	=	0	0	1	=	0	02	0 2-12
10	0	gold 10 guildr. piece	=	0	16	8	=	4	03	3 4-12
5	0	gold 5 do. do.	=	0	8	4	=	2	01	6 8-12
3	30	silver 3½ flor. piece	=	0	5	10	=	1	41	1 8-12
5	35	or ducat ..	=	0	9	3	=	2	23	8 6-12
2	42	or crown thaler	=	0	4	4	=	1	04	8 8-12
1	0	.. ..	=	0	1	8	=	0	40	3 4-12

1 florin is equal to 60 kreutzers.

Books are kept in Gulden a 60 kreutzer of the 20 gulden fuss, so called because the Cologne mark of fine silver is worth only 20 fl. Augsburg currency, while all other South German States reckon on the 24 gulden fuss.

COIN.—Gold (old). 1 Caroline=18*s.* 6*d.* English=$4.44.

½ caroline=9*s.* 3*d.* English=$2.22.

1 double max d'or=24*s.* 4*d.* English=$5.84.

1 max d'or=12*s.* 2*d.* English=$2.92.

1 ducat (new)=9*s.* 4*d.* English=$2.24.

Silver pieces of 3½ gulden, 1 gulden, ½ gulden, 1 kreutzer, 3 kreutzer, all in the 24 gulden fuss.

Weight.

1 pound=560 grammes French=1¼ pound avoirdupois.

1 cwt.=100 pounds=3,200 loth=12,800 quent.

1 Augsburg marc=16 loth=64 quent=256 pfenning=3,643 grains troy English.

Measure.

The foot=11½ inches English.

1 ruthe=10 feet=120 zoll or inches=1440 lines.

1 ell=2 41-48 feet=33¾ inches English.

1 klafter=6 feet=5¾ feet English.

FOR CORN.—1 scheffel=6 bushels 1 gallon English.

1 scheffel=6 metz=12 viertel=48 maas.

FOR LIQUORS.—Wine, 1 eymer=60 maas.
Beer, 1 " =60 "
1 maas=1⅓ pints English.

BELGIUM.

(*Principal Commercial City*, ANTWERP.)

Money (at par).

fr.	cts.			£	s.	d.		$	c.	m.
25	0	.. ..	=	1	0	0	=	4	84	0
1	25	.. ..	=	0	1	0	=	0	24	2
0	10	.. ..	=	0	0	1	=	0	02	0 2-12
25	0	or 1 gold Leopold	=	0	19	10	=	4	79	9 8-12
10	0	or 10 franc piece	=	0	7	10	=	1	89	5 8-12
5	0	or 5 franc piece	=	0	3	11	=	0	94	7 10-12
1	0	.. ..	=	0	0	9½	=	0	19	1 7-12

1 franc is equal to 100 centimes.

Weights and measures the same as in France.

BRAZILS.

(*Principal Commercial City*, Rio de Janeiro.)

Money.

reis.	£	s.	d.		$	c.	m.
6400 or gold piece =	1	15	9	=	8	65	1 6-12
4000 or gold piece of =	1	0	0	=	4	84	0
1200 or silver piece of =	0	4	2	=	1	00	8 4-12
960 " =	0	4	1	=	0	98	0 4-12
640 " =	0	2	9	=	0	66	5 6-12
320 " =	0	1	4	=	0	32	2 8-12
200 " =	0	0	8	=	0	16	1 4-12

1 mil reis is equal to 1000 reis.

The unit is the reis, as in Portugal.

Coin.—Gold dobra a 12,800 reis=$18.00.
Meia dobra a 6,400 reis=$9.00.
Moeda a 4000 reis=$5.75.

Silver.—Pieces of 1200 reis=$1.00. ; 400 reis=$0.33.
Pieces of 100 reis=$0.08.

Bank Notes are worth less than specie by about one third.

Exchange on London, 30d. sterling per milrea in bank notes.

Exchange on Paris, fr. 3.15 to fr. 3.20 per 1000 reis.

Weight.

1 quintal=4 arrobas a 32 arratels, (pounds.)
1 arratel (lb.)=11⅓ oz. avdp.
1 quintal=91½ lb. avdp.
Gold and silver weight is the arratel a 2.
Marcos a 8 onças a 8 oitavas a 72 granos.
1 marco=7 oz. 7 4-7 dwts. troy.

Diamonds, emeralds, rubies, pearls, &c. are sold by the quilate. Topazes by the oitava a 3 escrupulos a 3 quilates a 4 granos.

1 oitava=1 oz. 19 9-10 dwts. troy.
1 quilate=4 13-30 dwts. troy.

Measure.

1 pe (foot) 1=foot Eng.
1 palmo=9½ inches Eng.
1 braça=2 varas=8½ covados=10 palmas.
1 braça=2¾ yards Eng.
1 legoa (mile)=4¼ miles Eng.

Corn, Rice, Coffee, &c.—1 mayo=15 fanegas, each fanega=4 alqueires.

1 mayo=22½ bushels Eng.
1 fanega=11¾ gall.

Wine.—The same as in Portugal.

BREMEN.

(*One of the four Free Cities of Germany.*)

Money.

rigdl.	grosch.		£	s.	d.		$	c.	m.
6	6	=	1	0	0	=	4	84	0
0	24	=	0	1	0	=	0	24	2
1	0 or gold rigxdal.	=	0	3	4	=	0	80	6 8-12
0	36 or 36 groat piece	=	0	1	6	=	0	36	3
5	24 or Louis-d'or	=	0	16	0	=	3	87	2

1 thaler is equal to 72 groten.

BRUNSWICK AND HANOVER.

(*Principal Commercial Cities*, Brunswick and Hanover.)

Money.

tl.	grs.	pfn.		£	s.	d.		$	c.	m.
6	16	0	=	1	0	0	=	4	84	0
0	8	0	=	0	1	0	=	0	24	2
0	0	10	=	0	0	1	=	0	02	0 2-12
10	0	0 dble. Georged'or	=	1	12	4	=	7	72	4 8-12
5	0	0 or single "	=	0	16	2	=	3	91	2 4-12
1	0	0	=	0	3	0	=			
0	1	0 or 12 pfennings	=	0	0	1¼	=	0	02	5 5-24

1 thaler is equal to 24 groschen.

CHINA.

(*Principal Commercial City*, Canton.)

Money.

The Chinese reckon in taels, a 10 mace, a 10 candarin, a 10 cash.

1 tael=6*s.* 6*d.*=$1.56.

Coin.—They only have the cash or li. All other are imaginary. They use the piasters of Spain at 72 candarins. The East India Company take the tael only at 6*s.* 720 taels=1,000 dollars of Spain.

The exchange on London is 4*s.* 8*d.*, more or less, for one Spanish dollar.

Weight.

1 pecul=100 cattys (gin), a 16 taels (lyang), a 10 mazas (tachen), or 10 candarins (twin), a 10 cash (li).
1 pecul = 133⅓ pounds avoirdupois.
1 catty = 1⅓ pound "
1 tael = 1⅓ ounce "
1 catty (also the weight for gold and silver)=1 pound 7 3-5 ounces troy English; 1 tael=579 4-5 grains troy English.

The assay of gold and silver is done by 100 parts called toques. Silver must be 80-100 pure.

Measure.

The covid=14⅝ inches English.
1 covid=10 punts.

The Chinese use four different feet:

For mathematics = 13⅛ inches English.
For builders = 12 1-15 "
For engineers = 12⅔ "
For trade = 13⅓ "

1 li=180 fathoms of 10 feet of the engineers=2-5 of an English mile.

DENMARK.

(*Principal Commercial City*, Copenhagen.)

Money.

rigsd.	skil.		£	s.	d.		$	c.	m.
9	16	=	1	0	0	=	4	84	0
0	44	=	0	1	0	=	0	24	2
0	3¾	=	0	0	1	=	0	02	0 2-12
7	50 or 1 Christian d'or	=	0	16	3	=	3	93	2 6-12
2	0 or 1 species silver	=	0	4	4	=	1	04	8 8-12
1	0	=	0	2	2	=	0	52	4 4-12
0	16 or 1 mark ..	=	0	0	4½	=	0	09	1

1 rigsb. daler is equal to 96 skillings.
2 rigsbank daler=1 specie-daler=3 mark banco in Hamburg.
1 rigsbank daler=2*s.* 3*d.* English.
1 skilling=1 farthing=half a cent American.

Bank notes in specie daler are freely taken—100 specie daler for 200 rigsbank daler.

They draw generally on Hamburg at sight or 14 days after date, and the exchange on London is 9½ rigsbank daler for £1 sterling. Exchange on Paris (rarely) from fr. 2.60 to fr. 2.70 per rigsbank daler.

Weight.

1 pound=1 pound 1⅝ oz. avoirdupois.
1 pound=16 ounces=32 loth=128 quents.
1 ship-pound=320 pounds.
1 last=16½ do. or 52 cwt. of 100 pounds.

Gold and silver are sold by the pound=2 marks =16 ozs.=512 orts=8192 es. 1 mark=7 ozs. 4 1-5 dwts. Troy.

Measure.

1 foot=12⅜ inches English.
1 ell=24¾ inches English.
1 mile=4⅝ miles English.

For Corn.—1 toende=8 skieps=32 viertels.

1 toende=30 gallons 4½ pints English.
1 skiep=3 gallons 6½ pints English.
1 last=22 toendes.

EAST INDIES.

(*Principal Commercial Cities*, BOMBAY, BENGAL, CALCUTTA, *and* MADRAS.)

rup's.	ann.	pi.		£	s.	d.	$	c.	m.
10	8	0	..	= 1	0	0	= 4	84	0
0	8	4	..	= 0	1	0	= 0	24	2
0	0	8	..	= 0	0	1	= 0	02	0 2-12
16	0	0	gold mohur	= 1	9	0	= 7	01	8
1	0	0	rupee sicca	= 0	1	10½	= 0	45	3 9-12
0	8	0	half rupee	= 0	0	11¼	= 0	22	6 21-24

1 rupee is equal to 8 annas or 96 pice.

More particularly—

CALCUTTA. Money.

The Company's rupee=15-16 sicca rupee=1*s.* 11*d.* =$0.46.
1 rupee=16 anas; 1 ana=12 pice.

COIN—Gold: 1 mohur=15 rupees=33*s.* 2*d.* English=$8.02.6 4-12. Silver: 1 sicca rupee=2*s.* English =$0.48.4

Weight.

1 maund (factory maund), a 40 seers, a 16 chattacks.
1 maund=74 pounds 10 ounces avoirdupois.
1 seer=29⅘ ounces avoirdupois. The bazaar weight is 10 p. ct. heavier.
1 sicca=10 massa a 32 grains, or 4 punkhos.
1 sicca=178¾ grains troy Engl.

Measure.

1 cubit=18 inches English. 1 guz=1 yard English.
1 coss=4,000 cubits=1⅛ mile English.
Corn is sold by the khahoon of 40 maunds or 16 soallis a 20 pallies. 1 pallie=9⅓ pounds avoirdupois.

MADRAS. Money.

The same as Calcutta.

Weight.

1 candy=20 maunds=160 vis—6,400 pollams.
1 candy=500 lbs. avdp.

Measure.

Long measure the same as Calcutta.
FOR CORN—1 garee=400 mercals a 8 puddys or 84 allocks.
1 garee=135 bushels.

BOMBAY. Money.

1 rupee=100 reas. Value as in Calcutta.
Exchange on London, 2*s.*, more or less, for 1 Company's rupee.

Weight.

1 candy=20 maunds a 40 seers a 30 pice.
1 candy=560 lbs. avdp.

Measure.

1 covid=18 inches English.
FOR CORN—1 candy=8 parahas a 16 adowlies.
1 candy=24½ bushels.

EGYPT.

(*Principal Commercial City*, ALEXANDRIA.)

Money (at par.)

piast.	par.		£	s.	d.	$	c.	m.
97	20	.. ..	= 1	0	0	= 4	84	0
5	0	.. ..	= 0	1	0	= 0	24	2
0	17	.. ..	= 0	0	1	= 0	02	0 2-12
50	0	gold new sequin	= 0	10	4	= 2	50	0 8-12
12	0	silver new piast.	= 0	3	4	= 0	89	6 8-12
4	0	silver grush	= 0	1	2	= 0	28	2 4-12
1	0	piastre ..	= 0	0	2½	= 0	05	0 5-12

Wholesale payments are made in purses of 500 current piasters, chiefly in Span. dollars or piasters.
1 Sp. dollar=20 Egypt. piast.

1 piaster in Alexandria has 40 medinis or paras, or 100 good or 120 current aspers.
In Cairo 1 piaster=80 aspers or 33 paras.

COIN.—Ducatillo a 10, griscio a 30, piaster a 40, mahouib a 90, and zumabob a 120 paras. Also, zenzerli a 107, and mecchini a 146 zedinis.
Cotton is sold by cantaros. 1 cantaro=115 lb. Eng.
Coffee and Cotton are invoiced in Span. dollars.
Other goods in Egyptian Piasters.

Exchange on London, 80 piasters, more or less, for $1 sterlg.
Exchange on Paris, 315 a 320 per fr. 100.

Weight.

1 cantare a 100 rotoli.

The rotoli differ. There are rotolo forforo = 15 oz.; rotolo zauro = 33⅓ oz.; rotolo zadino = 21 5-16.; rotolo mina=26 5-7 oz.

The quintal of coffee in Cairo=103 3-5 lb. Eng.
1 oka=400 drachmas a 16 carat a 4 grain.
1 oka=3 lb. 2 oz. 17 2-5 dwt. troy.
1 drachma=1 dwt. 22½ grs.

Measure.

1 pik=26 4-5 in. Eng.
FOR CORN.—1 rebebe=36 galls. Eng.
1 kisloz=39 galls. Eng.

FRANCE.

(*Principal Commercial City*, PARIS.)

Money (at par.)

frs.	cts.		£	s.	d.	$	c.	m.
25	0	.. ..	= 1	0	0	= 4	84	0
1	25	.. ..	= 0	1	0	= 0	24	2
0	10	.. ..	= 0	0	1	= 0	02	0 2-12
20	0	or gold Napoleon	= 0	16	0	= 3	87	2
5	0	or silver do.	= 0	4	0	= 0	96	8
1	0	do. ..	= 0	0	9½	= 0	19	1 7-12
0	10	.. ..	= 0	0	1	= 0	02	0 2-12

1 franc weighs 5 grammes=100 centimes.

COIN.—Gold pieces of 100, 40, 20 and 10 francs.
Silver pieces of 5, 2, 1, ½ and ¼ francs.
Bank notes of 500 and 1000 francs.

Exchange on London, fr. 25.50 for £1 sterlg.
Exchange on New York, fr. 5.25 to 5.30 for $1.

Weights.

Milligramme	..	=	0.0154 grs.
Centigramme	..	=	0.1543
Décigramme	..	=	1.5434
Gramme ..	..	=	15.4340
Décagramme	..	=	154.3420

or 5·64 drams avoirdupois.
Hectogramme .. = 32.154 oz. troy, or 3·527 oz. avoirdupois.
Kilogramme=2 lbs. 8 oz. 3 dwt. 2 grs. troy, or 2 lbs. 3 oz. 4.652 drams avoirdupois.
Myriogramme .. = 26.795 lbs. troy, or 22·0485 lbs. avoirdupois.
Quintal=1 cwt. 3 qrs. 25 lbs. nearly.
Millier or bar=9 tons 16 cwt. 3 qrs. 12 lbs.

The weight of 1 cubic centimetre of pure water is taken as the foundation. It is called gramme.

1 myriagramme=10 kilogr.=100 hectogr.=1000 decagr.=10,000 grammes.
1 gramme=10 decigr.=100 centigr.=1000 milligr.
1 gramme=15 2-5 grains troy, or the kilogr.=15434 grains troy.
373¼ grammes=1 lb. troy.
453 3-5 grammes=1 lb. avdp.
1 kilogr.=2 lb. 3¼ oz. avdp.
1 quintal=100 kilogr.=220½ lb. avdp.

Measures.

Long Measure.

FRENCH.			ENGLISH.
Millimètre	..	=	0.03987 in.
Centimètre	..	=	0.39371
Décimètre	..	=	3.93710
*Metre**	.. ..	=	39.37100
Décamètre	..	=	32.80916 feet
Hectomètre	..	=	328.09167
Kilomètre	..	=	1093.63899 yds.
Myriomètre	..	=	10936.38900

or 6 miles, 1 furlong, 28 poles.

1 myriamètre=10 kilomètres=100 hectomètres=1000 Decam=10,000 Metres.

1 mètre=10 décimètres=100 centimètres=1000 millimètres.

The mètre is the 10,000,000th part of the northern meridian quadrant.

1 mètre=39 7-25 in. Eng.

1 lieue=1 myriametre=6¼ Eng. miles.

1 aune=1 1-5=47 1-6=in Eng.

Measures of Capacity.

Millitre ..	..	=	0.06103 cub. in.
Centilitre	..	=	0 61028
Décilitre	..	=	6.10280
Litre†	.. ..	=	61.02803

or 2·1135 wine pints.

Décalitre	..	=	610.28028 cub. in.

or 2·642 wine gallons.

Hectolitre	..	=	3.5317 cub. ft.

or 26.419 wine gallons, 22 imperial gallons, or 2.839 Winchester bushels.

Kilolitre ..	..	=	35.3171 cub. ft.

or 1 tun and 12 wine gallons.

Myriolitre	..	=	353.17146 cub. ft.

FOR WINE, &c.—1 litre=1 cubic décimètre.

1 myrialitre=10 kilol.=100 hectol.=1000 decal.=10,000 litres.

1 litre=10 decil.=100 centil.=1000 millit.

1 litre=1¾ pint Eng.

1 hectolitre=22 gallons Eng.

Superficial Measure.

Centiare ..	..	=	1·1960 sq. yds.
Are (a sq. décamètre)		=	119·6046
Décare ..	..	=	1196·0460
Hectare ..	..	=	11960·4604

or 2 acres, 1 rood, 35 perches.

Solid Measure.

Décistère	..	=	3·5317 cub. ft.
Stère (a cubic mètre)		=	35·3174
Décastère	..	=	353·1741

FRANKFORT ON THE MAIN.

AND THE SOUTHERN PARTS OF GERMANY.

Money.

1 gulden a 60 kreuzers a 4 pfennige.

1 gulden=$0.40=3 kreutzers=0.02.

COIN.—Ducats a $2.20.

Pieces of 3½ gulden=$1.40; 1 guld.=$0.40, and half gulden=$0.20.

Old pieces of 2 2-5 gulden=$0.96; ½=$0.48.

Exchange on London, 120 fl., m. or l., for £10 stg.

" Paris, fr. 2.10 a 2.15 per fl.

---

* *Mètre* is the fundamental unit of weights and measures; it is the ten-millionth part of the one-fourth of the terrestrial meridian.

† A cubic décimètre.

Money (at par).

florins.	kr.		£	s.	d.		$	c.	m.
12	0	.. ..	=1	0	0	=	4	84	0
0	36	.. ..	=0	1	0	=	0	24	2
9	48	or g. Louis-d'or	=0	16	1	=	3	89	2 2-12
5	35	or gold ducat	=0	9	3	=	2	23	8 6-12
2	42	or silver crown	=0	4	4	=	1	04	8 8-12
1	0	.. ..	=0	1	8	=	0	40	3 4-12

1 florin is equal to 60 kreutzers.

Weight.

1 cwt.=100 great or heavy pds.=108 small or light pds.

1 lb. heavy=17⅓ oz. avdp.

1 lb. light=2 mark=32 loth=128 quent=512 pfennig=15 1-20 oz. troy.

1 mark=7 oz. 10½ dwts. troy.

1 cwt. of 100 heavy or 108 light lbs.=111 lbs. avdp.

Gold and silver are sold by the mark.

1 carat of jewels=1 dwt. 7 5-7 gr. troy.

Measure.

1 foot=11¼ in. Engl.

1 foot=12 zoll=144 lines.

1 ell=21 5-9 in. Engl.

1 Francfort Brabant ell=27⅔ in. Engl.

FOR CORN.—1 malter a 4 simmer a 4 sechter a 4 gescheide.

1 malter=3 bush. 1¼ gall. Eng.

1 simmer=6 5-16 galls. Eng.

FOR LIQUORS.—1 ohm a 80 maas a 4 schoppen.

1 maas=1 gescheid=3 5-32 pints Eng.

1 ohm=31 5-16 galls.

1 fuder=6 ohms; 1 stuck=8 ohm.

GERMANY.

There can be properly no classification under this general head. See Frankfort on the Main, which is the principal commercial town of Germany.

GREECE.

(*Principal Commercial Cities*, ATHENS, NAUPLIA, ETC.)

Money.

drachm.	lept.		£	s.	d.		$	c.	m.
23	15	.. ..	=1	0	0	=	4	84	0
1	80	.. ..	=0	1	0	=	0	24	2
0	11	.. ..	=0	0	1	=	0	02	0 2-12
40	0	or gold piece	=1	10	6	=	7	38	1
5	0	or silv. piece	=0	3	9	=	0	90	7 6-12
1	0	.. ..	=0	0	8¾	=	0	17	6 11-24

1 drachme is equal to 100 leptas.

HAMBURG AND LUBECK

(*Commercial Cities of* GERMANY).

Money.

mk.	c. schil.	pfen.		£	s.	d.		$	c.	m.
13	8	0	..	=1	0	0	=	4	84	0
0	13½	0	..	=0	1	0	=	0	24	2
0	1	3	..	=0	0	1	=	0	02	0 2-12
8	0	0	or 1 ducat	=0	9	3	=	2	23	8 6-12
3	0	0	or 1 dol.cur.	=0	4	4	=	1	04	8 8-12
1	0	0	..	=0	1	2½	=	0	29	2 6-12
0	1	0	..	=0	0	0¾	=	0	01	5 3-24

1 mark current is equal to 16 schillings.

1 thaler=3 marks=48 schillinge; but they have two different values.

1st—According to the coin, called current;

2d—Imagined, used in trade, and called banco, generally 25 per cent. better than current.

1 mark currency = $0.26.

Exchange on London, 14 marks banco, m. or l., for £1 sterling.

" on Paris, fr. 1.50 to fr. 1.70 per mark banco.

Weight.

1 pound=16¼ oz. avdp. Engl.
1 pound=32 loth a 4 quent.
1 centner=111 lbs.=119¼ lbs. Engl.
1 ship pound=2½ cwts.=20 lies pound.
1 lies pound for shipping=14 lb.
1 " " land carriage =16 lbs.
1 stone flax, " " =20 "
1 " wood, etc. " " =10 "
For jewels the weight is the same as Berlin.

Measure.

Hamburg.		English.
1 foot	=	11.289 in.
100 commercial lbs. ..	=	106.838 lbs.
100 feet	=	94.021 feet.
100 ells	=	62.681 yds.
100 viertels	=	159·39 imperial gallons.
100 fass ..	=	18·135 imperial qurs.
1 last ..	=	11 imperial qrs.
1 ship last ..	=	3 tons.

1 foot=12 zoll=96 achtelzoll.
1 Rhineland foot in Hambro'=12⅓ in. Engl.
1 Hambro' ell=22⅔ in. Eng.
1 Brabant ell in Hambro'=27 in. Engl.
1 Hambro' mile=4 3-5 Engl. miles.

Grain.

Corn—Is sold by the last a 3 wispel a 10 scheffel a 2 wispel a 10 scheffel a 2 fass.
Barley—Is sold by the stock a 3 wispel a 10 scheffel a 3 fass.

1 fass=1 bush. 3 galls. 4½ pints Engl.
1 scheffel=2 bush. 7 gall. 1 pint.
1 wispel=29 bush.
1 last=10 quarters 7½ bush.

HOLLAND.

A part of the Netherlands.

(*Principal Commercial Cities*, Amsterdam, Haarlem, The Hague, Rotterdam, Leyden, &c.)

Money (at par.)

guilder.	cts.		£	s.	d.	$	c.	m.
12	0	.. .. =	1	0	0 =	4	84	0
0	60	.. .. =	0	1	0 =	0	24	2
0	5	.. .. =	0	0	1 =	0	02	0 2-12
10	0	gold 10 fl. piece =	0	16	6 =	3	99	3
5	55	or ducat .. =	0	9	3 =	2	23	8 6-12
1	0	or silver florin =	0	1	8 =	0	40	3 4-12

1 guilder is equal to 100 cents.

Weights and Measures.

Dutch.		English.
1 foot	=	11 1-7 in.
1 ell	=	27 1-12 in.
1 last for corn ..	=	10 qrs. 5½ bush. Winchester measure.
1 aam	=	41 wine gallons.
1 hoed	=	5 chaldr. Newcastle.
1 last for freight	=	4000 lbs.
1 last for ballast	=	2000 lbs.

LOMBARDY.

(*Principal Commercial Cities*, Venice *and* Milan.)

Money.

1 lira Austriaca = 100 centesimi or 20 soldi a 5 centesimi.
1 lira Austriaca = $0.16 cents.
The Austrian is the current coin, under other names.

2 gulden = 1 scudo nuovo = $0.96.
1 gulden = ½ scudo nuovo = $0.48.
½ gulden = ¼ scudo nuovo = $0.24.
⅙ gulden = 1 lira Austriaca = $0.16.

Exchange on London, 30 lira Austriache m. or l. for £1 sterlg.
Exchange on Paris, fr. 85.00 m. or l. per l. Aust. 100.

Weight.

1 libbra=1 kilogramme=2 lb 3¼ oz. avd.
1 libbra =10 oncie=100 grossi=1000 denari.
1 quintale=100 libbre.
1 rubbo=10 libbre.

Measure.

Equal to the French.
1 metro=10 palmi=100 diti=1000 adomi.
1 miglia=1000 metri.

Corn.—1 soma=1 hectolitre, French.
1 soma=10 mine=100 pinta=1000 coppi.

MEXICO AND MONTE VIDEO.

Mexico, *Capital of Republic of Mexico.*
Monte Video, *Capital of Republic of Uraguay (or Banda Oriental), S. A.*

Mexico. Money.

dols.	reals.		£	s.	d.		$	c.	m.
16	0	or gold doubloon =	3	5	0	=	15	73	0
8	0	or ½ do. =	1	12	6	=	7	86	5
4	0	or ¼ do. =	0	16	3	=	3	93	2 6-12
1	0	or 1-16 do. =	0	4	0	=	0	96	8
1	0	silv. dol. (8 reals) =	0	4	2	=	1	00	8 4-12
0	4	do. ½ dol. =	0	2	1	=	0	50	4 2-12
0	2	do. ¼ dol. =	0	1	0½	=	0	25	2 1-12
0	1	do. ⅛ dol. =	0	0	6¼	=	0	12	6 1-24

1 dollar is equal to 8 reals.
1 peso a 8 reales de plata a 4 cuartos.
1 peso=1 dollar U. S. currency.

The piaster or duros of 1833 and 1834 are about 6 per cent. less value.

Coin.—Gold doblones a 16 duros.
½, ¼ and ⅛ do.
Silver duros or dollars, ½, ¼ and ⅛.
Reales and ½ reales.

Monte Video. Money.

The peso or duro a 8 reales de plata a 100 centesimos.

This peso is not equal with the Spanish or Mexican, and is generally called the peso corriente.

1 peso corriente=$0.80, or 5 pesos corrientes = 4 pesos duro (Spanish silver dollar).

Exchange on London = 52 d. sterling for 1 peso duro.

Measure and Weight.

108 varas=100 yards English.
For the rest, see Spain.

NAPLES.

(*Principal Commercial City*, Naples, *the capital.*)

Money.

ducat.	grani.		£	s.	d.		$	c.	m.
6	3	.. .. =	1	0	0	=	4	84	0
0	30	.. .. =	0	1	0	=	0	24	2
0	2½	.. .. =	0	0	1	=	0	02	0 2-12
30	0	piece of .. =	5	0	0	=	24	20	0
1	0	silver ducat =	0	3	4	=	0	80	6 8-12
0	120	or dollar .. =	0	4	0	=	0	96	8
0	20	piece of .. =	0	0	8	=	0	16	1 4-12
9	10	piece of .. =	0	0	4	=	0	08	0 8-12

1 ducat is equal to 100 grani.
Ducati di regno a 10 carlini a 10 grani.
1 ducato=$0.90.

COIN.—Gold pieces of 6, 4 and 2 ducati, and pieces of 3 ducati or 1 oncia, and pieces of 2, 5 and 10 oncie.

Silver pieces of 12, 10, 6, &c. carlini.

Scudi of 12 carlini and ducati in silver of 10 carlini.

Exchange on London, 575 grani per £1 sterlg.

Exchange on Paris, 22 a 25 grani per 1 fr.

Weight.

1 cantaro=100 rotoli a 33⅓ oncie.
1 rotolo=1 lb. 15 3-7 oz. avdp.
The libbra for gold, silver, &c., has 12 oz.
360 trappesie, 7200 acini.
1 libbra=10 oz. 1¼ dwts. troy.

Measure.

1 palmo=12 oncie=60 minuti=120 punti.
1 palmo=10 10-27 in. Eng.
1 canna=8 palmi=2⅓ yards Eng.

CORN.—1 carro a 36 tomoli a 24 mass or 1 tomolo a 2 mezzetti a 4 quarti a 8 stoppeli=12 galls. 1½ pints Eng.

WINE.—1 carro=2 batti=24 barrili=1440 caraffi, in the country 1584 caraffi.
1 barile=9⅓ galls., 1 caraffo=1 5-22 pints.

Oil is sold by the salma a 16 staji a 256 quarti or 1536 misurelle, and weighs about 350 lbs. Eng.

The salma of Bari about 312 and of Gallipoli only 295 lbs. Eng.

1 quarto in measure=5-6 pint.
1 staja in measure=27 galls.

THE NETHERLANDS.

(*Principal Commercial City*, AMSTERDAM.)

Money.

1 gulden=100 cents=1*s.* 8*d.* English=$0.40.3 4-12
5 cents=1 stuiver=1*d.* English=$0.02.0 2-12.
2½ guilders=$1.00.

COIN.—Gold pieces of 10 and 5 gulden. Silver pieces of 3 and 1 gulden, 50, 25, 10 and 5 cents.

Old gold coin.—Ducats weighing 52 4-5 grains English, double ducats, ryders=14 gulden.

Butter is sold by the ton, which differs from the common ton=336 pounds Holl. 1 pound=1 5-12 avoirdupois. 1 ship-pound=300 pounds.

Exchange on London, 11 g. 80 cts., more or less, for £1 sterlg.

Exchange on Paris, 2 fr. 10 cts., more or less, per gulden.

Weight.

lb.		lood.		wigtj.		korrels.
1	=	10	=	100	=	1000
		1	=	10	=	100
				1	=	10

1 lb.=1 lb. 1⅝ oz. Avdp.

Measure.

The Ell=1 French metre=39⅜ inches English.

roede.		ell.		palm		duim.		streep.
1	=	10	=	100	=	1,000	=	10,000
		1	=	10	=	100	=	1,000
				1	=	10	=	100
						1	=	10

1 myl (mile)=1,000 ells=⅝ mile English.

FOR CORN.—1 mudde=2 bushels 6⅓ gallons.
1 mud=10 schepel=100 kop=1,000 maajtes.
1 last=30 mudden.

FOR LIQUORS.—1 vat=22 1-10 gallons English.
1 vat=100 kann=1,000 maatj.=10,000 vingerh.

NORWAY.

(*Principal Commercial City*, CHRISTIANA.)

Money.

sp. dol.	skil.		£	s.	d.		$	c.	m.
4	75	=	1	0	0	=	4	84	0
0	28	=	0	1	0	=	0	24	2
0	2¼	=	0	0	1	=	0	02	0 2-12
0	24 or 1 mark ..	=	0	0	9½	=	0	19	1 7-12
1	0 specie dollar	=	0	4	4	=	1	01	8 8-12
0	60 or 1 rigsbank dol	=	0	2	2	=	0	52	4 4-12
0	1 nearly ..	=	0	0	0½	=	0	01	0 1-12

1 specie dollar is equal to 120 skillings.

POLAND.

(*Principal Commerical City*, WARSAW.)

Money.

flor.	grosch.		£	s.	d.		$	c.	m.
42	0 .. .	=	1	0	0	=	4	84	0
2	3	=	0	1	0	=	0	24	2
0	5	=	0	0	1	=	0	02	0 2-12
18	15 or 1 gold ducat	=	0	9	3	=	2	23	8 6-12
8	0 or 1 rix dollar	=	0	4	0	=	0	96	8
1	0 or 1 silver florin	=	0	0	5¾	=	0	11	5 23-24

1 florin is equal to 30 groschen.

Formerly, the gulden a 30 graschm Polish.
1 gulden=$0.11½ cents.

At present the Russian coin is the only legal tender.

Bank notes of the Polish National Bank of 5,50 and 100 guilders.

Exchange on London, 32 Polish gulden M. or L. for £1 Sterling.

Exchange on Paris, fr. 60.50 a fr. 60.75 per 100 gulden.

Weight.

1 funt (lb.)=14 7-16 ounces avdp.
1 funt (lb.)=13⅓ ounces troy.
1 lb.=16 oz.=32 loth=128 drams a 3 scruples a 24 grains.
1 centner=3 stones=100 lbs.=87 7-8 lbs. avdp.
Wool is sold by the stone of 32 lbs.

Measure.

1 foot (stopa)=11¼ in. Eng.
1 ell (lokiee)=25 in. Eng.
1 mile=8 wersts=5 miles Eng.

CORN.—1 kwart=2 litre=1¾ pint Eng.
1 korzek=128 kwarts=28 gall. Eng.

PORTUGAL.

(*Principal Commercial City*, LISBON.)

Money.

reis.		£	s.	d.		$	c.	m.
4120	=	1	0	0	=	4	84	0
206	=	0	1	0	=	0	24	2
20 or 1 vintem ..	=	0	0	1⅕	=	0	02	2 33-48
6400 or gold Joannose	=	1	16	0	=	8	71	2
1000 silver crwn. or mil reis	=	0	4	8	=	1	12	9 4-12
400 or crusado ..	=	0	2	3	=	0	54	4 6-12

1 mil reis is equal to 1000 reis.

Accounts are kept in reis.

1 milrei (or 1000 reis)=2 1-12 new=2½ old cruzados=10 testons=25 reales; 1 rei=6 ceitis.

1 conto de reis (1 million reis)=£270 sterling =$1,296 (the dollar at the rate of 50 pence English).

1 milree=$1.25.
1 crusado velho=about $0.50.
1 crusado novo=about $0.60.

COIN.—Gold pieces of 24 and 12 thousand reis =$16.80 and $33.60.

Silver pieces, 1, ½, ¼, ⅛ cruzado.
Exchange on London, 1 milrei for 59 pence.
" on Paris, fr. 6.20 a fr. 6.30 per milrei.

Weight.

1 quintal a 4 arrobes a 32 libras a 2 marcas.
1 libra=1 lb. avdp. Eng.

Gold and Silver.—1 marco=8 onças=64 outavas=4608 grainos.
1 marca=½ lb.=8 8-20 oz. troy.
151 carats of jewels=1 oz. Eng. troy.

Measure.

The pe=12¾ in. Eng.
The vara=43 4-5 in. Eng.
The covado=26 7-10 in. Eng.
The passo geometrico=1⅔ vara.
1 mile=4 miles Eng.

Corn is sold by the moyo a 15 fanegas a 4 alqueiras a 4 quartos a 8 selamis.
1 moyo=23 bushels Eng.
1 fanega=11⅙ galls. Eng.

Wine and Oil.—1 tonelada a 2 pipas or botas=52 almudas=104 alquires or potes and 624 canadas.
1 almude of Lisbon=3 galls. 5 pints Eng.
1 " of Oporto=5 galls. 5 pints Eng.
1 canada=13 1-16 pints Eng.

PRUSSIA.

(*Principal Commercial City*, Berlin.)

Money.

thal.	sg.	pf.		£	s.	d.	$	c.	m.
6	20	0	.. ..	=1	0	0	=4	84	0
0	9	9	.. ..	=0	1	0	=0	24	2
0	0	10	.. ..	=0	0	1	=0	02	0 2-12
5	20	0	gold Frederick	=0	16	9	=4	05	3 6-12
1	0	0	silver thaler	=0	3	1	=0	74	6 2-12
0	1	0	silbergroschen	=0	0	1¼	=0	02	5 5-24

1 thaler=30 silver groschen a 12 pfenning.

Coins.—Friedrichs d'or=16*s.* 6*d.* English=$3.96. Double do. 33*s.*=$7.92. Half do. 8*s.* 3*d.*=$1.98. In silver pieces of 2, 1, ½, ⅓, ⅙, 1-12 thaler. Do of 2, 1, ½ groschen.

Bank notes of 1, 5, 50, 100, 500 thaler freely taken in the whole of Germany for their nominal value.

Wool is sold by the stein of 22 pounds=22¾ pounds avoirdupois.

Exchange on London, 6 thalers 25 gr., more or less, for £1 sterling. Do. Paris, fr. 3.75, more or less, per thaler.

Weight.

1 pound=467 7-10 grammes French=1 1-32 pound avoirdupois.
1 cwt.=110 pounds Pr.=113 7-16 lbs. avoirdupois.
1 last (shipping) is 4,000 pounds.

Gold and silver are sold by the mark=½ pound =7 oz. 10⅓ dwts. troy English.

The mark is=288 grains.

For assay of silver the mark is divided into 16 loth a 18 grs.; and of gold into 24 carats a 12 grs. 1 carat of jewels is=9-160 quent=1 dwt. 7 5-7 grains troy.

Measure.

The foot=12⅓ inches English.
1 ruthe=12 feet=144 zoll=1728 linien.
1 ell=25½ zoll=26¼ inches English.
1 faden=6 feet. 1 mile=4 2-5 miles English.
For Corn.—1 scheffel=1½ bushel.
1 scheffel=16 metz; 24 scheffel=1 wispel.

ROME.

(*Capital of the* Papal States.)

Money.

paoli.	baj.		£	s.	d.	$	c.	m.
46	0	.. ..	=1	0	0	=4	84	0
2	5	.. ..	=0	1	0	=0	24	2
0	2	.. ..	=0	0	1	=0	02	0 2-12
100	0	gold 10 scudi piece	=2	2	6	=10	28	5
10	0	silver scudo ..	=0	4	2	=1	00	8 4-12
1	0	.. ..	=0	0	5	=0	10	0 10-12

1 paoli is equal to 10 bajochi.

RUSSIA.

(*Principal Commercial City*, St. Petersburg.)

Money.

rouble.	kop.		£	s.	d.	$	c.	m.
6	33	.. ..	=1	0	0	=4	84	0
0	32	.. ..	=0	1	0	=0	24	2
0	2⅝	.. ..	=0	0	1	=0	02	0 2-12
5	15	gold half imper.	=0	16	3	=3	93	2 6-12
3	0	ducat ..	=0	9	2	=2	21	8 4-12
1	0	silver rouble	=0	3	2	=0	76	6 4-12

1 rouble is equal to 100 kopeks.

Coin.—Gold imperials of 10 and 5 roubles (silver). Silver, rouble, and pieces of 75, 50, 40, 30, &c., to 5 kopeks silver.
Bank notes from 1 to 1000 roubles silver.

Exchange on London, from 39d. to 42d. for 1 rouble silver.

Exchange on Paris, from fr. 4.10 to fr. 4.20 per rouble silver.

Weight and Measure.

Russian.		English.
1 arsheen*	..	= 28 in.
1 sashen†	..	= 7 feet.
100 feet ..	..	= 114¼ ft.
1 werst ..	..	= 5 furl. 12 poles.
1 lb. ..	..	= 6318.5 grs.
100 lbs. ..	..	= 90.26 lbs. avdp.
1 pood ..	..	= 36 lbs. 1 oz. 11 dr.
1 chetwert	..	= 5.952 Winc. bush.
100 do. ..	..	= 74.4 quarters.
1 wedro ..	..	= 3¼ wine gallons.

More particularly—

Weight.

1 pound (funt)=14½ oz. avdp.
1 pood=40 lb.=36¼ lbs. avdp.
1 bercowitz=10 poods=362½ lbs. avdp.
1 bruttolast=6 chetwerts.
(The funt is=95 solotnick. 1 sol.=96 doll.)

Measure.

1 foot = 1 foot Eng.
1 arsheen = 28 in. Eng.
1 sashen = 3 arsheens.
1 sashen=3 arsheens=7 feet=48 worsehecks=84 inches=1008 lines.
1 werst=500 sashen=⅝ mile Eng.

Corn, &c.—1 chetwert=4 pajok.
8 tschetwerick=32 tschewerka=64 garner.
1 chetwert=5 bushels, 6 galls., 2 pints, Eng.
1 tschetwerick=5 7-9 galls. Eng.
1 kuhl or sark=10 tschetwericki.
1 wedro=2¾ galls. Eng.
1 fass=40 wedroja.

---

* 1 arsheen=28 in. Eng.
† 1 sashen=3 arsheens.

SARDINIA.

(*Principal Commercial Cities*, Genoa and Turin.)

Money.

The lira nuova=1 franc a 100 centesimi=9¼*d*. Eng. =$0.18¾.

Coin.—Gold: Pieces a 20, 40, 80, and 100 lire nuove or $3.75, $7.50, $15.00, and $18.75. Silver scudi d'argento a 5 lire nuove. Pieces of 2 and 1 lire and 50 and 25 centesimi.

Bank notes of 5, 10, and 20 scudi.

Exchange on London, 25.50 lire, more or less, for £1 sterlg.

Exchange on Paris, 21 lire per fr. 20.

Weight.

IN GENOA. 1 peso grosso=12 1-6 oz. avdp.
1 peso sottile=1 lb. dwt. 18 gr. troy.

IN TURIN. 1 libbra=13 oz. avdp.

The Customs use the French kilogramme.

Gold and silver weight is the marco=8 uncie a 24 denari a 24 grani.

1 marco=8 oz. troy.

Measure.

IN GENOA. 1 palmo=9⅞ in. Eng.
For Corn—1 mina=3 bush. 2½ gall. Eng.
1 mina=8 quarti=96 gombette.
For Wine—1 barile=16⅛ galls. Eng.
1 mezzarola=2 barili=100 pinte.
For Oil—1 barile=14¼ galls. Eng.

IN TURIN. 1 piede liprando=1 foot 8½ in. Eng.
1 piede manelle=12⅜ in. Eng.
1 raso (ell)=23½ in. Eng.
For Corn—1 sacco=5 emine a 8 copi a 24 cucchiari.
1 sacco=25½ galls. Eng.
For Wine—1 brenta=10 4-5 galls.
1 carro=10 brenta a 36 pinte a 2 boccali.

SAXONY.

(*Principal Commercial Cities*, Dresden *and* Leipsic.)

Money.

rd.	gn.	pf.			£	s.	d.		$	c.	m.	
6	15	0	.. ..	=	1	0	0	=	4	84	0	
0	9	9	.. ..	=	0	1	0	=	0	24	2	
0	0	10	.. ..	=	0	0	1	=	0	02	0	2-12
5	12½	0	or August.-d'or	=	0	16	2	=	3	91	2	4-12
1	10	0	or specie thaler	=	0	3	11	=	0	94	7	10-12
1	0	0	currency ..	=	0	3	1	=	0	74	6	2-12
0	1	0	. ..	=	0	0	1¼	=	0	02	5	5-24

1 thaler a 30 groschen a 10 pfenninge.
1 thaler=2*s*. 11*d*. Eng.=$0.70.5 10-12.

Coin.—August d'or=16*s*. Eng.=$3.87.2.
Silver pieces of 2, 1, ⅓, 1-6, and 1-12 thaler.

Paper money is issued by the Government in notes of 10, 5, and 1 thaler.

By the Bank of Leipsic in notes of 20, 100, 200, 500, and 1000 thalers.

Also 1 thaler notes by the Leipsic Dresden Railway Company.

Exchange on London, 6 thaler 25 groschen, more or less, per £1.

Exchange on Paris, fr. 3.50 a fr. 3.75 per thaler.

Weight.

1 lb.=1 lb. 1⅝ oz. avdp. Eng.
1 cwt.=100 lbs.=1000 millas.

For the retail trade the lb. is divided into 32 loths, a 4 quents.

Measure.

1 foot=11⅛ in. Eng.
1 ell=3-5 French metre=24 in. Eng.

For Corn—1 schaffel = 100 litres French = 22 galls. nearly.
12 schaffels=1 malter, 2 malters=1 wispel.
1 wispel=66 bushels Eng.

For Liquids—1 oxhooft=1½ ohm=3 eimer=210 kanns.
1 fuder=4 oxhoofts.
1 kanne=1 litre=1¾ pints Eng.

SMYRNA AND THE LEVANT.

Money.

Like Constantinople. In the Levant are likewise used to a great extent, Spanish dollars and Dutch, Hungarian and Venetian ducats. Likewise German Conventions thaler=$0.96 to $1.00, being subject to variation.

Exchange on London, 105 piasters, more or less, for £1.

Exchange on Paris, fr. 4.75 to fr. 5 per piaster.

Weight.

1 cantaro=7½ battman=22½ chequis=45 okes=100 rotoli a 180 drachms.

The oka, as a gold and silver weight, has 400 drachms, and is equal to 3½ lbs. Troy.
1 cantaro = 127½ lbs. Troy.
1 rotolo = 1 lb. 4⅛ oz.

Goat's hair is sold by the chequi a 800 drachmas.
Silk is sold by the teffei a 610 drachmas.
Opium is sold by the teffei a 250 drachmas.
1 drachm=49 3-5 grains troy weight.

Measure.

1 pik = 27 in. Eng.

Corn.—The killow=11⅝ gall. Eng.

SPAIN.

(*Principal Commercial City*, Madrid.)

Money.

dols.	rls.			£	s.	d.		$	c.	m.	
4	14	barley ..	=	1	0	0	=	4	84	0	
0	5	.. ..	=	0	1	0	=	0	24	2	
16	0	or gold doubloon	=	3	6	0	=	15	97	2	
4	0	or gold pistole	=	0	16	6	=	3	99	3	
1	0	or silver dollar	=	0	4	3	=	1	02	8	6-12
0	1	or real vellon	=	0	0	2⅝	=	0	05	3	45-48

1 dollar is equal to twenty reals.

They use eight different sorts of money:—1. Castilian. 2. Mexican. 3. Catalonian. 4. Majorcan. 5. Valencian. 6. Arragon. 7. Navarre, and 8. The Canarian money.

The Castilian is the chief, and is 1 real de plate antigua=1 15-17 real de vellon=16 cuartos=34 maravedis de plata antigua=64 marav. de vellon =640 Castil. dineros.

10⅝ reales de plata antigua=1 piaster.
1 piaster or duro=4s. 4d. Eng.=$1.04 8 8-12.
1 real de plata=5d. Eng.=$0.10.0 10-12.

Coin.—Gold, 1 quadrupel pistole=8 escudos= $16 to $15.60=doblon or onza de Oro=$16 subdivided into ½, ¼, ⅛, and 1-16. Peso duro or dollar need not be described.

Exchange on London, 40d. sterling, more or less, per peso de plata antigua=48d. to 52d. Eng. per dollar.

Exchange on Paris, fr. 5.10 a fr. 5.30 per peso duro.

Weights and Measures.

Spanish.		English.
1 cana	=	21 inch. nearly.
100 "	=	58.514 yards.
100 quarteras	=	23.536 Win. qrs.
100 lbs.	=	88.215 lbs. avdp.

More particularly—

Weight.

1 Castilian marca=8 1-7 oz. avdp. or 7 oz. 3 4-25 dwts. troy, Eng.
1 marca=8 onzas=64 ochaves=4608 granos.
1 quintal macho=6 arrobas=150 libras.
800 marcas=152½ lbs. avdp.
1 quintal=4 arrobas=100 libras=101¾ lbs. avdp.
Jewels and pearls are weighed by the Castilian ounce a 140 quilates, a 4 granos.
1 oz.=431½ grains troy.

Measure.

1 pie=11⅛ in. Eng.
1 estado=2 varas=6 pies=5 ft. 6¾ in. Eng.
1 league=4¼ miles Eng.
FOR CORN.—1 cahir=12 fanegas a 12 celemines or almudos a 4 quartillos.
1 fanega=12⅛ galls. Eng.
FOR LIQUIDS.—1 cantaro or arroba mayor=8 azumbres=32 quartillos.
1 arroba mayor=3 galls. 3¾ pints Eng.
1 arroba menor for oil=2 galls. 5½ pints Eng.
1 moyo=16 cantaros. 1 pipa=27 cantaros.
1 bota=30 cantaros.

SWEDEN.

(*Principal Commercial City*, STOCKHOLM.)

Money.

rd.	skil.			£	s.	d.	$	c.	m.	
12	0	in banco	=	1	0	0	=4	84	0	
0	23	.. ..	=	0	1	0	=0	24	2	
0	2½	.. ..	=	0	0	1	=0	02	0	2-12
5	25	or 1 gold ducat..	=	0	9	2	=2	21	8	4-12
2	25	or 1 specie silver	=	0	4	4	=1	04	8	8-12
1	0	banco	=	0	1	8	=0	40	3	4-12
1	12½	or half specie silver	=	0	2	2	=0	52	4	4-12

1 rd. banco is equal to 48 skillings.
1 silver species is equal to 96 skillings.
1 riksdaler specie a 48 skillings=$1.05.

Payments are however made chiefly in bank notes of 8, 10, 12, 14, and 16 skillings, and 2, 3, 5, 6, 9, up to 50 riksdalers.

Banco=1 riksdaler specie.
Exchange on London, 12 dalers banco for £1 sterlg.
Exchange on Paris, fr. 2.10 to fr. 2.15 for 1 riksdal.

Weight.

1 skal pound = 15 oz. avdp.
1 schip pound = 400 skal lbs.
1 cwt. = 120 lbs.
1 scale of spelter = 165 lbs.
1 stone wool = 32 lbs.
1 mark (for gold) = 6 oz. 16 dwt. troy.

Measure.

1 foot =1 foot Eng.
1 faam=3 alnar=6 feet=17 verthum.
1 alnar=2 feet Eng.
CORN.—1 tonn=4 bush. Eng.
1 tonn=8 quarts=32 kappar=56 cans=448 quarrtiera.
WINE.—2 pipes=1 fuder=4 oxhoofte=12 eimer =720 stop.

SWITZERLAND.

(*Principal Commercial Cities*, GENEVA, BERN, BASLE.)

Money. Old System.

fr.	batz.	rap.			£	s.	d.		$	c.	m.	
17	7	5	..	=	1	0	0	=	4	84	0	
0	8	7	..	=	0	1	0	=	0	24	2	
0	0	7	..	=	0	0	1	=	0	02	0	2-12
4	0	0	piece of	=	0	4	8	=	1	12	9	4-12
1	0	0	or 10 batz	=	0	1	1½	=	0	27	2	8-12
0	1	0	..	=	0	0	1⅓	=	0	02	6	32-36

1 franc is equal to 10 batzen.

New System—as in France.

1 franc=10 batzen a 10 rappen or 1 livre a 20 sols a 12 deniers.
1 franc=1 livre=$0.27.
COIN.—Gold pistoles a 32 francs=$8.65.
" ½ pistoles a 16 francs=$4.32½.
" Ducats=$2.22.
Silver pieces of 40, 20, 10, and 5 batzen.

N. B.—Each Canton has besides these its own currency.

Exchange of Basle on London, 17 francs 5 rappes, more or less, for £1 sterling.

Exchange on Paris, fr. 1.50 per fr. 1, or 50 per cent. premium, more or less, in favor of Basle.

Weight.

1 cwt.=100 lbs.=50 kilogrammes=110¼ lbs. avdp. Eng.
1 lb.=½ kilogramme=1 lb. 1⅝ oz avdp. Eng.

Measure.

The basis is the Helvetian foot.
1 foot=3-10 French meter=11 17-20 in. Eng.
2 feet=1 ell; 4 feet=1 stab or staff.
16,000 feet=1 hour (mile)=3 Eng. miles.
FOR CORN.—1 malter=10 viertel=100 imir.
1 malter=4 bushels 1 gall. Eng
1 immir=3½ pints.
WINE.—1 ohm =100 maas (or measures).
1 ohm =33 galls. Eng.
1 maas =3½ pints Eng.

TURKEY.

(*Principal Commercial City*, CONSTANTINOPLE.)

Money.

pias.	par.		£	s.	d.	$	c.	m.	
109	0	.. ..	=1	0	0	=4	84	0	
5¼	0	.. ..	=0	1	0	=0	24	2	
0	18	.. ..	=0	0	1	=0	02	0	2-12
200	0	gold new dble. seq.	=1	11	0	=7	50	2	
100	0	" 1 seq. ..	=0	18	0	=3	35	6	
1	0	.. ..	=0	0	2¼	=0	04	5	9-24
22	0	or 1 Spanish dollar	=0	4	2	=1	00	8	4-12

Piaster a 40 paras a 3 aspers.
Also piaster (grush) a 100 aspers.
1 piaster=2½*d.* English=$0.05.
1 purse silver is 500 piasters.
1 purse gold is 30,000 piasters.
1 juk is 100,000 coined aspers.

The government or bank notes bear 8 per cent. interest.

Exchange on London, 104 piasters, more or less, for £1 sterling.

Exchange on Paris, from 400 to 410 piasters for 100 francs.

Weight.

1 pound, chequi=11⅓ oz. avoirdupois.
1 oka=2 lbs. 12 oz. avoirdupois.
1 oka=4 chequi=400 drachmas.
1 taffee=610 drachmas.
1 batman=6 okas.
1 cantaro=44 a 45 okas.
Gold and silver weight like Alexandria.
1 chequi opium=250 drachmas.
1 chequi goat-hair=800 drachmas.
PIECE GOODS.—1 mazzee=50 pieces.

Measure.

The large pik halebi, archim=27 9-10 inches Eng.
The small pik andassa=27 1-16 inches English.
FOR CORN.—The killow=7¼ gallons English.
1 fortin=4 killows=30 gallons English.
1 killow of rice should weigh 10 okas.
FOR LIQUORS.—1 almud=1 2-5 gallon English.
1 almud of oil should weigh 22 5-8 pounds avoirdupois.

TUSCANY.

(*Principal Commercial Cities*, FLORENCE *and* LEGHORN.)

Money.

1 lira Toscana=100 centesimi=7 4-5d. Eng.= $0.15 3-5.
1 lira Toscana=20 soldi=240 denari.
25 lire Toscane=21 francs.

COIN.—Gold:	Rusponi a 3 zecchini	=	$6 25
	Zecchini gigliati,	=	2 05
	Half "	=	1 03
Silver:	Francesconi a Leopoldini	=	0 96
	Half "	=	0 48
	Tallari	=	0 92
	Testoni	=	0 30
	Lire a 12 crazie, about		15

Exchange on London, 30 lire, m. or l., per £1.
" Paris, 80 to 85 centimes per lira.

Weights and Measures.

LEGHORN.		ENGLISH.
1 braccio	=	22.98 in.
155 bracci	=	100 yards.
1 sacco	=	2.0739 Winchester bushels.
4 sacci	=	1 imperial quarter nearly.
100 lbs.	=	74.864 lbs. avoirdupois.
1 centinajo	=	100 lbs.
1 rottolo	=	3 lbs.

More particularly—

Weight.

1 quintal=100 lbs.=1200 uncie a 24 denari.
1 lb. = 12 oz. avoirdupois.
1 quintal=74⅘ lbs. avoirdupois.
FOR GOLD.—1 lb. = 10 11-12 oz. troy, and is divided into 24 carati a 8 ottavi.
FOR SILVER, into 12 uncie a 24 denari.
Jewels are weighed by the carat a 4 grani.

Measure.

1 braccio	=	23 in. English
1 mile	=	1 mile, 48 yards, English.

The braccio used by builders=21 3-5 in. English.
FOR CORN.—1 sacco=3 staja=6 mines; 100 sacchi=201 bushels.
FOR WINE—1 barile=20 flaschi=80 mezzette= 160 quartuzzi=10 1-30 galls. Eng.
1 barile of oil=7⅝ galls English.

SHIPPING MEASUREMENT.

FOR GRAIN.—42 cubic feet=1 ton shipping measurement.

1 bushel	=	60 lbs.
1 bushel	=	2218¼ cubic inches.
8 bushels	=	1 quarter.
1 quarter	=	17745 cub. in. or 10.27 ft.

Therefore 1 ton will take 4 quarters and one-tenth
1 bushel being equal to 60 lbs.,
1 quarter will be equal to 480 lbs.,
1 ton=1968 lbs. or 17 cwt. 2 qrs. 0 lbs. fully.

1 ship of 200 tons measurement can therefore carry 820 quarters, but it generally can carry much more.

MISCELLANEOUS TABLE OF FOREIGN WEIGHTS AND MEASURES.

Arroba of Buenos Ayres ..		=25·36 lbs. U. S.
Amir, or Emir, of Stuttgard ..		=78 gallons.
Balsam Copaiva, 8 lbs. ..		=1 do.
Butt of wine		=130 do.
Canado of Balsam Copaiva ..		=30 pounds.
Chaldron coal, British Provinces		=36 bushels.
do. do. Cumberland ..		=58 do.
Cheki of opium (from Smyrna)		=1⅜ pound.
Coal, a railway wagon load, Pictou		=62 cwt.
Flax, head of, about		=6¾ pounds.
Foot, 100 feet St. Domingo ..		=106 60-100 feet.
Honey, 1 gallon		=12 pounds.
Linseed, one bushel		=47 do.
Mudd, or maud, of Rotterdam		=148 do.
Moyo of salt (Spain)		=70 bushels.
Modius of salt (from Ivica, Spain)		=40 do.
do. do. (Oporto & St. Ubes)		=23 do.
Mass (of Antwerp) ¼th of ohm		=10 gallons.
Ohm do.		=40 do.
Pounds of Austria, ..	100 lbs.	=123 60-100
do. Antwerp, ..	do.	=103 35-100
do. Bavaria, ..	do.	=123
Pounds of Belgium, ..	100 lbs.	=103 35-100
do. Brussels, ..	do.	=103 35-100
do. Bremen, ..	do.	=109 80-100
do. Berlin, ..	do.	=103 11-100
do. Hamburg, ..	do.	=106 80-100
do. Malaga, ..	do.	=101 44-100
do. Netherlands, ..	do.	=108 93-100
do. Portugal, ..	do.	=101 19-100
do. Prussia, ..	do.	=103 11-100
do. Rotterdam, ..	do.	=108 93-100
do. Spain, ..	do.	=101 44-100
do. St. Domingo, ..	do.	=107 93-100
do. Trieste, ..	do.	=123 60-100
do. Vienna, ..	do.	=123 60-100
Palm of Italy, of marble	..	=6 inches.
Quintal of France ..	..	=220 54-100 lbs.
Skippond of Gottenburg	..	=300 pounds.
do. Gefle ..	..	=314 1-10 lbs.
Salt, one barrel ..	..	=5¼ bushels.
Vara, Spanish	..	=8 feet.
Vara of Baracoa	..	=20 feet.

RATES OF FOREIGN MONEY OR CURRENCY, FIXED BY LAW.

The following condensed presentation of the United States value of Foreign Currencies, Weights and Measures, is to a considerable extent a repetition of what may be found in the foregoing Tables. It is here thus given, first, for the greater convenience of this condensed form; and secondly, as giving the specific values established by law in the United States, while that presented in the foregoing is the one recognized in London, estimated in Sterling Currency, and that reduced to Federal Currency, putting the pound at $4.84. The slight discrepancies between the two are thus accounted for, and the reader will bear in mind that the following are the popular values or rates at which these foreign coins pass in the U. S.

The Editor acknowledges his essential indebtedness for these to a volume, entitled "United States Tariff," &c., published by Messrs. Rich & Loutrel, New York, to whose courtesy we are indebted for the use of those Tables. In it may be found a great amount of valuable information to commercial men, respecting the Rates of Duties on foreign merchandise and other matters. The volume is compiled by E. D. Ogden, Esq., Entry Clerk in the New York Custom House, and is made the text book in all the Custom Houses throughout the United States and by the Departments at Washington.

	$ cts.				
Ducat of Naples, ...	80	or	100 grani		
Franc of France and Belgium, ...	18 6-10	"	100 centimes		
Florin of the Netherlands, ...	40	"	100 do.		
Florin of the Southern States of Germany, ..	40	"	60 kreutzers	of	4 pfennings
Florin of Austria and Trieste, ...	48½	"	60 do.	"	4 do.
Florin of Nuremburg and Frankfort, ...	40	"	60 do.	"	4 do.
Florin of Bohemia, ...	48½	"	60 do.	"	4 do.
Guilder of Netherlands, &c.—same as Florins.					
Lira of the Lombardo and Venetian Kingdom,	16	"	100 centisimi	"	100 millesemi
Livre of Leghorn, ...	16	"	20 soldi	"	12 denari
Lira of Tuscany, ...	16	"	20 soldi	"	12 denari
Lira of Sardinia, ...	18 6-10	"	4 reali	"	20 soldi
Livre of Genoa, ...	18 6-10	"	20 soldi	"	12 denari
Milrea of Portugal, ...	1 12	"	1000 reas		
Milrea of Madeira, ...	1 00	"	1000 do.		
Milrea of Azores, ...	83⅓	"	1000 do.		
Marc Banco of Hamburg, ...	35	"	16 shillings	"	12 pfennings
Ounce of Sicily, ...	2 40	"	30 tari	"	20 grani
Pound sterling of Great Britain, ...	4 84	"	20 shillings	"	12 pence
Pound sterling of Jamaica, ...	4 84				
Pound sterling of British Prov. of Nova Scotia, New Brunswick, Newfoundland and Canada,	4 00	"	20 do.	"	12 do.
Pagoda of India, ...	1 84	"	36 fanams	"	48 jittas
Real vellon of Spain, ...	5	"	34 maravedis		
Real plate of Spain, ...	10	"	34 do.		
Rupee Company and British India, ...	44½	"	16 annas	"	12 pice
Rix dollar (or thaler) of Prussia and the Northern States of Germany, ...	69	"	30 groschen	"	12 pfennings
Rix dollar (or thaler) of Bremen, ...	78¾	"	72 grotes	"	5 swares
Rix dollar (or thaler) of Berlin, Saxony & Leipsic,	69	"	30 groschen	"	12 pfennings
Rouble, silver, of Russia, ...	75	"	100 kopecks		
Specie dollar of Denmark, ...	1 05	"	6 marks	"	16 skillings
Specie dollar of Norway, ...	1 06	"	6 do.	"	16 do.
Specie dollar of Sweden, ...	1 06	"	48 skillings	"	12 'ore
Tale of China, ...	1 48	"	10 mace	"	100 candarems
Banco rix dollar of Sweden and Norway, ..	39¼				
Banco rix dollar of Denmark, ...	53				
Crown of Tuscany, ...	1 05	"	20 soldi	"	12 denari
Curacoa guilder, ...	40	"	20 stivers	"	12 pfennings
Leghorn dollar or pezzo, ...	90 76-100	"	20 soldi	"	12 denari
Livre of Catalonia, ...	53½	"	20 sueldos	"	12 dineros
Livre of Neufchatel, ...	26½	"	20 sols	"	12 deniers
Swiss livre, ...	27	"	100 centimes		
Scudi of Malta, ...	40	"	12 tair	"	20 grani
Scudi, Roman, ...	99 a 99½				
St. Gall guilder, ...	40 36-100	"	60 kreutzers	"	4 pfennings
Rix dollar of Batavia, ...	75	"	48 stivers		
Roman dollar, ...	1 05				
Rouble, paper, of Russia, ...		"	100 kopecks		Varies from 4 roubles 65 copecks to 4 roubles 84 copecks to the dollar.
Turkish piastre, ...	5	"	100 aspers		
Current mark, ...	28				
Florin of Prussia, ...	22¾				
Florin of Basle, ...	41				
Genoa livre, ...	21				
Livre tournois of France, ...	18½				

A TABLE OF FOREIGN WEIGHTS AND MEASURES,

REDUCED TO THE STANDARD OF THE UNITED STATES, AND AS RECEIVED AT THE UNITED STATES CUSTOM HOUSES.

ALEXANDRIA (Egypt).

Cantaro of 100 rottoli farforo of 15 oz. (avoirdupois) .. = 93¾ lbs.
100 rottoli zaydino of 21⅓ oz. = 133⅓ "
100 " zaura of 33 oz... = 207 "
100 " mina of 26⅔ oz... = 167 "
1 oke 400 drams of 16 carats each .. .. = 43 "

ALICANT (Spain).

Arroba .. .. = 27 lbs. 6 oz.
Quintal .. .. = 109⅝ lbs.

AMSTERDAM.

100 lbs. 1 centner .. .. .. = 108.93 lbs.
Last of grain.. .. .. .. = 85.25 bush.
Ahm of wine .. .. .. = 41.00 gall.
Amsterdam foot .. .. .. = 0.93 foot.
Antwerp foot .. .. .. = 0.94 "
Rhinland foot .. .. .. = 1.03 "
Amsterdam ell .. .. .. = 2.26 feet.
Ell of the Hague .. .. .. = 2.28 "
Ell of Brabant .. .. .. = 2.30 "
Medden or measure of coal = 2⅘ bush.

ANCONA (Italy).

100 lbs. Roman .. .. .. = 102.75 Ancona.
100 " Ancona .. .. = 73.75 lbs.

ARRAGON (Spain).

Libras of 100 lbs. .. .. = 77.01 lbs.
Quintal, 4 arrobas of 36 lbs. = 112.00 "

BASSORA (Persian Gulf).

Maund attary, 25 vakias tary = 28.05 lbs.
One vakia .. .. = 19 oz.

BATAVIA (E. Indies).

Large bahar .. .. = 4½ peculs.
Small " .. .. = 3 "
1 pecul .. .. = 100 catties.
1 catty .. .. = 16 tales.
1 pecul .. .. = 135 lbs. 10 oz.

BERGEN (Norway).

Shippond of 20 lisponds .. = 320 lbs.
Centner of 6¼ lisponds .. = 100 "
Lispond .. .. = 16 "
Waag, 3 bismar lbs. .. = 36 "
1 lb., 2 marcs, 16 oz., 32 loths.
100 Norway lbs. .. .. .. = 110.23 lbs.

CHRISTIANA (Norway).

Shippond .. .. = 352 lbs.

LAURWIG (Norway).

Shippond .. .. = 352 lbs.

BOMBAY.

Candy.. .. .. = 260 lbs.
Maund .. .. = 28 "
Seer .. .. = 11 1-5 oz.
Candy.. .. .. = 20 maunds.
Maund .. .. = 40 seers.
Seer .. .. = 30 pice.

BREMEN.

Shipfund .. .. = 2½ centners.
Centner .. .. = 116 lbs.
Waag of iron.. .. .. .. = 120 "
Stone of flax.. .. .. .. = 20 lbs.
Stone of wool .. .. .. = 10 "
Lispund .. .. = 14 "
100 lbs. .. .. = 109.8 "

CADIZ (Spain).

Quintal of 4 arrobas .. .. = 100 lbs.
1 lb., 2 marcs, 16 oz., or 256 adarms.
100 lbs. .. .. = 101.43 lbs.

CAIRO (Egypt).

Cantaro, 100 rottoli.. .. .. = 95 lbs.
1 rottoli .. .. = 144 drams.
Occa .. .. = 400 drams, or 26.39 lbs.
36 occas .. .. = 1 cantaro.

CHINA.

Tail .. .. = 1⅓ oz.
16 tails=1 catty .. .. .. = 1⅓ lb.
100 catties=1 picul .. .. = 133⅓ lbs.

CONSTANTINOPLE.

Quintal .. .. = 100 rottolis.
do. .. .. = 45 okes.
do. .. .. = 176 cheques.
do. .. .. = 127 lbs.
One oke .. .. = 2 lbs. 13 oz. 4 drams.

CALCUTTA.

Maund .. .. = 40 seers.
Seer .. .. = 16 chattacks.
English factory maund .. = 74 lbs. 10 oz.
Seer .. .. = 1 lb. 13 oz.
Chattack .. .. = 1 oz.
Bengal bezar maund is 10 per cent. heavier than the factory maund.
Bezar maund .. .. .. = 82 lbs. 2 oz. 2 1-13 drams.
Seer .. .. = 2 lbs. 13⅓ drams.
Chattack .. .. = 2 oz. 5-6 drams.

DENMARK.

100 lbs.=1 centner.. .. = 110.28 lbs.
Barrel or toende of corn .. = 3.95 bush.
Viertel of wine .. .. .. = 2.04 galls.
Copenhagen, or Rhineland ft.= 1.03 foot.
Centner or 100 lbs. Denmark = 110.28 lb.
Shipfund=20 lispunds .. = 320 lbs.
1 lispund .. .. = 16 "
1 bismerpund .. .. .. = 12 "
1 waag=3 bismerpunds .. = 36 "

ENGLAND.

Old ale gallon .. .. .. = 1.22 galls.
Imperial gallon .. .. .. = 1.20 "
Old wine " .. .. .. = 1.00 "
Quarter of grain, or 8 imperial bushels .. .. = 8.25 bush.
Imperial corn bushel, or 8 imperial gallons .. .. .. = 1.03 "
Old Winchester bushel .. = 1.00 "
Imperial yard .. .. .. = 36 inches.
Troy pound .. .. = 144-175ths of a lb. avoirdupois.
Newcastle chaldron .. .. = 36 bushels.
Stone .. .. = 16 lbs.
Tun of wine .. .. = 256 Imp. galls.

FRANCE.

Metre	=	3.28 feet.
Decimetre (1-10th metre)	=	3.94 inches.
Velt	=	2.00 galls.
Hectolitre	=	26.42 "
Decalitre	=	2.64 "
Litre	=	2.11 pints.
Kilolitre	=	35.32 feet
Hectolitre	=	2.84 bush.
Decalitre	=	9.08 quarts.
Millier	=	22.05 lbs.
Quintal	=	220.54 "
Killogramme	=	2.21 "
100 pounds	=	107.93 "
100 feet	=	106.60 feet.
Tun (of wine)	=	240.00 galls.

FLORENCE AND LEGHORN.

100 lbs. or 1 cantaro ..	=	74.86 lbs.
Moggio of grain	=	16.59 bush.
Barile of wine	=	12.04 galls.

GENOA.

100 lbs. or peso grosso ..	=	76.87 lbs.
100 " or peso sottile ..	=	63.89 "
Mina of grain	=	3.43 bush.
Mezzarola of wine	=	39.22 galls.

HAMBURG.

Last of grain	=	89.64 bush.
Ahm of wine	=	38.25 galls.
Hamburg foot	=	0.96 foot.
Ell	=	1.22 "
Shipfund, equal to 2½ centners, or 280 lbs. Hamburg	=	299 lbs.
1 centner	=	8 lispunds, or 112 lbs. Hamburg.
1 lispund	=	14 lbs. Hamburg.
1 stone of flax	=	20 " "
1 stone of wool	=	10 " "
1 stone of feathers	=	10 " "
100 lbs. Hamburg	=	106.8 lbs.

ITALY.

100 rottoli of 31 3-7 oz. each	=	196¼ lbs.
1 cantaro grosso	=	196¼ "

MADRAS.

Candy	=	500 lbs.
"	=	20 maunds.
Maund	=	8 bis.
Bis	=	8 seers.

MALACCA.

Pecul	=	135 lbs.
A pecul	=	100 catties, or 1600 tales.

MALTA.

100 lbs. 1 cantaro	=	174.50 lbs.
Salma of grain	=	8.22 bush.
Cantaro	=	100 rottoli.
Rottoli	=	30 oz.
1 cantaro (mercantile usage)	=	175 lbs.

NAPLES.

Cantaro grosso	=	196.50 lbs.
" picolo	=	106.00 "
Carro of grain	=	52.24 bush.
" wine	=	264.00 galls.

NETHERLANDS.

Ell	=	3.28 feet.
Mudde of Zak	=	284.00 bush.
Vat hectolitre	=	26.42 galls.
Kan litre	=	2.11 pints.
Pond killogramme	=	2.21 lbs.
100 pounds	=	108.93 "

PORTUGAL.

100 pounds	=	101.19 lbs.
22 pounds (1 arroba) ..	=	32.00 "
4 arrobas of 32 lbs. (1 quintal)	=	1.28 "
Alquiere	=	4.75 bush.
Mojo of grain	=	23.03 "
Last of salt	=	70.00 "
Almude of wine	=	4.37 galls.

PRUSSIA.

100 lbs. of 2 Cologne marks each	=	103.11 lbs.
Quintal, of 110 lbs... ..	=	113.42 "
Sheffel of grain	=	1.56 bush.
Eimar of wine	=	18.14 galls.
Ell of cloth	=	2.19 feet.
Foot	=	1.03 foot

ROME.

Rubbio of grain	=	8.36 bush.
Barile of wine	=	15.31 galls.
100 Roman lbs.	=	74.77 lbs.

RUSSIA.

100 lbs. of 32 loths each ..	=	90.26 lbs.
Chertwert of grain	=	5.95 bush.
Vedro of wine	=	3.25 galls.
Petersburg foot	=	1.18 foot.
Moscow foot	=	1.10 "
Pood	=	36.00 lbs.

SICILY.

Cantaro grosso	=	192.50 lbs.
" sottile	=	175 lbs.
100 pounds	=	70 "
Salma grossa of grain ..	=	9.77 bush.
" generale	=	7.85 "
" of wine	=	23.06 galls.

SPAIN.

Quintal, or 4 arrobas ..	=	101.44 lbs.
Arroba	=	25.36 "
" of wine	=	4.43 galls.
Fanega of grain	=	1.60 bush.

ST. GALL.

100 heavy lbs.	=	128 lbs.
100 light "	=	102 "

SURAT.

20 Surat maunds, or 10 Bengal factory maunds. ..	=	1 candy.
1 candy	=	746 lbs. 10 oz

SWEDEN.

100 lbs. or 5 lispunds ..	=	73.76 lbs.
Kan of corn	=	7.42 bush.
Last	=	75.00 "
Cann of wine	=	69.09 galls.
Ell of cloth	=	1.95 foot.
20 commercial lbs.	=	1 lispund.
20 lispunds	=	1 skeppund.

SMYRNA.

100 lbs. (1 quintal)	=	129.48 lbs.
Oke	=	2.83 "
Quillot of grain	=	1.46 bush.
Quillot of wine	=	13.50 galls.

TRIESTE.

100 pounds	=	123.60 lbs.
Stajo of grain	=	2.34 bush.
Orna or eimer of wine ..	=	14.94 galls.
Ell for woolens	=	2.22 feet.
" for silk	=	2.10 "

VENICE.

100 lbs. peso grosso	=	105.18 lbs.
100 " " sottile	=	66.04 "
Moggio of grain	=	9.08 bush.
Anifora of wine	=	137.00 galls.

TABLE

GIVING THE

CURRENCY, RATE OF INTEREST,

PENALTY FOR USURY,

AND LAWS IN REGARD TO COLLECTION OF DEBTS, &c.,

IN THE SEVERAL UNITED STATES.

The following items of information, it is believed, will be found convenient for business men, and useful in the "Counting-house and Family." They have been collected with much care, and original sources resorted to in the respective localities, for the most part. Yet, as the legislation in regard to some of these matters is changing, and what is true this year, in a given State, may not be entirely so the next, some caution will be required in relying too implicitly upon present statements, hereafter. They will serve, however, as a general guide, and are as valuable as any thing of the sort, from the nature of the case, can well be.

Although the Federal Currency is that established by law for the whole country, and that in common use in all the States, yet, as previous to its adoption the different States had different usages in these respects, that ancient usage, to some extent, continues. Thus, in Massachusetts, six shillings make a dollar, in New York, eight shillings, &c.

MAINE.

Currency.—The dollar is 6s.; 1s. is 16⅔c.; 6d. is 8⅓c.; 9d., 12½c., &c.

Interest.—Six per cent.

Penalty for Usury.—Usurious excess void. For debts contracted out of the State, the rates of interest in that State are supported by our laws; *i. e.* a debt contracted in California, interest 12 per cent., both parties remove here and note still due, interest continues the same as where it began.

Collection of Debts.—Real estate, and goods and chattels, may be attached and held as security to satisfy a judgment, which must be rendered by the appropriate court. Property possessed by a woman before marriage, remains hers after marriage, and not liable for husband's debts. Arrest for debt allowed if party about to leave the State, but if he disclose he is discharged, if he has not wherewithal to pay the debt. Certain specified property, for current support, exempt from attachment. There is a homestead exemption and mechanics' lien law.

NEW HAMPSHIRE.

Currency.—Same as Maine.

Interest.—Six per cent.

Penalty for Usury.—Forfeiture of three times the usury.

Collection of Debts.—There is a mechanics' lien and homestead exemption law. Certain specified property is also exempted from attachment. Other real and personal estate may be attached. Mortgages of personal property must be recorded in town clerk's office.

VERMONT.

Currency.—Same as Maine.

Interest.—Six per cent. Unusual interest legal when contracted for.

Penalty for Usury.—Excess not collectable, and when paid may be recovered back and costs.

Collection of Debts.—Real and personal property may be attached on mesne process, and persons residing in the State owing debtor exceeding $10 may be trusteed. No imprisonment on contract, except on affidavit that debtor is about to remove from the State and has money or property secreted. Mechanics have a lien for a limited time. Homestead exemption, $500. Household furniture, clothing, and tools, exempt from attachment.

MASSACHUSETTS.

Currency.—Same as Maine.

Interest.—Six per cent.

Penalty for Usury.—Three times the unlawful interest taken. A bank taking unlawful interest forfeits the debt.

Collection of Debts.—A mechanics' lien and homestead exemption law. Other specified property for family use and carrying on trade, exempt from attachment. Mortgages of personal property to be recorded by town clerk. Real and personal property not exempted, attachable. Imprisonment for debt not allowed except for fraud. Two thirds in value of the creditors may put a debtor into insolvency, when all his property shall be applied for equal benefit of all creditors in proportion to claims proved; or any creditor of $100 and upwards may, for specified causes, compel debtor to insolvency. Debtor complying with certain conditions and giving up all property, not further liable for any debts thereafter in the State. Married women have independent rights of property.

RHODE ISLAND

Currency.—Same as Maine.

Legal Interest.—Six per cent.

Penalty for Usury.—Forfeiture of excess.

Collection of Debts.—Mechanics' lien law. Specified property exempt from attachment; other property may be attached. Mortgages of personal property must be recorded in town clerk's office. Imprisonment for debt allowed, but the jail limits extend to the county. Here, as in most of the States, unwitnessed notes and ordinary book accounts can not be sued for after six years, unless a formal judgment of court shall have been had.

CONNECTICUT.

Currency.—Same as Maine.
Interest.—Six per cent.
Usury.—Forfeiture of all interest.
Collection of Debts.—A mechanics' lien law. Other specified property exempted from attachment. Mortgager of personal property may retain possession of it. Goods, chattels, and real estate of debtor may be attached, subject to be defeated by insolvency within sixty days. Person of debtor not liable to arrest. Wife's property at time of marriage, or subsequently acquired by devise or inheritance, not liable for husband's debts.

NEW YORK.

Currency.—Dollar, 8 shillings; 1s., 12½c.; 6d., 6¼c.
Legal Interest.—Seven per cent.
Penalty for Usury.—Voids the contract, but corporations can not set up usury as defense. Persons who take usury deemed guilty of a misdemeanor and liable to a fine not exceeding $100, or imprisonment not exceeding six months, or both.
Collection of Debts.—Certain specified property exempt from attachment; also a homestead exemption to value of $1000, and continued for benefit of widow and children until youngest child 21. But the deed conveying the property must show it intended to be held as such homestead, or a precise notice given and recorded to that effect. Mechanics, laborers, &c., in all cities and certain counties, have a lien on buildings, &c., for pay for labor, materials, &c., on such buildings. Chattel mortgages void unless filed with town or county clerks, or goods delivered. Personal arrest allowed in case of fraud, concealment, &c. Property owned by female at marriage not liable for husband's debts. Married woman may hold separate property, taken by inheritance, or by gift or bequest from any person other than the husband, and the same shall not be liable for the debts of the husband, nor subject to his disposal.

NEW JERSEY.

Currency.—7s. 6d. to the dollar.
Interest.—Six per cent.
Usury.—Forfeiture of whole amount.
Collection of Debts.—Homestead exemption to amount of $1000. Other specified property exempt from attachment. A mechanics' lien law. Ordinary debts outlawed in six years. Females exempt from arrest for debt. Widows' right of dower, one third husband's real estate.

PENNSYLVANIA.

Currency.—7s. 6d. to the dollar; 12½ cts. called a *levy*, an abbreviation of *eleven pence;* 6¼ cts. a *fip*, an abbreviation of *five pence* or *fippenny bit.*
Legal Interest.—Six per cent.
Penalty for Usury.—Forfeiture of usurious interest in action on the contract, and of the money lent in a penal action.
Collection of Debts.—Property to amount of $300, and clothing, school books, &c., exempt from attachment. Mechanics have lien on buildings for labor and materials in their construction in most of the counties. Arrest of person of debtor not allowed except for fraud or concealment. Six years voids debts by simple contract. Women's individual right in property continues after marriage, as before.

DELAWARE.

Currency.—7s. 6d. to the dollar.
Rate of Interest.—Six per cent.
Penalty for Usury.—Forfeiture of debt.
Collection of Debts.—Specified property, not exceeding $100, exempted from attachment. Person of debtor may not be arrested, except for fraud, concealment, &c. Limitation of debts, not of record, three years; for recovery of land, twenty years; note of hand, six years.

MARYLAND.

Currency.—7s. 6d. to the dollar, but shillings and pence are abolished in law and obsolete in popular use.
Interest.—Six per cent.
Usury.—Forfeiture of usury.
Collection of Debts.—Mechanics and men supplying material have a lien in Baltimore city and most of the counties for work done and materials furnished on and for the *construction* of buildings. Property belonging to a woman not liable for payment of husband's debts. Wearing apparel and bedding of debtor and family exempt from execution. Mortgages of personal property must be in writing, acknowledged, and recorded within twenty days of their date. Actions for debt, not on a sealed instrument, must be brought within three years; on sealed instruments within twelve years. No imprisonment for debt.

VIRGINIA.

Currency.—6s. to the dollar.
Interest.—Six per cent.
Usury.—Renders contract void, and in criminal action forfeits double the value of money lent.
Collection of Debts.—Mechanics have lien on land upon which they erect buildings, provided they build by contract in writing and recorded. Growing crops, not severed, not liable to distress or levy, except Indian corn, which may be taken after 15th October. Specified articles also exempted. Slaves not to be distrained or levied upon without debtor's consent, where other effects sufficient are shown to officer, and in his power to take. Mechanics' tools exempt to value of twenty-five dollars. Actions on unsealed instruments barred generally in five years; on sealed instruments in ten and twenty years. Imprisonment for debt abolished. In certain cases, debtor, when sued, may be held to bail; and in default of giving bail may be imprisoned. Married women may hold property separate from their husbands. Widow's dower, one third of real estate for life, and of personal estate absolutely after payment of debts, except only life estate in slaves.

Judgments give lien on real estate from first day of the term of the court at which they are rendered. Executions bind all the personalty which the debtor possesses, or to which he is entitled, from the moment they are in the hands of an officer who can by law levy them; and judgment debtor may be compelled, by interrogatories filed before a commissioner in chancery, to disclose upon oath all his effects, real, personal, and mixed, in his possession or under his control. If he answer said interrogatories fraudulently, or evasively, the commissioner may attach and commit him. Any one indebted to a judgment debtor may be garnished by the judgment creditor, and made to pay such creditor. Elegits now extend to all debtor's real estate. Judgment creditors may sue, at law or in equity, at their own costs, in name of sheriff or other officer, to recover any property of their debtors, on which they obtain a lien.

NORTH CAROLINA.

Currency.—10s. to the dollar.
Interest.—Six per cent.
Usury.—Voids the contract; lender forfeits double the amount of money lent.
Collection of Debts.—Specified property exempt from attachment. Actions on simple contract must be brought within three years; for land, seven years; by infants, feme coverts, or non compos mentis, within three years after disability removed; persons beyond seas, within eight years after title accrues. Possession for twenty-one years, under color of title, a bar to the State. Three years' possession of personal property gives title. Wife's real estate at time of marriage can not be sold or leased by husband without consent of wife. Deeds, mortgages, marriage settlements, &c., must be recorded, or are void as to creditors.

SOUTH CAROLINA.

Currency.—4s. 8d. to the dollar.
Interest.—Seven per cent.
Usury.—Forfeiture of interest with costs.
Collection of Debts.—Attachment holds against the property of a non-resident or absconding debtor, and the person of a debtor about to abscond. Actions for debt must be brought within four years; to recover possession of land, within ten years. Deeds of marriage settlement must be recorded. Mechanics have lien on building. Chattel mortgages void as against subsequent purchasers, unless recorded. Specified property, and a house and fifty acres of land, exempted from attachment, to $500.

GEORGIA.

Currency.—4s. 8d. to the dollar.
Interest.—Seven per cent.
Usury.—Usurious interest only void, principal and legal interest recoverable.
Collection of Debts.—All actions under the common law of England in force in this State. Mechanics have a lien on buildings they have built or repaired. Liens on river steam-boats for wages, provisions, supplies, and repairs; the same lien extends over mills for lumber, wages, provisions furnished, and repairs. There is a homestead exemption from levy and sale, but the property must not exceed in value $200. All conveyances of land must be recorded within six months; all mortgages, both of real and personal estate, must be recorded within ninety days. Actions on open accounts must be brought within four years; on promissory notes, unsealed, six years; for recovery of land, seven years; on bonds and other sealed instruments, twenty years. All property of whatever kind subject to attachment. Honest debtors' act in force; its operation is to release the debtor's person from arrest, but not his present or any future property from levy. Wives and widows are not exempt from the operation of the attachment law; but the persons of all women in Georgia are exempt from arrest under any civil process.

ALABAMA.

Currency.—Federal money only.
Interest.—Eight per cent.
Usury.—Forfeits all interest.
Collection of Debts.—Specified articles and homestead to value of $500 exempt from execution and sale. Mechanics' lien law. Actions on liquidated demands must be brought within six years; on open account, in three years. Mortgages of real and personal property must be recorded. Sale of goods over $200 must be evidenced by transfer of some portion of the goods, or payment of some portion of purchase money, or written contract. Attachment lies for debts, whether now due or not, in case of fraud in the debtor and non-residence. Arrest of person allowed, if fraud or concealment. Husband acquires no right to wife's property by marriage, so as to make it liable for his debts, but is entitled to its management and control during coverture; and husband and wife are jointly liable for family supplies.

MISSISSIPPI.

Currency.—8 bits (12½ cents) to the dollar.
Interest.—Six per cent., or by contract in writing *for money lent*, any rate of interest not exceeding ten per cent.
Usury.—Forfeiture of interest.

Collection of Debts.—No imprisonment of debtor. Mortgages and deeds of trust must be acknowledged and recorded. Specified property and a homestead exempted from execution and attachment. A mechanics' lien law. Actions on notes and bills, limited to six years; open accounts for goods sold, three years; bonds and sealed instruments, seven years; possession of land, ten years. Property of wife only sold by joint deed of herself and husband.

LOUISIANA.

Currency.—Federal money, only in New Orleans a picayune is 6¼ cents.
Interest.—Five per cent.; by agreement of parties, ten per cent. Bank interest, five to eight per cent.
Usury.—Forfeiture of interest.
Collection of Debts.—A mechanics' lien law. Specified property exempt from attachment. Women not subject to arrest for debt. Property owned by either party before marriage remaining such afterward. No imprisonment for debt.

FLORIDA.

Currency.—Federal money only.
Interest.—Six per cent., or by agreement, eight.
Usury.—Forfeits interest.
Collection of Debts.—Imprisonment for debt abolished. Specified property and forty acres of land exempt from attachment, not exceeding $200; also dwelling house to same amount by city or town resident. A mechanics' lien law. Mortgages of personal property must be recorded. Widow's dower, life interest in one third of real estate. Wife's property at marriage continues hers, and not liable for husband's debts.

TEXAS.

Currency.—Federal money.
Interest.—Eight per cent., or higher to twelve per cent., by agreement.
Usury.—Forfeits interest.
Collection of Debts.—Mortgages of personal property must be recorded, and may be set aside for valuable consideration, or possession given to mortgagee. Actions for debt on account must be brought within two years; on contract, four years; real estate, varying with circumstances. A homestead exemption; specified personal property also exempted from attachment. A mechanics' lien law. No imprisonment for debt. Property attachable of debtor *non est*. Widow's dower, life interest in one third real estate. Property of *feme sole at* marriage, if registered, remains hers independently.

TENNESSEE.

Currency.—6s. to the dollar.
Interest.—Six per cent.
Usury.—Fine at least $10.
Collection of Debts.—Specified property exempt from attachment. A mechanics' lien law. Mortgages of personal property must be recorded. No imprisonment for debt. Property of concealing or absconding debtor attachable. Actions for debts of account must be brought within three years. Widow's dower, one third of husband's estate at death. Married women, the twain are not one as to wife's property, in which she has an independent right. A homestead exemption.

KENTUCKY.

Currency.—6s. to the dollar.
Interest.—Six per cent.
Usury.—Forfeiture of usury and costs.
Collection of Debts.—Mortgages of personal and real property must be recorded. A mechanics' lien law in certain towns. Specified property exempt from attachment. Debtor is held to bail on specified conditions. Property attachable in case of concealment, proposed removal, absence, &c. *Feme covert* has independent rights in property, but husband not liable for wife's debts before marriage. Actions limited, on account, to one year.

OHIO.

Currency.—8s. to the dollar.
Interest.—Six per cent. As high as ten per cent. if stipulated in written instrument. Banks allowed only six per cent.
Usury.—Forfeiture of usury.
Collection of Debts.—Mechanics' lien. Specified property exempt from execution. A homestead exemption. Mortgages of personal property valid for one year if recorded. Lands not to be sold for less than two thirds of the appraised value. Attachments allowed in specified cases. First attachment of prior validity. Limitation laws: real estate, twenty-one years; written contracts, fifteen years; not written, six years. Widow's dower, one third of real estate.

INDIANA.

Currency.—6s. to the dollar.
Interest.—Six per cent.
Usury.—Forfeiture of usurious interest.

Collection of Debts.—Mechanics' lien law. Homestead exemption law. Specified property exempt from attachment. Mortgages of personal property must be acknowledged and recorded unless property transferred. Ordinary debts outlawed in six years; contracts in writing and real estate. Real and personal property not specially exempted may be taken on execution. Wife's real estate at or after coverture, not liable for husband's debts.

ILLINOIS.

Currency.—Federal money.
Interest.—Six per cent.; by agreement, as high as ten per cent.
Usury.—Forfeits entire interest.

Collection of Debts.—Widow's dower, one third of real estate. A mechanics' lien law. Homestead exemption law. Specified articles not attachable. Chattel mortgages must be acknowledged and recorded or property delivered. Body of debtor may be arrested for fraud or concealment.

MICHIGAN.

Currency.—8s. to the dollar.
Interest.—Seven per cent., yet as high as ten per cent. by agreement of parties.
Usury.—Voids the excess.
Collection of Debts.—There is a mechanics' lien law, and a homestead exemption law. Mortgages of personal property must be recorded, and then are void, as against other creditors or mortgagees, after one year, unless within thirty days preceding an authenticated certificate is attached to the instrument or record setting forth mortgagee's interest. Contracts for sale of goods invalid above $50, unless part of goods delivered, or something given to bind the bargain. Actions for ordinary debts must be brought within six years. Person of debtor may be arrested, if debtor about to remove property from State, or fraudulent concealment or intent to defraud. *Feme covert's* right to property possessed before marriage, or to which she becomes entitled subsequently, continues her separate property, and not liable for husband's debts, and she may alienate it as if unmarried.

MISSOURI.

Currency.—6s. to the dollar; bit, 12½ cts.; picayune, 6¼ cts.
Interest.—Six per cent.; by agreement, as high as ten.
Usury.—Forfeits usury and interest.

Collection of Debts.—Wife's dower, life estate in one third real, and specified personal property absolutely. Wife's property at marriage not liable for husband's old debts. No imprisonment for debt. Attachment of property in case of fraud, concealment, or removal of property, or non-residence. Property not specially exempt may be taken on execution. Mortgages of personal property must be recorded. Suits on open account debts must be brought within five years; on store accounts, two years; on notes, bonds, bills, &c., ten years. Specified property exempt from sale on execution. A mechanics' lien law.

IOWA.

Currency.—Federal money.
Interest.—Six per cent., and up to ten by agreement.
Usury.—Usurious interest recoverable.

Collection of Debts.—A mechanics' lien law. A household exemption law. Specified property exempt from attachment. Mortgages of personal property must be recorded. Ordinary indebtedness outlawed in five years; written contracts, as notes, &c., ten years. Person of debtor exempt from arrest. Married woman has rights in property independent of husband.

WISCONSIN.

Currency.—Federal money.
Interest.—Seven per cent.; as high as twelve by agreement.
Usury.—Forfeiture of entire debt.
Collection of Debts.—A mechanics' lien law. A homestead exemption. Mortgages of personal property must be filed or recorded. Actions for recovery of ordinary debts must be commenced within six years. No imprisonment for debt, but property of debtor attachable under certain circumstances. Real and personal estate of *feme sole* not liable for husband's debts.

MINNESOTA.

Currency.—Federal money.

Interest.—Seven per cent., or any higher rate if agreed in writing.

Usury.—No usury law.

Collection of Debts.—A mechanics' lien. A homestead exemption law. Specified property exempt from attachment. Mortgages of personal property, a copy must be filed with or recorded by county register. Imprisonment for debt abolished. Contracts for sale of goods must be in writing for amounts over $50, unless part of goods delivered, or part of purchase money or consideration paid. Real and personal estate of *feme sole* not liable for husband's debts after marriage. Widow's dower, life interest in one third real estate.

CALIFORNIA.

Currency.—Federal money, but usage not wholly established.

Interest.—Ten per cent.; any higher rate by contract not exceeding 18.

Usury.—Forfeiture of excess.

Collection of Debts.—Mechanics' lien law. Homestead exemption law. Specified property exempt from attachment. Mortgages of personal property, property must be transferred. Contracts void if over $200, unless in writing, or part payment made, or part goods delivered. Property may be attached, although debt not due, if fraud, concealment, or absconding. Wife holds in separate right property owned by her before marriage.

DISTRICT OF COLUMBIA.

Currency.—Federal money.

Interest.—Six per cent.

Usury.—Voids contracts at law, but a complainant in equity is relieved only as to the excess.

Collection of Debts.—Debts of $50 or less are recoverable speedily before a justice; above that, in Circuit Court. Where matter in controversy is $1000, appeal lies to Supreme Court. Money in the treasury cannot be attached, but a party having the apparent right to receive money from the treasury, may be enjoined from receiving the same by his assignee or other person having the substantial equitable title to that very fund. No bail in civil cases; no imprisonment for debt.

NOVA SCOTIA.

Currency.—5s. or ¼ pound to the dollar.

Interest.—Six per cent.

Penalty for Usury.—Forfeiture of treble the amount; does not extend to any hypothecation or agreement in writing entered into for money advanced upon the bottom of a ship or vessel, her cargo or freight.

Collection of Debts.—In the Supreme Court, major's and magistrate's courts by civil summons; *capias* where parties are about to quit the province. Limitation laws; written contracts under seal, twenty years; ordinary contracts, six years. Mortgages of personality, same as under the English law. Widow's dower, one third of real estate and one third of personality.

CANADA.

Currency.—4s. sterling equals 4s. 10½d. currency at the banks. Elsewhere, 4s. sterling equals 5s. currency. 1s. currency, 20 cents. 5s. currency to the dollar. $4 to the pound.

Interest.—Six per cent. at banks. Elsewhere, any rate of interest agreed upon; but no more than six per cent. can be recovered *at law*, even where a higher rate may have been stipulated.

Usury.—Penalties for usury abolished, except as regards banks.

Collection of Debts.—No homestead exemption. Specified articles not seizable. When married here, without a marriage contract, the wife's dower is the half of the real estate the husband has at the time of the marriage, or which he may acquire by inheritance during the marriage. Mortgages on real estate obtain precedence of payment according to the date of their registration. No mortgages obtainable on personal property. No seizure of estate for debt before judgment, except where a creditor swears his debtor is fraudulently concealing or disposing of it. No imprisonment for debt, except when a debtor is leaving the province of Canada with a fraudulent intent. Limitation laws: possession for thirty years creates a title; when proprietor is in a foreign country, twenty years.

www.ingramcontent.com/pod-product-compliance
Lightning Source LLC
LaVergne TN
LVHW020217110826
845151LV00003B/748

* 9 7 8 1 4 2 5 5 3 3 8 0 9 *